Merchandising:
Theory, Principles, and Practice

Merchandising:
Theory, Principles, and Practice

Grace I. Kunz
Iowa State University

Fairchild Books
New York

Dedication

To Dana and Debi for supporting me in the idea that textbooks are not so profound that parents can't write them.

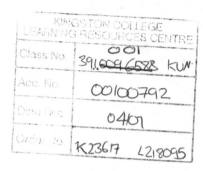
Cover Design: WHIZBANG! Studios
Cover Photo: WHIZBANG! Studios
Editor: Bette LaGow

Chapter Opener Credits:
Ch. 2: courtesy Richter Management Services, Inc.
Ch. 7: courtesy Anatomy™ Environmentally and Socially Responsible Products.
Ch. 8: photograph of GERBERdesigner Artworks™ System courtesy Gerber Garment Technology, Inc. Artworks™ is a trademark of Gerber Garment Technology, Inc.
Ch. 10: photograph © Elliott Kaufman.
Ch. 11: courtesy AP/Wide World Photos.
All others courtesy Fairchild Publications.

Copyright © 1998
Fairchild Publications, a division of ABC Media, Inc.

Library of Congress Catalog Card Number: 97-78088

ISBN: 1-56367-146-8

GST R 133004424

Printed in the United States of America

BRIEF CONTENTS

EXTENDED CONTENTS

PREFACE

Merchandising is planning, developing, and presenting product line(s) for identified target market(s) with regard to pricing, assorting, styling, and timing. Throughout the business sector, product lines must be planned, developed, and presented. Merchandising is most distinct as a business function among firms that deal with products that change frequently. Consequently, the foundations of merchandising principles are rooted in the apparel business. The textiles and apparel business is fascinating to study and, compared to other industries, has many unique characteristics. 1) Textile and apparel is a globalized business that now constitutes nearly one-tenth of world commerce (Cline, 1990); 2) In the United States, textiles and apparel are ranked second only to steel in terms of essential commodities for national defense (A Look at the Facts, 1992); 3) Quick Response business systems are revolutionizing business operation; 4) Apparel has long been recognized as having demand for more product change than any other consumer good; and, 5) Increasing vertical and horizontal integration has resulted in greater complexity of merchandising processes.

Most consumer goods manufacturers and retailers are facing some of the same kinds of conditions now being addressed by the textiles and apparel sector. These consumer goods firms are realizing more frequent product changes, shorter lead times, and attempts to maintain lower levels of inventory without sacrificing customer service. With current business trends, merchandising principles, particularly merchandise planning, are badly needed throughout the consumer goods sectors. Although merchandising is often regarded primarily as a retailing function, the principles are being applied in global manufacturing and retailing of all kinds of products.

The purpose of this book is to provide an academic foundation for integrating merchandising theory, principles, and practice to achieve the following:

- Demonstrate theory, principles, and practice of apparel merchandising and provide examples of application to other products.
- Provide a learner-centered, active learning text layout to accommodate multiple learning styles and multiple course objectives.
- Provide examples of merchandising practices for both manufacturing and retailing sectors.
- Focus on existing and developing merchandising technology.

- Develop a clearly stated, integrated merchandising language.
- Describe the role of merchandising related to other fundamental business functions.
- Examine the impact of Quick Response business systems on merchandising.

The text is targeted to the junior/senior collegiate level. Prerequisites are assumed to include a basic textile and apparel industries class and/or basic business classes including accounting, as well as understanding of product development processes. Computer applications related to merchandise planning and inventory management are highly recommended as a part of the course. A merchandising math class could either be a prerequisite or follow-up to this class. A merchandising course based on this text is an excellent prerequisite to a merchandising internship. This text can provide the foundation for graduate-level merchandising courses if the Recommended Resources at the end of each chapter are incorporated into the reading assignments.

Learning Activities and Cases are integrated into each chapter to provide an interactive, active learning environment. Many of the cases are drawn from the trade press to provide a "flavor" of the style and emphases of trade-related literature. The combination of Learning Activities in the chapters constitute more work than can be incorporated into any single semester. This is by design so the faculty can select the learning activities that are consistent with individual course goals and learning styles desired by the students and the faculty.

Acknowledgments

I appreciate the on-going support of my colleagues at Iowa State University, as well as many colleagues at other universities who encouraged me in this project. My graduate students, research assistants, and the graduate-level merchandising classes have provided invaluable literature search assistance and lively discussion of merchandising ideas. The research conducted by Dana Rupe, Jeong Won Song, and Tiing-Sheng Lin has provided key concepts, particularly in relation to merchandise planning. Claudia Lapadat, Keun Young Oh, and Bonnie Langreck wrote meticulous answers to Learning Activities and provided invaluable evaluation of questions and expectations. Special thanks to Heather Doe, Dr. Nancy Miller, and the junior level merchandising classes for testing and evaluating the manuscript. The undergraduate students' suggestions were the most valuable assistance I received, proof positive of the value of "asking the customer." In addition, a special note of appreciation to Dr. Joan Laughlin and Dr. Rita Kean at University of Nebraska–Lincoln for inspiring development of merchandising theory and Dr. Jean Hamilton at University of Missouri–Columbia for forever cheering me on.

Interaction with numerous apparel professionals, including alumni and recruiters, has provided on-going opportunities for testing ideas and implications. Special thanks to Dr. Russell King and his colleagues at North Carolina State University for developing the *Apparel Retail Model* (ARM), a computer simulation now called the *Sourcing Simulator,* and making it available to us. It has been incorporated into our merchandising classes and has been influential in much of our recent merchandising research. I also want to thank members of the Quick Response Leadership Committee of the American Apparel Manufacturers Association for providing feedback on merchandising-related concepts and ideas.

Appreciation goes to Pam Kirshen Fishman at Fairchild Publications for wanting to publish this book and Olga Kontzias at Fairchild for shepherding the prospectus and manuscript through review and publication. Special thanks to the numerous people who reviewed the prospectus and manuscript, including Diane Ellis, Meredith College; Cheryl Ann Farr, Oklahoma State University; Rita Kean, University of Nebraska–Lincoln; Judy K. Miler, University of Tennessee–Chattanooga; Nancy Miller, Iowa State University; and Teresa A. Summers, Louisiana State University. Your comments and questions provided necessary assistance in manuscript development.

Merchandising Theory

Merchandising Concepts

Learning Objectives

- Define merchandising.
- Introduce the fundamental components of the merchandising process.
- Examine the role of merchandising according to the Behavioral Theory of the Apparel Firm.

The textiles and apparel business is one of the most **globalized industries,** involving more than 10 percent of world business. The U.S. has the largest portion of this business with nearly 5,000 textile material manufacturers, 15,000 apparel manufacturers, 6,000 other fabricated textile manufacturers, and 150,000 textile and apparel retailers. The people of the United States consume more textiles and apparel than citizens of any other country—nearly 76 pounds of textile fiber per person in 1996. Most of the products imported to the U.S. are sourced by U.S.-based firms, primarily manufacturers and retailers. Consequently, the majority of the more than 200 countries in the world export textiles and apparel to the United States. At the same time, domestic apparel production is nearly equal to apparel imports at about $50 billion annually.

Textile and apparel trade associations have been aggressive in developing standards for technology and **Quick Response (QR)** business systems. Retailers are often the first to benefit from new technology related to acquisition and management of inventory in the trade system. Consequently, those retailers that benefited from apparel QR systems apply the same technology to other consumer products. Thus, technology standards developed and supported by the textiles and apparel industry are now being used by both manufacturers and retailers of a wide variety of consumer products. The leadership provided by the textiles and apparel industry has resulted in much broader application of QR systems than was originally conceived.

The textile industry produces three primary types of consumable goods: home textiles, industrial textiles, and apparel. Home textiles include carpets, draperies, upholstery, kitchen and bathroom towels, table linens, etc. Home textiles has been a growth industry over the last decade due primarily to an active home-building industry. Industrial textiles range from road-bed stabilizers to household insulation, from tents and awnings to heart valves. This application of "soft" materials to industrial problems has also resulted in a growth industry.

The apparel business exists to satisfy a fundamental human need—that of protecting and enhancing the appearance of the human body. Materials used for protecting the body as well as those regarded as aesthetically pleasing differ greatly among ethnic groups worldwide. Still, these materials usually have one characteristic in common—flexibility to comfortably accommodate the shape and movement of the human body. As a result, all production and distribution systems in the apparel business are uniquely adapted to handling **flexible materials.** "Soft" materials influence nearly every phase of the production and distribution process and are probably the greatest deterrent to automation of production processes. Thus much of apparel production remains labor intensive. Human hands are still often the most effective tools for picking up two pieces of fabric, matching the edges, and guiding them through a sewing machine. Soft materials also influence packaging and distribution methods. In the retail sector, hangers, racks, and display fixtures have to be designed to show garments made of flexible materials in an attractive manner.

Apparel has long been recognized as the most **change intensive** category of consumer products. In developed countries, the combination of fashion and seasonal influences results in major changes in product offerings, at both the wholesale and retail levels, several times a year. As economies develop, fashion becomes a factor in apparel as soon as people can afford it. Fashion influences are reflected in changes in styling, such as color, line, silhouette, pattern, shape, and acceptable fit. In addition, impacting product change are seasonal influences including the weather, annual holidays, and calendar-related events such as the beginning of the school year. Some manufacturers and retailers update apparel product offerings every two weeks, others every day. The process of planning, developing, and presenting product lines for identified target markets is called **merchandising.**

Merchandising Processes

Merchandising is necessary for most types of products. Automobile merchandisers determine the number of styles, colors, and sizes of vehicles to offer, how many to stock, and when to do price promotions. Grocery merchandisers decide how much space will be devoted to fresh, canned, frozen, and ready-to-eat foods and how assortments and pricing will differ at different times of the year. Video merchandisers determine assortment balance among adventure, romance, and classic movies and video games as well as how many of each title to have on hand. In the textiles and apparel business, merchandisers have a particularly strong role because of the intensive nature of product change.

Merchandising is integral to all parts of textile and apparel trade. Lines of textile fibers, yarns, and fabrics must be planned, developed, and presented. Lines of findings, such as like buttons, zippers, and thread must be merchandised for sale to finished-goods manufacturers. Most apparel manufacturers plan, develop, and present lines to be offered at wholesale markets for selection by retail buyers. At the same time, retail buyers merchandise lines for their retail customers. In these days of vertical integration, many apparel firms are merchandising for both the wholesale and retail sectors. (Read Case 1.1 and do Learning Activity 1.1.)

Definitions of Merchandising

There are many definitions of merchandising in print and probably dozens more in use in common practice, particularly in the apparel industry. P. H. Nystrom (1932) defined merchandising as "careful planning, capable styling and production or selecting and buying, and effective selling," (p. 4). By this definition, the primary mission of today's merchandisers seems unchanged. They continue to play an important role in the exchange process by providing products for consumption. Merchandisers must still understand customer demands, analyze sales trends, select, and present salable products (Fiorito & Fairhurst, 1993; Solomon, 1993). However, due to the competitive pressures in the apparel industry and the innovations required under QR business systems, the demands placed on merchandisers are changing.

R. C. Kean (1987) recognized these pressures when she explored the definition of merchandising, calling it one part of a marketing continuum. She said merchandising has usually been defined by function (i.e., planning, buying, etc.), rather than by concepts from which a theory could

CASE 1.1

Making a Wholesale Business Click

From *Catalog Age* (1996, March) p. 24.

With the luxury of a thriving catalog business carrying the brunt of the revenue and profit load, Venus Swimwear president and majority owner Daryle Scott has built a small, yet profitable wholesale arm.

Venus, a 12-year-old cataloger/manufacturer, each year mails several editions of its racy swimsuit catalog targeted at the junior-miss set as well as spin-off books of women's conservative swimwear and casual apparel. The private company, which won't reveal its annual sales, entered the wholesale business six years ago as a means of leveraging its manufacturing business. Although the wholesale business makes up just 10 percent of Venus' total revenue, Scott says wholesale brings in steady incremental income.

Venus wholesales primarily to mom-and-pop stores around the country rather than to big retail chains. Unlike many wholesalers, Venus doesn't negotiate prices or terms. "We're in a unique position in that our primary business is mail order," Scott says. "So we have our wholesale prices and terms, and that's it."

Because most other swimsuit catalogers' audiences overlap considerably with Venus', the company wholesales to only one cataloger. A spread of Venus swimsuits has appeared regularly for the past five years in Kristi's from Overton's, a swimsuit catalog produced by boating supplies mailer Overton's. "We supply Overton's because its target market is a bunch of boaters," Scott says.

So that neither book gains a competitive edge, Scott makes sure Kristi's prices are the same as Venus'. Although the two books' lists overlap 15 percent to 25 percent, "we mostly target different customers," says Overton's vice president of marketing, Jeff Parnell.

Other Catalog Wholesalers

Venus isn't the only cataloger that wholesales to other mailers. Gourmet foods cataloger/manufacturer American Spoon Foods, for instance, generates about 10 percent of its $2.5 million wholesale business through deals with several catalogers, according to president/CEO Justin Rashid.

"Our view is if customers prefer to buy from those catalogers we sell to, they're going to buy our goods from them no matter what," he says. "So we're not going to lose any of our own catalog customers as a result."

Learning Activity 1.1

Read Case 1.1 very carefully.

1. In what sense is Venus vertically integrated?

2. How have they maximized the potential sales by developing their product line?

3. In what way does Venus merchandise both for wholesale and retail?

ultimately be developed. Kean proposed the following definition: "Merchandising is the analysis and response to the changes (transformations) and processes (advances) which occur in the planning, negotiation, acquisition, and selling of products/services from their inception to their reception and use by the target customer" (p. 10–11). She proposed that perceptions of these functional words were changing due to internal changes in the industry.

As Kean foresaw, merchandisers are becoming more accountable for managing bottom-line profitability in contrast to the traditional measure of gross margin. This means merchandisers may be responsible for inventory turns, carrying costs, in-stock position, and distribution expenses in addition to traditional functions. Therefore, ensuring an in-stock position for the consumer while reducing average inventory is key, as is tailoring merchandise assortments to meet local demand (Solomon, 1993; Troyer & Denny, 1992).

In 1995, Kunz proposed the Behavioral Theory of the Apparel Firm (BTAF) in which merchandising and marketing are two of five constituencies necessary to operate an apparel firm. Kean saw merchandising as a subpart of marketing, whereas Kunz saw merchandising and marketing as interactive yet equivalent functions. Kunz used the Glock and Kunz (1990) definition of merchandising in the behavioral theory: "The planning, development, and presentation of product line(s) for identified target market(s) with regard to prices, assortments, styling, and timing" (p. 63). An alternative name for product line is merchandise line; these terms can be used interchangeably. The Glock and Kunz definition of merchandising is used as a foundation for this textbook.

Kunz also developed and presented a **Taxonomy of the Apparel Merchandising System (TAMS).** TAMS details the potential elements of each of the major components of the Glock and Kunz merchandising definition: line planning, line development, and line presentation. The taxonomy provides a useful framework for examining merchandising activities.

According to TAMS, **line planning** evolves in three major activities: synthesizing current issues and trends, evaluating past selling periods and merchandise classifications, and proposing plans for merchandise budgets and assortments for the specified selling period. Synthesis of merchandise budgets and assortment plans results in some combination of model stock plans, basic stock plans, and automated replenishment plans. Implicit to these plans is line concept, weeks of sale, price points, number and types of classifications, size ranges, and size and fit standards.

Line development occurs in several ways: by selecting finished goods at wholesale markets to fill the line plans, by product development, or via a combination of buying finished goods and product development (Glock & Kunz, 1995). Initial orders are placed for the desired merchandise and may represent 30 to 100 percent of the total inventory required. Reorders are placed according to agreements with vendors regarding merchandise replenishment, components of which include order processing, shipping, receiving, and distribution.

When product development is a part of line development, three phases evolve: pre-line adoption, line adoption, and post-line adoption product development. Pre-line adoption product development focuses on proposing designs, costs, and performance of merchandisible groups. Line adoption involves analysis of the salability of the proposed groups and deciding which designs should become styles in the line. Post-line adoption product development prepares the accepted styles for production. Focus is on perfecting garment fit, analysis of materials, doing detailed costing, writing style specifications, and developing production patterns.

Line presentation may occur internally within a firm, at wholesale, and/or at retail levels depending on the particular firm's strategies. Internal presentation involves evaluating line plans or presenting designs for adoption during the product development process. Wholesale presentation involves offering products for sale to retail buyers in show rooms at seasonal markets or by sales representatives when they call on retail buyers in their stores. Retail presentation involves many different types of retail stores as well as catalog, television, and computer selling. Strategies associated with merchandise presentation include pricing; visual display using fixtures, lighting, and space; providing product information via labels, tickets, and signage; serving customers; and managing inventory.

Merchandising As a Business Function

Merchandising was recognized as a key business function as early as 1924 (Copeland, 1924). In firms with a high rate of product change, merchandising is the function that coordinates the planning, development, and presentation of product lines (Glock & Kunz, 1990). While merchandising may not be recognized as a separate business function when focusing on basic/staple goods (since more merchandise is included in the assortments over a longer period of time), in firms that deal with fashion goods, merchandising processes are essential to the firm's operation.

Theoretical Foundations

The fundamental purpose of a **theory** is to describe, organize, and predict happenings in relation to something. Ultimately, the goal of theory development is to understand and describe a phenomenon and to be able to control and predict outcomes based on the presence and interaction of certain variables (Laughlin, 1993). In its simplest form, a theory consists of assumptions, constructs, and relationships among these constructs. **Assumptions** are the foundation from which a theory departs; **constructs** are the fundamental variables; and **relationships among constructs** determine potential outcomes when the theory is applied.

Two types of theories of the firm are used to describe a firm's decision making: economic and behavioral (Cyert, 1988). **Economic theories** emphasize profit maximization as is widely accepted in business practice. These theories play a strong role in business management, but even the best business strategies are limited by the human beings charged with executing them.

Behavioral theories of the firm provide an alternate way of thinking about how and why business firms operate as they do. These emphasize the role of human behavior, rather than economic factors, in explaining the activities of the firm. The key to a firm's survival is the ability to acquire and maintain resources, including people, money, and physical property. Major issues addressed include how organizational objectives are formed, how strategies evolve, and how decisions are reached within those strategies (Cyert, 1988; Cyert & March, 1963).

Fundamental Constructs from Behavioral Theories of the Firm

According to behavioral theories of the firm, the business firm is a coalition of individuals who have some common goals in relation to production, inventory, sales, market share, or profit (Cyert & March, 1963). Members of the firm's coalition are also members of interdependent, internal subcoalitions or constituencies (Pfeffer & Salancik, 1978). The primary constituencies correspond roughly to the major functional areas of specialization within a firm. Each constituency within the firm shares a common frame of reference and a relatively consistent set of goals and objectives, which may not be consistent with the other constituencies or with the overall goals of the firm. "A theory of the firm that does not give explicit recognition to the activities of these functional subunits fails to address their obvious importance in explaining firm behavior" (Anderson, 1982, p. 70).

Goals of the firm are achieved by negotiation to 1) determine the distribution of resources among internal constituencies; 2) resolve conflicts among the internal constituencies; and 3) determine resource exchanges with external coalitions. The power of an internal constituency is related to the importance of resource exchanges that are its responsibility. Contributing and managing the most critical resources results in the ability to direct and control the organization (Pfeffer & Salancik, 1978). The following theory of the apparel firm and the assumptions that emerge are based on fundamental constructs adopted from previously developed behavioral theories of the firm. These constructs are summarized in Table 1.1.

TABLE 1.1

Fundamental constructs adopted from previously developed behavioral theories of the firm.*

1. A business firm is a coalition of individuals who have some common goals.
2. Each firm/coalition is divided into interdependent, internal subcoalitions or constituencies corresponding to the functional divisions of a firm.
3. Constituencies negotiate resource exchanges inside and outside the firm.
4. Specialization occurs within the constituencies to enhance the effectiveness of negotiation.
5. Conflicting goals develop among the constituencies because of specialization.
6. Negotiation is the primary means of resolving conflicts.
7. The most powerful internal constituencies manage the most critical resources.
8. The most powerful external coalitions offer/control the most critical resources.

*Anderson (1982); Cyert & March (1963); and Pfeffer & Salancik (1978).

Learning Activity 1.2

Review the constructs of behavioral theories of the firm in Table 1.1.

1. How can you apply the concepts of constituencies and specialization from behavioral theory of the firm to situations in family life?

2. Can you think of experiences during your employment when conflicts developed because of different goals related to specialization of constituencies? Were problems resolved? According to the behavioral theory, how would you expect problems to be resolved?

3. What determines the power of a constituency? Does this concept apply in family life?

Behavioral Theory of the Apparel Firm (BTAF)

Apparel is the classic example of a consumer goods industry that experiences rapid product change. Products with rapid change have the greatest need for merchandising processes. Therefore it is appropriate that Behavioral Theory of the Apparel Firm (BTAF) (Kunz, 1995) provides the conceptual foundation for this merchandising textbook. The key economic unit in the apparel industry, as with any industry in the free enterprise system, is the firm. Some apparel firms are primarily manufacturers, others are primarily retailers. A manufacturer is involved in the formulation of the product; a retailer is involved in distributing goods to ultimate consumers. Some apparel firms are vertically integrated, that is, they are involved in some aspects of both manufacturing and retailing of apparel (Glock & Kunz, 1990). Thus, BTAF must accommodate multi-functional organizations and strategies.

Relationships of Internal Constituencies of the Apparel Firm.

It is traditional to represent a firm's organizational structure linearly. (See Figure 1.1.) Organizational structure represented in this way is reflective of top-down communication, limited interaction among divisions, and Theory-X management style that is, historically, typical of the apparel business (Arpan, De La Torre, & Toyne, 1982; Kunz, 1991; Scheller, 1993). Top-down communication means executives determine what is to be done and instruct accordingly. Interaction among a company's divisions may be limited because the activities of each are primarily dependent upon instructions from the division's executives. This mode of operation is consistent with the **Theory-X** management style, which is based on the assumptions that 1) employees really don't want to work, and 2) the primary motivation for work is money (McGregor, 1960).

For contemporary apparel firms, particularly those involved in QR business systems, the apparel business does not operate in a linear manner. Instead, these firms utilize a highly **interactive matrix** of complex decision making. To understand this matrix, it is essential to separate sequential events from decisions that cause events to happen. For example, a sequence of events might go as follows: fiber must be made before yarn can be made before fabric can be made. However, determining what type of fiber, what type of yarn, and what type of fabric should be made to satisfy customer needs requires interaction among people with multiple forms of expertise. Decision making is often most effective when it is highly interactive and multidimensional in its impact. **Theory-Y** management style (McGregor, 1960) incorporates multidimensional communication, problem solving, and empowerment in all parts of the organization. A behavioral view of the firm provides a more realistic and functionally positive view of these realities.

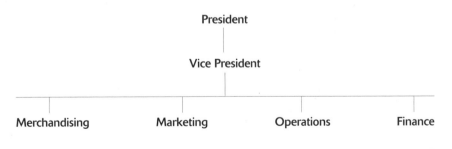

FIGURE 1.1

Traditional diagram of firm organization (Kunz, 1995).

Apparel firms can be viewed as **coalitions of employees** that share some common goals. (See Figure 1.2.) The apparel coalition/firm is divided into **five necessary internal constituencies,** or areas of specialization. They are: executive management, merchandising, marketing, operations, and finance. In the proposed model, these five constituencies encompass all the business functions that must be performed by an apparel firm.

External Coalitions and Environments

The apparel firm's constituencies interact both internally and with constituencies of **external coalitions** to provide the apparel firm with resources. These external coalitions include communities in which the firm resides, competitors, customers, families of employees, shareholders, and

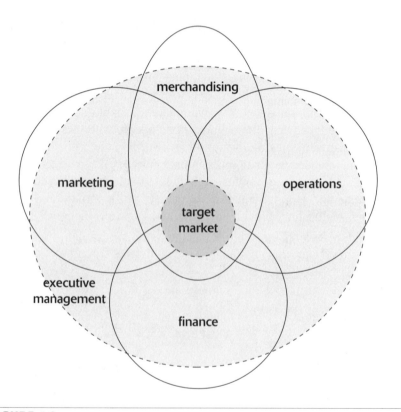

FIGURE 1.2

Interaction of the functional areas of specialization within an apparel firm according to the Behavioral Theory of the Apparel Firm (Kunz, 1995).

suppliers. The apparel firm and its external coalitions operate in many overlapping environments, including cultural, ecological, economic, political, regulatory, social, and technological. These environments may enhance or limit firm behavior. The external coalitions are not represented in Figure 1.2, but the permeable nature of the model implies opportunity for influence from external sources.

Learning Activity 1.3

Compare Figures 1.1 and 1.2.

1. How does line and shape of the models imply different relationships within the firm?

2. How does the implied working environment differ?

3. In which environment would you, as an employee, have the most independence, authority, and responsibility?

4. In which environment would you rather work? Why?

The Marketing Concept as a Philosophy of the Firm

The central focus of the model of firm organization (Figure 1.2) is on the target market. Satisfying the needs and wants of the firm's customers is assumed to be the central focus of decision making. This reflects the **marketing concept** in this theory of apparel firm. Supporting the marketing concept means the ability of a firm to meet its goals is partially dependent on satisfying the needs and wants of external coalitions that are exchange partners, particularly their customers (Houston, 1986). Note that the marketing concept is a philosophy of the firm as a whole; this is separate from the activities of the firm's marketing constituency. The marketing concept reflects a mode of operation for the firm that directs the agendas and activities of individual constituencies. Adoption of the marketing concept is a key factor in the success of apparel firms (Arpan, De La Torre, & Toyne, 1982; Cline, 1990).

Apparel firms specializing in manufacturing were once production driven, but now many realize the importance of being market driven. As such, they have adopted the marketing concept. **Production-driven** firms make and sell goods that can be produced conveniently and efficiently. Deadlines are determined by the production constituency. In contrast, a **market-driven** company evaluates opportunities in the market in relation to the firm's capabilities, and then merchandises, produces, and markets accordingly. In a market-driven firm, production schedules are planned based on sales forecasts and merchandise planning and development. Delivery deadlines are determined by the merchandising and marketing constituencies (Arpan, et al., 1982).

Some apparel retailers used to believe they were arbiters of taste—it was the retailer's job to tell customers what they should buy. Stanley Marcus has said that, in the early days of Neiman Marcus, establishing taste level was a merchandising responsibility. Most retailers today recognize their customers are likely to know their own minds. The retailer's success is dependent on figuring out what customers want, presenting it to them when they want it, and at a price they are willing to pay. Retail success is dependent on responding to customer wants, not dictating customer needs. This also reflects an adoption of the marketing concept.

The preceding scenarios include some key descriptions of concepts that contribute to the framework for the BTAF. A summary of these concepts is presented in Table 1.2.

Constituencies of the Firm

The five internal constituencies of the apparel firm (executive, merchandising, marketing, operations, and finance) form the fundamental theoretical constructs of the BTAF. The discussion of each construct includes primary

TABLE 1.2

Concepts in the apparel scenario.*

Apparel firm—a multi-functional and sometimes vertically integrated business involved in manufacturing and/or distributing apparel.

Constituencies of an apparel firm—five necessary internal areas of specialization encompassing all business functions including executive management, merchandising, marketing, operations, and finance.

Environments of an apparel firm—the complex of conditions that impact the nature of operation of an apparel firm, including cultural, ecological, economic, political, regulatory, social, and technological surroundings.

External coalitions of an apparel firm—constituencies and coalitions outside the apparel firm that impact its behavior, including communities in which the firm resides, competitors, customers, families of employees, shareholders, and suppliers.

Marketing concept—management philosophy of the apparel firm that recognizes that achieving a firm's goals is partially dependent on satisfying the needs and wants of the firm's external coalitions, particularly its customers.

Resources—people, money, and physical property required for operation of the firm's business.

*(Kunz, 1995).

responsibilities of the constituency, job titles that might be associated with each, and common measures of success. In a particular apparel firm, the actual number of areas of specialization and their titles may differ from those used as theoretical constructs in the model.

Executive Constituency

Responsible for the management of an apparel firm, the executive constituency is generally comprised of the heads of the other functional areas of specialization/constituencies and the owner/manager or chief executive officer/president. The **executive constituency** establishes goals for the organization and makes decisions that move the organization toward those goals. Fundamental management decisions include development of the firm's mission and business plan, including selection of target markets, identification of product lines, price ranges, and quality levels. The executive constituency sets the tone for the company and provides a foundation that allows employees to build the company and make it successful. Factors that influence the behavior of executives include the formal structure systems, plans, and policies of the firm; management/leadership style; corporate culture; and the environment in which the firm operates (Kotter & Heskett, 1992). Job titles often included in the executive constituency are owner/manager, president, chief executive or operating officer or financial officer (CEO, COO, CFO), vice president, director, and manager. The executive constituency's success is measured by its ability to achieve the firm's objectives and level a return on shareholder investments.

Merchandising Constituency

The **merchandising constituency** interprets customers' apparel preferences for the rest of the firm. "Merchandising is the planning, development, and presentation of product line(s) for identified target market(s) with regard to prices, assortments, styling, and timing" (Glock & Kunz, 1990, p. 30–31). Merchandising is a profit center, that is, the merchandising constituency is responsible for the product lines that provide the firm's primary source of income. While other constituencies provide services that are essential to the firm's operation, they are not sources of revenue. In fact, they are primarily cost centers. The merchandising constituency establishes the merchandising calendar; plans, develops, and edits product lines; and determines product presentation strategies (Bernard, 1987; Bertrand Frank Associates, 1982; Gioello, 1985; Glock & Kunz, 1990; Technical Advisory Committee, 1982). The merchandising constituency works with, and may also source, materials and production capacity for finished goods.

Merchandising involves directing and overseeing the development of the product lines from start to finish. The content of the line, fabrications, styling, diversity of assortments, pricing, mid-season changes, visual presentations, and timing are all part of the responsibilities and decision making of the merchandising constituency. Positions or job titles that might be a part of the merchandising constituency include buyer, designer, merchandise manager, merchandiser, product development manager, and product manager. Measures of merchandising success may include adjusted gross margin, average inventory, finished goods turnover, gross margin, gross margin return on inventory, maintained markup, markdown percentage, materials cost, piece goods turn, sales-per-square-foot, and sell-through.

Interestingly, as mentioned earlier, not all apparel firms have a defined merchandising constituency. When product lines are defined so that product change is not intense, merchandising responsibilities may be handled by the executive constituency or dispersed among other constituencies. Visualize Figure 1.2 without the merchandising constituency loop. Notice that the model nevertheless appears complete. A model of the behavioral theory of an apparel firm engaged primarily with basic/staple goods may omit the merchandising constituency.

Marketing Constituency

The **marketing constituency** is responsible for broadly defining a company's market, shaping, and strengthening the company's image and its products through promotion, optimizing sales opportunities, and developing alternate strategies for corporate growth (Bertrand Frank Associates, 1982). Marketing constituencies conduct market research, describe target customers, develop marketing strategies, set sales goals, and may sell products at wholesale and/or retail. This constituency also establishes the market position of a firm relative to competing firms, establishes the marketing calendar, and sets advertising and promotional objectives to attain sales goals. Positions or job titles included in the marketing constituency are advertising manager, manufacturer's representative, market researcher, public relations director, and sales manager. Marketing's success is measured by market share, advertising/sales ratios, and rate of sales increase.

Operations Constituency

The **operations constituency** manages the organization's resources of people and physical property. The focus of the operations constituency is very different when a firm is engaged primarily in manufacturing, as opposed to one that is engaged in retailing. Responsibilities include human resources, inventories, physical facilities and equipment, and quality control.

Employee turnover, materials and resource utilization, cost control, efficiency, productivity, and quality are concerns of the operations constituency. Depending on the firm's mission, the operations constituency may be involved in the operation and management of the firm's production and/or retailing facilities. Positions or job titles that might be a part of this constituency include manager of information, inventory controller, receiving manager, distribution manager, personnel manager, college relations manager, and recruiter. Other positions may include plant/store manager, apparel engineer, patternmaker, costing engineer, line manager, quality manager or engineer, and sewing machine operator. Measures of the success of the operations constituency include employee retention, stock/sales ratios, contribution margin, materials utilization, labor productivity, and break-even point.

Finance Constituency

The **finance constituency** personnel are responsible for evaluating the profitability of past business and setting goals for future business. They are additionally responsible for managing accounts receivable and payable, borrowing and spending money, and profit. Job titles included in the finance constituency include accountant, financial analyst, and investment manager. Measures of success include return on investment and profit. See Table 1.3 for a summary the responsibilities, job titles, and measures of success of each constituency.

Learning Activity 1.4

Distinguishing between merchandising and marketing.

The roles of merchandising and marketing are frequently confused. Sometimes the terms are even used interchangeably. One of the purposes of the BTAF is to clarify the responsibilities and relationships of each constituency. Make two lists: one of criteria descriptive of merchandising and the other of criteria descriptive of marketing. In what ways might these two areas of specialization conflict with one another? In what ways are these areas of specialization essential to one another? What are the benefits of a cooperative relationship between merchandising and marketing?

The Decision-Making Matrix

According to behavioral theories of the firm, specialization causes each constituency of the firm to develop its own goals and objectives. At the same time, constituencies must interact and coordinate their activities in order to achieve the common goals of the coalition/firm established by the executive constituency. *The goals of individual constituencies often conflict with*

TABLE 1.3

Theoretical constructs of the internal constituencies of the apparel firm.

Constituency	Responsibility	Job titles	Measures of success
Executive	Establishes the firm's goals and administers activities to achieve them.	Owner/manager, president, chief executive or operating officer or financial officer, vice president, director, manager.	Achievement of the firm's objectives; return on shareholder investment.
Merchandising	Plans, develops, and presents product lines.	Buyer, designer, merchandise manager, merchandiser, product development manager, product manager.	Adjusted gross margin, average inventory, finished goods turnover, gross margin, gross margin return on inventory, maintained markup, markdown percentage, materials cost, piece goods turn, sales-per-square-foot, sell-through.
Marketing	Defines target customer(s) and develops positioning and promotion strategies.	Advertising manager, manufacturer's representative, market researcher, public relations director, sales manager.	Market share, advertising/sales ratios, rate of sales increase, markdowns/sales ratios, growth.
Operations	Manages people and physical property.	Manager of information, inventory controller, receiving manager, distribution manager, personnel manager, college relations manager, recruiter, plant/store manager, apparel engineer, patternmaker, costing engineer, line manager, quality manager, sewing machine operator.	Employee retention, stock/sales ratios, contribution margin, materials utilization, labor productivity, and break-even point.
Finance	Manages monetary resources.	Accountant, financial analyst, investment manager.	Return on investment, profit, cash flow.

each other because of contrasting responsibilities and priorities. The ability of the firm to reach its goals may be limited by how successfully conflicts among constituencies are resolved. Although there is a normal human tendency to avoid confrontation, conflicts among constituencies can be resolved through negotiation. Such negotiation can emphasize the benefits of collaboration over competition.

Issues that commonly cause conflict among constituencies include sales forecasts, materials selection, number and types of merchandise classes and styles, size and timing of purchase orders or production runs, levels of inventory, and quantities and types of fixtures or equipment. Each constituency's perspectives on these issues differ in relation to timing of decisions and levels of investment. Functional priorities of constituencies also differ. For example, the merchandising constituency recognizes the need for diversity of styling, color, and price to satisfy customers' needs. Yet from the standpoint of the operations constituency, diversity and efficiency are not compatible (Technical Advisory Committee, 1982). The finance constituency usually seeks to limit merchandise investment while marketing may seek brand identity and product differentiation through what may be regarded by the operations constituency as frivolous and costly advertising campaigns. Interactions and conflict resolution among internal constituencies and interactions of internal constituencies with external coalitions and environments provide the basis for the decision-making matrix.

Executive Interactions

Cohesiveness of purpose among constituencies may well depend on the strength of leadership from the executive constituency. As described earlier, the executive constituency provides the glue that cements the functional divisions into a whole. Sam Walton was a classic example of a leader able to inspire unified support for a firm's goals—the goals necessary to grow a small discount shop into the international Wal-Mart discount chain. The executive constituency often establishes the firm's goals with input from the firm's other constituencies. The management/leadership process includes interactions related to planning, coordinating, directing, negotiating, allocating, motivating, and evaluating activities of all the firm's constituencies. The ability of executives to inspire resourceful cooperation among constituencies while carrying out the varied responsibilities required for the firm to reach its goals may determine the firm's overall productivity.

The executive constituency also interacts intensively with external coalitions and environments. Executives are responsible to shareholders first and foremost. They are the primary representatives of the firm in the community at large. Their presence is often required on boards of charitable organizations and chambers of commerce. Their interaction in the economic and political environment of the community may be essential to maintain community support for the firm.

Merchandising Interactions

As illustrated in Figure 1.2, the merchandising constituency provides an integrative function among the four divisions involved with the product line (Bernard, 1987; Bertrand Frank Associates, 1982; Brauth & Brown, 1989; Brown & Brauth 1989; Glock & Kunz, 1990; Kunz, 1986; Mellon & Brown, 1989). The merchandising constituency is responsible for decision making with regard to product lines, using input from the other constituencies, and interpreting the needs and wants of the target market while considering the economic, social, and cultural environments of the firm. Merchandising negotiates differences in goals and priorities that exist among the firm's internal constituencies related to product lines.

Responsibilities of the merchandising constituency and its interactions with other constituencies vary according to the size of the firm. Merchandising is sometimes described generally as buying and selling (Copeland, 1924; Kotsiopulos, 1987), and in small firms the merchandising constituency tends to be responsible for both. As firms grow, buying and selling is eventually separated and assigned to different constituencies, with the planning and acquisition remaining the primary function of the merchandising constituency. The selling function may become the responsibility of the marketing or operations constituency. In this scenario, the merchandising constituency loses direct control of presentation and sale of goods. Merchandisers must work with market representatives or retail department managers on an informal basis since merchandisers do not have formal power in the marketing or operations constituencies. This is a source of conflict between merchandisers who plan and develop the goods and the constituency responsible for selling the goods. In addition, the finance constituency may impose strict limits on investment in merchandise, particularly when firms are in financial distress. The merchandising constituency, however, continues to be regarded as the primary revenue source because of its responsibility for planning and developing the product lines (Cyert, 1988).

Another major responsibility of the merchandising constituency is negotiating with external coalitions. Internal constituencies that negotiate vital resource exchanges with external coalitions come to have greater power within the firm (Anderson, 1982). The merchandising constituency's acquisition negotiations are vital to the firm because the product line is the firm's primary profit center.

At the same time, external coalitions that control vital resources have greater control and influence over the firm's activities (Pfeffer & Salancik, 1978). Suppliers with well-established product lines or highly desired brand names are in the best position to influence merchandisers. They can demand minimum quantities, floor space, specialized display fixtures, advertising, limited markdowns, etc. External coalitions that offer what merchandising constituencies regard as essential resources (e.g., materials, styles, brands) have the power to influence allocation of the firm's resources.

Marketing Interactions

The marketing calendar, including the key dates within each selling period, provides a framework for planning strategies for the entire apparel firm. Market research conducted or contracted by the marketing constituency provides the basis for establishing sales goals for the company, product line, departments and/or classifications. Sales goals are functional in guiding resource allocation within the firm.

Using market research and other interactions with external coalitions, the marketing constituency is in the best position to communicate information to internal constituencies about the nature of the target market, customer preferences, nature of the competition, and positioning strategies. Marketing constituencies interact with and evaluate customer and competitor external coalitions. Sales representatives, manufacturer's representatives and retail sales associates have the most direct contact with buyers at the retail and consumer levels. The marketing constituency provides feedback from retail buyers, competitors and consumers to the company's other divisions. Marketing also monitors competitors' business activities and plans and implements appropriate positioning strategies to benefit the entire firm.

Operations Interactions

Interactions of the operations constituency may vary greatly depending on the size of the firm, its mission, and whether it owns retailing and/or production facilities. The latter usually involves significant investment in real estate requiring interaction by operations with the executive and finance constituencies and perhaps the marketing and merchandising constituencies. Numerous external coalitions and environments may also be involved.

In this model the operations constituency also includes the human resources area of specialization. Labor is a strong source of interaction both inside and outside the firm. The performance and productivity of the labor force is of great concern to the entire firm, since both retailing and manufacturing-based apparel businesses tend to be labor intensive. The operations constituency collaborates in the development and administration of remuneration systems and benefit packages for employees. As a result, the operations constituency may also have the most direct interaction with the external coalitions composed of the employees' families. Operations may also strongly influence company policy relative to hours of work per week, overtime pay, types of reimbursement, etc., which may affect all family members. Issues such as labor costs, robotization, and safety regulation stimulate interactions for operations constituencies. Economic, technological, and regulatory external environments particularly affect the operations constituency.

Finance Interactions

The control function of the finance constituency creates extensive and sometimes stressful interactions with the other divisions. Finance prepares reports on which the executive constituency bases productivity assessment of the other constituencies and plans for future development. Finance also provides feedback to all other constituencies regarding their performance through management information systems and/or daily, weekly, monthly, and annual reports. Finance is responsible for paying the bills and collecting accounts receivable.

In addition, the finance constituency examines and acquires the necessary financial resources to operate the firm. Interactions with external coalitions may include borrowing money from financial firms, paying vendors for goods and services, and collecting charge accounts from customers. Firms that have heavy debts may become finance-driven instead of market-driven, which would seem contrary to the success of the firm.

The interactions of constituencies provide the foundation for the decision making matrix. These interactions, both within and outside the firm, are summarized in Table 1.4.

Summary of Relationships Among a Firm's Internal Constituencies

1. The apparel coalition is divided into five major constituencies: upper management and four functional areas of specialization including merchandising, marketing, operations, and finance.
2. Each constituency has goals and responsibilities related to their particular functions within the firm.
3. Goals and responsibilities of one constituency contribute in their own way to those of the total firm, but are not likely to be exactly the same as goals and responsibilities of other areas.
4. Goals and responsibilities of constituencies may conflict with one another.

5. Conflicts are resolved through negotiation.
6. The merchandising constituency negotiates/arbitrates differences among constituencies and provides an integrative function in relation to the product line.
7. The power of a constituency is related to the value of the resource exchanges it negotiates.
8. Business decisions frequently involve a complex matrix of information sources.
9. Business decisions have multi-faceted impact on both internal constituencies and external coalitions.

TABLE 1.4

The likely internal and external interactions of constituencies of the apparel firm as foundations for the decision making matrix.*

	LIKELY INTERACTIONS		
Constituency	**Internal Constituencies**	**External Coalitions**	**Environments**
Executive	foundation of firm merchandising marketing operations finance	shareholders suppliers customers communities	economic social cultural political
Merchandising	integrative function related to product line executive marketing operations finance	suppliers customers competitors	economic social cultural technological
Marketing	executive merchandising operations finance	customers competitors communities	economic social cultural political ecological
Operations	executive merchandising marketing finance	suppliers communities families of employees	economic cultural regulatory technological ecological
Finance	executive merchandising operations marketing	customers suppliers communities	economic political technological regulatory

*(Kunz, 1995).

CASE 1.2

Pamida's Focus: Small Towns in a Big Way.

From Johnson, J. L. (1995, December). *Discount Merchandiser,* pp. 20–30.

Pamida's new prototype stores are relatively small at 42,500 square feet. The chain's target markets are also on the small side—rural towns with populations of 10,000 to 15,000. This pocket-size focus is paying off for the chain: The 15 percent of its stores in the new, smaller prototype mode account for about 20 percent of Pamida's annual volume of approximately $750 million. And going forward, the company expects to be doing $1 billion in sales by the year 1999. In other words Pamida is getting bigger by looking after small, out-of-the-way places.

"We don't compete directly against some of the national chains, which is one of the reasons we're a bit healthier than some of the others," explains Steven S. Fishman, chairman and CEO of Omaha, NE-based Pamida. "Mentally, our competition is ourselves. We discuss that a lot, versus worrying about what others are doing."

By the end of 1995, Pamida will have 17 new prototype stores in place in Indiana, Ohio, Michigan and Nebraska. "We plan to add six to eight new markets a year for the next five years," Fishman reports. "For us, a market is one location. While we have been opening new stores, we have also closed 20 during the same period. We don't intend to open more outside the current 15-state trading area, unless, of course, something becomes available. In four years, we will probably have about 45 percent of our chain in the new prototype format.

"Basically, we try to place ourselves in the middle of what's around us. We try to insulate ourselves in population bases of 15,000 or less. And we want to be at least 15 or 20 miles from competition. We look for markets that aren't going to grow so dramatically that eventually we will face competition.

"For example, in 1992 we competed with Wal-Mart in 28 percent of our markets. Today, we're indirect competition with Wal-Mart in only 16 percent of our markets, and we will continue to compete in fewer and fewer markets in the future."

Pamida recently opened a prototype store in Blair, NE, north of Omaha. There is a Wal-Mart Supercenter 25 miles west in Fremont. Twenty miles toward Omaha, there's a Wal-Mart discount store, and 25 miles south is a Target Supercenter. "It wouldn't make

much sense for a national company to open a large store in this size market," says Fishman. "We aim to give our customers good reason to shop Pamida instead of driving 25 or 30 miles to a larger store. We try to keep them at home whenever possible.

"Over 65 percent of our business is in routine purchases, not stimulated by promotions, or any of the 52 weekly tabs we run throughout the year. What brings them into the store is top-of-mind needs: toothpaste, T-shirts, socks, snacks, and so forth."

Staying close to home is preferable for several reasons. Fishman explains: "One, it's handy. Two, our prices are as competitive as those in national chains. Three, and most important to us, our apparel offering is beginning to include national brands that are not normally found in discount stores. You will see, for example, B.U.M. Equipment, and Bugle Boy. In shoes, we have Converse, Reebok, and Keds. We want to carry more branded merchandise but acquiring it is a slow process. In other categories we have AT&T, Sony, General Electric, Duracell, Rubbermaid, T-Fal, Mattel, and Fisher Price. We offer the best quality merchandise available at nationally competitive prices to meet the basic needs of our customers."

Disappearing "Discount"

Pamida, which for many, many years carried the descriptive word "discount" next to its name, has eliminated the word completely from its new prototypical store. Now the word does not appear anywhere in the new stores.

Yet Pamida competes directly with discounters. "We have no choice," Fishman concurs. "We still have to offer what the consumer wants on a day in, day out basis. When you live in a small town, there are three basic necessities that are required to keep the consumer in town: great general merchandise, great groceries, and great health care and/or pharmacy."

Of the 180-plus stores Pamida currently operates, 40 have pharmacies. "They are a critical strategy to our future growth," Fishman declares. "When it comes to health care and prescriptions, many people will drive 20 or 30 miles to save money. So we have to be competitive with Wal-Mart and Target. Walgreen's and Osco Drug are here too. They're great at what they do."

Last year, Pamida's apparel business pulled in almost 25 percent of its total business. "That's up from

22.5 percent a couple of years ago," Fishman says. "We'd love to increase it to 27 or 28 percent, which we think is a realistic goal. At the same time, we are not going to turn our back on merchandise that made this company—day in and day out needs—such as home furnishing and hardgoods. As for apparel, we stress daily wants and needs, and casual weekend wear. We are not in the dress business and don't intend to go into it. When people think of Pamida it's socks, underwear, T-shirts, blue jeans, and fleece.

A Fashionable Floor

"In our new prototype stores, about 45 percent of the sales floor is allocated to ready-to-wear, and sales are about 30 to 40 percent higher than in our average store. The older traditional stores devoted about 75 percent of the floor space to hardgoods, and about 25 percent to ready-to-wear.

"In the new stores, we have moved home furnishings into the center core of the store, along with stationery, domestics, housewares, and RTA furniture—which is a major move for us. And our overall average margins are up substantially in the new stores—maybe a couple of full points in all."

In addition to moving ahead with its new store format, Pamida plans sizable capital investments in technology, anywhere from $6 to $7 million, "a very large amount for us to be spending on systems," Fishman admits. "This is a company that for many years starved itself from an investment standpoint. We recognize that if we are going to play in the big time, we will have to do things differently . . . we will go off the mainframe computer and put a PC on every buyer's desk . . . invest in software to help people make better and quicker decisions."

"In essence, we are going to put information in the hands of those using it, to help them make better decisions. The information will be tailored for an individual—focused without excess data to contend with. The user will be able to organize it in a spreadsheet as he or she wants: by season, by style, by category, It will all be extremely user-friendly."

Since April 1994, Pamida has been scanning every item. "But we don't have accurate on-hand information by SKU," explains Frank A. Washburn, executive vice president at Pamida. "By the end of July 1996, we plan to have 100 percent SKU-level inventory, so that we will be able to tell by store and item exactly what's on hand and what's been sold. It's the minimum requirement if your are going to be a thriving retailer today. Our biggest investment is in inventory. You have to have the right quantity of product at the right location when the customer wants it."

The Cutting Edge Dilemma

History doesn't always repeat itself. Weather, a constant variable, can have a major influence on shopping behavior. "I think most replenishment programs are based on about three years' worth of history," Washburn notes. "They don't take into account a drought or an extremely wet summer. That is still part of the buyer's decision-making process. It still takes a buyer to understand how much of a particular product will sell, depending on the advertising program, store space, and such variables as fashion and color. The buyer who guesses that the Cabbage Patch Doll will be a hit is going to be a hero. The one who misses it won't be. You can't predict that with a computer."

Is Pamida's corporate culture changing? In what direction is it heading? Answers Fishman: "We're driven to win as a team. No one is going to be successful as an individual. We have to communicate with one another, which we talk a lot about. Instead of berating someone for making a mistake, we encourage them to make a decision and then make sure that the experience is a learning one, and that they don't make the same mistake the next time."

"It's important to recognize that this is a relatively small company spread across 2,200 miles from one end to the other. We've got to have people who can make good decisions. We can't have the telephone ringing all the time at headquarters. We encourage our people to make good, sound decisions every day-no matter at what level. Our culture is headed in that direction-communication and empowerment.

"We talk about being a family, which some people think is a little corny. We employ 6,500 to 7,000 people, but whenever a decision is made, it affects the lives of husbands, wives, children—probably 30,000 or 40,000 people in all. We can't afford to make too many bad decisions. Otherwise, we won't be around. It's scary."

Learning Activity 1.5

Read Case 1.2.

Analyze the case relative to the behavioral theory of the firm.

1. Describe the dimensions of Pamida's market positioning strategy.

2. According to the behavioral theory of the firm, what constituency is responsible for market position?

3. What merchandise classifications are included in Pamida's product line?

4. According to the behavioral theory of the firm, what constituency is in charge of the product line?

5. At Pamida, what types of interactions would you expect between the merchandising and marketing constituencies?

6. In what other ways does Pamida exemplify the behavioral theory of the firm?

Summary of Theoretical Assumptions of BTAF

1. An apparel firm can consist of any combination of manufacturing and/or distribution functions.
2. A firm is a coalition of individuals with some common goals.
3. The coalition is made up of sub-coalitions, or constituencies, that conform to the functional areas of specialization of the firm.
4. Five constituencies perform all the business functions required for the apparel firm's operation.
5. Overall goals of the coalition are formulated by the executive constituency.
6. The focus of the coalition is on the customer and satisfying the customer's needs within the limitations of the firm.
7. The inter-relationships among constituencies form the internal decision-making matrix for the firm.

Summary

The apparel industry is the classic example of a business operation in an environment of intense product change. Merchandising has a key role and a central business function when product change is frequent. While merchandising has many definitions, they nevertheless have similar meanings. This textbook is based on the Glock and Kunz (1990) definition: "Merchandising is the planning, development, and presentation of product lines for identified target market(s) with regard to prices, assortments, styling, and timing." Merchandise/line planning is a process that results in a framework for line development. Merchandise/line development is a process that determines the actual goods to fill out the line plan. Merchandise/line presentation results in evaluation of the effectiveness of line planning and line development. Merchandise/line presentation may take place internal to a firm, in wholesale markets, or in retail markets.

Behavioral Theory of the Apparel Firm addresses the role of the merchandising process in achieving a firm's goals. According to the behavioral theory, a firm is a coalition of individuals with some common goals. An apparel firm can consist of any combination of manufacturing and/or retailing functions. The focus of the coalition is on the customer and satisfying the customer's needs within the limitations of the firm. The coalition is made up of sub-coalitions or constituencies that conform to the firm's functional areas of specialization. Five constituencies perform all the business functions required for the apparel firm operation. The overall goals of the coalition are formulated by the executive constituency. The merchandising constituency is in charge of coordinating the planning, development, and presentation of the product line. The marketing constituency defines target customer(s) and develops positioning and promotion strategies for the firm. The operations constituency manages people and physical property, and the finance constituency manages financial resources. The inter-relationships among constituencies form the internal decision-making matrix for the firm.

Key Concepts

apparel firm
arbiters of taste
areas of specialization
assumptions
behavioral theories of the firm
behavioral theory of the apparel firm (BTAF)
change-intensive products
coalition of employees
constructs
economic theories of the firm
environments of apparel firms
executive constituency
external coalitions

finance constituency
firm
flexible materials
globalized industry
interactive decision-making matrix
internal constituencies of the firm
manufacturer
market-driven
marketing concept
marketing constituency
merchandise/line development
merchandise/line planning
merchandise/line presentation

merchandising
merchandising constituency
operations constituency
overlapping environments
production-driven
Quick Response (QR)
resources
retailer
Theory-X management style
Theory-Y management style

Integrated Learning Activity 1.6

Create a puzzle representing the textiles and apparel industry and BTAF. Select a piece of heavy paper and a piece of transparent film, each about eight or nine inches square. Divide the heavy paper into five equal-sized strips. Write one of the following titles on each strip: ultimate consumption, retailing, apparel manufacturing, materials manufacturing, fiber production/manufacturing. Cut the transparent film into four equal size strips. On the strips of transparent film, write the following titles: merchandising, marketing, operations, finance.

With the class divided into critical thinking teams, use the strips of paper and film to create models representing industry operation. Think through definition of terms and relationships among business functions. When teams are satisfied with their organization of the strips, think through the assumptions upon which their models are based. Report outcomes to the class.

Recommended Resources

Bernard, H. (1987, January). Vertical ventures. *Apparel Industry Magazine,* pp. 56–58.
Brauth, B., & Brown, P. (1989, June). Merchandising malpractice. *Apparel Industry Magazine,* pp. 108–110.
Drinkard, G. (1992). Quick Response—the perfect partnership: A hard goods vendor perspective. *Proceedings of the Quick Response 92 Conference,* 59–73.
Five thousand Sears vendors to use EDI. (1990, September). *Apparel Industry Magazine, 51,* 38.
Hartnett, M. (1993, September). Buyers: Endangered species? *Stores, 75,* 53–55.
Heinsen, B., Holohan, J., Muldowney, K., & Williams, B. (1992). The role of the merchant—implementing quick response. *Proceedings of the Quick Response 92 Conference, 58.*
Houston, F. S. (1986, April). The marketing concept: What it is and what it is not. *Journal of Marketing, 50,* 81-87.

References

Anderson, P. E. (1982, Spring). Marketing, strategic planning and the theory of a firm. *Journal of Marketing, 46,* 15–26.
Arpan, J. S., De La Torre, J., & Toyne, B. (1982). *The U.S. apparel industry: International challenge, domestic response* (Research Monograph No. 88). Atlanta: Georgia State University, Business Publications Division.
Bernard, H. (1987, January). Vertical ventures. *Apparel Industry Magazine,* pp. 56–58.
Bertrand Frank Associates. (1982). *Profitable merchandising of apparel.* New York: National Knitwear & Sportswear Association.
Brauth, B., & Brown, P. (1989, June). Merchandising malpractice. *Apparel Industry Magazine,* pp. 108–110.
Brown, P., & Brauth, B. (1989, August). Merchandising methods. *Apparel Industry Magazine,* pp. 78–82.
Cline, W. R. (1990). *The future of world trade in textiles and apparel.* Washington, DC: Institute for International Economics.

Copeland, M. T. (1924). *Principles of merchandising.* Chicago: A. W. Shaw.

Cyert, R. M. (1988). *The economic theory of organization and the firm.* New York: Harvester-Wheatsheaf.

Cyert, R. M., & March, J. G. (1963). *A behavioral theory of the firm.* Englewood Cliffs, NJ: Prentice Hall.

Fiorito, S. S., & Fairhurst, A. E. (1993). Comparison of buyers' job content in large and small retail firms. *Clothing and Textiles Research Journal, (11)*3, 8–15.

Gioello, D. (1985, March). A merchandising checklist. *Bobbin,* pp. 155–158.

Glock, R. E., & Kunz, G. I. (1990). *Apparel manufacturing: Sewn products analysis.* New York: Macmillan.

Glock, R. E., & Kunz, G. I. (1995). *Apparel manufacturing: Sewn product analysis (2nd ed).* Englewood Cliffs, NJ: Prentice Hall.

Houston, F. S. (1986, April). The marketing concept: What it is and what it is not. *Journal of Marketing, 50,* 81–87

Kean, R. C. (1987). Definition of merchandising: Is it time for a change? In R. C. Kean (Ed.), *Theory building in apparel merchandising* (pp. 8–11). Lincoln: University of Nebraska-Lincoln.

Kotsiopulos, A. (1987). The need to identify merchandising content and generalizations. In R. C. Kean (Ed.), *Theory building in apparel merchandising* (pp. 12–14). Lincoln: University of Nebraska-Lincoln.

Kotter, J. P., & Heskett, J. L. (1992). *Corporate culture and performance.* New York: Free Press.

Kunz, G. I. (1986). Career development of college graduates employed in retailing. *Dissertation Abstracts International, 46,* 3619-A. (University Microfilm No. DA604886).

Kunz, G. I. (1991). EDI, JIT, FM, MM, QA, QR, UPS, VAM: The magnitude of change for a new socio-technical interface. *[TC]² Report,* pp. 6–7.

Kunz, G. I. (1995). Behavioral theory of the apparel firm: A beginning. *Clothing and Textiles Research Journal, 13*(4), 252–261.

Laughlin, J. (1993). *Toward a contextual understanding of theoretical development in textiles and clothing.* Unpublished manuscript, University of Nebraska-Lincoln.

McGregor, D. M. (1960). *The human side of enterprise.* New York: McGraw-Hill.

Mellon, C., & Brown, P. (1989, November). Using real time. *Apparel Industry Magazine,* pp. 54–60.

Nystrom, P. H. (1932). *Fashion merchandising.* New York: The Ronald Press Co.

Pfeffer, J. & Salancik, G. R. (1978). *The external control of organizations: A resource dependence perspective.* New York: Harper and Row.

Scheller, H. P. (1993). *Apparel quality through the perception of apparel production managers and operators.* Unpublished masters thesis, Iowa State University, Ames.

Solomon, B. (1993, July). Will there be a miracle on 34th Street? *Management Review, 82,* 33–36.

Technical Advisory Committee of American Apparel Manufacturers Association. (1982). *Fashion in apparel manufacturing: Coping with style variation.* 1982 Report of the Technical Advisory Committee. Arlington, VA: Author.

Troyer, C., & Denny, D. (1992, May). Quick response evolution. *Discount Merchandiser, 32*(5), 104–105, 107.

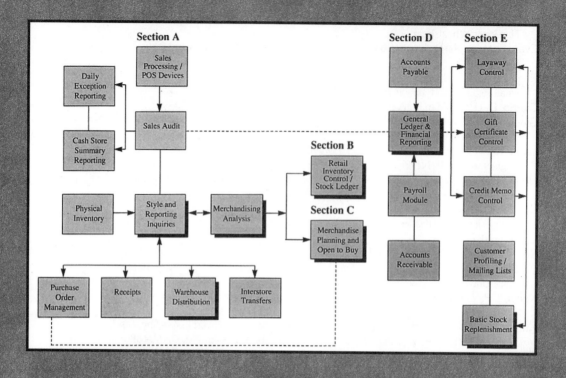

Section A

Sales Processing / POS Devices

Daily Exception Reporting

Sales Audit

Cash Store Summary Reporting

Physical Inventory

Style and Reporting Inquiries

Merchandising Analysis

Section B

Retail Inventory Control / Stock Ledger

Section C

Merchandise Planning and Open to Buy

Purchase Order Management

Receipts

Warehouse Distribution

Interstore Transfers

Section D

Accounts Payable

General Ledger & Financial Reporting

Payroll Module

Accounts Receivable

Section E

Layaway Control

Gift Certificate Control

Credit Memo Control

Customer Profiling / Mailing Lists

Basic Stock Replenishment

Merchandising Technology

Learning Objectives

- Define merchandising technology.
- Evaluate concepts of Quick Response business systems.
- Discuss the role of merchandising in a Quick Response universe.
- Incorporate Quick Response and Diffusion of Innovation theory into Behavioral Theory of the Apparel Firm.

When an apparel firm introduces Quick Response (QR) business systems and technologies, the assumptions regarding the firm's purpose and operation fundamentally change. Organizational learning is required. Purveyors of technology often express frustration that, when businesses acquire new technology, they seldom use it to capacity; only a few select functions are utilized (Kunz, 1991). Few apparel firms are investing enough time and other resources to successfully implement QR strategies (Black, 1992). Consequently, their return on the investment in new technology is seldom optimized.

Role of Merchandising Technology

Technology is defined by Schon (1967) as "any tool or technique, any product or process, any physical equipment or method of doing or making, by which human capability is extended" (p. 1). Galbraith (1978) defined technology as "the systematic application of scientific or other organized knowledge to practical tasks" (p. 12). This definition is extended by Pacey (1983) as "the application of scientific and other knowledge to practical tasks by ordered systems that involve people and organizations, living things and machines" (p. 6). Pacey's definition includes social and cultural impacts, as well as technical aspects.

Considering these definitions of technology, merchandising itself is a kind of technology. The impact of merchandising technology may have some effect on consumer behavior, industrial and economic structure and activity, and furthermore, on human life, ideas, and creative activity. Therefore, using a broad definition, we can call merchandising technology the systematic application of scientific knowledge and technique to merchandising in ways that reflect social and cultural value. Or to fully implement the Glock and Kunz definition of merchandising (1990), merchandising technology may be the systematic application of scientific knowledge and techniques to planning, developing, and presenting product lines in ways that reflect social and cultural value.

The ultimate goal of merchandising technology is to use time effectively, increase merchandising accuracy, and optimize benefits to the firm and the consumer. In today's markets, scientific knowledge and techniques relate primarily to use of computers, information systems, telecommunications, and related hardware and software. The operational definition of **merchandising technology** used in this text reflects this more limited perspective: *"Merchandising technology is the systematic application of information technology and telecommunications to planning, developing, and presenting product lines in ways that reflect social and cultural value."*

Learning Activity 2.1

Think through the sequence of definitions related to merchandising technology.

1. What are some examples of merchandising technology as experienced by retail customers?

2. Why is it important that technology "reflect social and cultural value"?

Quick Response Business Systems

In the U.S., the textiles and apparel industry has recognized that to survive in a globally competitive environment, firms must become more effective in serving their customers. This means operating within shorter time frames and making more accurate and timely decisions. This movement to compress the apparel time line from product concept to delivery to consumer—and to make more informed decisions based on up-to-the minute information—has been termed "Quick Response" (QR). Associations within the American textile and apparel industry have been leaders in developing technology and standard practices to support QR business systems (Blackburn, 1991; Hammond, 1993; Sheridan, 1994), although progress has been slower than expected by many of the QR pioneers. Today, most progressive manufacturers and retailers are using some aspects of QR business systems (Kurt Salmon Associates, 1994).

A QR system can trigger a series of benefits. First and foremost is increased sales due to an increased retail in-stock position. Simply stated, this means having the product the customer wants on the shelf or the rack when the customer wants it. Therefore, more merchandise is sold at first price, resulting in higher financial outcomes. Improved sales at retail benefits the entire supply and distribution system. Realistically, the ultimate consumer pays the price for the entire apparel business system.

QR systems increase sales with lower inventory levels and reduced carrying costs (Bravman, 1993). Additional advantages include the accuracy of information, time savings due to reduced data entry, and increased distribution efficiency (Gilman, 1989). These benefits can be recognized throughout the supply and distribution matrix, creating a win-win situation for all firms involved.

Quick Response Conferences

Annual Quick Response trade conferences commonly attract up to 1,600 attendees, primarily apparel manufacturing people who pay over $800 to attend. Automatic Identification Manufacturers, Inc. (AIM USA) and Voluntary Interindustry Communications Standards (VICS) have sponsored the QR conferences since 1992. The purpose of the conferences is to inspire apparel professionals and other business people to effectively adopt QR business systems. Presenters include representatives of major retailers including Belk Stores, Dayton Hudson Corp, The Home Depot, Kmart, Mercantile Stores, Saks Fifth Avenue, Sears, Strawbridge & Clothier, and Target Stores; major apparel manufacturers such as Brown Group Inc., Haggar, Jockey International, Levi Strauss, Norton McNaughton, Phillips Van Huesen, Sara Lee, and VF Corp.; and major materials suppliers, including Delta Mills, Springs Industries, and Pillowtex Corp. Other major consumer goods companies are also represented, including EKCO Housewares, Florsheim Shoe Company, Hartz Mountain Corp, Lenox China and Crystal, Proctor and Gamble, and SuperValue Inc. Other presenters are representatives of consulting firms, computer software companies, and educators. It is not surprising that most presenters represent large companies. Research has shown that large companies are more likely to adopt QR business strategies (Kincade & Cassill, 1993).

Fundamentals of Quick Response

The textiles and apparel industry operates in a constantly changing business environment. Factors contributing to the recent complexity of the industry include low wages in developing countries, the U.S. trade deficit, the formation of the World Trade Organization (WTO), the Multi-Fiber Arrangement (MFA), the North American Free Trade Agreement (NAFTA), currency fluctuations, the surge of leveraged buyouts and consolidations of manufacturing and retail businesses, as well as increasing global competition (Anderson Consulting, 1994; Glock & Kunz, 1995; Hunter, 1990; Kean, 1987). Additionally, U.S. retail markets are saturated with malls, stores, and merchandise; distribution channels are clogged with inventory and customers are more demanding (Johnson, 1992). Stiffening global competition is forcing firms to compress lead and cycle times as a condition of competitive survival (Blackburn, 1991; Mooney & Hessel, 1990; Kurt Salmon Associates, 1994). In an attempt to combat and manage these factors, QR business systems are being developed, implemented, and updated.

QR has been defined in a variety of ways. Usually, QR is associated with the sophisticated technology that facilitates the process. However, technology is simply one part of the equation, not the definition of QR. Similarly, QR is often defined by what it can accomplish, for example, lower carrying costs, higher gross margins, etc. Again, these accomplishments do not represent what QR *is*, but are instead some of its outcomes. For the purposes of this textbook, the following **Quick Response** definition was developed: *Quick Response is a comprehensive business strategy incorporating time-based competition, agility, and partnering to optimize the supply system, the distribution system, and service to customers.* The supply system includes manufacturing and associated activities related to materials and finished goods. The distribution system includes wholesale markets, merchandise handling and transportation, and retailing.

Customer-Driven Business System

The fundamental premise of QR is that merchandise systems are customer driven. Knowing what is selling over the retail counter **real-time** (right now) is essential. The process begins when a customer makes a purchase at a retail store and the sale is recorded via a **point of sale (POS)** system using a **scanner** and a **universal product code (UPC).** The style, size, color, and other pertinent data related to the product is relayed via **electronic data interchange (EDI)** to the retailer's and vendor's data systems and to the vendor's materials suppliers. Action on replacement depends on predetermined agreements and/or automatic replenishment models. In less than a week the product is manufactured using a flexible production system then delivered to the retailer shelf-ready, using drop shipment or cross-docking strategies. High levels of collaboration and team-work are required throughout the process. The goal is to optimize sales at first price based on minimum inventory throughout the supply system.

POS information is available primarily through the use of UPCs and retail scanning, combined with EDI among vendors and their suppliers. A UPC is a 12-digit code representing a unique product. It is a standard for "identifying merchandise to the lowest level of detail necessary for tracking and ordering merchandise" (Anderson Consulting, 1994, p. 5). This bar code is scanned electronically at the retail counter when a consumer makes a purchase, providing up-to-the-minute (real-time) sales information. The data can then be used for analyzing business and making future decisions on reorders and new product introductions, as well as for forecasting and inventory management. Other benefits include increased speed and accuracy at checkout by eliminating manual entry.

The real-time sales data captured at POS, in addition to other information, can be transmitted electronically and shared throughout the apparel supply chain via EDI, which is the computer-to-computer exchange of business documents, such as sales information, purchase orders or invoices. Information is moved electronically in a standard, structured, retrievable format that allows the data to be transmitted without rekeying from one business or location to another. EDI's benefits include reduced order lead-times, better customer service, better accuracy, increased information availability, and timely information receipt. Firms that have implemented communication technology have realized more benefits than they anticipated. According to one study, benefits of EDI exceeded expectations for users, customers, and suppliers (Walton, 1994).

Retail sales associates and everyone involved with data entry and management, however, need to understand the importance of accuracy at the UPC level when scanning merchandise. This allows replenishment and other merchandise decisions to be based on accurate data, thus maintaining **data integrity.** Data have integrity when merchandise reality is accurately represented, i.e., when every activity relative to a product is correctly recorded: pricing, repricing, receiving, transferring, selling, returning, etc. Maintaining data integrity can be a serious challenge; some tests have reported that as much as 60 percent of data being transferred via EDI are in error. Data integrity is a key in a customer-driven business system based on information technology.

Time-Based Competition

The QR movement is a form of time-based competition that has transformed the way merchandise is conceived, produced, brought to market, and sold (Blackburn, 1991). **Time-based competition** means time is recognized as the firm's most fundamental resource (Blackburn, 1991). Much of the development of the global market has been driven by firms seeking the lowest costs for materials and labor. Focusing on the increased amount of business that can be generated by shorter time-lines, instead of focusing on doing business at the lowest possible cost, requires a great change in the mode of thinking by business executives. In behavioral theory jargon, high levels of cooperation are required among internal business constituencies and with external coalitions to reduce time-lines. With time-based competition, business processes and decision making must be prompt, accurate, and agile in adjusting to the needs of target customers and business partners (Fralix & Off, 1993).

Levi Strauss and VF Corp have been leaders in the QR movement. They have implemented EDI with suppliers and customers and changed production to more flexible manufacturing systems. Still, much remains to be done. Levi's present strategy is to regionalize distribution centers (DC) so no retail customer is more than two days' transportation time from a Levi's DC (Knill, 1994). When production trims cycle times, distribution becomes an area of emphasis because there is no point in trimming production time if the product will be held up in warehousing or distribution. The role of the transportation partner is critical (Carrier is key, 1993). Distribution, like retail sales, takes advantage of scanning, UPC, and EDI technologies, requires partnerships with transportation companies, as well as close coordination among production plants, distribution centers, and retail stores.

Agility

A QR system is a market-oriented system wherein merchandise is "pulled" through the system in response to consumer desires (Houston, 1986; Kunz, 1995). It is consistent with the behavioral theory of the firm in that the marketing concept is implicit to the system; the QR system contrasts with traditionally "pushing" goods on consumers (Kurt Salmon Associates, 1994). Agile firms are dynamic, context specific, change-embracing, and growth oriented (Goldman, Nagel, & Preiss, 1995). **Agility** requires information-based decision-making along with flexible supply and distribution systems. Agile business systems result in the timely offering of goods desired by customers in the appropriate styles, quantities, and qualities. Determining these factors is primarily a merchandising responsibility. A futuristic vision of agile manufacturing follows:

> ". . . you hustle over the "QuickFit Tailors" outlet in your local shopping mall. There, after selecting the style and fabric you want, a technician escorts you into a booth where a sophisticated 3-D optical body-scanning device measures and records your precise body dimensions.
>
> The data are then converted to a 2-D pattern design that is transmitted by modem to an apparel-manufacturing plant, where it is matched to a pattern in an existing database. After the computerized system makes any necessary adjustments [in pattern dimensions], the pattern is relayed to a high-speed single-ply laser cutter that automatically cuts the pieces for your suit. These are immediately routed to a flexible, team-based production line that does the final sewing and packages the garment for express shipment back to the Quick-Fit shop.
>
> Four days after placing your order, you have a high-quality, custom-tailored suit—at a price comparable to ready-made (Sheridan, 1994, p. 43)."

Agile business systems usually include **flexible manufacturing systems** such as modular and unit production systems. Agility also includes concepts of **Just-In-Time (JIT)** inventory management. JIT is "a business philosophy that focuses on removing waste from all the organization's internal activities and from external exchange activities" (O'Neal & Bertrand, 1991). Principles of **Total Quality Management (TQM)** are also consistent and in some ways implicit to agility. TQM requires organizing an operation to give timely response, deliver first quality, and get the order right the first time and on time. Technologies inherent to this goal include computer-integrated manufacturing (CIM) and flexible manufacturing in small lots (Beckert, Knill, Rohan, & Weimer, 1990). The use of computer-aided design (CAD) systems allows both the retailer and vendor to quickly and inexpensively alter designs prior to production and engage in joint product development (Bernard, 1987). These technologies and more contribute to agile business systems.

Partnering

QR strategy includes the establishment of business partnerships and procedures to speed the flow of both information within the trade matrix and merchandise to ultimate consumers (Anderson Consulting, 1994; Blackburn, 1991). **Strategic partnering** (Charron & Straviitz, 1993; Zimmerman, 1993) or value-adding partnership is the term for this relationship (Johnston & Lawrence, 1988). Unusual levels of cooperation, collaboration, and trust are required within firms and among suppliers and customers to make the strategic partnering work. The communication of financial information within and among apparel firms requires a new way of relating to peers, suppliers, and customers—a drastic contrast to traditional adversarial relationships among firms in the trade system. Changing this alienated relationship to a cooperative one is a great challenge.

External Partnering

Partnership tactics include timely sharing of sales and inventory information; joint, up-front planning among materials suppliers, manufacturers, and retailers; optimizing logistics to ensure faster processing and transit time; and reducing total inventory by more frequent ordering (Rouland, 1991). The goal of partnerships, like the overall goal of QR, is to optimize the entire supply and distribution system by producing a win-win situation via cooperation. Organizations must extend their narrow view of simply buying and selling to a multi-faceted view of the entire system. They must understand all components involved in producing and moving materials and goods to the ultimate consumer.

Working in an environment where strategic partnerships are the norm requires a paradigm shift for the apparel industry (Tappscott & Caston, 1993); this change in philosophy must be supported by senior management (Blackburn, 1991; Kunz, 1991; Knill, 1994). This is where the importance of training and education and learning comes in. Retailers, vendors, suppliers, and manufacturers must make a concerted effort to understand how to work in partnerships. Employees will embrace change more readily if they are included in the process from the beginning, especially if their feedback has been solicited (Blackburn, 1991; Kunz, 1991).

Internal Partnering

Not only are organizations required to rethink external relationships, but internal functions must also be reevaluated in a QR environment. In many firms, developing internal collaboration is a greater problem than developing partnerships with suppliers and customers. Because QR requires several areas of the apparel firm to function as a whole—sharing, analyzing, and reacting to real-time sales data—management must remove traditional functional barriers so that executives, marketers, merchandisers, production managers, finance managers, and/or store managers can work together toward a unified purpose (It's all in, 1990). Many times this is accomplished through the use of teams (Henricks, 1993)—multi-functional and cross-functional teams comprised of members from a firm's different constituencies. Discussion among team members provides perspectives from different areas of specialization for problem solving and developing policy. The result is a more comprehensive view of issues and solutions that are easier to implement.

Organizational structures are becoming flatter and more team-oriented because of access to information (Tapscott & Caston, 1993). Information provides a foundation for organizational learning. For example, at Girbaud, President and CEO Bob Stec believes in making information instantaneously available to everybody in the company, so whoever needs it can make decisions with it. "When you do that, " he says, "you can empower people with the information to make the right decisions" (Henricks, 1993, p. 16).

Merchandising Issues

Despite efforts to move toward QR systems, many business problems persist, including the escalating percentage of markdowns being taken at retail, high levels of stockouts, lower gross margins, excess inventory, and increasing prices. Many of these problems stem from the lack of adequate forecasting and merchandise-planning systems to aid in the merchandising process (Black, 1992; Chanil, 1992). Traditionally, a crystal ball has been a key piece of equipment for merchandisers (Brown & Brauth, 1989; Hartnett, 1993). Today, however, technology is being developed and implemented to take some of the guesswork out of merchandising, providing merchandisers with tangible information upon which to base decisions.

It would seem apt that merchandisers would be highly involved in the exploration, development, and acquisition of new technology (Drinkard, 1992; Fallon, 1992). However, recent observations at Quick Response, Riscon, Bobbin, and other conferences and trade shows related to apparel technology reveal poor attendance by both manufacturing and retailing merchandisers. The vast majority of those in attendance represent the operations and information-systems areas of their firms. The challenge today is to take QR from an operations, management information system-driven function to a merchant-driven responsibility (Blackburn, 1991).

Learning Activity 2.2
Concepts of QR.

1. Think through your work experiences in terms of evidence of the concepts of QR. What experiences can you think of that exemplify time-based competition? Agility? Partnerships among suppliers and vendors?

2. What problems have you experienced that might have been solved had QR been in use?

CASE 2.1
Kiosk Data Supports Manufacturing Flexibility

From DeWitt, J. W. (1995, May). *Apparel Industry Magazine,* pp. 42–46.

"In survey after survey, women continue to state that bra shopping is one of the worst, if not the worst, shopping experience they go through," says Jeremy A. Konko, director of business planning and development for Sara Lee Intimates. Naturally, reducing bra-shopping trauma is a priority for Konko, whose company makes the Bali line of bras and other underwear for department stores. In the process, Bali should be able to collect customer demographics and preferences that give the company a better idea of what it should be manufacturing. Armed with such knowledge, Bali could be more flexible in its response to customer demands.

The solution they are currently testing involves an interactive kiosk and they are finding that solving the customer's fit problems has put a wealth of consumer information in their hands-information that may eventually allow Bali to mass customize its bras and sell direct to the consumers. "We believe we have a higher quality and better fitting product, so who better to sell it than ourselves?" Konko says. "With this kiosk, we have a Bali representative on the floor who is never late, never cranky, and knows a whole lot about our product."

A major reason why women have so many problems finding suitable bras is, Konko believes, "a lack of knowledge—on the part the consumer as well as the sales associates in the stores." Thus an adequate remedy requires education. Enter the multimedia interactive kiosk, dubbed the Bali Solution Center. At this kiosk, women are not only presented with the full line of Bali products, but can also watch full-motion videos that tell them, for example, how to properly fit a bra.

Complete Information and Control

Bali's first interactive kiosk has been in consumer testing at a Hecht's Department Store in Cary, N.C. Al Williams, the store's general manager, reports that he's "very happy" with the kiosk. "It's an attention-getter and a good customer service tool within the intimate apparel area."

The Bali Solution Center is designed to provide consumers with a wide range of information, all accessible through a touch-screen television monitor. It includes a complete catalog of all Bali products—bra styles, panty styles, etc. Each product can be accessed in full color simply by touching the on-screen menu, and the consumer can also request black-and-white printouts of product information.

Furthermore, by answering a few questions, the system will search for items by category. "For example, say she wants to see all underwires with lace available in a 36C cup," Konko explains. "The kiosk not only brings up a picture of the bras but also, at a touch, gives verbal descriptions of the bras and their prices."

But that's just the basics. The exciting part comes when consumers access the kiosk's 10 full-motion, TV-quality videos, which were created to address the major problems women have in finding a properly fitting bra.

The two main videos instruct the consumer in bra fitting and taking measurements. "One features a model wearing a Bali bra and a professional fitter describing how the bra should fit, how an underwire should feel, how much give there should be in the band, an so on," Konko explains. "The other video tells exactly where measurements should be taken and how to take them, so the consumer gets a comfortable fit."

The other eight videos are short 45-second to one-minute segments. These address the most common bra problems including underwire discomfort, bra strap slipping, bounce, etc.—and recommend the types of Bali bras that can solve them. One key virtue is that throughout the entire process of using the kiosk, "the customer has complete control," Konko emphasizes. "For instance, she doesn't have to watch the videos to the end."

Transparent Technology

The technology behind the Bali Solution Center is deliberately designed to be invisible to the consumer, says Stan Eskridge, president of Raleigh, NC-based InteractiVisions, developer of the multimedia interactive kiosk.

"To the customer, it's simply a television product," Eskridge explains. "We use a standard TV monitor with a touch-screen mounted on it. It's the same kind of television that consumers have at home. That's important, because that way we don't get a technophobic response." The system's hardware is straight forward—it's simply a 486 PC with optical disk drives for the video.

One key virtue is that the system allows virtually real-time, on-line access from a remote site, courtesy of AT&T's nationwide data communications network. "Thus we can provide Sara Lee with all the feedback from point-of-sale, and we can change the content at any time," Eskridge notes.

More specifically, "we can get results daily from the system. It tells us how many people interacted with the screen, what sizes they looked at, and what time of the day they used it," Konko says. "And except for the video, which comes off the laser disk drive, we can change everything over the phone, including both prices and the voice-over. We can actually snip a single word out or add a new color."

Buoyed by the kiosk's success, Sara Lee Intimates will deploy 10 or so more units in other retail stores during the next fiscal year, Konko says. These units will have an additional feature—direct order fulfillment. "If the store is out of a particular style, or doesn't carry it, then the consumer can swipe her credit card, order it directly from the kiosk and have delivered to her home. It depends on the results from these kiosks as to how far we go from there."

Perhaps most significant is the degree of control that the kiosk provides Sara Lee Intimates. "I think that this product, in combination with the AT&T network, provides an ability to manage content at the point-of-sale unlike anything else on the market today," Eskridge says.

Learning Activity 2.3

Read Case 2.1 very carefully.

1. Because of the kiosk, what kind of information is available to the manufacturer and the retailer that would not routinely be available?

2. How can the kiosk contribute to making merchandise systems customer-driven?

3. What are the advantages to the retailer of a customer-driven system?

4. What are the advantages to the manufacturer of a customer-driven system?

Theoretical Foundations of Technology Innovation

Four theoretical viewpoints are considered here as a basis for examining innovation of technology: theories of the firm, theories of management style, organizational learning, and diffusion of innovation. Theories of the firm and theories of management style were introduced in Chapter 1. A brief overview of these theories follows.

Theories of the Firm and Theories of Management Style

Behavioral theories of the firm emphasize the role of human behavior in explaining the activities of the firm, while economic theories emphasize profit maximization (Anderson, 1982). According to the behavioral theory of the firm, employees form constituencies related to their areas of specialization within the firm. The executive constituency provides leadership and sets the tone for the firm's operation. Other constituencies develop their own objectives that may or may not directly relate to the objectives of the firm. Conflicts frequently develop between constituencies because of different objectives and responsibilities. Conflicts may be resolved through negotiation. Constituencies that control the firm's key resources tend to have the most power in negotiation. The success of the firm is dependent on the ability of the executive constituency to unify the employees to support the firm's objectives.

Apparel firms, historically, have been autocratically operated firms. Top-down communication has been the norm. Most QR strategies require that executives/managers change from being "bosses" (Theory-X Management Style) to being "leaders" (Theory-Y Management Style). Leaders, under Theory-Y management style, engage the whole human being into his/her work based on the assumption that employees are capable, desire respect and responsibility, and want the opportunity to be creative and solve problems. Employees are empowered with both the responsibility and authority to make decisions regarding the use of the firm's resources (McGregor, 1960). Successful implementation of QR technology is dependent on stimulating employees to accept technology, learn to use it, and see it as a positive influence in their work environment.

Organizational Learning

Training is a relatively short-term activity involving teaching how to produce specific, predetermined results as quickly as possible. In training, there is a correct way and an incorrect way to perform the task, one right answer and a lot of wrong ones. In contrast, **learning** is the result of educating for longer-term outcomes (Barr & Tagg, 1995). Benefits of learning may be less immediate, its goals are less clear cut. Definitions of right and wrong become much less distinct because of asking questions differently and because of problem solving in a more complex manner.

It is one thing to teach employees skills that will help them do their present jobs better (training) and something else to expose them to information or situations that will enable them to perform better in a variety of possible jobs (learning). In the first case, management expects an immediate payoff. The trained person can go straight back to the job and start to do something differently, and this difference will be a good thing for the organization. In the longer term learning process, exactly when or how the organization will benefit is not as readily apparent.

Firms engage in training when they perceive the short-term benefits to the organization will outweigh the costs. The worth of human performance (W) is equal to or greater than the value of a person's accomplishments on the job (V) divided by the cost of behavior that goes into producing the accomplishments (C): $W \geq V/C$. It is impossible to talk about training without measuring a return on the investment. When deciding to train to cure a performance discrepancy, the first step is to figure out how much the discrepancy is costing the firm.

Implementing QR strategies and merchandising technology requires organizational learning. A **learning organization** is "an organization that is continually expanding its capacity to create its future" (Senge, 1990, p. 14). Learning involves vision, critical thinking, and problem solving. Through learning, pupils understand how and why something works the way it does. Understanding *why* is the key difference between training and learning.

For example, firms launch training programs for quality improvement. These programs are designed to teach employees specific processes that will improve quality. Initially, significant improvements occur. But over time many organizations reach a plateau because employees have been trained in only a specific process, not in problem solving for on-going quality improvement. They have not been empowered to think for themselves. They don't know how or haven't been allowed to take the next steps on their own.

In contrast, a learning organization is one that continuously improves. Because employees are encouraged to use their intelligence and implement their own ideas, improvements do not stop when the process they were taught in training is in place. Instead, employees determine the next logical step and initiate on-going improvements.

Educating for learning involves risk for the firm since the learner/employee may acquire new competencies and be ready to seek out new opportunities when the firm does not have a new job available. If it is not possible to enrich the current job, the employee may seek a new job elsewhere, taking the new learning with him or her. The possibility of this outcome has made some organizations cautious about providing education with learning outcomes. This perspective is extremely short-sighted, because it deprives the firm of the full engagement of employees' intellect during the time they are employed by the firm.

Theory of Diffusion of Innovations

Rogers (1983) identified five characteristics of an innovation or new technology that determine its **rate of adoption** by members of a social system. These attributes are: relative advantage, compatibility, complexity, trialability, and observability. **Relative advantage** is the degree to which an innovation is perceived as better than the idea it replaces. **Compatibility** refers to the perception of how consistent the innovation is with existing values, past experiences, and needs of the potential adopters. **Complexity** is the perceived difficulty involved in understanding and using the innovation. **Trialability** describes the ease with which the innovation may be experimented with on a limited basis. Finally, **observability** refers to the degree to which the results of an innovation are visible to others. Although these are not the only qualities that affect adoption rates, "past research indicates that they are the most important characteristics of innovations in explaining rate of adoption" (Rogers, p. 16).

Rogers also outlines a two-stage process model for the adoption of innovations within the organization. These sequential stages are called initiation and implementation. The **initiation** phase is the decision to adopt the technology; the **implementation** stage occurs as the technology is put to use. Difficulties may result from the fact that the individuals usually involved in the initiation process are often a different group of than the implementers. In addition, the organizational structure that supports the initiation may be resistant to implementing of an innovation.

Summary of Concepts of Quick Response and Technology Innovation

1. Fundamental concepts of Behavioral Theory of the Apparel Firm (BTAF) are consistent with the fundamental concepts of Quick Response (QR) and Diffusion of Innovation.
2. Theory-Y management style and the associated empowerment are essential to successfully implement QR-related business strategies and new technology.
3. Executive leadership is essential to implement change.
4. Modification of both formal and informal organizational structure is necessary to fully implement QR systems.
5. Because of the underlying assumptions related to human behavior, it is unlikely that groups using Theory Y can operate effectively within a Theory-X management structure.
6. The characteristics of a particular technology may limit its rate of adoption. Organizational learning is required for successful innovation.
8. Both initiators and implementors of technology innovation must be adequately educated to support the process.

CASE 2.2

A Failure of Merchandising Technology Innovation

Based on research conducted by Sarah Cosbey and Grace I. Kunz at Iowa State University, Ames, IA.

The Company

The purpose of this case study is to examine the people and events involved in a technology innovation failure. We were seeking the multiple realities of the many people associated with introduction of new technology throughout the organization, thus, naturalistic, field research methods were employed. Sources of data included interviews based on an interview guide, informal interviews, and field observation.

The setting is an apparel manufacturer specializing in athletic wear, particularly uniforms and "letter" jackets that identify athletes with certain teams. The firm features a quick response turn-around time from order placement to delivery of finished goods. This is achieved in part by stocking pre-cut basic garment parts that can be assembled in the color combinations specified by different teams.

Sales representatives are part of the marketing department and work from a catalog of styles and selected sales samples. They assist customers in selecting garment styles and color combinations. Logos are custom designed by the art department as desired by customers. The firm does not offer the lowest prices in the market; instead they provide good quality and the best service as their strategic advantages.

Initiation of Technology

A few of the manufacturing executives identified development of garment design as a bottleneck in the merchandising/product development operation. They decided they needed a computer aided design (CAD) system to create visualizations of garment designs. They believed the illustrations produced on the CAD system would help the company to do the following: provide a "blueprint" for design development, reduce the number sample garments produced, assist in the development of more innovative design ideas, and maintain and/or improve company image with customers and competition.

As is sometimes the case with companies that deal primarily with basic types of goods, in this company, product development is a division of what is called the marketing department. Because garment design ideas are first visualized by product developers, it seemed logical to the technology initiators that the

CAD system should be implemented in product development. They acquired over $40,000 worth of hardware and software and put it in place in the product development area. Two years later the system was pushed aside; sitting unused; four years later the system was being used in ways only utilizing a few of its functions.

Implementation, Phase One

An enthusiastic, recent graduate of a textiles and clothing program was hired, sent to California for two weeks training on the CAD system, then put in place in product development. Numerous problems soon became apparent. It was assumed the other product development people would give the CAD operator work. They didn't. Sales representatives who asked for design development found the CAD operator was not skilled enough to execute what they wanted on the spot. It turned out the person hired to run the CAD system was not very skilled in computer operation nor aggressive in learning how to solve problems. Perceptions of complexity of the system dominated perceptions of the technology. After about six months of frustration on her part and others, she resigned and left the company, taking the California training with her. The CAD system sat idle for several months. The technology initiative was generally regarded as a failure.

Implementation, Phase Two

To get the CAD system operating again, the technology initiators hired a summer intern from a neighboring university who had learned the CAD system as a part of her coursework. She was friendly, out-going person who was comfortable with her computer expertise. She was quickly able to impress the product developers, the sales representatives, and the art department with the relative advantages of the system. The initiators were pleased with her contributions to the company during her three-month internship. However, none of the product developers were prepared to take up CAD when she left, so once again, the system was idle.

Implementation, Phase Three

The technology initiators decided their mistake had been placing the CAD in the product development area; it should have been placed in the art

continued

department. They decided to hire the CAD company to come to the headquarters and train two people on the system: one as the regular operator and one as a backup. Their logic was that the art department was familiar with graphical software and learning new technologies was an on-going part of their activities. In addition, the individual chosen as the primary operator would be given "ownership" of the system, and mastering CAD would be his or her sole responsibility. Under this arrangement, marketing (product development and sales) would place orders, so to speak, with the CAD artist to obtain garment illustrations.

Two individuals were chosen for training by the art department manager, who expressed a priority for an individual with a strong personality to be able to deal with the marketing/sales people who were regarded as being unreasonable in their demands on the art department. The art department manager, however, selected the person she thought she could work with most compatibly, and rearranged the department so the CAD would be located close to the manager. That way the manager could assist the CAD operator in dealing with the difficult marketing/sales people. As implementation proceeded, the primary CAD artist attempted to gain competence and the secondary user had little access because he was fully employed elsewhere.

Two years have elapsed. A recent check on the status of the system revealed that it is being used for designing signs and to some extent for catalog layout—certainly not the primary uses to maximize the investment in technology.

Sources of Implementation Problems According to Theory

The initiators started out by placing CAD in product development, then they moved to the art department, and eventually planned to have still other individuals use it. Even after members of the art department were trained on it, management still saw product development as the primary users. The initiators failed to recognize the rivalry between the art and marketing departments. The two departments were forced to work together everyday. The marketing department thought the art department was too slow and the art department thought marketing was too demanding. Marketing employees did not like the art department manager. CAD was moved from market-

ing, where it failed, and forced on the art department, creating resentment on both sides. All interviewees acknowledged the strain between art and marketing except the director of marketing, who took over the art department just prior to Phase Three of implementation. The restructuring was viewed as a means of facilitating CAD implementation.

The concept of a firm's internal constituencies having conflicting goals was exemplified by the tension between the art and marketing departments. However, the tension was not acknowledged by management and no effort was made to negotiate a solution to the problems. Theories of management style also lend some insight into the difficulty in implementing CAD. Although employees said they were very happy with their jobs and they all expressed a certain amount of ease in interaction with superiors and other departments, the situation indicates there was not adequate communication within the firm. The firm seemed to be operating primarily with a top-down communication system within the confines of a Theory-X management style. More teamwork in the technology initiation phase may have eased the implementation phase. The first CAD operator may have been screened more carefully for computer skills or a more assertive art department employee might have been selected as the third operator.

There was an obvious need for organizational learning beyond the technical training for CAD operators. The art and marketing departments needed to work out a more productive working relationship. The sales people, the art department, and product development all needed help in understanding what the CAD system could do, how it could help them with their jobs, and how they could expect to work with the CAD operator. Individuals were not relieved of other job responsibilities in order to concentrate on perfecting skills and developing new professional relationships necessary to successful technology implementation.

The case study confirmed the relevance of Rogers' concepts of innovators and implementers and the behavioral theory of the apparel firm. Lack of collaboration between initiators and implementers was decidedly a problem. The excitement and inspiration of the initiators must be transferred to the implementers and their work environment must be modified to support implementation of technology.

Learning Activity 2.4

Innovation of Technology

Think through Case 2.2. Based on the behavioral theory of the apparel firm and Roger's diffusion of innovation theory, design a process for introduction of a CAD system into the product development area. Be sure to consider management style and organizational learning in the process.

Incorporating Quick Response into the Behavioral Theory of the Apparel Firm

Integrating the concepts of Quick Response, organizational learning, and diffusion of innovation into Behavioral Theory of the Apparel Firm expands the horizons of the theory. The expanded theory includes a definition of a sixth construct and constituency, as well as modifications of assumptions, constructs, and propositions.

Definition of a QR Construct and Constituency

As Hammond (1993) pointed out, many Quick Response business systems, as they are presently operating, are implementing only part of a QR business system. Information technology and telecommunications systems tend to be the core aspects of these implementations. The EDI, UPC, and automated replenishment systems tend to be based primarily on sales history. These systems have realized many benefits from basic/staple goods where forecasts can be adequately based on sales history and little merchandise planning is required.

Firms are forming QR areas of specialization at both the wholesale and retail levels. QR constituencies cut across all other divisions and seek teamwork support from other areas. New positions include QR Director, QR Coordinator, EDI Director, UPC Supervisor, as well as support positions (Hare, 1992; Parr, 1993). QR Directors tend to have experience in merchandising or marketing because they must understand the product side of the business. Nevertheless, firms with QR constituencies keep minimal numbers of their people directly involved in QR.

Partnering often focuses on sharing necessary sales data; agility may focus on "just-in-case," instead of "just-in-time." Goods are made-to-stock instead of made-to-order so they can be quickly re-supplied to retailers. As a result, manufacturers bear the inventory expense for the retailers. However, despite only partial implementation of QR, average retail inventories are lower, there are fewer stockouts and fewer lost sales, and more merchandise is sold at first price, showing financial gains associated with even this minimal implementation of QR systems. See Figure 2.1, for a visual representation of a firm with partial implementation of a QR system.

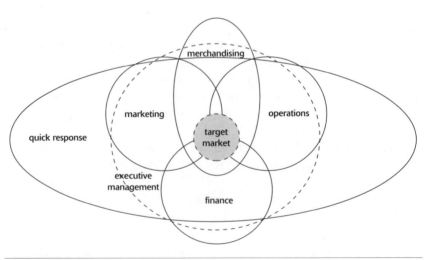

FIGURE 2.1.

Interaction of the functional areas of specialization of an apparel firm operating with selectively implemented and fully implemented Quick Response business systems.

The areas of specialization in the QR model are the same as in the BTAF with the addition of a QR area as a construct. The QR "propeller" is shown cutting across the organizational matrix. Only a few members of the firm's coalition are involved with QR, although perhaps it seems they all should be. Usually, a few people are selected to lead initiation and implementation strategies. Outside coalitions can access the firm's technology by connecting to the ends of the QR propeller.

Levi's has defined the nature of its QR "propeller." The company announced a $400-million commitment to QR in 1994 and the investment reportedly soon ballooned to $850 million. Levi's is focusing its QR efforts on time-based competition in its merchandising handling areas. This system supports its extensive automated replenishment systems already in place (Nannery, 1996).

Fully Implemented QR

The QR models in Figure 2.1 demonstrate the interactive organizational matrix of an apparel firm being operated with selectively implemented QR (as with Levi's) and fully implemented QR business systems. When QR fully incorporates time-based competition, agility, and partnering, the QR "propeller" expands into a "wing." Remember, under BTAF, customers are the driving force—the propeller of an apparel firm. With fully implemented QR, the majority of the firm is overlapped by the QR wing. This implies joint decision making and teamwork involving most people and all aspects of the firm's operation with QR business strategies. Outside coalitions have easier access to the technology of the firm by connecting anywhere on the QR wing.

Assumptions of BTAF with a QR Construct (BTAF/QR)

1. An apparel firm can consist of any combination of manufacturing and/or distribution functions.
2. A firm is a coalition of individuals with some common goals.
3. The coalition is made up of sub-coalitions or constituencies that conform to the functional areas of specialization of the firm.
4. Six constituencies perform all the business functions required for operation of the apparel firm.
5. Overall goals of the coalition are formulated by the executive constituency.
6. The focus of the coalition is on the customer and satisfying the customer's needs within the limitations of the firm.

7. The inter-relationships among constituencies form the internal decision-making matrix for the firm.
8. Time-based competition will change the firms decision-making priorities and measures of success.
9. Agility will contribute to the ability of the firm to satisfy customer wants and needs.
10. Partnering will provide information to optimize the ability to achieve the firm's goals.

Decision Making in a QR Universe

The addition of the QR construct expands the focus of the BTAF beyond interactions of internal constituencies to interactions of the firm and its constituencies with external coalitions, particularly its trading partners. Words used to describe the apparel industry and industries in general tend to imply linearity: trade channel, pipeline, supply chain, etc. In reality, however, firms within the apparel industry and their associated manufacturing and distribution processes do not have linear relationships with each other. While certain events are sequential (e.g., cotton must grow before it can be harvested and spun into yarn; patterns must be made and fabrics cut before garments can be sewn), products are manufactured and distributed through a complex matrix of integrated decision making within the firm, between the firm and its suppliers and customers, and between the firm and its interlocking environments. Many of the perceived "problems" that arise in the manufacturing and distribution process are related to violations of an erroneous assumption of linearity (Scheller, 1993). *The assumption of linearity is the problem.*

If decision making is regarded as interactive and individuals/teams are given the information, education, and power to make decisions, the "problems" become resolvable issues that are a normal part of doing business. Effective solutions can be developed because the people who are dealing with the "problems" have the authority, responsibility, and ability to find solutions.

For QR systems to operate successfully, unusual levels of cooperation, collaboration, and trust are required among suppliers and customers throughout the **trade universe.** In this case, *a universe is defined as all firms, collectively, that are subjects of consideration at one time.* Breaking down traditional adversarial relationships among suppliers and customers to the point of electronically sharing data requires new paradigms in industrial relations. To be involved in time-based competition, business executives and their employees must believe that is possible to create a win/win situation through collaboration.

Strategic partnering results in an informal form of vertical integration. This is occurring at a time when formal vertical integration is also on the increase. Manufacturers' outlet malls, one of the most obvious forms of forward vertical integration, is one of the few areas of retailing that is growing. At the same time, retailers are adding product-development divisions to modify their sourcing capabilities, thus creating backward vertical integration. Both formal and informal vertical integration provide control over both product and process, as well as the time required for both. Clearly control of product and process is regarded as a strategic advantage in today's apparel markets. Figure 2.2 is an example of a multi-dimensional apparel trade universe operating under assumptions of BTAF and BTAF/QR.

Some firms are retailers, some are manufacturers of finished goods, some are manufacturers of materials. Some of the firms have defined merchandising constituencies; some don't. Some firms (those with QR wings) are fully engaged in QR. Think about the huge amount of information being shared by firms fully engaged in QR. Is it possible that full commitment to QR might actually limit the flexibility of the firm to adjust the other changes in the firm's environment?

For firms partially engaged in QR (those with QR propellers), the QR connections may be primarily electronic: UPC, EDI, and perhaps some automated replenishment. Some firms are isolates; they are not directly connected to other firms in the universe. Firms without propellers or wings are not engaged in QR. Those with propellers but not attached to other firms may have failed in QR partnerships or be new to QR and seeking partnerships. Which firms will be able to optimize the benefits of QR? Will the isolates starve and die?

Merchandising in a QR Universe

Hammond (1993) emphasized the difficulties associated with full implementation of QR business systems. Most firms focus on some aspects of QR and do not attempt full implementation. She particularly identified components of the textile and apparel industry's culture that must change, including focus on the short-term, hostility of interfirm relationships, lack of attention to human resources, and inadequate production flexibility. See Table 2.1 for a summary of factors that remain to be implemented in many firms for QR systems to fully succeed.

While some firms have successfully overcome the challenges listed in Table 2.1, most have not. As indicated by the table, merchandising technology is a component of the QR business system needing development and implementation. *The problems associated with forecasting and merchandise*

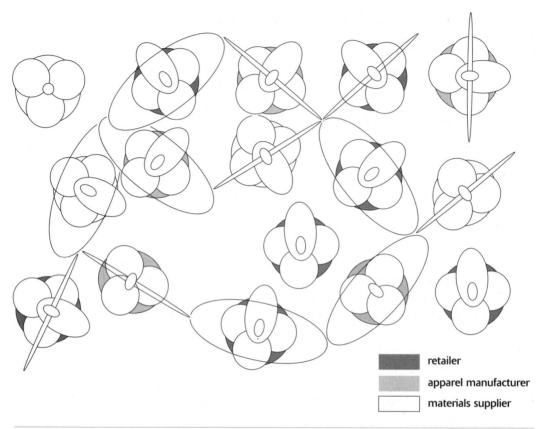

retailer

apparel manufacturer

materials supplier

FIGURE 2.2.

Example of a Quick Response universe operating under assumptions Behavioral Theory of the Apparel Firm.

Learning Activity 2.5

Examine Table 2.1.

1. What are merchandising-related issues for manufacturers regarding QR implementation?

2. What are merchandising-related issues for retailers regarding QR implementation?

3. Are there merchandising-related issues requiring joint activity?

4. How might Accurate Response help solve other problems in the apparel business system?

planning are seen as the greatest challenges in the current market (Fisher, Hammond, Obermeyer, & Raman, 1994; Hammond, 1993; Reda, 1994). For some firms, Quick Response should be **Accurate Response.** *Accurate*

TABLE 2.1

Challenges remaining to be overcome by QR business systems*
(Items in italics are merchandising-related issues.)

Manufacturing	Joint Activity	Retailing
• Provide adequate learning opportunities to support QR systems	• Fully implement necessary technology to support QR activities	• Provide adequate learning opportunities to support QR systems
• Improve efficiency by negotiating resolutions of conflicts among internal constituencies	• Replace adversarial customer and supplier relationships with cooperative partnerships	• Improve efficiency by negotiating resolutions of conflicts among internal constituencies
• *Improve basis of forecasting beyond sales history*	• *Incorporate demand uncertainty into planning processes*	• *Improve basis of forecastinb beyond sales history*
• Shift production emphasis from direct labor costs to total product costs and bottom line returns	• *Plan merchandise assortments and track inventory at full SKU level*	• *Shift merchandising focus from percent gross margin to bottom-line returns*
• Use short-cycle manufacturing so final product decisions can be close to point of sale	• Use automated replenishment systems for basic and staple goods	• *Plan assortments and manage inventory by individual store rather than by aggregate chain*
• Ship merchandise floor-ready		• *Place smaller initial orders and replenish based on POS data*

*Based on Hammond (1993); Fisher, Hammond, Obermeyer, & Raman (1994); and Reda, (1994).

Response is determining what forecasters can and cannot predict well and redesigning their merchandise planning processes to minimize the impact of inaccurate forecasts (Fisher, Hammond, Obermeyer, & Raman, 1994, p. 84).

Some merchandisers are using the wealth of information available from technological innovations, such as UPCs, scanning, and EDI, to make more accurate and timely decisions. Such support systems allow merchandisers to react more quickly to definite information, rather than relying on sales representatives, trade journals, fashion magazines, or instinct (Shim & Kotsiopulos, 1991). But most of the systems, or the *use* of the systems, do not provide adequate usable information. Having a lot of information is not enough; it must be usable information. The textile and apparel industry has come a long way, but much remains to be done to optimize the effectiveness of QR systems. (Do Learning Activity 2.5.)

Sources and Capabilities of Merchandising Technology

There are two primary sources of merchandising technology: proprietary systems and commercial systems. **Proprietary systems** are developed by individual firms for their own use. For example, Sears' SAMS system (Sears Apparel Merchandising System) has generated much publicity (Sears, 1993). Firms usually hire consultants to assist operations/MIS (management information system) and merchandising personnel to tailor the systems to the firm's product lines and priorities. Proprietary systems are usually regarded as trade secrets.

Commercial systems for merchandising technology are available for sale from computer software and consulting firms. The software is often designed in several parts so the buyer can purchase only the components desired for implementation. The cost of the software probably includes some sort of a service package for training, updates, and problem solving. A merchandising technology software system may cost anywhere from a few thousand dollars to over a million, depending on its capabilities and the size of the firm it will serve. The focus of the following discussion is on commercially available software.

Report of Merchandising Technology Available at Retail Systems '95

One hundred and twenty-eight vendors were listed in the directory of commercially available retail technology displayed at Retail Systems 1995 trade conference in Chicago, IL. Of those described in the directory, 36 identified themselves as "merchandising systems," while nine were listed as "advertising systems." There was no category called marketing. A content analysis of the descriptions of merchandising technology from the show directory provided the functions listed in Table 2.2.

Based on discussions with the firms' representatives, their descriptions of merchandise management and inventory management were closely associated. Automated replenishment tended to be offered in association with forecasting and warehouse/distribution center inventory management. Forecasting was also viewed as a component of automated replenishment systems and was based primarily on POS data. Customer profiling was not always described in relation to forecasting. Store management systems tended to have strong accounting relationships and did not always include multi-tier applications, that is, headquarters and stores integration. Space management systems focused primarily on planogramming for grocery and drug stores. Two firms had some soft goods applications for visual merchandising, but the term "visual merchandising" was not used by the vendors.

TABLE 2.2

Most frequently mentioned functions of technology from firms listed in the merchandising category in the Retail Systems 95 Show Directory.

Functions Mentioned in Directory	Number of Times Mentioned
Merchandise Management	9
Inventory Management	7
Store Management System	7
Automated Replenishment	6
Multi-Tier Applications	5
Customer Profiling	4
Forecasting	4
Space Management	4
Merchandise Planning	4
Warehouse/Distribution Center Inventory Management	3

Four firms identified **merchandise planning** as a feature of their software. Systems were based primarily on dollar planning and open-to-buy with some opportunity for unit planning and/or merchandise allocation to stores. When the four vendors that claimed to provide technology for merchandise planning were asked about assortment planning, one sales representative said they had it, one said they could do it but it was not a strong system, two said they were working on systems that should be available in late 1995. **Assortment planning** was the topic of a three-hour workshop featured at the show. The title of the workshop was "Assortment Planning: The Next Frontier." The speaker promised to clarify the definitions of merchandise planning, merchandise management and assortment planning.

Three descriptions of merchandising technology systems from the Retail Systems '95 directory are shown below. The descriptions provide a feeling for the services the systems are intended to provide. They all claimed to provide merchandise planning. The descriptions of these three systems were selected based on the comprehensiveness of their capabilities. The first, ARTHUR Planning, is offered by Comshare Retail, based in Wilmington, DE. The second is offered by JDA Software, Inc., Scottsdale, AZ, and the system title is Merchandise Management System (MMS). The third is Richter Automated Merchandising System (RAMS) from Richter Management Services, Inc., Montreal, Quebec.

> "ARTHUR Planning (ARTHUR) is a powerful merchandise planning, decision-assist application that enables retailers to create detailed plans from a customer and store perspective, analyze valuable information and test merchandise

strategies before resources are committed. ARTHUR Planning Server simplifies the management of large planning environments without restricting the freedom of individual planners. NEW PLATFORMS! Now available on UNIX, OS2 and Windows NT. ARTHUR Performance Tracking gives retailers the performance information they need to spot trends and opportunities while there is still time to act."

"Merchandise Management System (MMS) is a fully integrated system that offers a wide range of applications including ad planning and control, inventory, warehouse, sales audit and analysis, automated replenishment, purchase order management, polling, store data interchange, and financials. Featured applications in Distributed Store System include back office, price management, report writer, point of sale, credit authorization, layaway, multiple currencies, in-store merchandising, and communication. Open Database Merchandise System (ODBMS) provides an open and sophisticated tool for sales analysis and margin management and supports multiple databases and multiple operating systems."

"The Richter Automated Merchandising System (RAMS) is fully integrated computer system for both softgoods and hardgoods retailers. The software can function under all major UNIX/AIX operating environments. The package contains modular software including merchandise planning, open to buy, purchase order management, receipts, distribution, full inventory control, sales audit, merchandising analysis, and financial applications. Sophisticated modules are also available for stock replenishment, customer profiling, suggested transfers, event management, gift registry, and EDI. An EIS and ad-hoc query system are provided to enhance available applications."

MMS integrates with ARTHUR. ARTHUR focuses on what the vendors called **"front-end" merchandising activities,** while MMS focuses more on **"back-end" merchandising activities,** including inventory management. ARTHUR reported numerous inquiries from apparel manufacturing firms that are looking for merchandise-planning technology.

The third system, RAMS, can also serve both the apparel retail and manufacturing firms. RAMS can be implemented gradually as it has five modules. Section A is the basic stand-alone system that can interface with the rest, providing complete style and inventory control as well as merchandising analysis. Section B automates retail inventory control; Section C adds merchandise planning and open-to-buy. Section D includes accounting applications, such as integrated accounts payable, purchase order, and merchandise receiving system. Section E includes other aspects of retail operations such as layaway control, customer profiling, and stock replenishment.

While 28 percent of the vendors at Retail Systems '95 claimed to offer merchandising systems, only a few offered support for "front-end" merchandising planning processes. The merchandising planning processes supported by the systems, for the most part, were dollar planning and open-to-buy. Little support is available for the assortment planning functions that were identified by Hammond and others as necessary initiatives to fully implement QR business systems.

Making Quick Response into Accurate Response

A Quick Response constituency can become an Accurate Response (AR) constituency by defining the firm's commitment to QR to include effective forecasting and merchandise planning systems. Apparel firms are also changing their organizational structures to facilitate QR. Some organizations are becoming flatter, with middle management levels disappearing and teamwork becoming the norm (Stec, 1993). Managers are learning how to become leaders. The development of commitment to QR requires executive management's profound endorsement, active involvement, and on-going support. At the same time, they must be receptive to and comfortable with the technology that supports QR. Through executive leadership, all constituencies can come to recognize the common goals related to QR, including improving the performance of QR systems already in place. In addition, technology implementation, forecasting, and merchandise planning must be improved. Measures of AR success include improved stock turn, gross margin return on inventory, employee retention, and customer service; reduced average inventory and increased merchandise sold at first price. The merchandising constituency is highly involved in AR with new forecasting and merchandise planning technology.

Merchandising Technology Theory

Constructs, assumptions, and propositions are fundamental results of the inductive process of theory development. The constructs and assumptions related to Behavioral Theory of the Apparel Firm in a Quick Response System have already been discussed. Propositions describe the next level of complexity in theory development; they predict outcomes related to interactions of constructs. Propositions are tested through trial and error in the business sector and are sometimes treated as hypotheses, becoming the basis of research to test the theory.

Overview of Potential Outcomes of QR

The outcomes of QR for basic and staple merchandise are obvious. It truly becomes possible to have the right product at the right place at the right time. Salable products are on the retail shelf, salable products are manufactured and materials for salable products are produced. Automatic replenishment systems based on model stocks can be developed and basic stock models can be automatically modified by computer based on rate of sale.

The benefits related to what is sometimes called "the Quick Response movement" accrue throughout the consumer goods business systems. These benefits include increased sales, reduced markdowns, increased stock turn, lower average inventories, increased gross margin return on inventory, increased adjusted gross margin, and satisfied customers (Hunter, 1990). Implementation of QR strategies requires discarding traditional apparel business paradigms in favor of human-empowerment strategies and technology-based systems.

QR systems are more frequently applied to basic/staple goods than to fashion/seasonal goods, although Kincade & Cassill (1993) found no significant difference. Fundamentally, the time period that fashion and seasonal goods are salable is so short, usually less than 12 weeks, that the merchandising process is believed to test even the best of QR strategies.

Expectations of those responsible for the planning, developing, and presentation of product lines are becoming more complex and require a broader base of expertise. Merchandising trends include increasing complexity of line and product development with fewer weeks of sale for individual styles and less defined selling seasons. Channels of distribution in the market are more complex, with multiple sourcing methods including both finished goods and product development with domestic and international sources. At the same time, the new emphasis on QR relationships will have a profound impact on merchandising.

Propositions Related to Merchandising Technology

1. The concept of the selling season will be replaced by weeks of sale, with new merchandise being strategically introduced on a continual basis.
2. Merchandise planning, development, and presentation will extend to the SKU level.
3. The seasonal wholesale market will be replaced, at least in part, by joint product development.
4. Consolidation will occur in the number of retailers and manufacturers in the market.
5. Consolidation will occur in the number of vendors and customers with which each firm works.
6. Merchandising processes will be based on merchandise classifications.

7. Assortment planning model stocks will provide the basis of initial deliveries; the rest of inventory supply will be customer-driven.

8. Automatic replenishment model stocks will control flow of basic/staple goods.

9. Measures of merchandising success will include not only an established level of gross margin and/or sales per square foot but, more importantly, gross margin dollars, total revenue, gross margin return on investment, and gross margin adjusted for delivery and carrying costs.

10. In many cases, not all of a firm's products will be on QR systems, but QR products will be given priority by both suppliers and buyers.

11. Merchandising decisions will be based on information about products, suppliers, and customers-more information than merchandisers have ever dreamed possible.

Summary

A paradigm shift is required of both people and firms in order to adapt to changes required by implementing merchandising technology consistent with QR business systems. Merchandising technology is one part of the total QR business system. Until now, the focus of merchandising aspects of QR systems has been on "back-end" merchandising processes, including inventory management that is sometimes performed by the operations constituency. Merchandise planning and, in particular, assortment planning have been neglected. Customer purchases may drive automated replenishment, but merchandisers still must decide when merchandise needs to be added or dropped from the line and what, at what price, and how much to include in an assortment.

Technology and technology standards for EDI, UPC, POS, and inventory management are well established, but not necessarily at the SKU level. Inadequate training on new technology systems reduces effectiveness of more information. Education can help reduce employees' resistance to implementation of merchandising technology.

Strategic vendor partnering is a top priority for retailers because retailers are the first beneficiaries of improved inventory management. Many firms say they are partnering but are not truly operating as equals. Establishment of collaborative and cooperative relationships among business partners is essential for on-going success. Human qualities of judgment, insight, and creativity are even more important in the presence of QR technology. Gaining a consistent level of excellence throughout out the business system is essential.

Because of compatible assumptions, the concepts of QR business systems can be integrated into Behavioral Theory of the Apparel Firm. The QR construct is defined and represented in a modification of the BTAF model by a propeller that cuts across the constituency matrix of the apparel coalition. The thickness of the propeller can indicate the level of involvement in QR systems. The QR propellers of individual firms join in QR relationships to create an extended integrated universe incorporating the apparel business system. BTAF assumptions can be modified to include the QR construct and propositions are proposed related to merchandising technology.

Key Concepts

accurate response (AR)
agility
assortment planning
back-end merchandising
  activities
commercial systems
customer-driven business
  systems
data integrity
electronic data inter-
  change (EDI)
front-end merchandising
  activities

implementation of
  technology
initiation of technology
Just-in-Time (JIT)
learning
learning organization
merchandise planning
merchandising technology
proprietary systems
scanning
strategic partnering
technology

theory of diffusion of
  innovation
time-based competition
Total Quality Manage-
  ment (TQM)
trade universe
training
Universal Product Code
  (UPC)

Integrated Learning Activity 2.6

1. What is involved in "front-end" merchandising versus "back-end" merchandising? What are some possible reasons why "back-end" systems have had more attention from technology developers?

2. Think through the relationships indicated by Figure 2.2, the Quick Response Universe. Can a business system operate effectively when it is so closely vertically and horizontally integrated? What are the advantages and disadvantages of formal and informal vertical integration?

Recommended Resources

Goldman, S. L., Nagel, R. N., & Preiss, K. (1995). *Agile competitors and virtual organizations: Strategies for enriching the consumer.* New York: Van Nostrand Reinhold.

Hammond, J. H. (1993) Quick response in retail/manufacturing channels. In S. P. Bradley, J. A. Hausmen, & R. L. Nolan, (Eds). *Globalization, technology, and competition: The fusion of computer and telecommunications in the 1990s.* (pp. 185–215). Boston: Harvard Business School Press.

IMRA focuses on merchandising. (1992, June). *Discount Merchandiser, 32,* 12 & 16.

Knill, B. (1994). Quick response too slow for the '90s. [Automatic Data Collection Management Section] *Industry Week, 243*(16), 16–21.

Needed: 3-way partnering of chains, vendors, suppliers or QR nets nothing, says mercantile (1994, October). *Chain Store Age Executive, 70*(10), 54–56.

Redman, J. M., Chiappina, P., & Clausen, F. (1994). A strategy for modernizing the apparel industry. *Issues in Science and Technology, 11,* 61–67.

References

Anderson Consulting. (1994). *Quick response.* Charlotte, SC: Arthur Anderson & Co.

Anderson, P. E. (1982, Spring). Marketing, strategic planning and the theory of a firm. *Journal of Marketing, 46,* 15–26.

Barr, R. G., & Tagg, J. (1995, November/December). From teaching to learning—A new paradigm for undergraduate education. *Change,* 13–25.

Beckert, B., Knill, B., Rohan, T., & Weimer, G. (1990). Integrated manufacturing: New wizards of management. *Industry Week, 239*(6), 60–84.

Bernard, H. (1987, November). Retailers realize CAD benefits. *Apparel Industry Magazine, 48,* 69, 72, 74–75.

Black, S. S. (1992, April). More turns on the road ahead. *Bobbin, 33,* 18–21.

Blackburn, J. D. (1991). The quick-response movement in the apparel industry: A case study in time-compressing supply chains. In J. D. Blackburn (Ed.), *Time-based competition: The next battleground in American manufacturing.* Homewood, IL: Irwin.

Bravman, R. (1993). Quick response: An introduction. *Proceedings of the Quick Response 93 Conference,* 1–8.

Brown, P., & Brauth, B. (1989, August). Merchandising methods. *Apparel Industry Magazine, 50,* 78, 80, 82, & 110.

Carrier is key to QR success. (1993). [Proceedings from the Inventory Pipeline Management Through Partnerships and Technology Conference]. *Chain Store Age Executive, 69*(10), 136–137.

Chanil, D. (1992, July). Partnerships: Illusion or reality? *Discount Merchandiser, 32,* 20–26, 58.

Charron, P., & Straviitz, R. (1993). Strategic partnering. *Proceedings of the Quick Response 93 Conference,* 339–362

Drinkard, G. (1992). Quick response—the perfect partnership: A hard goods vendor perspective. *Proceedings of the Quick Response 92 Conference,* 59–73.

Fallon, B. (1992). A successful quick response trading partnership. *Proceedings of the Quick Response 92 Conference,* 276–281.

Fisher, M. L., Hammond, J. H., Obermeyer, W. R., & Raman, A. (1994, May–June). Making supply meet demand in an uncertain world. *Harvard Business Review, 72,* 83–93.

Fralix, M., & Off, J. (1993). A changing soft goods industry: A look at today and tomorrow. *ITAA Proceedings 1993,* 44–47.

Galbraith, J. K. (1978). *The new industrial state* (3rd ed.). Boston: Houghton Mifflin.

Gilman, A. (1989). Assessing quick response benefits. *Chain Store Age Executive, 65*(5), 314.

Glock, R. E., & Kunz, G. I. (1990). *Apparel manufacturing: Sewn products analysis.* New York: Macmillan.

Glock, R. E., & Kunz, G. I. (1995). *Apparel manufacturing: Sewn product analysis (2nd ed).* Englewook Cliffs, NJ: Prentice Hall.

Hammond, J. H. (1993) Quick response in retail/manufacturing channels. In S. P. Bradley, J. A. Hausman, & R. L. Nolan (Eds.). *Globalization, technology, and competition: The fusion of computers and telecommunications in the 1990s.* Boston: Harvard Business School Press.

Hare, D. (1993). The role of the quick response director. *Proceedings of the Quick Response 92 Conference,* 243–248.

Hartnett, M. (1993, September). Buyers: Endangered species? *Stores, 75,* 53–55.

Henricks, M. (1993). Girbaud re-invents the apparel company. *Apparel Industry Magazine, 54,* 12, 14, 16.

Houston, F. S. (1986, April). The marketing concept: What it is and what it is not. *Journal of Marketing, 50,* 81–87.

Hunter, A. (1990). *Quick response in apparel manufacturing: A survey of the American scene.* Manchester, England: The Textiles Institute.

It's all in the implementation. (1990). *Chain Store Age Executive, 66*(5), 205–207.

Johnson, S. (1992). Retail systems: No longer business as usual. *Journal of Systems, 43*(8), 8–10, 34–35.

Johnston, R., & Lawrence, P. R. (1988, July–August). Beyond vertical integration—the rise of the value-adding partnership. *Harvard Business Review, 4,* 94–101.

Kean, R. C. (1987). Definition of merchandising: Is it time for a change? In R. C. Kean (Ed.), *Theory building in apparel merchandising,* (pp. 8–11). Lincoln: University of Nebraska.

Kincade, D., & Cassill, N. (1993). Company demographics on adoption of quick response by North Carolina apparel manufacturers. *Clothing & Textiles Research Journal, 11*(3), 23–30.

Knill, B. (1990, March). Quick response: Now for the hard part. *Material Handling Engineering, 45,* 67–68, 72, 74, 77–78.

Knill, B. (1994). Quick response: Slow but inevitable [Automatic Data Collection Management Section]. *Industry Week, 243*(16), 8–15.

Kunz, G. I. (1991, May). EDI, JIT, FM, MM, QA, UPS, VAM: The magnitude of change for a new socio-technical interface. *[TCI² Report,* pp. 6–7.

Kunz, G. I. (1995). Behavioral theory of the apparel firm: A beginning. *Clothing and Textiles Research Journal, 13*(4), 252–261.

Kurt Salmon Associates. (1994). *The quick response handbook.* Princeton, NJ: Author.

McGregor, D. (1960). *The human side of enterprise.* New York: McGraw-Hill.

Mooney, M., & Hessel, M. (1990). Quick response management helps organizations that are pressed for time. *National Productivity Review, 9*(4), 419–427.

Nannery, M. (1996, March 29). Levi's expects new QR service department on-line by June. *Daily News Record,* p. 3.

O'Neal, C., & Bertrand, K. (1991). *Developing a winning JIT marketing strategy.* Englewood Cliffs, NJ: Prentice Hall.

Pacey, A. (1983). *The culture of technology.* Oxford, England: Basil Blackball.

Parr, M. (1993). The role of a quick response director. *Proceedings of the Quick Response 93 Conference,* 15–32.

Reda, S. (1994, April). Floor-ready merchandise. *Stores, 76,* 41–44.

Rogers, E. M. (1983). *Diffusion of innovations* (3rd ed.). New York: Free Press.

Rouland, R. (1991, January). Target: Partnerships in progress. *Discount Merchandiser, 31,* 37–39.

Rouland, R. (1992). Partnerships aren't perfect. *Discount Merchandiser,* pp. 24–25.

Scheller, H. P. (1993). *Apparel quality through the perception of apparel production managers and operators.* Unpublished masters thesis, Iowa State University, Ames.

Schon, D. A. (1967). *The process of invention, technology and change.* New York: Delacorte Press.

Sears' merchandise allocation system helps spur turnaround (October, 1993). *Chain Store Age Executive, 69*(10), 20–23, 26–31.

Senge, P. M. (1990). *The fifth discipline: The art of practice in the learning organization.* New York: Doubleday.

Sheridan, J. H. (1994, March 21). A vision of agility. *Industry Week [Supplement], 243,* 43–46.

Shim, S., & Kotsiopulos, A. (1991). Information-seeking patterns of retail apparel buyers. *Clothing & Textiles Research Journal, 10*(1), 20–30.

Stec, B. (1993). The ultimate consumer connection. *Proceedings of the Quick Response 93 Conference,* 85–92.

Tapscott, D., & Caston, A. (1993). *Paradigm shift: The new promise of information technology.* New York: McGraw-Hill.

Walton, L. W. (1994). Electronic data interchange (EDI): A study of its usage and adoption within marketing and logistics channels. *Transportation Journal, 34*(2), 37–45.

Zimmerman, R. M. (1993). Strategic partnering roundtable [Summary remarks]. *Proceedings of the Quick Response 93 Conference,* 79–84.

ZuHone, L. M., & Morganosky, M. A. (1995). Exchange relationships between apparel retailers and manufacturers. *Clothing and Textiles Research Journal, 13*(1), 57–64.

Merchandising Systems

Learning Objectives

- Explore the Taxonomy of Apparel Merchandising System (TAMS).
- Examine dimensions of product lines and define dimensions of product change.
- Discuss context of merchandising based on TAMS and examine measures of success.
- Relate fundamentals of income statements to merchandise planning and controlling processes.

The **Taxonomy of Apparel Merchandising Systems (TAMS)** was developed as a comprehensive description of elements of a merchandising system—an extended definition of merchandising within the context of the Behavioral Theory of the Apparel Firm with Quick Response Universe (BTAF/QR). Think of the egg-shaped merchandising portion of the model; TAMS describes the planning, development, and presentation of product lines as merchandisers interact and collaborate with the firm's constituencies and with outside coalitions, particularly vendors and customers.

Assumptions Related to TAMS

Take a few minutes to examine TAMS in Figure 3.1. The white portions of TAMS detail elements of the merchandising process related to planning, developing, and presenting product lines. These elements are commonly regarded as merchandising responsibilities. The shaded segments of TAMS represent areas closely associated with merchandising process, but usually not direct responsibilities of merchandisers. In small firms, a single

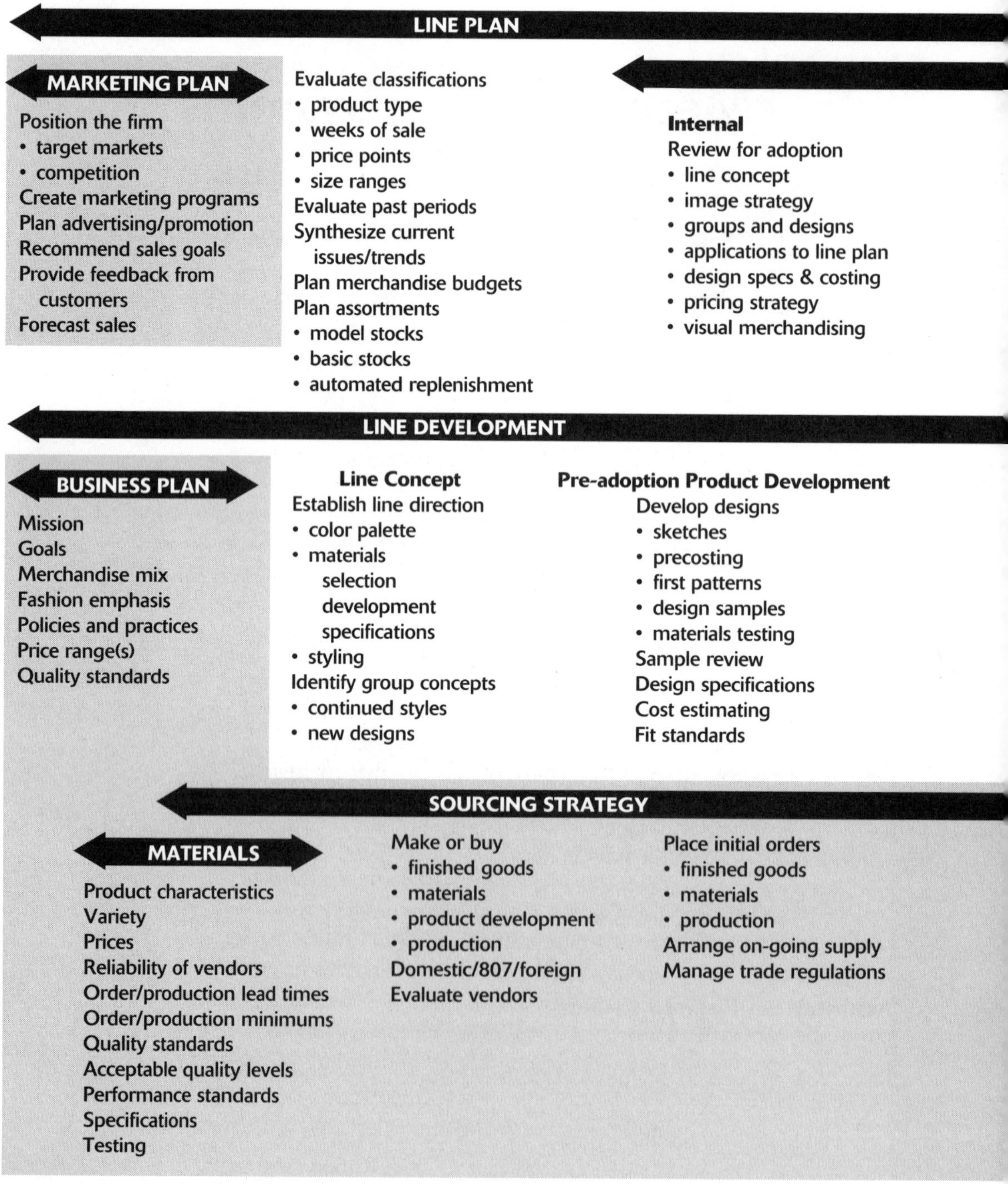

LINE PLAN

MARKETING PLAN

Position the firm
• target markets
• competition
Create marketing programs
Plan advertising/promotion
Recommend sales goals
Provide feedback from
   customers
Forecast sales

Evaluate classifications
• product type
• weeks of sale
• price points
• size ranges
Evaluate past periods
Synthesize current
   issues/trends
Plan merchandise budgets
Plan assortments
• model stocks
• basic stocks
• automated replenishment

Internal
Review for adoption
• line concept
• image strategy
• groups and designs
• applications to line plan
• design specs & costing
• pricing strategy
• visual merchandising

LINE DEVELOPMENT

BUSINESS PLAN

Mission
Goals
Merchandise mix
Fashion emphasis
Policies and practices
Price range(s)
Quality standards

Line Concept
Establish line direction
• color palette
• materials
   selection
   development
   specifications
• styling
Identify group concepts
• continued styles
• new designs

Pre-adoption Product Development
Develop designs
• sketches
• precosting
• first patterns
• design samples
• materials testing
Sample review
Design specifications
Cost estimating
Fit standards

SOURCING STRATEGY

MATERIALS

Product characteristics
Variety
Prices
Reliability of vendors
Order/production lead times
Order/production minimums
Quality standards
Acceptable quality levels
Performance standards
Specifications
Testing

Make or buy
• finished goods
• materials
• product development
• production
Domestic/807/foreign
Evaluate vendors

Place initial orders
• finished goods
• materials
• production
Arrange on-going supply
Manage trade regulations

FIGURE 3.1

Taxonomy of the Apparel Merchandising System (TAMS): interactive, concurrent, and sequential components of merchandising defined as the planning, development, and presentation of product lines (Developed by G. I. Kunz).

LINE PLAN

LINE PRESENTATION

Wholesale

Line preview
- line concept
- image strategy
- assortment strategy
- style appeal
- marketing strategy
- pricing strategy
- visual merchandising

Line/style release
- fashion shows
- wholesale markets
- sales presentations
- trunk shows

Customer service

Retail

Specialty   Hanger/shelf appeal
Department   Display space
Discount   Fixtures/lighting
Off price   Signage/labels/ticketing
Mfg. outlet   Pricing strategy
Catalog   Delivery strategy
Television   Customer service
Computer   Inventory management

LINE DEVELOPMENT

Line Adoption

Establish prices
Assign styles/sizes/colors to
   line plan
Balance assortments diversity/-
   volume/allocation
Establish gross margin
Produce sales/photo/catalog
   samples

Post-Adoption Product Development

Perfect styling and fit
Engineer production patterns
Test materials & assembly methods
Develop style samples
Develop style/quality specifications
- styling
- fit
- materials
- assembly methods
Detailed costing
Pattern grading

SOURCING STRATEGY

PRODUCTION

Production Planning

Make or buy
Style assignment
Make to order/stock
Cut order planning
Marker making
Engineering specifications
Capacity/workflow
Plant layout/startup
Methods development
Training

Assembly & Finishing

Production scheduling
Work study
Ergonomics
Quality control
Spreading
Cutting
Sewing
Pressing
Finishing
Actual costs

Packaging & Distribution

Labeling/ticketing
Packaging
Hangar or shelf ready
Shipping methods
Loading
Handling

merchandiser may be responsible for the white portions of TAMS as well as parts of the shaded portions. In large firms, a particular merchandisers job may include only a few elements of one of the white portions.

At first glance, TAMS may appear static, but in fact, merchandising is a **dynamic process** of intense change. Notice the double-ended arrows related to each segment of TAMS. These indicate influence of each segment throughout time. Visualize the TAMS model as rolled into a cylinder; the arrows related to line planning circumnavigate the cylinder, reflecting endless change and responsiveness of line plans to influences within and outside the firm. Peer into the center of the cylinder and visualize a spider-web-like network of electronic data interchange (EDI) connecting constituencies within the firm, and coalitions outside the firm, with information related to the product line.

The **merchandising cycle** represented by TAMS is one year, beginning the first week of February and ending the last week of January. The cycle begins in February because January apparel sales are primarily the clearance of fall and holiday stocks in preparation for the new spring and summer selling periods. In some firms, the selling period concept has merged into a concept called **weeks of sale.** For example, at JCPenney, "week 1" is the first week of February. Thus, certain merchandise groups might be planned for retail sale from week 5 through week 15, that is, four weeks in March, four weeks in April, and two weeks of May. Merchandise groups overlap one another in the merchandise plan to provide adequate variety for customers and a continuous supply of new merchandise.

As a merchandiser, it is common to work on several different **selling periods** at the same time. To apply the TAMS model to this idea, a merchandiser can be concurrently planning, developing, and presenting different parts of the same line. This makes for a great deal of variety and challenge in the life of a merchandiser.

A **product line** consists of a combination of styles that 1) satisfy similar or related customer needs; 2) can be sold within the targeted price range; and 3) marketed with similar strategies. The terms product line and merchandise line are used interchangeably. Apparel manufacturers and retailers commonly plan, develop, and present two to eight lines a year depending on their fashion focus. Selling periods are traditionally defined as spring, summer, back to school, early fall, late fall, holiday, and cruise.

Large apparel firms may have several product lines for each selling period, with each product line marketed at a different price range, under a different label and targeted to a different market segment (Reda, 1994, January). This gives the firm broader market coverage. Each of these lines may have a different merchandise manager.

Line Planning

As shown in TAMS, line planning is a dynamic, ongoing process throughout the merchandising cycle. Notice that line planning is somewhat concurrent with the development of line concept, a component of line development. Notice also that materials sourcing may precede the initiation of line planning for a particular selling period. Materials often provide inspiration for development of line concept.

Line planning requires assessment of the present, analysis of the past, and projection for the future. Line plans are based on and integrated with the overall business and marketing plans, as well as information provided by the operations and finance constituencies. The primary elements of the line planning process are synthesis of current issues, evaluation of past seasons, and development of merchandise budgets and assortment plans. **Current issues** might include positioning of new local, domestic, or international competitors with similar merchandise classifications, as well as economic, social, and cultural influences on fashion trends and potential sales. **Evaluation of past periods** usually includes detailed analysis of the same selling period last year, as well as an examination of the current selling period for any relevant trends. For the past season, planners seek to understand customer spending patterns in relation to merchandise classifications, identification of hot selling merchandise groups and styles, and influences of pricing.

Classification analysis results in establishing priorities for weeks of sale, price points, size ranges, and size standards. **Merchandise budgets** identify planned dollar investment by category or classification and open-to-buy. **Assortment plans** may include model stocks, basic stocks, and automated replenishment. Merchandise plans may identify merchandise to be continued in stock, but only provide criteria for the selection of new merchandise to be introduced into the line. The identification of the actual new merchandise is a function of line development.

Line Development

Line development includes the processes required to translate a line plan into real merchandise. The length of time allowed for line development varies greatly from one firm to the next depending on the nature of the merchandise offered and the types of line development processes used. Sometimes the process is highly formalized, with numerous planning meetings involving a merchandising team; in other firms the process may be almost haphazard in nature. The line plan is a guide for line development and is always subject to review. Adjustments are often needed to make the line more marketable, producible, and salable.

If the line will be sold at wholesale, it must be completed in time for presentation to the sales staff. If the firm is vertically integrated and sells all of its merchandise through its own retail outlets, the wholesale selling process is unnecessary. Line development may be completed with a final internal management review. In any case, the line development timeline is determined by when the merchandise must appear on the retail sales floor. The first phase of line development is formulating the line concept. Once this is agreed upon there are two means of completing line development: finished goods buying/sourcing and/or product development.

Line Concept

A line concept includes the look and appeal that contributes to the identity and salability of the line. The first element of line concept is establishing **line direction,** which is related to trends in color, styling, and fabrications as interpreted for the firm's target customers.

The second element is to establish merchandise **group concepts** within the line concepts. Group concepts are factors that give unanimity to merchandise groups, enabling manufacturers and retailers to sell them together. Group concepts may be communicated by style features, repetition of color or fabric, coordinated print designs, and so forth. Based on group concepts, sales history, and sales forecasts, decisions are made as to which styles from the past season's line should be carried over and which should be replaced. To minimize product-development costs and risks associated with introducing new styles, firms must identify high-volume styles that, with no change or minimal change, can continue to be top sellers.

Finished Goods Buying/Sourcing

Retail buyers/merchandisers often travel to wholesale markets or work with manufacturers' representatives in their stores to select merchandise from apparel manufacturers' lines. **Wholesale markets** provide a setting for linking the work of merchandisers at the wholesale level with those at the retail level. **Sales representatives** are often instrumental in developing retail assortments and writing purchase orders.

Merchandise plans provide the framework for developing balanced assortments. Good coordination within merchandise groups is critical to sales success. The more merchandise groups mix, match, and complement each other, the greater the potential for multiple sales, higher total sales volume, and gross margin. A well-planned variety of styles is essential to make a fashion statement, inspire the retail buyer and ultimate consumer, and to make an effective presentation on the retail sales floor.

Both manufacturer and retailer merchandisers may be involved in sourcing finished goods in the world market. More often than not, however, they are also involved in some form of product development.

Product Development

Product development is the design and engineering of products to be serviceable, producible, salable, and profitable (Glock & Kunz, 1995). In the apparel industry, product development evolves in three phases: preadoption, adoption, and post-adoption. The line plan, combined with the line concept, provides the framework for this process. **Pre-adoption product development** focuses on analysis, creativity, and the formation of product groups that are unique while reflecting the line concept. Design is an important element in this phase.

The **line adoption** process may be one of the most stressful periods for designers and merchandisers. In some firms, line adoption occurs during a series of day-long meetings involving elaborate presentations of line concept, group concepts with story boards, design samples, design specifications, fit analysis, and cost estimates. In other firms, line adoption is more gradual, occurring during on-going short meetings where a few designs or merchandise groups are evaluated at a time. No matter the format, this is when decisions are made about what styles and merchandise groups will be included in the line and how the styles will be applied to the line plan. Decisions are made about what merchandise groups will be adopted, what designs will become styles in the line, model stocks, gross margins, prices, and expected volume for each merchandise group.

During the **post-adoption** phase of product development, styles are prepared for production. The process includes perfecting styling and fit, engineering production patterns, testing materials and assembly methods, developing style and quality specifications, developing detailed costs, and grading patterns. Early phases of **production planning** are concurrent with postadoption product development. Merchandisers must be knowledgeable about merchandising, marketing, and production in order to develop products and product lines that are salable and financially productive.

Line Presentation

Line presentation involves evaluating the line in order to make it visible and salable. The power of appeal (Scheller, 1993), also known as hanger or shelf appeal, attracts attention, causing retail buyers and ultimate consumers to stop, take a longer look, and ultimately purchase. Successful merchandise groups have hanger and shelf appeal for both retail buyers and target customers. Customer loyalty develops when expectations are satisfied from one season to the next. Line presentation occurs internally within a firm at line adoption, at wholesale to retail buyers, and at retail to ultimate consumers.

Internal Line Presentations

The purpose of internal line-adoption presentations is to develop consensus and support for the proposed additions of specific products to the line plan. Product developers often include articulation of the line concept and image strategy for the coming selling period in their adoption presentations. They describe proposed merchandise groups and styles to be carried over into the next selling period, along with any proposed modifications. New groups, and each proposed design within a group, are described and evaluated. Other considerations discussed are the application of the proposed merchandise groups and designs to the line plan, cost estimates, pricing strategies, and visual merchandising strategies for the retail sales floor.

Wholesale Line Presentation

There are two aspects of wholesale line presentation: **line preview** and **line release.** Line preview is the presentation of the planned and adopted product line to the sales force. The purpose of line preview is to communicate the line concept and to help sales representatives to effectively sell the line the way it was conceived. Feedback from the sales force with regard to the proposed product line can be very helpful when refining merchandise groups and styles in the post adoption product development process. Line release marks the beginning of promotion for the new selling period. The line may be released via an elaborate fashion show attended by the fashion press. Other firms may release their line by distributing sales samples to the sales force. In any case, line release marks the first opportunity for the public to view the new line.

Retail Line Presentation

The purpose of retail line presentation is to sell the line to ultimate consumers. Strategies used for retail line presentation vary depending on the type of retailer. For example, specialty and department stores have different types of store layout and fixturing than discount, off-price, and manufacturer's outlet stores. Obviously, retail merchandise presentation in catalog, television, and computer formats take on very different forms. Issues they have in common, however, include merchandise appeal, use of space, fixturing, lighting, signage, pricing and delivery strategies, customer service, and inventory management.

The Taxonomy of Apparel Merchandising Systems is based on a series of assumptions related to merchandising processes and the relationships among constituencies as described by the Behavioral Theory of the Apparel Firm. Table 3.1 summarizes those assumptions.

TABLE 3.1

Summary of assumptions of the TAMS.

1. Merchandising is a functional constituency of an apparel firm.
2. The apparel firm can be a manufacturer, a retailer, or be vertically integrated.
3. The dynamic merchandising process takes place in the context of a firm's business and financial plans and marketing strategy.
4. The three fundamental components of the merchandising process are line/merchandise planning, line/merchandise development, and line/merchandise presentation.
5. TAMS has vertical and horizontal dimensions; elements located vertically on the model tend to happen simultaneously, while elements located horizontally tend to be sequential.
6. The dimensions of product lines that merchandisers are responsible for include pricing, assortments, styling, and timing.
7. Merchandisers work closely with, and may be involved in sourcing materials and production.
8. The merchandising cycle is one year beginning February 1 and ending January 31.
9. A merchandising cycle is divided into several overlapping selling periods depending on the nature of the merchandise and customer demand defined by weeks of sale.

Learning Activity 3.2

Assumptions of TAMS

What is an assumption? What is the role of the assumptions when using and applying the components of TAMS?

CASE 3.1

ShopKo: A Clear Vision

From Roach, L. (1995). *Discount Merchandiser,* pp. 24–26.

"We should hit the magic number very soon," predicts an excited Terry MacDonald, ShopKo's senior vice president of marketing, "Two billion dollars by the end of next fiscal year." The Green Bay, WI-based chain saw sales of $1.85 billion in fiscal 1995, a 6.6 percent increase over the previous year. Comp-store sales increased by 0.7 percent and net earnings were $37.8 million, up from $32.1 million—strong numbers in retail's trying year of bankruptcies and reorganizations.

"The Vision 2000 strategy is really behind all the growth we've experienced, " says MacDonald. "It is a concept that is really working." Since its inception in 1991, Vision 2000 has been the buzzword for change in the company, which recently celebrated its 33rd anniversary. The strategy was created to ensure longevity through differentiation, by focusing on flexibility and experimentation. At the close of 1995, 75 percent of all ShopKo stores will be remodeled or updated to fit the Vision 2000 mold. The newest entry, a 77,000-square-foot unit in Belvidere, IL, represent "ShopKo at its very best," says Dale P. Kramer, president and CEO. "We've evaluated what works and what doesn't," adds MacDonald. "In some ways we've gone beyond the original Vision 2000 concept. A customer would not have seen a ShopKo like the Belvidere store a year ago. The hallmarks of a Vision 2000 store are super-wide aisles, good lighting and merchandise stacked neatly to the ceiling but there have been some significant changes.

"We are really trying to differentiate ourselves, primarily with our pharmacy/optical operation, which accounts for a quarter of our annual sales," MacDonald continues. "The pharmacy/optical department is run on an EDLP (everyday-low-price) strategy; the rest of the company is now run on a high/low, sale-driven

pricing structure. We've been really promoting this category and it has been very good to us."

Fine-Tuning

For the rest of the store, the move from EDLP to a sale-driven strategy is signaled by the new signage gracing the store bearing the catch phrase "Great Value, Great Price." Again, ShopKo's need for differentiation, particularly from Wal-Mart, the chief competitor in many of the small- to medium-sized markets ShopKo is targeting, drove the transition, says MacDonald. "We needed a way to show customers that we have a great deal of merchandise in-stock and at a great price," he explains. "The term 'EDLP' is very identifiable with Wal-Mart. ShopKo wanted to communicate a unique, effective message."

The Category Killer

As part of the evolving Vision 2000 concept, ShopKo has pared down its assortment to concentrate on "categories that are part of our heritage and categories that represent avenues of growth," says MacDonald. Seasonal items "have always done well at ShopKo," he adds, "but we've really taken our strengths in that category and worked on becoming a real category killer. Halloween has always been big with us; this year we've made a dramatic statement throughout the store. Also, Christmas items, especially tree-trimming merchandise, is terrific for us. ShopKo has a huge custom-order tree business."

The domestics category also evolved into an area of primary focus. "We are tying to become a dominant retailer in solid color sheets," says MacDonald. "ShopKo can't compete with the depth of Bed, Bath and Beyond, and Linens 'n Things, but we can compete in select categories. Our shot is going to be the solid-color sheets-we're stocking as many colors as we can. This area, including bed pillows, has been

---

Learning Activity 3.3

Read Case 3.1 very carefully.

1. Examine how the merchandising dimensions of products lines (pricing, assortments, styling and timing) are being incorporated into ShopKo's Vision 2000.

2. In contrast, what are the dimensions of ShopKo's marketing strategy?

phenomenal. We've worked hard at making a strong statement."

ShopKo has adopted the "store-within-a-store" concept for its health and beauty care department, using cosmetic specialty stores and upscale department stores as models. "We want to stand for cosmetics," states MacDonald. "ShopKo is building the hottest categories—aromatherapy, scents and bath products to get that department-store look within a discount store. There is a Wal-Mart and a Kmart less than 50 miles from the Belvidere store. We want people to walk into this ShopKo and say 'this is really different.'"

In apparel, ShopKo has eliminated all dressy and work-related clothing "because they represented a small piece of our sales and required a large part of our space and inventory. We're moving into the casual-wear leisure look. Aerobic wear has increased five-fold in the past year," says MacDonald. "Casual wear is something we can do well. It's impossible for us to follow high fashion, but we can stock quality, trend-driven apparel.

"The concentration has been on denim this year, and plaid, running a theme through all the apparel de-partments," he continues. "The softlines side has made many changes in the past few years, moving toward what you would see in a specialty store, like The Gap."

A smaller number of categories have been stream-lined to fit the Vision 2000 concept. "About a year ago we had to make some hard choices as to what categories should be of primary focus. As a result, some had to decrease," says MacDonald. "The paint, automotive, and tool categories have been condensed to about half the usual space. We've stocked them with a convenience mentality as opposed to a traffic mentality. This left space for other booming cate-gories, such as storage."

The next Vision 2000 store will open in the sum-mer of 1996 in Pullman, WA, and using the Belvidere store as a model, will parlay the best aspects of that store into a new interpretation of the concept. "We recognize the need for flexibility," says MacDonald. "But we also recognize that we've found our niche. ShopKo is a second-tier-city player; we're comfort-able in a medium-sized market. It's been very good to us."

Dimensions of Product Lines

According to the Glock and Kunz (1995) definition of merchandising, the dimensions of product lines considered by both manufacturers and retail merchandisers include prices, assortments, styling, and timing. A firm may focus on a particular price range of merchandise, such as budget and lower-moderate or upper-moderate, and better **price ranges,** depending on their target customer. Merchandisers select or develop products, select materials, and perhaps recommend performance and quality characteristics that can be executed within this price range. They also help set list prices for manufacturers and first prices for retailers. List prices provide the foun-dation for pricing in the manufacturing sector; first prices are the basis of pricing in the retail sector. Merchandisers are also instrumental in determin-ing when goods will be marked down, and by how much. Chapter 5 focuses on the pricing process.

A **merchandise assortment** is determined by the relative number styles, colors, and sizes included in the line. Apparel merchandise assortments are structured by related product groupings called collections, groups or stories. Merchandise groups may be described as diverse or focused, depending on average volume per SKU for the assortment (VSA). A SKU is a stock-keeping unit determined by a combination of style, size, and color. Research has shown that the lower the volume per SKU, the lower the financial productivity of the assortment. Assortment diversity needs to be considered when developing pricing strategies in order to generate adequate gross margin. Assortments are thoroughly investigated in Chapter 7.

Styling refers to the appearance of a product. It involves selecting or developing product design—the creative, functional, and fashion aspects of line—and product development. Styling must be consistent with the firm's positioning strategy in terms of the relative number of fashion and/or basic goods in an assortment. If a firm defines itself as fashion forward, most styles it includes in a line must convey fashion leadership. If a firm defines itself as offering classics, then the styles included in the line should reflect time-tested favorites. Style choices for a particular selling period are framed by the development of the line concept. In the line-development process, specific styles are selected or developed to fill out the line plan.

Timing is determined by the nature of merchandise classifications in relation to the merchandising cycle. Timing of merchandise presentation at the wholesale and at retail levels determines merchandise, marketing, and production schedules. The merchandising calendar for a manufacturer who sells wholesale is likely to be based on key market dates relating to major selling periods in the retail sector. A retail merchandising calendar defines the total merchandising cycle into selling periods for particular merchandise classifications. It also considers the timing of major selling periods and special promotions. A **selling period** is defined by an opening date, a closing date, and the overall selling trend. The calendar also might identify the potential for extending the selling period beyond the initial plan.

A component of timing that is extremely important for both manufactures and retail merchandisers is the turn-around time between order placement and delivery of the goods to the retail sales floor. For both branded and private-label goods, the time required from developing a concept for new merchandise to having the group ready to go into production is crucial, as is the time from beginning production until the goods can be delivered to the retail sales floor. Timing is a key factor in merchandising success.

Dimensions of Product Change

Dealing with the demand for constantly changing products may be one the most challenging and interesting aspects of apparel merchandising. The explanation of the demand for intense product change is often attributed to fashion. However, understanding fashion change is a subject of some complexity.

> Psychologists speak of fashion as the seeking of individuality; sociologists see class competition and social conformity to norms of dress; economists see a pursuit of the scarce; aestheticians view the artistic components and ideals of beauty; historians offer evolutionary explanations for changes in designs. Literally hundreds of viewpoints unfold, from a literature more immense than for any phenomenon of consumer behavior (Sproles, 1985, p. 55).

The stages of the fashion process are often discussed in relation to a bell-shaped curve representing levels of fashion acceptance. Sproles (1985) provides a meta-theory approach to understanding fashion change (See Table 3.2); he emphasizes the complexity of perspectives on what drives fashion change.

Merchandising Perspectives on Product Change

From a merchandising perspective, "fashion is a continuing process of change in the styles of dress that are accepted and followed by segments of the public at any particular time" (Jarnow, Judelle, & Guerreiro, 1981). A second aspect of product change—seasonal change—is often confused with fashion change by both academicians and apparel professionals. The terms "seasonal goods" and "fashion goods" are often used interchangeably, as are the terms "basics" and "staples." However, when fashion change is separated from seasonal change, this clarifies the characteristics of product change with which merchandisers must contend. Distinguishing between "fashion" and "seasonal" and "basic" and "staple" are essential first steps.

Fashion goods are products that experience demand for change in styling. Style is the characteristic or distinctive appearance of a product, the combination of features that makes it different from other products of the same type (Troxell & Judelle, 1981). Fashion goods require frequent change in styling in order to maintain acceptance from consumers. For example, the salable life of junior dress styles may be only about eight weeks.

In contrast, products that have little demand for style change are called **basic goods.** Basic goods, with little or no change in styling, may be

TABLE 3.2

The framework for a general fashion theory*

Stages of the Fashion Process	Explanatory Models
Invention and Introduction	Aesthetic (art movements, ideals of beauty) Business (market infrastructure) Cultural (subcultural leadership) Historical (historical resurrection, historical continuity)
Fashion Leadership	Aesthetic (art movements, ideals of beauty, aesthetic perception) Communications (symbolic communications, adoption and diffusion) Cultural (social conflict) Economic (scarcity, conspicuous consumption) Psychological (individuality) Sociological (trickle down)
Increasing Social Visibility	Aesthetic (aesthetic perception) Business (market infrastructure, mass market) Communications (adoption and diffusion) Geographical (spatial diffusion) Psychological (uniqueness) Sociological (collective behavior)
Conformity Within and Across Social Groups	Communications (adoption and diffusion) Economic (demand) Geographic (spatial diffusion) Psychological (conformity)
Social Saturation	Business (mass market, market infrastructure) Economic (demand) Psychological (individuality) Sociological (collective behavior)
Decline and Obsolescence	Business (mass market, market infrastructure) Communications (adoption and diffusion, symbolic communications) Economic (demand) Historical (historical continuity) Psychological (individuality)

*Based on Sproles (1985), pp. 66.

salable in the same styles up to 52 weeks a year and perhaps for several years.

Seasonal goods experience change in demand related to a combination of factors associated with the calendar year, including ethnic and cultural traditions, seasonal events, and weather changes. Holidays and the beginning and ending of the school year have a major impact on the demand for certain types of products. Some seasonal goods sell only a few weeks out of the year.

In contrast to these seasonal products, products that have little change in demand relative to the time of the year are called **staple goods.** Staple goods sell 52 weeks a year at similar rates. Change in demand related to the time of the year may or may not include a corresponding demand for change in styling.

A Perceptual Map of Product Change

Figure 3.2 is a Perceptual Map of Product Change. Some apparel products are highly fashionable; others are highly seasonal. Some are both seasonal and fashionable; others are neither. The impact of these aspects of product

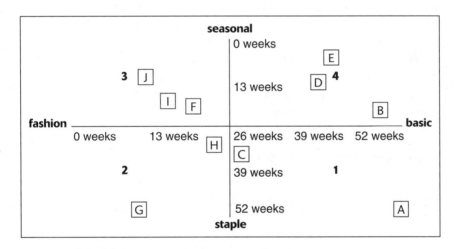

Types of ShopKo Products in Each Quadrant

Sector 1. Basic/Staple goods
    A. tools
    C. interior paint
Sector 2. Fashion/Staple goods
    G. aerobics
    H. solid color sheets

Sector 3. Fashion/Seasonal goods
    F. casual wear
    I. plaid
    J. denim
Sector 4. Basic/Seasonal goods
    B. exterior paint
    D. Christmas holiday decorations
    E. custom Christmas trees

FIGURE 3.2

A Perceptual Map of Product Change (Based on Kunz, 1988.)

change on merchandise planning and positioning can be visualized through the use of this perceptual map, which is a graphic means of plotting fashion and seasonal variation in consumer demand for selected products.

Fashion/Basic Continuum   Think of a completely basic product as one with no demand for styling changes through a 52-week merchandising cycle. At the other extreme, think of a fashion product that experiences weekly demands for styling change. Putting these two scenarios opposite each other on a line results in a continuum related to demand for change in styling. At one extreme are completely basic products with infrequent demand for style change. At the other extreme are high-fashion or fad items requiring very frequent changes in styling. This continuum is represented horizontally in Figure 3.1.

Seasonal/Staple Continuum   A completely staple product experiences no change in demand related to the time of year, while a completely seasonal product would be salable for only one week. The seasonal/staple continuum is represented vertically in Figure 3.2.

Four sectors are created by the intersecting these two continuums. These are useful in describing product characteristics in relation to product change. Table 3.3 provides a summary of definitions related to the Perceptual Map of Product Change.

Assessment of Product Change at ShopKo

Some aspects of ShopKo's product line are included in Case 3.1. Merchandise categories and classifications included in ShopKo's merchandise mix are: quality, trend-driven apparel, including casual wear similar to Gap's; aerobic wear; denim, and plaid; Halloween and Christmas; tree trimming and custom-order trees; cosmetics, scents, bath; solid color sheets; paint, automotive, tools, and storage. What products have demand for change in styling and how often? What products have change in demand related to the time of the year? How do these products relate to the perceptual map of product change?

Sector 1 represents products that are basic *and* staple. Products in this sector experience the least product change. The same or similar styles in the similar fabrics and colors are stocked year around. Manufacturers of staple, basic goods may produce and promote only one line a year, a 52-week selling period. These products may have only slight changes in color and trim from one year to the next. Probably the most basic and staple category in ShopKo's merchandise mix is tools. Tools might be positioned in

TABLE 3.3

Summary of definitions related to Perceptual Map of Product Change.

Merchandising—the planning, development, and presentation of product line(s) for identified target market(s) with regard to prices, assortments, styling, and timing.

Merchandising cycle—one-year period from February 1 to January 31.

Weeks of sale—time period during the merchandising cycle that a particular classification of merchandise is salable.

Merchandise classification—group of products that are reasonable substitutes for each other from the perspective of customers; similar in function, selling period, and price.

Styling—characteristic or distinctive appearance of a product, the combination of features that makes it different from other products of the same type.

Fashion Goods—classifications that experience frequent demand for change in styling during a merchandising cycle.

Basic Goods—classifications that experience little demand for change in styling during a merchandising cycle.

Staple Goods—classifications that are in continuous demand throughout a merchandising cycle; demand is not greatly affected by the time of the year.

Seasonal Goods—classifications that experience changes in market demand during a merchandising cycle related to ethnic and cultural events, holidays, and weather changes.

Sector 1 at "A" on the perceptual map. Basic/staple merchandise lends itself to standardized stocks and computer-based reordering systems.

What fashion and seasonal aspects are associated with paint? Exterior paint is much more seasonal than interior paint because of the weather, but interior paint probably comes in more fashion colors. Exterior paint might be positioned in Sector 4 at "B" as a basic/seasonal good with a 26-week selling period, while interior paint might be positioned in Sector 1 at "C" as a basic/staple with a 26-week selling period. Because exterior paint may be salable for only about 26 weeks a year, the shelf space can be available to other goods during the off season. At the same time, interior paint with a 26-week selling period is stocked year around, but new colors are brought in the other 26 weeks to complement the other stock.

The selling period for Christmas decorations begins earlier and earlier, with presentation beginning in late September for about a 12-week selling period. At the same, time products are relatively basic from one year to the next. Holiday decorations are a basic/seasonal product, positioned at "D" in Sector 4. The selling period for custom Christmas trees is probably less than four weeks annually, with some style change required in the decorations from year to year, but not during the selling season. Custom Christmas trees might be positioned at "E" in Sector 4.

Products that experience subtle fashion change from one season to the next are sometimes called "fashion basics." ("Fashion basics" is an apparel industry term for what are commonly called "classics" in the fashion literature.) ShopKo's Gap-like casual wear might be regarded as fashion basics. They probably have three or four selling periods a year of 15 to 20 weeks each. Casual wear might be positioned at "F" in Sector 3. Modification of fabrications and color assortments are probably the primary merchandising tactics.

Aerobics wear, while being offered in stock year around, may show the greatest impact of fashion with the most frequent changes in styling related to color and garment design. Aerobics wear may be a fashion/staple at "G" in Sector 2. Solid color sheets may also be a fashion/staple stocked year around with two different color systems a year with a 26-week selling season for each. Solid color sheets might be positioned in Sector 2 at "H". Plaid and denim are probably a nod toward fashion for youth and junior sizes. Plaid may be the most frequently changing category in the ShopKo assortment. It would fit in the fashion/seasonal category with a selling period of eight to ten weeks. Plaid might be positioned in Sector 3 at "I".

Uses of the Perceptual Map

Merchandise classifications might be more accurately placed on the perceptual map by analyzing sales figures that reflect changes in rate of sale during each week of the year. Clearly, the length of time that a particular style or classification is salable may be limited either by consumer expectation for fashion change or by the seasonal nature of the product. Merchandisers must understand what aspect of product change limits salability and makes merchandise plans accordingly.

Point-of-sale data (POS) combined with EDI makes appropriate information easily accessible to both manufacturers and retail merchandisers. Raw sales figures reflect two things: 1) the results of decisions made by merchandisers and marketers related to selection, presentation, and promotion of goods, and 2) customers' preferences relative to the merchandise offered.

Fashion and seasonal changes are two aspects of product change that strongly influence merchandisers' decisions, who often have their salaries and/or number of assigned departments or classifications varied according to the "difficulty" of the merchandise. Difficulty of the assignment is highly related to the amount of change in the merchandise.

CASE 3.2

French Facelifts

From D'Aulnay, S. (1995, October 30) *Daily News Record,* p. 6.

France may not be a country with a department store mentality, but department store executives here are attempting to change that. In the past, department stores used to be synonymous with bazaars—everything for everyone at every price. But that era is finished. Highly selective, consumer-friendly concepts are all the rage this year.

Leading the way was Left Bank store Bon Marche, which changed from a dusty neighborhood store into an elegant up-market emporium. Last year, Bon Marche gave birth to Balthazar, a redesigned men's department that could almost stand on its own as a specialty store.

Then this summer, Printemps and Galeries Lafayette each kicked into high gear. Printemps launched a more focused, user-friendly concept in a Paris suburb, while Galeries Lafayette unveiled its redesigned flagship men's department. The catalyst for much of the fine-tuning trend is Printemps president Philippe Vindry, who did a short stint at Bon Marche, spearheading that store's restructuring project, before returning to Printemps to oversee its three-year $100 million reorganization program.

"Printemps has launched into a great challenge," Vindry said, adding that the changes involve merchandising, a complete remodeling and improvement of services, and a modernization of the computer systems. "The strategic concept is to have a department store with the spirit of a boutique," Vindry explained.

The first stage was the complete refurbishing of the street level of its Velizy store, which features Brummell along with tabletops, linens, toys, and children's wear.

Brummell is a multiple-use name for the Printemps chain. It is the name of the men's department (which in Paris is a freestanding unit), as well as the store's private men's label, and, partly because of its multiplicity, its image needed realigning. The store label had stretched its price points so much that it had diluted its image. Now, the price range will be drastically reduced, from eight price points to four in suits, for example.

Previously, there were eight price points going from 995 francs ($199), permanent promotion price,

to a high of 2,295 francs ($459). In between there was a choice: 1,195,1,295, 1,395, 1,495, 1,595, and 1,895 francs.

Now the price policy has been rationalized with an emphasis on a consistent manufacturing quality. The difference is in the fabrics and in the margins taken: 1,195 francs ($239); 1,395 ($279); 1,695 ($339); 1,995 ($399).

Michel Silvey, general merchandise manager for men's and children's fashion, explained: "Brummell had become more of a store name with a wide price range than a consistent brand. So we're redefining Brummell as a brand with a new product, quality and price policy. The price difference will be in the fabric, so that consumers can recognize the product. It creates stability. We got caught up in the price spiral and consumers couldn't recognize (the Brummell brand) anymore."

The realignment is expected to reap rewards for the company. According to Silvy: "The Brummell brand currently represents 25 percent of total men's sales, but our objective is to reach 40 percent."

"It's also important to have a stability in the production. One of our priorities in the next two years is to find reliable partnerships with manufacturers," Silvy added.

He is planning a strong advertising campaign to promote Brummell as a store name, and will offer a leaflet, describing the history of Brummell an some fashion consultancy tips. "This will help position Brummell not just as a men's department within a store but as a specialty store," he added.

"If the department store wants to have a future, it has to offer a feasible alternative to prestigious boutiques," Silvey said. "We want to give more space for brands to better express their identity. This will lead us to eliminate brands according to profitability in order to have a focused representation in the market."

Brummell will be divided into six universes: traditional city, contemporary city, leisure accessories, shoes and homewear/underwear. The traditional city sector will feature the private label as well as brands like Yves Saint Laurent, Pierre Cardin, and de Fursac, while the contemporary city sector will have the private label as well as multiproduct as well as Kenzo, Armani Jeans and Le Garage shirts. The leisure

continued

universe will contain Levi's and Lee Cooper for jeans, Quiksilver for outdoors, Esprit for contemporary sportswear, Marlboro Classics for the authentic look, as well as New Man and McGregor for traditional sportswear.

"Consumers expect a focus, a clarity of product offering and visibility," said Silvey, adding that service will be a key focus. "The first reason for a non-purchase is the lack of size and color," he said. "We've focused our policy on managing our stock."

Part of that management of stock is reflected in Printemps' recent decision to open two discount stores, named Carre des Affaires Printemps. One is located near Nantes and the second will open in December just outside Toulouse. "This a new way of handling our leftover stock and it enables us to better update our collections," said Vindry.

At Galeries Lafayette, the goals were to clarify the presentation and reposition the range of products in the medium to up-market. Priority was given to international brands and to the four private labels. "We're setting up a new policy for men's wear geared to the international image," said Pierre Pellarrey, manager of the men's department.

"We were inspired by department stores like Barney's New York and Harrods in London, but we kept in mind that the French mentality is very different," Pellarrey explained. Among the new international brands Pellarrey introduced were Aquascutum raincoats, Barbaur outerwear, a Paul Smith corner, as well as DKNY. The latter marks the launch of that brand in the French market. Galeries also has the exclusive in France for Calvin Klein underwear.

The Armani corner was enlarged and Dior will reappear "because it's an important French brand," he said. In the jeans department alongside Levi's, Lee and Liberto, Pellarrey decided to concentrate on designer jeans from Armani, Girbaud, DKNY, Paul Smith and Faconnable.

"We have a very important percentage of international consumers. Our competition is more the international department stores than the multi-brand shops," said Pellarrey. "The lesson is what we see in the U.S.—we must specialize. The time of bazaar-style department stores that have everything is over. We can't please everyone and we mustn't target all and everything."

The Galeries Lafayette chain operates 30 stores in France with additional units in Singapore, Japan, Moscow and Korea. A new store is opening in Berlin this month.

The Printemps chain currently has 17 fully owned stores and 18 affiliates stores in France. Outside France, the group has 12 affiliated stores remaining after the destruction of its two Kobe stores by the Japanese earthquake. Five more stores will soon be added to the chain-Lisbon and Istanbul in 1996, and Tagu in Korea, Tauyuan in Taiwan and Dlian in China in 1997. Also under consideration are sites in Peking, India, and Arab Emirates and South America, "but nothing is signed yet, " said Vindry, adding that the U.S. is not on the list of prospects.

Learning Activity 3.4

Using the Perceptual Map of Product Change

1. What are the principles guiding the development of the merchandising system at Printemps?

2. What are the principles guiding the development of the merchandising system at Galeries Lafayette?

3. Develop a Perceptual Map of Product Change for the merchandise classifications at either Printemps or Galeries Lafayette.

Context of Merchandising

As explained by the BTAF, merchandising is one of five essential, interactive business constituencies including executive management, marketing, operations, and finance. Executive management is responsible for development of the business plan that defines the business and establishes long- and short-term goals. Marketing defines and describes target customers, shapes the image of the company, and develops strategies for growth. Merchandising plans, develops, and presents product lines. Operations and finance manage the firm's resources: people, property, and money. One of the ways the interactive productivity of a firm's constituencies is assessed is via an income statement or Profit and Loss Statement (P&L), as it is sometimes called.

Income Statements

An **income statement** is a summary of a firm's revenue and expenses for a defined period of time. Income statements are commonly prepared on a monthly, quarterly, and/or annual basis (Berman & Evans, 1995). Frequently assessing revenue and profitability allows a firm to update plans, modify strategies in a timely way, and to be proactive rather than reactive in the business environment. For a small firm, a single income statement per period may suffice. But in large complex organizations, many income statements may be prepared to examine financial productivity of different parts of the firm. Income statements are commonly prepared for each tier in an organization and often for individual components within each tier.

A primary purpose of an income statement is to demonstrate whether the firm has made a profit for the period. Profit is an essential component of business operation in a capitalistic system. Profit may be stated in different ways: gross profit, operating profit, net profit, dollar or percentage profit or before- and after-tax profit. Gross profit, commonly called gross margin, is closely associated with merchandising responsibilities.

Income statements include nine basic elements that can be grouped into two categories: income measurements and income modifications (Lewison, 1994).

Income measurements include the following:

- **gross sales** is total dollar revenue received by a firm from the sale of goods and services.

- **net sales** is actual revenue from the sale of goods and services (gross sales—customer returns and allowances).
- **gross margin** is the revenue available for covering operating expenses and generating profit; sometimes called gross profit (net sales—cost of goods sold).
- **operating profit** is what remains after all financial obligations related to operating the business are met (gross margin—operating expenses).
- **net profit** before taxes is the figure on which the firm pays income tax.

Income modifications include the following:

- **customer returns and allowances** is cancellation of sales because of merchandise returns and refunds or price adjustments related to customer dissatisfaction.
- **cost of goods sold** is the amount the firm has paid to acquire or produce the merchandise sold (cost of merchandise available for sale—cost value of remaining inventory).
- **operating expense** is all costs associated with operating a business other than cost of merchandise sold.
- **other income and/or expenses** is additional revenue or costs related to operating the firm other than from selling goods and services.

In the first column of Table 3.4, measures of income are left justified; modifications of income are indented. Each measure of income has a corresponding modification in an income statement with the amounts reported in dollars in the second column.

Income statements often also include **merchandising and operating ratios** associated with measures of income and income modifications. See the third column of Table 3.4. The ratios are commonly stated as a percentage of net sales. Cost of goods sold and gross margin ratios are primary responsibilities of merchandisers. Responsibilities for the other ratios in the income statement are shared with marketing and operations constituencies. Ratio analysis often provides the most important information in the income statement besides profit. Past ratios and present ratios can be compared to identify trends (Lewison, 1994). Ratios generated by a particular firm can also be compared to other firms in the same business to identify advantages and disadvantages in the way a firm is conducting its business. Ratios are also reported across industries to identify general trends and problems in business operation.

TABLE 3.4

Basic income statement.

Gross Sales	$2,200	110%
Customer Returns and Allowances	$ 200	10%
Net Sales	$2,000	100%
Cost of Goods Sold	$1,000	50%
Gross Margin	$1,000	50%
Expenses	$ 900	45%
Operating Profit	$ 100	5%
Other Income	$ 100	5%
Net Profit Before Taxes	$ 200	10%

Relationships of Income Measurements, Income Modifications, and Associated Ratios

Income measurements are different expressions of revenue gained while running a business for a defined period. Income modifications are the reasons for the differences in income measurements. Table 3.5 demonstrates the mathematical relationships among income measurements, income modifications, merchandising ratios, and operating ratios.

Gross sales is total revenue received from sale of goods and services in a time period including both cash and credit sales. Unfortunately, not all goods sold stay sold. There are many reasons why customers return goods for refund or exchange. Many firms have liberal return policies, which grant customers a full refund. Allowances, a reduced price, or other form of credit may be granted to customers because merchandise is unsatisfactory for some reason. The ratio of gross sales to net sales is greater than 100 percent because gross sales is more than net sales: gross sales = net sales + customer returns and allowances.

Returns and allowances in relation to net sales may vary widely depending on the nature of a firm and its return policies. Catalog operations may have returns that total up to 40 percent of net sales, which is a real problem. Returns and allowances are part of manufacturer/retailer relationships, as well as the retailer-customer relationships. Retail merchandisers frequently request to return merchandise to the manufacturer that is unsatisfactory for some reason, i.e., it was shipped late, it was not what was ordered, or the quality was unsatisfactory. Sometimes they negotiate an allowance on the goods, that is, a price reduction, so the merchandise can be sold at a lower price and still provide adequate gross margin. In this case, the retailer would not return the merchandise.

TABLE 3.5

Calculation of a basic income statement and associated ratios and common merchandising and operating ratios.

Calculating Dollar Values	Calculating Ratios	Common Ratios
Gross Sales	gross sales ÷ net sales × 100	101% to 140%
− Customer Returns & Allowances	customer r & a ÷ net sales × 100	1% to 40%
Net Sales	net sales = 100%	100%
− Cost of Goods Sold	cost of goods sold ÷ net sales × 100	55% to 70%
Gross Margin	gross margin ÷ net sales × 100	30% to 45% of net sales
− Operating Expense	operating expense ÷ net sales × 100	18% to 35% of net sales
Operating Profit	operating profit ÷ net sales × 100	1% to 15% of net sales
± Other Income and/or Expenses	other income/expenses ÷ net sales × 100	0% to any number
Net Profit Before Taxes	net profit before taxes ÷ net sales × 100	1% to 12% of net sales

Net sales is the foundation of the income statement. It is the amount of merchandise actually sold in dollars during a specified time period: gross sales less customer returns and allowances. Net sales is the most realistic measure of revenue gained from operating a firm. All numbers and merchandising and operating ratios in the income statement relate directly to net sales. Net sales is 100 percent in relation to all ratios.

Cost of goods sold is calculated with consideration for inventory on hand at the beginning of the period; purchases of new merchandise with related transportation charges and cash discounts during the period; and alteration and workroom costs associated with sales. The difference between net sales and cost of goods sold is gross margin.

Gross margin is a measure of the amount of money available to cover all of the firm's expenses, except cost of merchandise, which is the only expense already accounted for. Any excess of gross margin over expenses results in operating profit. The merchandising ratio of gross margin in relation to net sales commonly runs from 30 to 45 percent in the retail sector depending on type of retail operation. Discounters commonly have lower percent gross margin than department stores, specialty stores are usually higher. Manufacturers commonly operate on lower percent gross margin than retailers.

Operating expenses cover all general and administrative costs incurred to run the business (rent, utilities, supplies, maintenance, and payroll) other than cost of merchandise and taxes. To realize a profit, operating expense must be less than gross margin. The ratio of operating expense to net sales is insightful in relation to a firm's profitability. Wal-Mart is known for its low operating expense ratio of less than 20 percent, which is credited, in part, to its efficient methods of distributing merchandise. For comparison, Aileen (as reported in Case 3.3) had an operating expense ratio of 39 percent. Every dollar a firm reduces its operating expense goes directly to the bottom line operating profit.

Operating profit is the measure of a firm's efficiency in managing the relationship between gross margin and operating expenses. Operating profit is the expression of profit commonly reported in the trade press and referred to when only the word "profit" is used. Firms may have negative operating profit (loss) for some periods for many reasons, for instance, unanticipated shifts in the market resulting in a decline in sales or large capital expenditures. However, successful continuation of a business depends on profit. Firms must show profit in order to grow, and growth is essential in today's market. Growth requires the reinvestment of profits into the business. Operating profits of 2 to 15 percent of net sales are common for apparel firms. But a firm may still be considered successful with a ratio of operating profits in relation to net sales as low as one percent.

Other income and expenses are commonly derived from activities associated with the business other than sales of goods and services. One common source of income in the retail sector is selling goods on credit with a service/interest charge on accounts receivable. Other income and associated expenses added to operating profit results in **net profit.** Net profit is the basis of the firm's tax liability.

Merchandisers play key roles in relation to a firm's income statement because they are usually responsible for planning what and how much merchandise will be acquired or produced, what it will cost, and how it will be priced for sale. These decisions are closely associated with cost of goods sold and gross margin on the income statement. Gross margin is a key factor because it determines how much money is available to pay marketing, operations, and financial expenses.

Income Statements for Mike's Bikes

Read Company Profile 3.1, Mike's Bikes, Part 1. Table 3.6 shows the beginning of an income statement for Mike's Bikes. An income statement is like a financial puzzle. Given a few dollar figures or ratios, the rest of the statement can be calculated. It is an excellent way to estimate the financial well-being and the merchandising effectiveness of a firm.

To complete the Mike's Bikes Income Statement, complete the easy numbers first. In an income statement, net sales = 100 percent and the

COMPANY PROFILE 3.1

Mike's Bikes, Part 1

Mike's Bikes is a "family"-owned partnership operated by Michelle Grant and Kevin Dana, long-time companions and avid bikers. They met 10 years ago on RAGBRAI, an annual week-long bike ride across Iowa that attracts 10,000 bikers annually. At the time they met, Michelle was a financial analyst for a computer company in San Jose, California, and Kevin was a salesman for an aluminum company based in Chicago. Two years later, they decided to join forces and turn their hobby into their profession. They resigned their positions and took up housekeeping in West Des Moines, Iowa, surrounded by the highest average income area of the state. They created Mike's Bikes, a specialty store for serious biker hobbyists. The name "Mike" was created by combining the first two letters of each of their first names.

They chose Des Moines as the site for their shop because the state capital has an extensive bike path system, a large contingent of dedicated leisure bikers, and commuters are increasingly using bikes as transportation to work. The State of Iowa and the *Des Moines Register* host RAGBRAI, which attracts the attention of national and international serious recreational bikers.

The climate in Iowa allows biking through three seasons of the year. Michelle and Kevin planned from the beginning to close the store during February, when business would be slow anyway, to allow them and their bike riding employees to vacation with their bikes in other parts of the country or the world. Mike's Bikes has been in business eight years and now generates $1,500,000 in annual sales.

Michelle and Kevin brought complementary expertise to the business. Michelle is in charge of the operations and finance; Kevin is in charge of marketing and merchandising. Together they comprise the management team. The 10,000-square foot store is located in a strip mall within a mile of a major regional mall. Other stores in the strip mall include a Lands' End outlet, a computer store, an office supply store, a book store, and TCBY yogurt store. Mike's Bikes has one full-time and four part-time employees, all dedicated bikers.

The store is open six days a week; they are closed Mondays. Hours are 10 to 8 each day. The primary selling season is April through August, with holiday sales in November and December. Seventy percent of their business occurs March through August. As originally planned, the store is closed during the month of February.

The merchandise mix includes three categories: bikes, apparel, and accessories. They also have a bike service department.

Operating expenses, including their own salaries of $35,000 each are 38 percent of sales leaving only a 3 percent operating profit. Michelle and Kevin have considered opening a store in another location, but fear it would limit their time to enjoy their sport.

TABLE 3.6

Numbers from Company Profile for 1996 Mike's Bikes Income Statement.

Gross Sales		
Customer Returns and Allowances	negligible	
Net Sales	$1,500,000	
Cost of Goods Sold		
Gross Margin		
Expenses		38%
Operating Profit		3%
Other Income		
Net Profit Before Taxes		

profile reports that customer returns and allowances are negligible. If returns and allowances are calculated at 0.5% then

Customer returns and allowances is net sales × 0.5% = $7,500
Gross Sales is net sales + returns and allowances = $1,507,500
Gross sales operating ratio is % net sales + % returns and
    allowances = 100.5%
Expenses is 38% × net sales = $570,000
Operating profit is 3% × net sales = $45,000
Gross margin = expenses + operating profit = $615,000
Cost of goods sold = net sales − gross margin = $885,000

No mention is made in the company profile about additional income or expense. If there is none, then for Mike's Bikes, operating profit = net profit. A different sequence of calculations will work to figure out Mike's Bikes Income Statement. The sequence doesn't matter as long as all the numbers make sense together. Table 3.7 shows the completed income statement.

TABLE 3.7

Estimated 1996 Income Statement for Mike's Bikes.

Gross Sales	$1,507,500	100.5%
Customer Returns and Allowances	7,500	0.5%
Net Sales	1,500,000	100%
Cost of Goods Sold	885,000	59%
Gross Margin	615,000	41%
Expenses	570,000	38%
Operating Profit	45,000	3%
Other Income	0	0
Net Profit Before Taxes	$45,000	3%

Learning Activity 3.5

Income Statements

1. If Mike's Bikes were able to reduce operating expenses by 5 percent how would gross margin be affected? How would operating profit be affected? Why?

2. If Mike's Bikes were forced to increase cost of goods sold by 3 percent, how would gross margin be affected? How would operating profit be affected? Why?

3. Create an income statement for Aileen from the information given in Case 3.3. Use Table 3.4 as a model. Insert the numbers given and calculate the rest. How can you check to be sure your numbers make sense?

4. Based on the income statement for Aileen, what options does the firm have to achieve a net profit goal of 15 percent?

CASE 3.3

Aileen Banks on Outlets

From Washaw, A. H. (1992, May). *Apparel Industry Magazine, 53*(5), p. 64.

Outlet, once a dirty word to many retailers, is now a sophisticated $57 billion industry. Though many apparel manufacturers are only dabbling in this distribution channel, Aileen, a Martinsville, VA-based women's sportswear and knitted goods maker, has banked its future on the success of outlet retailing.

From 1985 to 1991, Aileen's outlet retail sales grew from $12 million to nearly $58 million, while other channels were failing. In 1987, the company lost $3.5 million because of idle factories. In 1989, the company lost $5.3 million in wholesale business.

Recovery began in 1990, thanks to a combination of selling underutilized equipment, modernizing operation, re-engineering and simplifying plants, closing unprofitable stores, re-merchandising its apparel line and improving inventory management. Aileen also got a little help from a growing consumer interest in outlets.

By the end of 1991, the company's sales were up 9 percent, mostly from new outlet stores. Operating profit was at 9 percent and gross margin increased to 48 percent of sales, an all-time high. Selling and administrative expenses were at 39 percent, a little high for an outlet store operation. Aileen will have to achieve a 49 percent gross margin or reduce expenses in order to get operating profits to 10 percent. Well-run outlet stores should generate at least 15 percent operating income.

Breaking From the Pack

There are several reasons why Aileen's outlet channel is successful. Most outlets succeed by offering the same merchandise available in department and specialty stores, but at a lower price. Aileen has no traditional retail presence and isn't providing a recognizable discount. The company's success is an indication of the strength of outlet malls and the consumer traffic they generate.

This trend also indicates an opportunity for apparel manufacturers to use distressed brands, either owned or bought to create an outlet business for themselves. It's not easy or cheap, but it's an avenue for controlled growth and diversity. Aileen has carved a great niche in the value channel and has proven the virtues of the outlet store business. With its feet now on solid ground, the company is in a position to follow one of three paths: grow a traditional retail business, develop a competitive private label/wholesale business, or stay where it is.

Benchmarks of a Firm's Success

Each constituency in an apparel firm tends to have measures of success particularly related to its responsibilities. Some business executives declare, "You get what you measure." Table 3.8 summarizes some of the issues particularly related to the responsibilities of each constituency and benchmarks that might be used to measure success. Benchmarks (points of comparison) provide indicators of levels of success. The merchandising responsibility is to provide a product line that generates revenue to support the necessary activities of the other constituencies to run the business.

As might be expected, the measures of success related to the executive constituency focus on broad issues integrating the entire firm. Marketing measures focus on market position and growth in sales and market share. Operations measures focus on management of people and physical property. Finance measures relate to management and growth of financial resources. Merchandising measures relate to planning, development, and presentation of product lines.

TABLE 3.8

Indicators of Business Success.*

EXECUTIVE	
Issue for Analysis	**Benchmark**
1. Has the firm achieved its financial goals?	1. Profit, market share, GMROI
2. Has the firm achieved its goals related to social responsibility?	2. Community support, environmentalism
3. Does return on shareholders' investments meet expectations?	3. Achieved plan
4. Has the firm achieved its goals related to its employees?	4. Employee satisfaction and retention
5. Has the firm achieved its goals in relation to customers?	5. Sales growth, customer loyalty
6. Has the firm achieved its goals in relation to suppliers?	6. Vendor partnerships

MERCHANDISING	
1. What is average initial markup?	1. 48 percent might be regarded as minimum; over 58 percent is more and more common
2. What are markdowns as a percent of sales by classification?	2. Markdowns for fashion/seasonal goods (may be over 15 percent) will be much higher than basic/staple goods (less than 5 percent)
3. Are markdowns taken regularly based on rate of sale?	3. A minimum of every 26 weeks, preferably every two to four weeks
4. What is maintained markup by classification?	4. Under 39% is a problem for many firms; over 46 percent is good
5. Is open-to-buy updated as indicated by sales for each classification every few weeks?	5. Open-to-buy needs to adjusted frequently to reflect rate of sale of various merchandise classifications
6. What is the annual rate of merchandise turnover by classification?	6. Less than 1 is a problem; over 7 is very good
7. How much of present inventory is merchandise purchased for this selling period?	7. Less than 50 percent is a problem; close to 100 percent is best
8. What are the weeks of sale for each selling period for each merchandise classification?	8. Weeks for fashion/seasonal goods: 10–26; weeks for basic/seasonal goods: 26–52
9. What are the peak selling weeks for each selling season for each classification?	9. Usually one-half to two-thirds of the way through the selling period
10. What is the best size scale by classification?	10. Merchandise should be bought in the same size ratios that it sells
11. What is profitability by resource?	11. Gross margin, quality, late deliveries, charge backs

(continued)

*Based in part on criteria developed by Retail Merchandising Services Automation,Inc., of Riverside, CA (RMSA) and Quick Response Leadership Committee of American Apparel Manufacturer's Association.

TABLE 3.8

Indicators of Business Success.* *continued*

MARKETING

1. What are annual advertising costs as a percent of sales?
2. What are markdowns as a percent of sales for whole operation?
3. Have goals for market share been achieved?
4. Have goals for sales increases been achieved?

1. Over 6 percent may be too high; less than 1 percent may be too low
2. Ten percent may be acceptable, over 20 percent can be a big problem
3. Market share goals met or exceeded
4. Sales goals met or exceeded

OPERATIONS

1. What are operating expenses as a percent of sales?
2. What is the total annual payroll expense as a percent of sales?
3. What are the annual selling costs (sales personnel wages and commissions) as a percent of sales?
4. What was last year's inventory shrinkage as a percent of sales?
5. Do you transfer non-selling merchandise from non-selling to selling stores?
6. What is rental costs as a percent of sales?
7. What are annual utility costs as a percent of sales?
8. What is the annual rate of merchandise turnover for the whole organization?

1. Over 43 percent is probably a big problem; less than 30 percent is probably good
2. Over 21 percent is probably a big problem; less than 13 percent is probably very good
3. Over 15 percent is probably a big problem; less than 6 percent is very good
4. Over 4 percent is a big problem; less than ½ percent is probably very good
5. Yes
6. Over 11 percent is a problem; less than 4 percent is probably very good
7. Over 1½ percent is probably a problem; less than ¼ percent is probably very good
8. Less than 1 is a big problem; over 7 is very good

FINANCE

1. Is the level of fixed expense reasonable?
2. Is the level of variable expense reasonable?
3. Is cash flow adequate to cover expenses without reducing resources?
4. Is growth adequate to achieve goals?

Learning Activity 3.6

Measures of Success

1. Examine Table 3.8. What is the nature of the measures of success for each constituency? What is the nature of a benchmark? What does it mean to say "you get what you measure"?

2. Read Case 3.4. What measures of success are being altered by Macy's new strategy for their Herald Square store? Will benchmarks change?

CASE 3.4

Macy's Kahn Planning to Polish Macy's Herald Square Flagship

Based on *Daily News Record,* Tuesday April 2, 1996, p. 10.

In a sweeping three-year plan, Hal Kahn is looking to restore the luster to the Macy's Herald Square flagship by adding more fashionable and better-priced goods and undertaking $50 million in renovations. In a interview here [New York], the chairman and CEO of Macy's East said: "Every floor will be impacted by improvements, enhancements and upgrades."

The project, extending from 1996 to 1998, could resolve the great paradox on 34th Street. Macy's Herald Square is the world's largest and most trafficked department store, attracting 30,000 to 50,000 people daily and 50,000 to 75,000 each day around Christmas. Yet it is also among the most maligned—criticized for being too moderate, too confusing to shop and lacking price credibility. "It used to have a great personality," said one fashion executive. "It's lost it. It's cheap and deep."

To some extent, Kahn agreed, saying that because of the Macy's bankruptcy from January 1992 to December 1994, "we became very predictable, very safe." But last year, Macy's began to add some zip to the selling floor—a strategy that will continue in 1996. "We want to take more risks," Kahn said.

The prime objective is to give Herald Square more of a lifestyle approach by bringing together labels and like categories of merchandise. The reason: "People don't have as much time to shop," Kahn explained. "We're repositioning the store so customers don't have to walk all over and then discover that shoes are on four or five different floors. The goal is to be dominant in a classification, not to split a classification."

Another major objective is to restore price credibility. That will entail cutting back on price promoting and reducing the ubiquitous 25-percent off point-of-sale signs at Macy's. "We want to be more credible in the way merchandise is ticketed and less promotional," Kahn said.

The intention is also to cut four one-day sales and maybe six to seven storewide events over the next two to three years. Currently, Macy's stages about 14 or 15 one-day sales annually. "The issue is not just one-day sales. We have to earn the business rather than promote."

The 85-unit Macy's East division of Federated Department Stores posted $4.6 billion in sales last year and is eyeing a 2 to 3.5 percent sales gain this year. The year's results will be affected by how many sales promotions get yanked out of the calendar. Over the next two or three years, promotions that span periods accounting for about $200 million in volume chainwide could be eliminated, Kahn said.

"The goal is not to grow volume, but to grow margins and fashion," Kahn explained. "volume is not the key word. There will be small increases in volume as we reduce promotional activity. As we expand our business to better prices, vendors that are priced to be 50 to 40 percent off will have a smaller percentage of our floor space," he added.

"There is nothing wrong with merchandise on sale at the end of the season. Those interim ups and downs are when you lose your credibility."

Other big changes in store for the flagship include the elimination of the Arcade on the main floor to give more room to cosmetics, and the enhancement of the private-label business to emphasize exclusivity. Space devoted to children's wear will be reduced and moderate goods will get pushed to the back of the store," Kahn said, "to really focus on the better and the best. The best resources are those not broadly distributed [which] offer fashion and are priced to sell at regular price, not to promote."

Overall, Kahn said Macy's East had "a strong 1995" and although December was slow due to snow, Macy's came very close to the sales projection for the year an added over 1.5 percent to profits as a percentage of sales. Kahn declined to say what the profit rate was.

The next three sections of this textbook are based on the definition of merchandising. Section Two deals with line planning, Section Three with line development and presentation, and Section Four with career opportunities. The merchandising measures of success and their benchmarks will be revisited numerous times throughout these discussions.

Summary

The Taxonomy of Apparel Merchandising Systems (TAMS) was developed to comprehensively describe elements of a merchandising system. TAMS is viewed as an extended definition of merchandising in the context of the Behavioral Theory of the Apparel Firm with Quick Response universe (BTAF/QR). Merchandising is a dynamic process of intense change. The merchandising cycle represented by TAMS is one year, beginning February 1 and ending January 31. A product line *consists of a combination of styles that satisfy similar or related customer needs, can be sold within the targeted price range, and marketed with similar strategies.* Line planning requires assessment of the present, analysis of the past, and projection for the future.

Line development includes the processes required to translate a line plan into real merchandise. A line concept includes the look and appeal that contributes to the identity and salability of the line. **Wholesale markets** provide a setting for linking the work of merchandisers at the wholesale level with those at the retail level. **Sales representatives** are often instrumental in developing assortments and writing purchase orders. In the apparel industry, product development evolves in three phases: pre-adoption, adoption, and post-adoption. The line plan combined with the line concept provide the framework for product development.

Line presentation includes evaluating the line to make it visible and salable. The power of appeal (Scheller, 1993), also known as hanger or shelf appeal, attracts the attention of retail buyers and ultimate consumers, causing them to stop, take a longer look, and finally purchase.

The dimensions of product lines considered by both manufacturers and retail merchandisers include prices, assortments, styling, and timing. Merchandisers select or develop products, select materials, and perhaps recommend performance and quality characteristics that can be executed within the price range. A merchandise **assortment** *is determined by the relative number styles, colors, and sizes included in the line.* **Styling** refers to the appearance of a product and involves selecting or developing product design; the creative, functional, and fashion aspects of line, as well as product development. Styling needs to be consistent with the firm's positioning strategy in terms of the relative number of fashion and basic goods in an assortment. **Timing** is determined by the nature of merchandise classifications in relation to the merchandising cycle. Timing of merchandise presentation at wholesale and at retail determines merchandise, marketing, and production schedules.

The terms "seasonal goods" and "fashion goods" are often used interchangeably, as are the terms "basics" and "staples." However, when fashion change is separated from seasonal change, this clarifies the characteristics of product change with which merchandisers have to deal. One can visualize the impact of these changes on merchandise planning and positioning through the use of a perceptual map. Merchandise classifications might be more accurately placed on the perceptual map by analyzing sales figures that reflect changes in rate of sale during each week of the year. Point-of-sale (POS) data combined with EDI make appropriate information easily accessible to both manufacturers and retail merchandisers.

As explained by the BTAF, merchandising is one of five essential, inter-active business constituencies, the others are: executive management, mar-keting, operations, and finance. Each constituency measures its success in relation to its responsibilities. Income Statements are common measures of success. Benchmarks provide indicators of levels of success. The merchan-dising measures of success and their benchmarks will be revisited numer-ous times throughout the following chapters.

Key Concepts

basic goods
benchmarks
cost of goods sold
dimensions of product lines
dynamic merchandising process
fashion goods
fashion theory
finished goods buying/sourcing
gross margin
income measurements
income modifications
income statement

internal line presentation
line adoption
line concept
line development
line plan
materials sourcing
measures of success
merchandise assortment
merchandise line
merchandise plan
merchandising cycle
net sales
operating profit
perceptual map

post-adoption product development
pre-adoption product development
product line
production sourcing
retail line presentation
seasonal goods
selling period
staple goods
taxonomy
weeks of sale
wholesale line presentation

Integrated Learning Activity 3.7

Begin a profile of a local apparel firm that you can observe as you work your way through the rest of this course. The profile of the firm you select will provide a foundation for later projects related to the planning, development, and presentation of product lines. Resources you might use to develop the profile include 1) annual reports and articles in the trade press (available at the library); 2) interviews with ex-ecutives; and 3) your own critical observation and analysis.

Include the following in your initial draft of the profile:

a) Name, address, type of retail firm, type of location (strip mall, downtown busi-ness district, etc.), and mission of the firm (select one that includes apparel in their assortment).

b) Number of stores owned by the firm and general locations.

c) Target/mass market customer strategy using demographic and lifestyle variables (mean family income in US is $45,000) and competing firms in local market area.

d) Describe how merchandise is presented for sale: layout, fixturing, etc.

e) Estimate and provide evidence of financial status (profitable/nonprofitable; growing/stable/shrinking).

f) Describe social, economic, and fashion trends that might impact the firm.

If possible, compile the profile on a word processor so it can be modified easily as you learn more about the firm.

Recommended Resources

Barrett, G. (1993). Changing measures of performance. *Proceedings of the Quick Response 93 Conference,* 245–252.

Chanil, D. (1993, July). Grappling with changes in retail. *Discount Merchandiser, 33*(7), 28–32, 37, & 71.

Hart, E., Salfin, C., & Spevach, R. (1993, April 7). Matrix remakes marketing methods. *Daily News Record,* p. 1+.

Setren, M. (1993). Changing measures of performance. *Proceedings of the Quick Response 93 Conference,* 253–260.

Sproles, G. B. (1985). Behavioral science theories of fashion. In M. R. Solomon (Ed.), *The psychology of fashion,* pp. 55–70. Lexington, MA: Lexington Books.

References

Berman, B. B., & Evans, J. R. (1995). *Retail management.* Englewood Cliffs, NJ: Prentice Hall.

Glock, R. E., & Kunz, G. I. (1995). *Apparel manufacturing: Sewn product analysis* (2nd ed.). Englewood Cliffs, NJ: Prentice Hall.

Jarnow, J. A., Judelle, B., & Guerreiro, M. (1981). *Inside the fashion business* (3rd ed). New York: Wiley.

Kunz, G. I. (1988). Apparel merchandising: A model for product change. In R. C. Kean (Ed.). *Theory building in apparel merchandising* (pp. 15–21). Lincoln: University of Nebraska.

Lewison, D. M. (1994). *Retailing* (5th ed.). New York: Macmillan.

Quick Response Leadership Committee. (1996). *Measurements of excellence.* American Apparel Manufacturers Association: Author.

Reda, S. (1994, March). Planning systems. *Stores, 76,* 34–37.

Retail Merchandising Services Automation, Inc. (1985). *Retail intelligent forecasting: Merchandise planning for the future.* (1995). Riverside, CA: Author.

Scheller, H. P. (1993). Apparel quality through the perception of apparel production managers and operators. Unpublished masters thesis, Iowa State University, Ames.

Sproles, G. B. (1985). Behavioral science theories of fashion. In M. R. Solomon (Ed.). *The psychology of fashion* (p. 66). Lexington, MA: Lexington Books.

Troxell, M. D., & Judelle, B. J. (1981). *Fashion merchandising.* New York: McGraw-Hill.

SECTION TWO

Merchandise Planning

Fundamentals of Merchandise Planning

Learning Objectives

- Apply concepts of merchandise classification systems to facilitate planning.
- Become acquainted with the background and current trends related to merchandise planning and merchandise planning technology.
- Analyze past seasons and synthesize current issues/trends to provide a foundation for forecasting.

Merchandise planning processes have not kept pace with other business technologies. A review of the continuing declines in gross margin, adjusted gross margin, stock turnover, and gross margin return on inventory confirm the existence of inadequate merchandise planning processes in both wholesale and retail sectors. The historic use of line planning processes have always recognized the need for forecasting sales; but today technology is available to support more sophisticated forecasting. Effective forecasting, integrated with classification-level merchandise budgets and assortment plans, provides a necessary framework for productive merchandising systems.

Overview of Line Planning Processes

Up until the 1960s, merchandising planning and inventory management were done manually. Purchase orders, price tickets, inventory records, and sales slips were all hand written. To resupply merchandise, goods on the sales floor and in the stockroom were physically counted and reorders were based on sales. Another method was using a tear-off ticket system where half of the price ticket was removed when an item was sold. Tickets were put in a bag and sent on a daily or weekly basis to the accounting department to update the perpetual inventory system. Tracking sales at the SKU level was helpful, but extremely time consuming.

During the 1960s, large firms acquired mainframe computers that initially were used primarily for record keeping. More sophisticated cash registers provided more detailed sales information to retailers. The introduction of micro-computers in the 1970s made point-of-sale data systems more affordable for smaller firms. Extensive sales reports began to be provided to merchandisers on a weekly and sometimes a daily basis. Many merchants resisted the new technology and continued to use their traditional "black-book" system of merchandise planning and line development. Among other things, "black-books" included notes on fashion trends and "hot numbers," sketchy dollar plans, and reminders of reliability of vendors.

At the same time, the introduction of new technology in the manufacturing sector increased the capability for product change. Improved communication technology and increased travel made customers more aware of a broader range of fashion choices. Consequently, frequency of fads increased and rate of fashion change in general increased. Shorter selling periods became common—26 weeks to 14 weeks to 10 weeks to even 8 weeks for some products. Demand increased for more diversity of assortments. The retail discount industry became full-blown, throwing traditional department store and specialty store pricing systems into disarray.

Firms in the 1980s focused on expense control to protect profits. More and more merchandise was sourced abroad to reduce merchandise costs. Retailers reduced customer service to control selling costs. At the same time, more forms of retailing became available with increased use of mail order, television shopping, and on-line computer services. It became obvious that cost control was not enough to protect market share and provide for growth.

In the 1990s, in part because of the influence of QR business systems, attention has turned to refining business processes beyond cost control. Effective merchandise planning has been recognized as a necessary means of reducing inventory investment and markdowns while increasing customer satisfaction and sales at first price.

Traditional Line Planning

Line-planning processes are often described as top-down, bottom-up, or interactive. **Top-down planning** means the executive constituency develops the business plan and, based on growth projections, prescribes sales goals and dollar investment in merchandise, usually for a six-month period or a year. Funds are then allocated, usually by department, for the acquisition of merchandise for each selling period. The plans developed by the executive constituency often prescribe the goals, levels of dollar investment, and measures of success for each constituency.

With top-down planning, the focus is often on sales goals. This may lead the merchandising constituency to over-buy (retail sector) or over-produce (manufacturing sector) because of the penalties related to lost business. Setting goals also for merchandise turnover, maintained margins, and gross margin return on inventory provides a more balanced perspective on merchandising performance. If sales do not meet expectations, across-the-board cuts in inventory may be implemented, resulting in high rates of markdowns because of excess goods in some categories and massive lost sales in other categories where demand is strong.

Bottom-up planning means the analysis begins with what was sold: how much, what kind, when, and at what price. Projections are made for the coming period and investment in merchandise is based on previous sales. Classification-level plans are combined into department or line estimates and eventually merged into a company plan. Bottom-up planning may be used particularly in smaller firms where everyone knows the product line and thinks they understand the reasons for events in the past selling period. The bottom-up plan may or may not be based on substantive data. Data-based bottom-up plans may be the most realistic merchandise plans, since they match plans to needs at the store level. When bottom-up plans are not merged into a cohesive plan for the entire firm, the constituencies may lack common goals and the firm may appear to lack direction. (Interactive planning is described under Contemporary Line Planning.)

Phases of Line Planning

Traditionally, line plans took the form of two six-month plans a year. The six-month plans had two phases: 1) dollar planning and 2) unit planning. **Six-month plans** established available levels of investment for merchandise lines and product classifications for each selling period and each month of the year. Last period's sales provided the primary basis for six-month plans with possible consideration for the marketing strategy, profit goals, and sales forecasts. Six-month plans required a great deal of time and attention on the part of merchandisers, with much numerical manipulation to develop appropriate numbers for the dollar plans. Consequently, once the plans were set they tended to be static. The plans were in place and merchandisers were expected to carry them out. Merchandisers were expected to "make plan" regardless of intervening circumstances.

Dollar plans were usually based on an assumption of improvement for the coming period: improved sales, increased turnover, improved profit margins, and reduced markdowns. The dollar allocation to departments or merchandise categories determined the amount of merchandise that could be made available for sale, but did *not* outline strategies to support other improvements. A six-month plan, however, did not detail strategies required to achieve the improvements. The **dollar open-to-buy** was usually determined based on the difference between planned sales and the combination of inventory already owned and on-order. The purpose of open-to-buy is to prevent over investment in merchandise.

Unit plans could be based on bottom-up planning but were usually based on top-down dollar plans. The quantity (units) of goods that could be made available during the selling period was determined by dividing the dollar allocation by average merchandise price. Unit open-to-buy could also be determined by dividing dollar open-to-buy by average price. Unit plans may have been developed to the SKU level to examine exactly how many styles, sizes, and colors could be made available in each classification.

During the 1980s and '90s, as the size of retailers exploded through growth, mergers, and consolidations, merchandising systems became more centralized and dependent on dollar plans with less and less planning to the store level or SKU level. Most existing computer systems could not handle the detailed data required to break down line plans to the SKU level. Consequently, store-level assortments were frequently neglected, resulting in lost sales in combination with high rates of markdowns.

The conceptual simplicity of traditional six-month plans is dated in current merchandising environments. Today, dollars should follow merchandise sales rather than using dollar plans to limit merchandise availability.

Contemporary Line Planning

Large and complex firms have many tiers in their organizational structures that influence the levels and the manner in which merchandise might be planned. Figure 4.1 has a pyramid shape, representing a firm with the possibility of five different tiers in its organizational structure. Pyramids can be used to represent a firm's organizational structure for various reasons. Numbers of employees are normally relatively few at the top and many at the bottom. At the pyramid's peak is the conglomerate tier, followed by tiers entitled group, corporate, division, and individual store or production unit. The actual number of tiers and the language used to describe them varies by firm. Merchandise planning may start at the corporate tier, then proceed through and be integrated with all of the lower tiers.

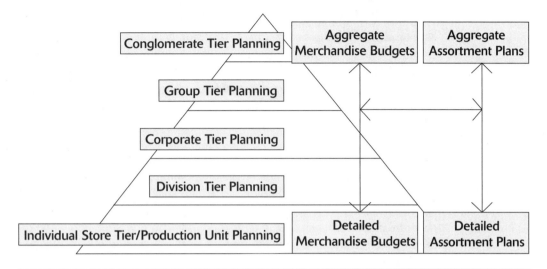

FIGURE 4.1

Tiers in an organizational pyramid in relation to planning merchandise budgets and assortments. (model developed by Grace I. Kunz).

For example, according to its 1996 annual report, Dayton Hudson Corporation is a retail *conglomerate* that includes several relatively independent corporate units including Target, Mervyns, and Department Stores. The Department Stores corporate unit includes the divisions Dayton's and Marshall Field. Within both Dayton's and Marshall Field are dozens of individual department stores.

VF Corporation is an apparel manufacturing conglomerate that includes several business groups: Jeanswear, Decorated Knitwear, Intimate Apparel, Playwear, and Specialty Apparel. Each business group has several divisions. Jeanswear includes Lee, Wrangler, and Girbaud; Decorated Knitwear includes Bassett-Walker, JanSport, and Cutler Sports. Both VF and Dayton Hudson count their sales in billions of dollars. Some forms of merchandise planning may occur in all tiers of each pyramid.

In contrast, Mark Shale, an upscale, Chicago-based specialty chain, has eight stores. Mark Shale has only two tiers: the corporate tier and individual store tier. Independent retail chains and small retail firms with one or a few stores may start the merchandise planning process at the corporate or individual store tier levels of the organizational pyramid. Mark Shale has a proprietary merchandise planning and management system that supports merchandise planning at the store, classification, sub-classification, and SKU levels. Mark Shale may be the exception rather than the rule, as many firms are dependent on commercially available merchandise-planning systems.

Merchandise Budgets and Assortment Plans

Merchandise budgets for a merchandising cycle identify planned sales, dollar investment, and open-to-buy by merchandise category, department or classification. The merchandising cycle may be broken into selling periods for classifications. **Assortment plans** may include model stocks, basic stocks, and automated replenishment. The closer to the peak of the pyramid, the more aggregated the merchandise planning and the more likely that merchandise budgets will be the primary form of planning. The closer to the base of the pyramid, the more detailed the planning and the more likely that assortment-type merchandise planning will be used, hence greater need for detailed planning of merchandise assortments. The lower in the pyramid the firm plans, the greater the need for a sophisticated merchandise-planning computer system and the more power and capacity required of that system. Parts of a firm's merchandise mix may be planned at any or all of these tiers.

Merchandise planning for private-label goods that are internationally sourced may take place at the conglomerate, group, or corporate tiers. Desire for economies of scale may encourage high-level coordination of these activities. Private-label goods are often intended to offer good value to consumers while contributing to the improvement of overall gross margin, thus merchandise cost is an important sourcing factor. By combining orders from several divisions or corporate units economy of scale can often be achieved. If smaller firms are members of corporate buying offices, these offices may assist in merchandise planning and/or engage in buying for its members, similar to conglomerate or division-level activity in large organizations.

Interactive Planning

Interactive planning is consistent with QR business systems and the use of information technology. **Interactive planning** is a combination of the top-down and bottom-up systems previously described. It is a teamwork approach with input from all of the firm's constituencies. Information technology systems make it possible for everyone in the firm, regardless of organizational tier or constituency, to have access to the appropriate data and reports. However, a common problem with information systems is that data are not presented in usable form. Different forms of detailed information can be developed to meet specific needs, but this often requires "tailor-made" reports developed by a firm's management information system (MIS) team. Selling patterns for several periods may need to be analyzed to determine the most accurate perspective on trends. The information will be used very differently by the constituencies because of their areas of specialization.

With interactive planning, within the groups or divisions in each tier, the executive constituency negotiates broad guidelines in relation to the firm's goals. Estimates for the line plan are also developed by the merchandising constituency using bottom-up planning methods at the merchandise classification level. The marketing constituency develops sales and promotion plans based on the business plan. The finance constituency plans needs for cash flow, revenue, and profit. The operations constituency plans human resource needs, renovation of property, and logistics for handling merchandise. The plans proposed by each constituency are negotiated into a company-wide plan that provides guidance for the decisions of managers throughout the merchandising cycle. Interactive plans result in the most accurate merchandise plans, but are also stressful and time consuming because of all the negotiation involved. From the perspective of saving time, top-down planning is probably most efficient, but the process may result in unrealistic plans and often alienates the employees who are expected to carry them out.

Technological Support for Line Planning

To help understand the status of merchandising technology, Iowa State University conducted a telephone survey of computer software companies claiming to offer software systems that aid in merchandise planning (Rupe, Song, & Kunz, 1994). A sample of 47 companies and contact persons from each were chosen from the 1994 National Retail Federation's Software Directory. The sample represented all companies that indicated their software possessed merchandise planning functions with IBM-DOS compatible software. The survey consisted of 30 yes/no questions regarding the particular features of the software. The remainder of the survey was eight brief, open-ended questions addressing frequency of use. The response rate for the survey was 38 percent with 18 out of 47 possible firms participating. See Table 4.1 for a summary of the findings.

For the most part, merchandising technology uses the language of traditional merchandise planning. **Basic merchandise planning** features, including top-down and bottom-up dollar planning and unit planning, were offered by 67 percent of the systems. Less than 10 percent of the systems offered space-planning technology.

Inventory management was the most commonly available feature of the merchandising technology systems and the most frequently used.

TABLE 4.1

Findings of merchandising-technology systems telephone survey.

Merchandise Planning Features	Availability	Other Merchandising Features	Availability
Basic planning tools		**Inventory management**	
• top-down dollar planning	67%	• inventory updates	83%
• bottom-up dollar planning	67%	• current on-hands	83%
• unit level planning	67%	• current on-orders	83%
• planning based on floor or shelf space allocation.	less than 10%	• POS integration	94%
		• EDI capabilities	61%
Detailed planning tools		**Forecasting features**	
• planning at the store level	94%	• in-season trending	83%
• at the day level	28%	• consumer demand	72%
• at the SKU level	50%	• statement of trends	72%
• historical data	89%	• price changes	67%
• seasonal factors	72%	• style pre-testing	27%
• actual in-season data	78%		
• location/region factors	67%	**System requirements**	
• demographics	39%	• mid-range PCs	100%
• suppliers' characteristics	33%	• training required	2 days to 1 week.
• season transition planning	50%		

Information provided by 83 percent of systems included inventory up-dates, current on-hands and current on-orders. Integration with point-of-sale (POS) was provided by 94 percent of systems but only 61 percent had electronic data interchange (EDI) capabilities.

The least commonly used system features were in the group called **de-tailed planning,** which encompassed a wide variation in availability. Only 28 percent of the systems allowed planning on a day-to-day basis, while only 50 percent provided planning at the stock-keeping unit (SKU) level. Utilizing historic data was possible with 89 percent of systems, and 72 percent could incorporate seasonal factors. Actual seasonal data could be incorporated by 78 percent of systems, location and region factors by 67 percent, and demographics by only 38 percent. Suppliers characteristics could be accounted for by 33 percent of the systems and season transition planning by 50 percent. Planning at the SKU level, as well as other infor-mation supplied by detailed planning features, is essential for determining assortments for QR systems.

Forecasting is regarded as a primary problem by those involved with QR, so it is not surprising that forecasting was the most frequently requested feature for merchandising technology systems. In-season trending was supplied by 83 percent of the systems, consumer demand and trends by 72 percent, and price changes by 67 percent. However, only 27 percent of the systems provide a feature incorporating style testing.

Only two-thirds of the systems offered the basic planning features and the lack of use of detailed planning is an indicator of the overall lack of sophistication of merchandising-planning systems in use. At the same time the fact that forecasting features are the most frequently requested recognizes the need to improve merchandise planning accuracy. Most of the features identified as "detailed planning" can potentially contribute to planning accuracy. It is clear that merchandising technology systems are not being fully utilized for effective merchandise planning.

Learning Activity 4.1

Line planning fundamentals

1. How does merchandise planning relate to merchandise development and presentation?

2. What are the key differences between traditional line planning and contemporary line planning?

3. What features of merchandise planning technology identified in Table 4.1 support each tier of the merchandise planning pyramid in Figure 4.1?

Forecast-Based Merchandise Plans

Members of the Quick Response leadership committee of the American Apparel Manufacturers Association frequently express frustration with the inaccuracy of forecasting. They are frustrated because their own merchandisers cannot present merchandise plans that incorporate accurate forecasts to facilitate efficiency in production processes. They are also frustrated that their retail partners are ineffective in forecasting demand, even with the short time lines associated with QR systems. *The purpose of merchandise forecasts is to provide a foundation for planning optimal levels of inventory for satisfied customers while achieving the firm's goals for each selling period in the merchandising cycle.* Three elements of analysis are considered here in relation to forecast-based merchandise plans: merchandise classifications, past selling periods, and current issues and trends.

Analysis of Merchandise Classifications

Perhaps the most critical merchandising problem is that of having—on demand—the type of merchandise sought by customers (Taylor, 1970). An effective merchandise classification system contributes to having the right merchandise; it facilitates planning, development, and presentation of product lines, as well as the shopping and merchandise selection by customers. Classifying merchandise is the process of arranging the merchandise mix into groups based on the criterion of the end-user (Taylor, 1970). Criterion might include functional use, quality, size range, rate and type of product change, and product characteristics.

A merchandise classification system consists of a set of names and code numbers for breaking down the total merchandise mix into consistent identifiable groups. A classification system enables the following activities:

- evaluating consistent merchandise groups for sales potential, profitability or expense reduction.
- better timing of beginning, peak(s), and end of selling periods.
- eliminating unplanned duplication of merchandise.
- planning dollar sales and stocks with reasonable precision.
- developing realistic dollar open-to-buy.
- facilitating communication among managers, sales associates, merchandisers, sales representatives, and distribution managers.
- providing appropriate space for storage and/or display (Taylor, 1970).

Effective classification systems may include the following categories:

- class and subclass codes
- class and subclass descriptions
- seasonal indicators for each class and subclass
- age limit/markdown time for each class or subclass
- price lines or price ranges
- allowable cost
- minimum initial markup percentage
- preferred resources (Taylor, 1970, p. 15)

Classification information in relation to inventory and sales records (including when products were sold, at what price, gross margin generated, rates of markdowns, and joboff rates) provides a substantive foundation for continuing, increasing, decreasing, or modifying the merchandise in a product class. Fashion may, in part, dictate movements among classes in merchandise assortments. Classification systems may be modified as types of merchandise are added to the assortment. Over-classifying, or having too detailed a classification system, may generate meaningless information.

Breaking Down a Merchandise Assortment

There is a great deal of inconsistency in the use of language describing merchandise. Therefore, the terms used here reflect a simple system that makes sense within this context, but may differ from systems you read about in other texts or experience as customers or employees of apparel firms. A detailed classification system must be learned in the context of a particular firm.

A total **merchandise mix** is the complete offering of a particular manufacturer or retailer. This mix is comprised of **categories** of merchandise. For example, the merchandise mix offered by a men's specialty retailer may include the categories of suits, outerwear, casual wear, furnishings, and accessories. Categories may be broken down further into **classes and subclasses.** Classes within the suit category may be single-breasted, double-breasted, and formal. Subclasses within the single-breasted class may be solids, stripes, and tweeds. Subclasses may, in turn, be broken into merchandise **groups.** Subclasses and groups are described by assortment factors that make up a stock keeping unit (SKU). For apparel, SKUs are usually defined by style, size, and color. To summarize, the breakdown of a merchandise mix goes from categories to classes to subclasses to groups to assortment factors. See Table 4.2 for other examples of breaking down a merchandise assortment.

The purpose of the line plan is to provide a foundation for balanced assortments. A **balanced assortment** is one that has a well-planned variety of styles, sizes, and colors for special appeal to a specific market. A primary goal of merchandise planning is offering balanced assortments. At the same time, the firm must sell each style or merchandise group in adequate numbers to meet volume and profit goals. A balanced assortment results in satisfied customers and meets merchandising goals. A balanced assortment results in:

1. adequate variety to attract target customers
2. adequate inventory to prevent stockouts
3. minimum investment in slow-moving goods
4. minimum investment in inventory
5. maximum gross margin
6. maximum gross margin return on inventory
7. maximum stock turn

TABLE 4.2

Examples of fundamental levels in a merchandise classification system.

Possible Categories Within a Merchandise Mix and Classes in Each

Apparel	*Accessories*	*Cosmetics*	*Sporting Goods*
men's	fine jewelry	make-up	hunting
women's	costume jewelry	hair products	fishing
children's	belts	perfume	golf
	scarves	bath products	tennis
	gloves		camping

Subclasses Within Selected Classes

Children's Apparel	*Gloves*	*Hair Products*	*Hunting*
newborn	men's leather	shampoo	guns
infants	women's leather	rinse	knives
toddlers	winter gloves	color	ammunition
preteen	winter mittens		gun cases
girls			jackets/vests
boys			gloves
outerwear			

Merchandise Groups Within Selected Subclasses

Newborn			*Guns*
pajamas			hand guns
undershirts			hunting rifles
diapers			target rifles
diaper covers			shotguns
shirts			
pants			
dresses			
layettes			

Assortment Factors for Selected Subclasses and Merchandise Groups

Layettes	*Leather Gloves*	*Hair Color*	*Hunting Rifles*
price point	style	men's	price point
brand	size	women's	brand
style	color	brand	style
color		type	caliber

A balanced assortment may contribute more to merchandising success than any other activity. That said, it is also nearly impossible to achieve. In the list of results related to balanced assortments, improvement of one factor decreases the effectiveness of others. For example, minimum inventory (4) is sure to cause stockouts (2); an attractive variety of merchandise (1) may not allow minimum investment in slow-moving goods (3). Planning and developing balanced assortments is an ongoing merchandising challenge.

CASE 4.1

Talbots Thrives with Innovative Synergies, Consumer Research

From Reda, S. (1995, July). *Stores,* pp. 34–35.

When executives at Talbots decide where to open a new store, as they plan to do scores of times this year, they use a road map that sometimes leads them to locations that other techniques of market analysis would have overlooked.

Talbots' method, which has worked with almost complete success in recent years, calls for placing stores in clusters of ZIP codes where the company's catalog customers have already spent $150,000 on classic women's and children's apparel.

That store-location strategy is a good example of the Hingham, MA-based company's innovative efforts to take advantage of synergies between its retail and catalog businesses. Such policies, along with a commitment to intensive consumer research and a clearly articulated stylistic vision, have enabled Talbots to thrive and expand in the face of the ongoing slump in the women's apparel business.

Last year, while other women's apparel chains selling flimsy floral dresses, sheer blouses and other trendy items peaked out comparable-store sales increase of just 1 percent to 2 percent, Talbots' classic blue blazers, white cardigans and Khaki slacks yielded store-for-store sales gains of 9.5 percent, a 19-percent hike in net sales to $879.6 million and a 30 percent increase in net income.

Even as many of their competitors are pulling the reins in on store expansion and merchandising experimentation, Talbots plans to open 65 new stores this year, debut five shoe and accessory stores, introduce infant and toddler sizes at the burgeoning Talbots Kids units, and increase the company's presence internationally.

"We're a very focused company. We are classic women's clothing," says president and chief executive officer Arnold Zetcher. "That's what we've been and that's what we're going to be in the future. Women have reached a point in their lives where they don't want to light a match to their closet every other season," he explains. "They have a different set of priorities than they had five or six years ago. Today it's exceptional quality at reasonable prices, a comfortable shopping experience, and knowledgeable service that they value."

Zetcher, who took the helm in 1988 just as Jusco, a Japanese retail conglomerate, bought the chain from

General Mills, makes clear that the company's success did not happen overnight. A brief foray into fast-changing fashion in 1990 caused operating profits to slump by 40 percent and led to a $7 million loss. The company quickly shifted gears and regained its footing, though the slip-up taught Zetcher a valuable lesson.

Ever since, building and maintaining close relationships with shoppers has been the watchword at Talbots, whose founding credo—"Do what's right for the customer"—originated in 1947. Consumer focus groups held throughout the year are attended by the whole senior management team, and an annual benchmark survey in which customers voice their likes and dislikes is required reading.

"We've constantly got our ear to the ground to find out what our shoppers want. They've been very loyal to us and we're willing to do whatever we can to keep it that way," says Zetcher, whose company was ranked first among specialty store retailers in a 1994 survey by *Consumer Reports.*

Continually probing shoppers' needs and wants has led to many changes and new avenues of growth for the company. A decision to increase the proportion of private label to 95 percent and a commitment to making the stores more comfortable with amenities such as spacious fitting rooms both were fueled by customer dialogue.

In addition, the recently launched Talbot Babies collection was conceived during a focus group. Next month a 700- to 800-sq.-ft area within four to five Talbots Kids stores will be assigned to the new baby merchandise.

Talbots' trump card is the opportunity created by the combination of catalog and store operations, which are run as an integrated business. Utilizing the customer information and demographic data gathered from the catalog database, executives have managed to substantially increase the efficiency of the total business. They have also been able to reduce out-of-stock position and lessen the risk associated with brand extension and new store locations.

"By using our catalog database to determine where to open new stores, we have taken virtually all of the risk out of store site selection. We know exactly where our customers are," explains Zetcher, who reports that the company has opened several highly

continued

profitable stores in markets that might otherwise have been ignored. Generally, once catalog sales in an area exceed $150,000, it can support a store. Over the past four years, 95 percent of Talbots new stores have become profitable in their first year of operation.

Exploiting this synergy between catalog an store-based retailing has also served the company in the development of new business lines. The expansion of petites and the introduction of Talbots Kids and Talbots Intimates stores were all based on the strong acceptance those merchandise categories first received in the catalog. The latest catalog spin-off, Talbots Shoes and Accessories, will debut this fall. Plans call for four to five stores to open adjacent to Talbot's misses units.

Although retail analysts aren't sure whether Talbots' expansions into new fields will be successful, they do seem convinced it will continue to defy the slump in women's apparel. Harry Ikenson, senior director of New York-based Rodman & Renshaw, estimates total sales growth of 12 percent in 1995 to $990.9 million, and a 5.5 percent increase in comp-store sales.

"There are a number of facets to Talbots' business that point to continued growth," explains Ikenson. "They have a fair pricing policy, which reinforces their credibility with shoppers. They have superior customer service that is professional and knowledgeable without being pushy. And they've figured out how to update the classics with enough fashion to keep it interesting but not so much that it alienates today's somewhat less fashion-forward shopper."

In the first quarter of this year, Talbots once again posted industry leading figures. The company tallied $230.6 million in sales—a 13 percent increase compared with the first quarter of the previous year, and store-for-store sales in units open for at least a year were up 3.7 percent.

Talbots is also planning to continue expanding internationally. It opened a store in Britain last September, and plans to open two more stores this fall. In Canada, where the first Talbots store debuted in 1991, four new stores are planned, bringing the total there to 16. In addition, there are 12 Talbots stores in Japan. These units are operated by Jusco, which retains a 63 percent stake in the publicly traded company.

Learning Activity 4.2

Read Case 4.1 very carefully.

1. Create a merchandise classification chart reflecting how Talbots has structured their business and merchandise mix into categories, classes, and subclasses. What are the advantages and disadvantages of using merchandise classifications in this way?

2. What measures of merchandising success are reported in this article? What other measures do you need to know to really know how well off the company is?

Buying Patterns and Sales History by Classification

For most merchandise classifications, the merchandising cycle is divided into selling and transition periods reflecting the buying cycles of customers. Key questions to answer when doing a merchandising cycle selling analysis for a particular merchandise classification include the following:

- During which weeks does each selling period begin?
- During which weeks does each selling period end?
- How many peaks are in each selling period?
- During which weeks do the peaks occur in each selling period?
- What merchandising activities influence the sales per week?

Table 4.3 describes sales by weeks in the merchandising cycle for men's furnishings. The merchandising cycle shown here is consistent with 4-5-4 calendar commonly used by retailers for accounting purposes. The 4-5-4 calendar defines the fiscal year from February through January, the same as the merchandising cycle; 4-5-4 stands for the number of weeks in each month for each quarter. For example, for the first quarter, the days of the month are manipulated so that there are four weeks in February, five weeks in March, and four weeks in April. To accomplish this, week one of the merchandising/4-5-4 calendar actually includes a few days of January (Donnellan, 1996).

National holidays and religious events that commonly influence sales, or are often used as a basis for promotional events (special purchases of merchandise or price promotions) are identified in relation to weeks of sale. The beginning and the end of each selling period is identified by week. In addition, timing of major promotional activities is identified along with timing of semi-annual clearances.

Figure 4.2 provides another interpretation of the selling periods in the merchandising cycle for men's furnishings. The vertical axis is weekly sales for the classification, the horizontal axis is weeks in the merchandising cycle beginning with week number one on February 1. The line segments represent four different selling periods and four transition periods. Selling period number one is 13 weeks, number two is nine weeks, number three is 14 weeks, and number four is six weeks. Transition periods number one and number three are each two weeks; number two and number four are each three weeks. Semi-annual merchandise clearance is included in transitions number two and number four.

An experienced merchandiser can look at these tables and graphs and understand the significance of a particular week in the merchandising cycle. Relationships to holidays or cultural events, as well as merchandising activities that might have influenced sales in different weeks, are readily recalled. But even excellent merchandisers can't synthesize outcomes for forecasting without some systematic analysis of a variety of data. The current season needs to be compared to a similar interpretation of selling periods for last year and for other previous years' merchandising cycles. Look for similarities and differences in timing and rate of sale for the same

TABLE 4.3

Calendar-related events and selling cycles by weeks in the merchandising cycle for men's furnishings.

Month	Week	Event	Selling Cycle
Feb.	1		begin period #1
	2		sales peak #1
	3	Valentine's Day	
	4	President's Day	
Mar	5		
	6		
	7	St. Patrick's Day	
	8		
	9		
Apr.	10		
	11	Jewish Passover	
	12	Easter Sunday	
	13		end period #1
May	14		transition #1
	15		begin period #2
	16	Mother's Day	
	17		
June	18	Memorial Day	
	19		sales peak #2
	20	Father's Day	
	21		
	22		
July	23	Independence Day	begin semi-annual clearance
	24		end period #2
	25		pre-season sale
	26		end semi-annual clearance
Aug	27		begin period #3
	28		peak pre-season sale
	29		end pre-season sale
	30		
Sep	31		
	32	Labor Day	
	33		
	34		sales peak #3
	35	Jewish New Year	
Oct	36	Yom Kippur	
	37	Columbus Day	
	38		
	39		
Nov	40	Halloween	
	41	Veteran's Day	end period #3

TABLE 4.3 (continued)

Calendar-related events and selling cycles by weeks in the merchandising cycle for men's furnishings.

Month	Week	Event	Selling Cycle
	42		transition #3
	43	Thanksgiving	begin period #4
Dec	44		
	45	Hanukkah	
	46		
	47		sales peak #4
	48	Christmas	begin semi-annual clearance
Jan	49	New Year's Day	end period #4
	50		transition #4
	51	M.L.King's Birthday	
	52		end semi-annual clearance

weeks. Statistical analysis can help interpret when differences really matter. Then, consider reasons for similarities and differences and determine which information provides the best foundation for planning for the coming merchandising cycle.

Many aspects beyond the sales history need to be considered to determine what aspects of sales history are unique to a particular selling period:

• What factors influenced the beginning and end of the selling periods?

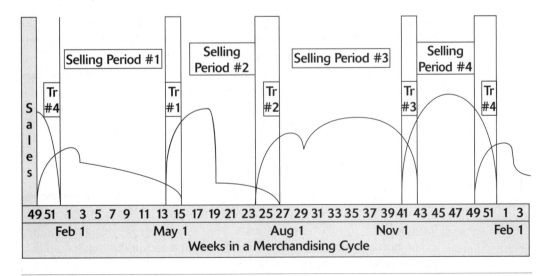

FIGURE 4.2

Illustration of selling and transition periods in a merchandising cycle for men's furnishings.

- Did the timing of merchandise delivery influence sales?
- Were inventory levels appropriate?
- Were sales lost because of unbalanced assortments?
- Were sales lost because of missed reorder opportunities?
- Were weather conditions a factor in any of the selling periods?
- What caused selling peaks?
- Would similar selling peaks be expected this year?
- For multi-store operations, were distribution plans effective by classification?
- How much and what kind of merchandise remains from past season by store?
- How much and what kind of merchandise was transferred among stores?
- How might distribution plans be modified to balance assortments?
- Is remaining merchandise salable at regular price?

Regional and Local Economic and Cultural Influences

A mistake that is often made in the merchandise planning process is not looking beyond what can be directly derived from sales data. The Behavioral Theory of the Apparel Firm (BTAF) (Kunz, 1995) identifies essential external coalitions and environments that influence a firm's success. The **external coalitions** include communities in which the firm resides, competitors, customers, families of employees, shareholders, and suppliers. A systematic analysis for forecast-based merchandise plans includes these coalitions. Market research, focus groups, and brief telephone surveys for example, can provide insights into the firm's perceived role in the community, which creates satisfied customers.

The apparel firm and its external coalitions operate in many **overlapping environments,** including cultural, ecological, economic, political, regulatory, social, and technological. During certain times these environments require particular attention in the merchandise planning process.

During-the-Period Trend Analysis

Merchandise planning is an on-going, dynamic process. A merchandise plan is only good as long as it meets the needs of the firm and its customers. Plans should be reviewed at least every four weeks and modified as the need becomes apparent. Trend analysis needs to be conducted during the current selling period, because after the period ends it may be too late for planning the same selling period for next year. Trend analysis might develop during the season as follows:

Evaluate fast sellers
- determine the appeal of the product—quality, style, color, fit, price, other
- reorder for continued sales potential, if time permits
- rework merchandise presentation to feature similar and related merchandise
- update trend analysis

Evaluate slow sellers
- determine the problem with the product—quality, style, color, fit, price, other
- rework merchandise presentation to better display merchandise
- markdown promptly if price is too high
- consider stage of fashion cycle
- update trend analysis

End-of-Period Trend Analysis

Analyzing overall productivity by classification is the final component of classification analysis. In a multi-store operation it may be useful to look at combined statistics for a classification by store. (See Table 4.4.) The evaluation criteria includes sales volume, turnover, markdown percentage, maintained markup, and current sales trend. The means are presented for each criteria at the bottom of the table. **Sales volume** is total sales for the classification during the selling period being evaluated. **Turnover** is the number of times average inventory on hand was sold. **Percent markdown** is markdown dollars as a percent of net sales. **Maintained markup** is the difference between cost of merchandise, including its transportation, and

TABLE 4.4

History of merchandise classification by store.*

History of		Classification		Selling Period	
Store	**Sales Volume**	**Turnover**	**% Markdown**	**% Maintained Markup**	**% Change in Sales**
1	20,500	2.0	22.0	41.0	+16.6
2	18,700	3.1	10.7	50.3	+8.5
3	48,500	4.2	12.2	49.9	−5.9
4	67,000	4.3	10.9	52.1	−6.4
5	52,000	3.7	18.7	46.6	+11.0
6	48,000	3.3	15.5	45.1	+5.1
Mean	42,450	3.43	15.0	47.5	+4.82

*Based on a table from Retail Merchandising Services Automation, Inc., Riverside California.

CASE 4.2

Trends for Pantyhose Manufacturers in Cosmetics Numbers?

From Dortch, S. (1997, April). *Hosiery News,* pp. 30–31. (Reprinted from *American Demographics Magazine,* March 1997).

It's been a few years since musician Janet Jackson appeared on the cover of Rolling Stone magazine wearing neither clothes nor makeup. That appearance helped usher in a trend in neutral-colored makeup that appears to be ending—much to the relief of cosmetics makers. Color is back, from the red-black lipstick popularized by Chanel's "Vamp" line to Revlon's "Virtual Violet" collection.

The current upswing in color cosmetics follows a 10-year period of decline in cosmetics users. In 1996, 88 percent of women aged 18 and older said they used makeup of some kind in the past six months, compared with 92 percent ten years earlier, according to Mediamark Research of New York City. Color cosmetics include foundation, powder, blushes, lip color, and eye makeup, such as shadow and mascara. The share declined across all age groups, including women aged 18 to 24. They are a prized market for cosmetics makers because they are the most likely of all U.S. women to wear makeup, at 91 percent in 1996. They are also thought to be experimental and willing to spend money to try new products. Yet the share of 18-to-24-year-olds using any cosmetics declined 4 percent points between 1986 and 1996.

One reason for the decline is changing fashion. In the early 1990's, supermodels such as Kate Moss pop-ularized an androgynous style for women. Hip body shapes were slim and boyish, with feminine curves and roundness de-emphasized. Cosmetics followed suit, with many women adopting a minimalists approach to their facial makeup. But there's more to it, as well. "The generation of women in their 20s are willing to look more natural," say Candace Corlett, President of the special markets division of Research 100, a Princeton, new Jersey-based market research firm. "They're not as driven to get made up, so they don't wear makeup like the women in their 20s did 20 years ago."

Revlon, Inc., of New York City, helped launch the natural-look trend with colors that helped women look like they were wearing no makeup at all, Corlett says. The same company gets a lot of credit for makeup's current shift back to color, color, and more color. Revlon got the ball rolling with its ColorStay brand long-wearing lipstick. "It's been a major improvement in the lipstick market." Corlett says. "And another thing is the extraordinary colors available."

The availability of new, long-wearing lipsticks hasn't yet resulted in an overall increase in the share of women who are lipstick users. There is modest growth among women aged 18-24, at 81 percent in 1996, up from 76 percent ten year earlier. But rates for all women declined 3 percentage points over the period, to 77 percent in 1996.

Cosmetic makers are reaping benefits anyway, though. For one thing, women who like color cosmetics may be using more of them. "When you start

---

selling price. **Percent change in sales** reflects the sales trend as compared.to the previous selling period. It is clear that a quick perusal of these figures does not reveal how the classification should be planned for the next selling period. Additional analysis including serious reflection is required to make merchandising decisions. A similar comparison should be made among classifications to evaluate their relative productivity. (Read Case 4.2 and do Learning Activity 4.3 here.)

Merchandise Planning at Sport Obermeyer Using Accurate Response

(The following discussion is based on two articles: Fisher, M. L., Obermeyer, W., Hammond, J., & Raman, A. (1994, May–June). Making supply

playing with colors, you change colors more often." Corlett says. But perhaps more importantly, women appear less price-resistant when faced with long-lasting products and exciting colors. "They have everyone signing on for higher-priced lipstick," Corlett says. "The big revolution is the willingness of madam consumer to pay almost department-store prices for cosmetics in drug stores and mass retail outlets." For instance, ColorStay lipstick retails in drug stores for around $9.

Sales data suggest that color products for lips are indeed a bright spot on the non-prestige cosmetics market, which includes purchases made in most outlets other than department stores. Both dollar sales volume and unit volume posted above-average one-year increases for the year ended October 27, 1996, according to Information Resources, Inc., of Chicago. Annual sales of lip-color products in food, drug, and mass retail stores rose 12 percent to more than $494 million, compared with a 7 percent increase for all cosmetic products, including nail products. Unit volume rose 5 percent, to 11 million, compared with 2 percent for all cosmetic products sold through these three types of stores.

Women who shop for color cosmetics outside department stores face some obstacles. It's often harder to sample cosmetics in drug, grocery, and mass retail stores. And there are seldom salespeople to help women identify the best products for them. Yet that doesn't stop them from spending million on cosmetics each year in non-department store outlets.

Dollar sales may increase as cosmetic prices rise, and unit sales may grow when established makeup users buy more products. But the cosmetic industry may also be able to look forward to increasing numbers of women using color cosmetics. Growth could be modest to the year 2000, at about 2 percent. At that rate, 91.6 million U.S. women aged 18 and older may be cosmetic users in 2000. The pace could pick up a bit to 2007, when almost 95 million women may have used makeup in the past six months. Growth will not be uniform across age groups.

Young women aren't necessarily a slow growth market for color cosmetics, especially Hispanic women. "This is a great opportunity, and a marketer's dream," says Tony de La Ossa, director of U.S. market segmentation for Avon Products, Inc. of New York City. Hispanic women have a younger median age than all U.S. women, at 27.1, compared with 36. And their numbers are growing rapidly through immigration and high birth rates. The Census Bureau projects the number of Hispanic women aged 15 and older may grown 38 percent between 1997 and 2007, to 13.7 million. In addition, Hispanic women wear makeup with emphatic color—a tendency that doesn't appear to change with mainstream fashion.

Learning Activity 4.3

Trends for Pantyhose Manufacturers in Cosmetics Numbers?

1. Read Case 4.2 very carefully. Identify the different sources of data that provide information for this overview of trends in the cosmetics business.

2. What are the trends in cosmetics that could provide guidance for planning merchandise budgets and assortments?

3. How and why might cosmetic trends be informative in planning hosiery budgets and assortments?

meet demand. *Harvard Business Review,* 72, 83–90; and Fisher, M., Obermeyer, W., Hammond, J., & Raman, A. (1994, February). Accurate response: The key to profiting from QR. *Bobbin,* 35, 48, 50–52, 54–57, 59–62. The combined academic expertise of Marshall L. Fisher from the Wharton School at University of Pennsylvania and Janice H. Hammond and Ananth Raman at Harvard University with Walter R. Obermeyer, principal of Sport Obermeyer, Ltd. in Aspen, CO, resulted in re-engineering the merchandising planning process.)

Accurate Response combines QR practices with a new planning paradigm that maximizes profit by explicitly measuring forecast risk and then optimizing production to minimize stockouts and markdowns. Accurate Response appropriately *focuses attention on the result* (accurately producing the styles and colors customers want by responding to early market signals), *rather than the means* (lead time reduction). Costs associated with implementing Accurate Response are less than one-tenth of one percent of sales and the savings are at least 20 times that. Profits in the apparel industry average three percent of sales, so the savings are great enough to increase profits at Sport Obermeyer by 66 percent.

Sport Obermeyer designs and manufactures fashion skiwear (parkas, pants, suits, shells, jackets, sweaters, turtlenecks, and accessories). The merchandise is sold primarily through specialty ski shops. The primary retail selling period is about 26 weeks long, depending on the length of the ski season in different parts of the country.

Obermeyer is a dominant company in the fashion skiwear market. More than 95 percent of Obermeyer's products are new styles each year. Obermeyer works with long lead times. The design process begins two years ahead of the retail selling period, and line adoption one year ahead. Production of components and garments begins in January in a variety of locales, including Hong Kong, China, Japan, Korea, Jamaica, Bangladesh, and the United States. Retail orders are received between February and May. Finished goods are shipped to Obermeyer's distribution center in Denver and then allocated to stores according to purchase orders in time for the beginning of the retail selling period in November. Obermeyer implemented numerous QR projects related to order processing and materials management to improve overall performance.

Forecast-Based Merchandise Plans

Traditionally, in November each year, shortly after line adoption (about one year prior to the retail selling period), a six-member buying committee (president, vice president, merchandiser, and managers of marketing, production, and customer service) reviewed the new line and, through a consensus process, forecasted sales for each style and color. Analysis of the forecasts relative to sales revealed the forecasts were accurate for about half of the company's products. The problem was, before the season began, there was no way of knowing which half of the products were accurately forecast.

In an attempt to improve the buying committee's forecasts, they modified the process so each member of the committee forecasts independently, rather than through consensus. They found the independent forecasts were better predictors of sales than those formed by consensus. They also were able to indicate which styles were being accurately forecasted by looking at the standard deviation among the independent forecasts for a single style. (See Table 4.5.)

Table 4.5 shows the forecasts made by each member of the buying committee for a portion of the adult outerwear line. The overall forecast is

TABLE 4.5

Computing Forecast and Standard Deviation from Buying Committee Estimates.*

STYLE	Carolyn	Malinda	Laura	Kenny	Wally	Klaus	Overall Forecast	Standard Deviation
			INDIVIDUAL FORECASTS					
WOMEN'S PARKAS								
Nell	4000	3000	3500	3200	4100	2200	3333	1284
Stardust	3500	2800	3300	2300	2700	2800	2900	792
Tantric	2500	2600	2000	2100	1500	1800	2083	761
Blue Ribbon	1000	1200	1200	1000	700	1200	1050	361
SHELLS								
Blondie	4100	4000	3400	4200	3000	4000	3783	867
Pamela	2000	1800	2200	2100	2000	2000	2017	243
Taylor	1100	1000	800	850	1400	1600	1125	577
SUITS								
Ruthie	1200	1000	1300	1800	1400	1500	1367	499
Switchback	1200	800	1100	950	1100	1200	1058	285
Audacious	700	1000	800	450	600	600	692	348
MEN'S PARKAS								
Ski Chute	800	1200	800	850	1000	1000	942	285
Helicopter	1800	1000	800	1150	900	1600	1208	736
Snowcat	1100	1200	1100	1150	900	1000	1075	198
Big Burn	800	1400	1500	1350	800	1700	1258	684
SHELLS								
Quad	1000	800	900	1100	600		880	344
Zermatt	600	300	600	550	400		490	240
SUITS								
Gondola	1800	1200	1200	1700	1500		1480	496
Innsbruck	800	600	500	800	1000		740	349
Ravine	500	1000	900	650	650		740	366
Cirque	400	500	300	250	400		370	174
Snowbird	500	700	1100	600	450		670	463

*Fisher, Obermeyer, Hammond, & Raman (1994).

the **mean** of the individual forecasts. To obtain the standard deviation, the **variance** of individual forecasts is determined by squaring the difference between each individual forecast and the overall forecast, summing the variances, and dividing by the number of individual forecasts.

The **standard deviation** for a style is estimated as twice the square root of the variance. A scale factor of two was chosen to equal the actual forecast errors from previous periods. Some styles were not forecast by all members of the committee; these are shown as blanks on the table and all calculations are done on the available individual forecasts. Obermeyer offers each style in about four colors, so the buying committee members also forecast the demand for each style/color combination. The same method is used to compute the forecast and standard deviation for style/color combinations.

Notice in Table 4.5 that the more the members of the buying committee disagree about the sales potential of a style, the larger the standard deviation. The hypothesis is: If the buying committee disagrees on the sales potential of a style, demand uncertainty is greater for that style. Standard deviation provides a way to identify those styles and colors that are accurately forecast and can be produced with low risk of bad production forcasts. These styles are put into production early, reserving production capacity later in the merchandising cycle for products with uncertain forecasts.

A program called **Early Write** is specifically directed toward improving merchandise forecasts for styles where the buying committee did not agree or had high standard deviations. For Early Write, a select group of customers representing about 20 percent of sales is invited to the home office to place orders a month earlier than everyone else. Obermeyer uses these orders to re-evaluate the accuracy of their forecasts. The Early Write orders represent a very small amount of sales data, but provide information that substantially improves forecasts. The retail buyers are closer to the ultimate consumer than the Obermeyer buying team, thus they provide additional insight into the salability of the styles. The Early Write orders have priority for shipping, so these retailers receive their merchandise earlier than other retailers. Early Write also gives Obermeyer the potential to increase the "square-footage days" that goods are displayed by retailers. This is a key to achieving excellent sell-through in a short selling period.

Forecasting Principles Demonstrated by Obermeyer

1. Invest technology and people's time into forecast-based merchandise plans.
2. Identify what can and cannot be accurately forecast.
3. Early in the process, seek diversity of opinion rather than consensus.

4. Put accurately forecast products into early production.
5. Reserve later production for less accurately forecast goods.
6. Provide opportunities for other experts to assist with poorly forecast goods.
7. Use appropriate, systematic methods for on-going analysis of effectiveness of forecasts.

Learning Activity 4.4

Forecasting

1. In the case of Sport Obermeyer, how does standard deviation help distinguish between good forecasts and bad forecasts?

2. Can the principles demonstrated by the Sport Obermeyer case be applied to forecast-based merchandise plans in the retail sector? How?

Summary

Computerization of merchandise planning and other merchandising-related processes has had a profound effect on merchandising systems, even though this planning technology has not kept pace with the other functions of a firm. The development of intense competition in both manufacturing and retailing's global markets during the 1980s resulted in a focus on price competition. Merchandisers traveled the world seeking lower merchandise costs. In the 1990s, QR business systems focus on the benefits of saving time and have recognized the essential need for forecast-based merchandise plans.

An effective merchandise classification system is an essential foundation for merchandise planning. The language used for merchandise classification varies greatly among firms. Therefore, a simple system of commonly used terms is presented in this text. The merchandise mix is made up of categories, which can be further broken down into classes and subclasses. Subclasses may be divided into merchandise groups. Groups are described according to assortment factors; for apparel these are usually style, size, and color.

Forecasting is the most frequently requested feature in merchandise technology systems. Early forms of merchandising technology had forecasting based primarily on sales history. Today's firms focus on planning merchandise budgets and merchandise assortments based on more diverse forms of information. For example: 1) priorities of each of the firm's constituencies in relation to the firm's goals; 2) events impacting the firm's external coalitions, and 3) influences of a firm's environments.

Sport Obermeyer has developed a forecasting system based on the concept of identifying what goods can be accurately forecast and sourcing them early and by developing additional information on goods that cannot be accurately forecast and sourcing them later. Obermeyer uses standard deviation among individual's forecasts as a measure of forecast accuracy.

Key Concepts

Accurate Response (AR)
assortment plans
balanced assortments
bottom-up planning
dollar plans
external coalitions
forecasting
interactive planning
mean
merchandise budgets
merchandise categories
merchandise classes
merchandise groups

merchandise mix
merchandise subclasses
merchandising cycle
overlapping environments
percent change in sales
percent markdown
percent maintained
  markup
sales volume
selling periods
six-month plans
standard deviation

tiers in organizational
  pyramid
top-down planning
transition periods
turnover
unit plans
variance

Integrated Learning Activity 4.5

1. Review the company profile that you began with Integrated Learning Activity 3.7. Summarize the issues that are particularly pertinent to line planning. Add the following:

   a) Describe product lines, including categories and classifications of merchandise, based on your observations.

   b) Identify primary suppliers/brand names/private-label merchandise.

   c) Describe how you would expect their merchandise classes to relate to the Perceptual Map of Product Change, Figure 3.2.

   d) Choose two merchandise classes or subclasses, one that is fashion/seasonal and the other that is basic/staple. Develop a merchandise calendar for each using Table 4.3 as a model.

2. Read Case 4.3. very carefully. Assume you are going to open a "gently used" children's clothing store. Develop a classification system for the merchandise you will carry and establish criteria for accepting goods. Will each classification be consigned or purchased outright? Why?

CASE 4.3

Second-Hand Items, First-Rate Bargains

From Myers, M. (1996, April 1). *Des Moines Register,* pp. 1T–2T.

"Some people turn their noses up at used clothes, some people consider these their best clothes, and some buy used items just for play clothes," explained Patti Johnson about people who buy and sell kids' wear on consignment.

It's no secret to parents, grandparents, and gift-givers that kids' clothes don't come cheap.

Johnston, owner of Kids' Stuff consignment store on Des Moines' east side, believes that's one reason the children's consignment business involves a lot of loyal, repeat customers.

"Usually, if they come in after they've just had a baby, they'll stay with until they've outgrown the store," she said.

Outfitting children from head to toe—tops, bottoms, socks, shoes, hair accessories, coats—can be both expensive and tedious. Then, quicker than you can capture the Kodak moment, the clothes are too small.

Still, if there's no one to pass the "previously loved" outfits to, there are good alternatives.

Charitable organizations like Disabled American Veterans (DAV), Goodwill and the Salvation Army accept good, used clothing as well as other home items. And in many cases, you can claim a portion of the value of donated merchandise as a deduction on income taxes if you itemize your return and get a receipt.

Garage sales are another option. All you need is the ambition to clean up the items, set prices, sweep out the garage, make signs and place ads, then hang around the house all day waiting for customers to take interest in your merchandise.

But increasingly consumers are turning to consignment stores—to cash in on outgrown or unwanted stuff and to buy the "next size up" or a different version in bargain-priced used goods. In the Des Moines area alone [population 200,000], there are nearly a dozen stores that resell children's apparel. Some cater exclusively to the kiddie market; some also accept adult clothing; and many also take books, toys, baby equipment and other children's paraphernalia.

Johnston, who has been operating her store for 10 years, sells clothing for newborns to preteens, plus children's furniture, books, toys, decorations, and miscellaneous articles.

Like most dealers, she offers a consignment customer 50 percent of the resale price of the item. "But, I'm really picky about what I take," she said. "I don't have to take a bunch of junk, because I can fill the store up with good stuff."

There are also consignment stores that carry clothing in all sizes, rather than dealing exclusively in kids' wear. Rachel Sykes, co-owner of Elite Repeat in Ankeny, can outfit a whole family. Her children's goods are in a back room with a few toys and books, and adult clothing and items are in the front of the store.

She, too, closely scrutinizes merchandise offered for resale. Elite Repeat, which deals with a lot of dance wear, takes mainly higher-priced clothing and name-brand items rather than play clothes.

"We don't do a lot with casual clothes or play wear, because it's so affordable through stores like Wal-Mart and Target," Sykes said.

"We take things you have invested a lot of money in and want to recoup something from because it's still in good shape. I require customers to wash and iron clothing and hang it. If the clothing requires dry cleaning, I need proof of that—like the receipt," Sykes said.

In typical consignment agreements, whether a store deals in children's clothing exclusively or family apparel, the store contracts to keep items for 90 days. After that they are put on sale, donated to emergency shelters or other charitable agencies, or must be reclaimed by the owners.

A few stores will keep items indefinitely and store them off season, then offer them for sale the following year. ABC Children's Store in Des Moines is one such shop. Out-of-season clothing is kept in a basement storage area but remains handy if needed out of season, say, for a vacation.

Kay Wieland, who co-owns ABC with daughter Gail Bates, said the store does a mixture of buying outright and taking consignments. However, in outright purchases, the seller is offered a price that is "just a little more than garage sale prices"—about a fourth to a third of what the store will mark them.

continued

That's in comparison to consignments, where the seller gets 50 percent of the selling price. Often, Wieland said, ABC will buy a customer's consignment "leftovers" and put the items on a sale rack. The store also takes the loss on any items that are shoplifted.

"The customer can't use a loss, but we can take it off our taxes," she said.

Last summer, Christie Jarchow opened Kidsignment, a new children's consignment store in Grimes. "Since I just started, there's nothing I'll say 'no' to taking right now," she said.

Jarchow plans to carry children's clothing in sizes 0 to 7 and "all sorts of baby equipment and toys." For customers who consign, she offers in-store credit and will also manage clients' accounts as they consign, sell and purchase items.

"I'm still trying to figure out what the Grimes community wants the most," she said. "So far, it's mainly name-brand clothing."

For those who don't want to wait through a consignment period to make money on their goods, it is often possible to sell items outright to a resale store.

Once Upon a Child, a franchise outlet in Clive run by Shari Balberg, handles children's clothing, toys and accessories. Items are purchased outright, never consigned. Other Iowa Once Upon a Child stores are in Cedar Rapids, Waterloo and Sioux City.

Her main requirement for items, she said, is that they are freshly laundered and not stained or torn. Baby equipment and toys, equally big sellers, are checked against a list of manufacturers' recalls, so a customer can be sure that although the merchandise has "previous experience," it is of good quality.

Another franchise operation is Play It Again Sports, which, like Once Upon a Child, is a division of Minneapolis' Grow Biz International. There are two Des Moines outlets, both owned by Joe Schneider and his father, Dennis. Joe Schneider said of lot of used sporting goods for such children's activities as Little League and hockey are purchased outright. The stores also take in larger items—bicycles and fitness equipment—on consignment. Some athletic clothes for children and adults are available, but they must show only minimal wear to be accepted for resale.

Recommended Resources

Fisher, M., Obermeyer, W., Hammond, J., & Raman, A. (1994, February). Accurate response: The key to profiting from QR. *Bobbin, 35,* 48, 50–52, 54–57, 59–62.

McEntire, M. A. (1994). Consumer responsive product development. *Proceedings of the Quick Response 94 Conference,* 67–70.

Needed: 3-way partnering of chains, vendors, suppliers or QR nets nothing, says mercantile (1994, October). *Chain Store Age Executive, 70*(10), 54–56.

Reda, S. (1994, March). Planning systems. *Stores, 76,* 34–37.

References

Donnellan, J. (1996). *Merchandise buying and management.* New York: Fairchild.

Fisher, M. L., Obermeyer, W., Hammond, J., & Raman, A. (1994, May–June). Making supply meet demand. *Harvard Business Review, 72,* 83–90.

Fisher, M., Obermeyer, W., Hammond, J., & Raman, A. (1994, February). Accurate response: The key to profiting from QR. *Bobbin, 35,* 48, 50–52, 54–57, 59–62.

Hart, E., Salfin, C., & Spevach, R. (1993, April 7). Matrix remakes marketing methods. *Daily News Record,* p. 1+.

Reda, S. (1994, March). Planning systems. *Stores, 76,* 34–37.

Retail Merchandising Services Automation, Inc. (1995). *Retail intelligent forecasting: Merchandise planning for the future.* Riverside, CA: Author.

Sears' merchandise allocation system helps spur turnaround (October, 1993). *Chain Store Age Executive, 69*(10), 20–23, 26–31.

Skinner R. C. (1992). Fashion forecasting at Oxford Shirtings. *Proceedings of the Quick Response 92 Conference,* 90–107.

Solomon, B. (1993, July). Will there be a miracle on 34th Street? *Management Review, 82,* 33–36.

Taylor, C. G. (1970). *Merchandise assortment planning: The key to retailing profit.* New York: National Retail Merchants Association.

5

Merchandising Perspectives on Pricing

Learning Objectives

- Analyze the intricacies of pricing language.
- Examine the relationships among manufacturer pricing, retailer pricing, and customer perceptions of pricing.
- Apply components of pricing strategies as administered by consumer goods firms.

Prices and pricing have become major issues in consumer goods merchandising as increasing quantities are sold at less than the original ticketed price. The price-cutting practice is particularly pervasive with apparel and in department stores where over 75 percent of goods are being sold "on sale" (Kaufmann, Smith, & Ortmeyer, 1994). "A major contributor to retail price deflation has been the heightened value and price sensitivity of consumers" (Levy, 1994, p. 1).

Price has become the primary component of consumer goods advertising. Selling at less than "regular" retail price has become so common that many consumers have been conditioned not to buy if a product is not "on sale." Looking forward, firms will have to recognize that price is an important component, but not the only component of merchandising. One study has shown that only 10 to 15 percent of customers are so focused on product cost that they will sacrifice convenience to find the lowest price. The rest can be satisfied with a fair price along with selection, quality, and fast checkout (Reda, 1994).

Pricing Relationships in the Trade Matrix

Price is the amount asked for or received in exchange for a product. **Cost** is the value given up in order to receive goods or services; the amount invested in order to have a product. The relationship between selling price and merchandise cost determines **gross margin,** the traditional measure of merchandising success. Firms engaged in consumer goods businesses administer the prices of their products with regard to market conditions, merchandise costs, and what they perceive to be customer's priorities. For the most part, consumer goods are differentiated products, that is, a particular firm's products are identifiable from similar products produced or distributed by competing firms. Prices are set by the individual firms, not by impersonal market forces that establish prices for commodities such as steel, corn, or cotton. Effective pricing assists in meeting gross margin goals, meeting volume goals, and covering costs. Achievement of these goals contributes to accomplishing the firm's mission.

Pricing practices in wholesale and retail sectors are based on a combination of legal regulation, tradition, and strategic marketing. A combination of federal, state, and local laws determine what types of pricing practices are legal. Table 5.1 includes a list of federal laws regulating pricing activity. The impact of these laws is discussed within context of the appropriate pricing practices.

A Language of Price

A firm's business plan usually includes the price range(s) within which it plans to compete. For apparel, general price ranges are commonly described as **low-end, budget, moderate, better, bridge, and designer.**

TABLE 5.1

Federal laws regulating pricing.

Sherman Antitrust Act, 1890
- prevents development of monopolies
- protects competition
- makes horizontal price fixing illegal

Federal Trade Commission Act, 1914, Amended 1938
- established Federal Trade Commission (FTC) as a regulating body
- regulates truth in price advertising

Robinson-Patman Act, 1936
- removed advantages of large companies

Consumer Goods Pricing Act, 1975
- terminated all interstate resale price maintenance and fair trade regulations
- made it illegal for manufacturers to specify retail prices and take action to be sure distributors and retailers use them

Apparel is generally manufactured to be retailed within a particular price range; retail merchandisers select products at wholesale to be retailed within a similar price range. When customers are not well informed about product attributes, they may use price as a surrogate for quality (Tellis, 1986). They may assume that if the price is high, the quality is high. This may allow merchandisers to exploit their customers by buying lower quality goods and selling them at a higher price, at least until customers find product performance is inadequate.

Pricing terminology is not used consistently throughout the trade and academic literature. For purposes of clarity in this text, a set of commonly used pricing terms are defined and used throughout. Readers are encouraged, however, when reading other publications or talking with merchandising professionals, to keep in mind the context in which the language relative to price is offered to clearly understand its meaning. To make it easier to refer back to the definition of terms, they are presented in Table 5.2 in alphabetical order.

TABLE 5.2

Definition of pricing terms.

- **above-market**—price set in the upper range of prices for a particular product type; includes additional markup on first price or higher than average initial markup.
- **additional markup cancellation**—reduction in above-market/premium price to first price.
- **additional markup**—difference between first price and above-market/premium price.
- **adjusted gross margin**—gross margin less transportation and distribution expense.
- **at-market price**—similar to competitors offering the same products.
- **below-market price**—less than competitors offering the same products; may be based on lower than normal markup.
- **billed cost**—list price less quantity and trade discounts as stated on an invoice.
- **cash discount**—reduction in billed cost as incentive to pay the invoice on time.
- **clearance price**—price asked when increasing the appeal of goods to customers for purposes of inventory management.
- **comparison price**—price offered in advertising or on price tickets as representative of "regular price" or the value of the product.

- **contract dating**—terms of a purchase agreement that determine when an invoice is due to be paid.
- **distressed goods**—merchandise unsalable during a selling period using established outlets for first quality goods.
- **first price**—original retail price; may or may not be the same as list price or the price the customer first sees on a price ticket; *first price is the base price for retail price structures.*
- **initial markup**—difference between wholesale price (billed cost) and first price.
- **job-off price**—price for selling distressed goods to a jobber or diverter; may be sold by the piece or by weight.
- **keystone markup**—traditional markup on apparel; 50% markup on retail; 100% markup on cost.
- **list price**—suggested retail price used in manufacturer's/wholesaler's catalogs and price sheets; an estimate of the value of the product to the ultimate consumer; *list price is the base price for wholesale price structures.*
- **manufacturer's wholesale price**—list price less quantity, seasonal, and trade discounts.

TABLE 5.2 (continued)

- **markdown cancellation**—elimination of a markdown to restore first price; may be accompanied by another markdown or an additional markup to establish the next price a customer will see.
- **markdown**—difference between first price and promotional or clearance price.
- **permanent markdown**—reduction in price reflecting decline in merchandise value based on salability.
- **predatory pricing**—illegally selling items at very low markup or below merchandise cost to eliminate competition.
- **premium price**—see above-market price.
- **price lining**—"offering merchandise at a limited number of price points that should reflect differences in merchandise quality" (Mason, Mayer, Ezell, 1984); selling items of varying costs for the same price.
- **price points**—specified prices representing a price line.
- **pricing strategy**—particular combination of pricing components designed to appeal to a firm's target customers and contribute to achieving a firm's goals.
- **promotional price**—price intended to increase total revenue by generating additional customer traffic.
- **quantity discount**—reduction from list price related to efficiencies of volume of purchase.

- **reference price**—see comparison price.
- **regular price**—price perceived to be the "usual" or "normal" price for a product.
- **retail merchandise cost**—wholesale price less discounts and allowances; may include transportation costs.
- **sales promotion**—a marketing strategy intended to increase total revenue.
- **seasonal discount**—reduction from list price relating to time of purchase in a selling period; a manufacturer may offer pre-selling period, late-selling period, and end-of-the-selling-period discounts.
- **selling price**—price a customer pays for a product; wholesale price in the manufacturing sector; may be higher or lower than first price in the retail sector.
- **shipping terms**—determines who pays the freight costs and when ownership of products is transferred; free on board (FOB); cost, insurance, freight (CIF); free along side the ship (FAS).
- **temporary markdown**—reduction in price for sales promotion; markdown will be canceled at end of sale period.
- **trade discount**—reduction from list price granted to a firm that performs some marketing or distribution function.
- **wholesale price**—list price less quantity, seasonal, and trade discounts.

Learning Activity 5.1

Using the list of definitions in Table 5.2, do the following:

1. Identify all of those that include the word price. How do these terms relate to each other?

2. Identify all the terms that include the word discount. How do these terms relate to each other?

3. Identify all the terms that include the word cost. How do these terms relate to each other?

4. Read Case 5.1 very carefully. What are the central pricing issues in the case? How will the resolution of the case impact manufacturers? How will the resolution of the case impact retailers? How will the resolution of the case impact consumers?

CASE 5.1

Reebok and FTC Settle Price-Fixing Charges

From Novak, V., & Pereira, J. (1995, May 5). *Wall Street Journal,* pp. B1, B8.

The Federal Trade Commission, along with all 50 state attorneys general, yesterday announced an agreement with **Reebok International Ltd.** settling government charges that Reebok and its Rockport Co. subsidiary tried to fix the prices of their footwear with retailers.

According to the FTC's new director of competition, William Baer, Reebok coerced retailers into agreeing to keep prices above certain levels. Some retailers raised their prices by as much as 30 percent to stay in line with what they assumed was a minimum retail price, said Mr. Baer, because they feared Reebok would cut off their supplies or not fill orders.

Reebok, based in Stoughton, Mass., and Rockport control about a quarter of the market in athletic and casual footwear, Mr. Baer noted. The alleged price-fixing agreements between Reebok and its retailers meant that shoppers who needed a new pair of running shoes couldn't find them discounted. They also meant retailers who wanted to cut prices to bring in customers felt they couldn't do so.

The case also signals that the FTC's new chairman, Robert Pitofsky, intends to pursue this once-moribund area of anti-trust law, vertical price fixing, staff members indicated.

In the proposed consent decree Reebok and Rockport didn't admit guilt, but agreed not to try to set or control the prices at which retailers sell or advertise their brands—and not to threaten retailers with suspension or termination if they don't go along with suggested prices. The FTC will accept public comment on the proposed settlement for 60 days, after which the commission will decide whether to make it final.

In their settlement with the states, the companies also agreed to pay $9.5 million. About $1.5 million of that will cover the cost of the litigation, and the rest will be distributed among the states to improve public and nonprofit athletic facilities and services.

In a news release, Reebok stated that "investigations by both the Federal Trade Commission and the National Association of Attorneys General of the athletic footwear industry failed, in this view, to establish any evidence of wrongdoing by Reebok and Rockport." The company said it entered into the consent

decrees to "avoid the considerable expense of protracted litigation." A company spokeswoman declined further comment.

Though the FTC's Mr. Pitofsky didn't participate in the commission's 3-1 vote to bring the case—it occurred just before he came on board in March—Mr. Baer made it clear that vertical price-fixing cases are a priority for the new chairman. "I think that's a trend you will see continued," he said. "There is real consumer injury when there are agreements between retailers and manufacturers" that prevent discounting.

In the 1980s, this area of law was virtually mothballed. At the Justice Department, in fact, then antitrust chief William Baxter was so publicly opposed to it that an alarmed Congress attached an amendment to an appropriations bill in 1983 preventing the department from spending money to try to alter or overturn the law's prohibition on this sort of price-fixing, known as resale price maintenance. The conservatives' theory was that discount retailers would be free riders because full-service retailers would promote products and have salespeople to demonstrate products to consumers, but consumers would go to discounters to actually buy the products.

At the Clinton Justice Department, Assistant Attorney General Anne Bingamon has initiated three vertical price-fixing cases involving hockey skates, suntan products, and toys. The FTC has filed three since 1991—including one in 1993 against Stride Rite that settled allegations that it coerced retailers into selling its Keds shoes within certain price ranges.

In fact, analysts say that athletic-footwear manufacturers routinely pressure retailers to sell their shoes at suggested retail prices. Both retailers and manufacturers benefit from such pricing policies, analysts note. A brand's image remains untarnished, and retailers can breathe easier knowing that rival stores won't be drumming up business through special discounts and promotions.

"But Reebok was one of the few in the industry to ever put such a policy in writing, " said Rich Wilner, athletics editor for *Footwear News,* a trade publication.

In the fall of 1992, Reebok insisted through what was called a Centennial Plan that retailers keep prices inflated during certain brisker shopping periods of the year. Retailers objected, citing soft retail sales, and some even threatened to drop orders of certain Reebok

continued

CASE 5.1 (continued)

lines, analysts said. It was around that time that a number of disgruntled retailers—including Sportmart Inc. of Niles, Ill. and Oshmann's Sporting Goods of Houston —approached federal regulators to discuss the industry's practice, according to one industry source. Under the Centennial Plan, "retailers were not allowed to price the shoes below a suggested price level for the upper end premier shoes and not allowed to discount a shoe more than 10% on less expensive lines, said Kevin Nasca, an assistant attorney general for the state of Massachusetts. "The implied threat was that supplies would be cut off, existing orders wouldn't be filled, and future orders wouldn't be taken," he said.

Investigations into other footwear and sporting goods companies have been launched as well, according to a government investigator. The investigator declined to name those companies.

The U. S. athletic-footwear market, however, has been in a slump over the past couple of years and price-fixing pressure has eased, analysts say. "The technology-hungry customer was paying $100 for a pair of sneakers, partly because that's what the fashion was back in the 1980's," said John Horan, publisher of Sporting Goods Intelligence, an industry newsletter. "But the fashion-oriented customer today is going to much lower-priced shoes."

The average price of a pair of sneakers for men is about $43; the average price of a pair of women's sneakers is about $38 today, according to Sporting Goods Manufacturers Association. A fashion shift toward hiking boots and an outdoorsy look has also helped lower sneaker prices, said Mr. Horan.

Perceptions of Price

Quick Response (QR) business systems require that merchandisers are informed about pricing throughout the trade matrix in order to be effective negotiators of contracts and agreements related to development, acquisition, and sale of merchandise. As discussed in Chapter 2, *"QR is a comprehensive business strategy incorporating time-based competition, agility, and partnering to optimize the supply system, the distribution system and service to customers."* The fundamental premise of QR is partnering, including collaboration and cooperation in all processes required to improve speed of processing and service to consumers. QR has improved communications among firms actively participating, but price structures within the textiles and apparel trade matrix remain based primarily on industry tradition. In spite of their interdependence, apparel manufacturers and retailers may be intolerant of one another's pricing practices when each has little understanding of the other's cost structures and pricing strategies. At the same time, retail customers are often shocked to find out that what retailers call 50 percent markup (keystone markup) actually represents a retail price that is more than double the billed cost of the merchandise.

Table 5.3 demonstrates relationships among pricing factors as viewed by manufacturers, retailers, and consumers. The pricing factors are accom-

TABLE 5.3

Relationships among pricing factors as viewed by manufacturers, retailers, and consumers.

Manufacturer Pricing		Retailer Pricing		Retail Customer's View of Pricing	
		premium price	**$110**	**regular price**	**$110**
list price	**$105[1]**				
quantity/seasonal discounts	−5%	additional markup	+10%		
reduced list price	**$100**	**first price**	**$100[5]**		
		planned average markdown	−20%	special sale	−27%
		planned average selling price	**$ 80**	**bargain price**	**$ 80**
trade discount	−50%	initial markup	−50%	great sale	−55%
wholesale price	**$ 50**	**planned cost**	**$ 50**	**clearance price**	**$ 49.50[10]**
advertising/markdown discounts	−10%	advertising/markdown discounts	−10%		
billed cost	$ 45	billed cost	$ 45		
production cost	−$ 32				
$ gross margin	**$ 13**	**$ gross margin**	**$ 35[6]**		
% gross margin	**28.89%[2]**	**% gross margin**	**43.75%[7]**		
cash discount on billed cost	−8%	cash discount on billed cost	−8%		
reduced billed cost	$ 41.40[3]	reduced billed cost	$ 41.40[3]		
reimbursed shipping expense	+$ 2	shipping expense	+$ 2		
amount received	$ 43.40	amount remitted	$ 43.40		
other expenses	−$ 2	other expenses	+$ 3		
production cost	−$ 32	net cost of goods	$ 46.40		
$ adjusted gross margin	**$ 9.40**	**$ adjusted gross margin**	**$ 33.60[8]**		
% adjusted gross margin	**21.66%[4]**	**% adjusted gross margin**	**42%[9]**		

[1]price changes in wholesale sector are based on list price or reduced list price
[2][(billed cost − production cost) / billed cost] × 100
[3]billed cost − cash discount
[4][amount received − (production cost + other expense) / amount received] × 100
[5]all price changes in the retail sector are based on first price
[6]planned average selling price − billed cost
[7][(planned average selling price − billed cost) / planned average selling price] × 100
[8]planned average selling price − net cost of goods
[9][(planned average selling price − net cost of goods) / planned average selling price] × 100
[10]regular price − great sale percent

> ### *Learning Activity 5.2*
>
> #### Pricing in the Trade Matrix
>
> 1. Use the definitions of terms to interpret the relationships displayed in Table 5.3. Examine particularly how the bold faced items relate to each other from the manufacturer's, retailer's, and customer's perspective.
>
> 2. Think through how the numbers in each column relate to each other mathematically. In particular, examine $ and % gross margin and $ and % adjusted gross margin.

panied by a simple mathematical example to clarify the relationships. Table 5.3 can be interpreted both vertically and horizontally. Note in this scenario that the list price and the first price—the manufacturers' and retailers' planning prices—are not seen by the retail customer because a premium price is used. The customer sees a premium price and the markdowns as related to that premium price—not the first price, which is the retailer's basis of determining price. What the customer perceives as a bargain price may be the retailer's planned average selling price, one that is expected to provide adequate gross margin for successful business. Some regard retail pricing practices such as this to be deceptive, yet the practice has become widespread in what is known as high-low or promotional pricing. The average selling price indicates that the retail merchandiser plans that most merchandise will be sold at substantially less than the premium/comparison price offered the customer. The gross margin realized on the merchandise relates to average price. (Review the Income Statement discussed in Chapter 3.) Gross margin is a common measure of merchandising success. The significance of the pricing relationships demonstrated in Table 5.3 will become more apparent as you work your way through the chapter.

Wholesale price, in the manufacturing sector, may be reduced to billed cost in the retail sector. After two substantial markdowns the clearance price still exceeds the billed cost of the merchandise. This means the clearance price will cover the cost of the merchandise and make some small contribution toward other business expenses.

The issue of whom should be able to control the price of a product offered to the ultimate consumer is an ongoing debate between manufacturers and retailers. A 1977 lower court decision was upheld in 1988 by the U.S. Supreme Court allowing manufacturers to "reasonably decide to protect some dealers from price competition so that the favored dealers would be profitable enough to promote the products adequately and to provide good display, service, and repair facilities." The court said a manufacturer restricting distribution to price-cutting retailers would not necessarily be violating the Sherman Antitrust Act. The decision was regarded as especially relevant to apparel and electronic industries (Manufacturers can refuse, 1988). More recently the Federal Trade Commission announced the settlement of a case against Reebok International Ltd. related to charges that Reebok coerced retailers into restricting price reductions to the amounts and time periods specified by Reebok (Novak & Pereira, 1995). Prosecuting restraint-of-trade cases was a low priority for the Reagan administration, but the Federal Trade Commission has become much more active during the Clinton administration. See Case 5.1, Reebok and FTC Settle Price Fixing Charges, for a more extensive example of this issue.

Pricing Mechanics

Merchandisers set and manipulate prices on merchandise within the context of a firm's pricing strategy. They also frequently negotiate contracts for purchase of materials to be made into finished goods and/or merchandise to be sold either at wholesale or retail. Methods used to calculate costs and prices are sometimes very elaborate, other times very simple. The methods often reflect an accounting perspective of inventory management rather than a merchandising perspective of planning, development, and presentation of product lines. The key elements of retailer's pricing from a merchandising perspective have been selected for discussion here. Factors related to manufacturer's pricing and wholesale price structures are discussed in Chapter 9, Global Sourcing. A detailed study of the many mathematical manipulations that relate to pricing are left to a merchandising mathematics course.

Retail Pricing

First price is the original retail price. This may or may not be the same as list price or the price the customer first sees on a price ticket. *First price is the base price for retail price structures.* First price is determined by adding initial markup to wholesale price. Normally, retail prices are set before merchandise is delivered, therefore the exact amount to be paid for the merchandise is not yet determined. Relationships of markups and markdowns determining retail price are shown in Table 5.4.

Markups

Initial markup (IMU) establishes the difference between wholesale price (planned cost) and first price. Initial markup is often reported both in terms of percentage and dollars. Two methods may be used, resulting in very different implied results: markup based on retail and markup based on

TABLE 5.4

Determining retail price.

wholesale price
+ *initial markup*
= **first price**
+ *additional markup*
= premium price
− *markup cancellation*
= first price
− *temporary markdown*
= promotional price
+ *markdown cancellation*
= first price
− *permanent markdown*
= clearance price

cost. To interpret %IMU correctly, it is essential to know how it was calculated. Percent IMU based on cost implies a much higher level of $IMU than %IMU based on retail when, in fact, $IMU is the same. See Table 5.5. An initial markup of $7 results in 58.34%IMU based on retail and 140%IMU based on cost. The financial impact for the firm is the same but appearance is very different.

Markup based on cost is commonly used on non-apparel, basic/staple type of goods that are stocked year around and have few price changes. Consumer goods with a very high price-per-item, such as fur coats and automobiles, also usually use markup based on cost.

It is common for manufacturers to use initial markup based on cost when thinking of their wholesale prices, and use markup based on retail for list prices. Initial markup based on retail is the system commonly used in the retail sector, particularly for apparel and other products that experience high rates of fashion and seasonal change. Markup based on retail is

TABLE 5.5

Comparison of percent initial markup (%IMU) when calculated as based on retail and based on cost.

$ Initial Markup	% Initial Markup Based on Retail	% Initial Markup Based on Cost
first price $12 − initial markup $ 7 mechandise cost $ 5	$\%IMU = \dfrac{\text{first price} - \text{planned cost}}{\text{first price}} \times 100$	$\%IMU = \dfrac{\text{first price} - \text{planned cost}}{\text{billed cost}} \times 100$
	$\mathbf{58.34\%IMU} = \dfrac{\$12 - \$5}{\$12} \times 100$	$\mathbf{140\%IMU} = \dfrac{\$12 - \$5}{\$5} \times 100$

consistent with the retail method of calculating inventory where merchandise value is recorded at retail rather than cost. Permanent price reductions result in the reduction of the value of inventory as an asset, a much more realistic assessment for fashion and seasonal goods.

Additional markup (AMU) is the difference between first price and premium price. Premium prices are commonly used for status/prestige pricing strategies and as a comparison price for high-low/promotional and quick markdown pricing strategies. Premium price is adjusted downward by canceling additional markup and recalculating with a lower percent additional markup.

Markdowns

Once first price is established based on initial markup, all price changes are based on first price. Markdowns are calculated as a percent reduction on first price. If additional markdowns are to be taken, the original markdown is canceled and a greater markdown is taken based on first price. For example, assume a firm has a pricing strategy where it uses 30-percent, 40-percent, and 50-percent markdowns for clearance, each for one week during the last three weeks of a ten-week selling period. Table 5.6 shows a correct system for calculating a series of markdowns.

Each time a new clearance price is calculated it is based on the first price of $30. Assuming 50-percent markup on retail for first price, a 50-percent markdown on first price means the merchandise is being cleared at cost based on the third markdown. Using first price as the base price for all price changes provides a systematic, logical method of price change. Ignoring the concept of markdown cancellation causes serious problems.

The results of an inexperienced merchandiser calculating markdowns without understanding the concept of markdown cancellation is shown in Table 5.7. A merchandising manager, when reviewing the financial records of the sale, would find the merchandise being sold at well below cost with both the second and third markdowns. While customers may find these uncommonly low prices very gratifying, they would have devastating effect on the gross margin produced by the merchandise group.

TABLE 5.6

Markdown calculation (based on first price of $30, 50%IMU on retail).

	1st Markdown		2nd Markdown		3rd Markdown
First Price	$30	1st	$30	2nd	$30
% Markdown	− 30%	markdown is	− 40%	markdown is	− 50%
Clearance Price	$21	canceled	$18	canceled	$15

TABLE 5.7

Incorrect markdown calculation (based on first price of $30, 50%IMU on retail).

	1st Markdown		2nd Markdown		3rd Markdown
First Price	$30	1st	$21	2nd	$12.60
% Markdown	− 30%	markdown is	− 40%	markdown is	− 50%
Clearance Price	$21	not canceled	$12.60	not canceled	$6.30

Learning Activity 5.3

Retailer Pricing

1. Examine the differences in results when percent initial markup is based on cost and on retail. Set up three different experiments based on the following examples using Table 5.5 as a model:

   - 14-karat gold chain with a planned cost of $140 and a dollar markup of $150.
   - baseballs with a first price of $6 and planned cost of $4.
   - video tapes with a dollar markup of $.90 and a first price of $2.99.

2. If a group of boy's shirts had no price changes and all sold at first price, what would be the relationship between initial markup and gross margin?

3. Correctly calculate the clearance prices for a camera with a first price of $50 and markdowns of 20, 30 and 40 percent.

Strategic Pricing

The type of pricing strategy employed by a firm is a key business decision determined by executive management with input from the merchandising and marketing constituencies. The merchandising constituency is then responsible for selecting merchandise that can be priced according to the strategy and sold in adequate quantities to meet the firm's goals. Merchandisers determine list or first price, depending on whether they are working in the wholesale or retail sector, and subsequent price changes according to the pricing strategy. The marketing constituency helps carry out the pricing strategy by developing and managing appropriate advertising and promotions.

Six to twelve different pricing strategies, or policies as they are sometimes called, are frequently itemized in the pricing literature and retailing textbooks. A **pricing strategy** is a particular combination of pricing components designed to appeal to a firm's target customers and contribute to achieving the firm's goals. For purposes of discussion here, a taxonomy of pricing was developed relating six different pricing strategies with six different pricing components. **Pricing components** are variables of pricing strategies that can be applied in different ways. The mode of applying these pricing components determines their internal consistency and their ability to support the firm's mission and strategic goals. There are three fundamental purposes for the development of a consistent pricing strategy:

1. Stimulate regular shopping by target customers;
2. Optimize sale of available merchandise; and
3. Provide guidelines for consistent administration of price.

With rare exceptions, firms are dependent on regular, established relationships with suppliers and customers. Customer loyalty has been seriously undermined by the prevalence of promotional pricing in today's retail markets. If a firm wants to be known as "a purveyor of fine quality merchandise in a high-service environment," then their pricing strategy should support that image. If a firm wants to be known as a "source of better than average quality/status merchandise at less than average price," then their pricing strategy must correspond. If the firm wants to be known as a "source of a wide variety of serviceable consumer goods available everyday at good value," then the pricing strategy should reflect this.

"Optimize" means to make the most effective use of, to make as good or as effective as possible. Discussions of pricing strategies are usually placed within the economic assumption that the purpose of pricing is to maximize profit. To *maximize* is to make as great as possible. However, at any given time, maximizing profit may or may not contribute to the firm's other goals. Therefore, the purpose here—to optimize sale of available merchandise—recognizes the behavioral context and the complexity of interactions that must occur to successfully distribute merchandise to ultimate consumers. In a merchandising environment, all desirable things cannot be maximized, but outcomes can be optimized by making strategic use of opportunities.

Price administration is a profound challenge because of the variety of people involved in establishing, publishing, and changing prices. Consistent pricing practice improves communication with customers. For example, some retailers may consistently use even dollar prices on regular merchandise and odd-price endings on sale merchandise. This practice can become quickly apparent to new customers, making it easy for them to identify the desired merchandise. From a record-keeping perspective, consistent application of a pricing system helps prevent and detect errors.

Strategic Pricing Fundamentals

Pricing strategies face the economic reality of a downward sloping demand curve. There may be very rare instances where increasing a price results in increased quantities purchased in the market. For most part, however, the higher the price for a particular product, the smaller the quantity purchased; conversely, the lower the price the larger the quantity purchased. The fundamental questions are: How high should the price be set? How much and how often should prices change? What will happen to unsold merchandise?

Setting the Price

The relationship between price and quantity purchased is called the **price elasticity** of demand. When price is **inelastic,** the quantity purchased is relatively unaffected by a small price change. Thus, a slightly higher price results in an increase in total revenue because only a few less items are purchased and the higher price more than compensates for this. At the same time, a slightly lower price results in a decrease in total revenue because, while only a few more items are purchased, it is nevertheless not enough to compensate for the lower price. When price is **elastic,** a slightly higher price results in a decrease in total revenue; the number purchased is noticeably less because of the higher price. A slightly lower price results in an increase in total revenue because of the increase in the number purchased. **Unit elasticity** means a higher or lower price has no impact on total revenue; a higher price results in a proportional quantity decrease and a lower price results in a proportional quantity increase so that total revenue is unaffected. Assuming other things being equal, price elasticity of demand determines the financial impact of the price level at which a price is set.

Apparel and other differentiated products are generally regarded as relatively inelastic in relation to price. A small increase or decrease in price will have relatively little impact on the quantity purchased in a particular time period. This means if a merchant desires large increase in quantity sold, a much larger discount must be taken than when dealing with goods with elastic demand. Consequently a "sale" of apparel is seldom advertised with less than 20-percent discount.

Price elasticity is evaluated against total revenue, while merchandising success tends to be evaluated against gross margin. Fundamentally, assuming merchandise costs stay the same and merchandise is salable, a price increase results in greater gross margin and a price decrease results in less gross margin on a per-item basis. Gross margin determines the number of dollars available to pay the firm's expenses beyond the cost of the merchandise. Consequently, price changes must be planned into the pricing strategy to consider both total revenue and gross margin. Setting the price and changing the price are among the many components of a complete pricing strategy.

Changing Prices

Women's apparel has long been regarded as the primary domain of fashion change because of customer demand for frequent change in styling. Fashion influence has expanded to include most apparel and many other consumer products, such as toys. Historically, women's apparel has had higher levels of markup and higher levels of markdowns than men's apparel, although the difference has narrowed since the 1960s. The magnitude of markups and markdowns are now greater for juniors and teens than any other apparel group (Pashigian, 1988). The role of fashion in men's wear has increased significantly in recent years and teen and junior apparel may be the fashion leader in today's markets.

The rate of fashion change has increased over time, as has the variety of products available. Pashigian suggests the increase in fashion influence is due to the supply side rather than the demand side. Improvements in technology and ready access to global markets make a wider variety of goods available, increasing the complexity of merchandise selection for both retail buyers and ultimate consumers.

Based on uncertainty theory, Pashigian and Bowen (1991) attributed the difference in markup and markdown rates to 1) rate of product change associated with fashion; 2) the time of the year; and, 3) the variety of product offering. A retail buyer faces greater uncertainty in product selection and in price-setting when dealing with fashion/seasonal goods. Fashion goods require higher rates of markdowns than basic goods because of their greater uncertainty relative to choosing the most desirable items and judging what price customers will pay. Seasonal influences require judgment in determining when and how long the product will be salable at what price. Increasing variety of product offerings increases risk of incomplete assortments and stockouts. Merchandisers must decide how much of each group of goods to order, where to set the price, when and how much to reorder, and when to mark-down broken assortments.

There are three times during a selling period when markdowns might be taken: pre-selling period, main or within-selling period, and end-of-selling period or clearance (Pashigian, 1988). Price elasticity of demand may vary at different stages of the selling cycle. Markdowns have to be higher to stimulate sales for clearance than for pre-selling period sales. Pre-selling period price promotions may be 10 percent off; main selling period price promotions may be advertised at 20 percent off, and clearance prices at the end of the selling period are frequently 50 percent off. The characteristics of products sold on clearance differ from those sold during the pre-selling period and main selling period. The most desirable goods sell early, while the less desirable goods remain for clearance sales. It takes a larger discount to move leftover merchandise and broken assortments at the end of the selling period. Markdowns peak in July and January, which are the primary clearance periods for the main spring and fall selling periods.

"...the relative profitability of shorter markdown periods are greater than longer markdown periods" (Levy and Howard, 1988, p. 56). When merchandise is marked down for an extended period and still no one buys it, customers may conclude there is something wrong with it. When the markdown period is short, customers may perceive they are in competition for scarce resources and thus place more value on the merchandise. These observations provide support for brief pre-selling period price promotions, limited times for main selling period "sales," and limited times for clearance.

Handling Unsold and Distressed Merchandise

A **clearance sale** toward the end of the selling period is a common way to sell discontinued merchandise and broken assortments. This often involves a series of markdowns over a specified period of time. Another option available is to **job-off** the leftover merchandise to a diverter or wholesaler. The advantage to the retailer here is a relatively short clearance period can be followed by removing all unwanted merchandise from inventory. This frees space to display new merchandise so customers can focus on it. The disadvantage is the job-off price which may be as low as 10 percent of merchandise cost (Levy and Howard, 1988).

A third option for disposing of unwanted merchandise is **consolidation** in a few stores or into a single area of a store. For example, Paul Harris has successfully used consolidation of distressed merchandise in stores where demand is high for high-value merchandise. The merchandise is shipped to a prescribed location for a consolidation sale at very low prices. For example, stores in college towns have been successful in clearing unwanted merchandise from other stores in their region. Consolidation may allow the retailer to recover more total revenue than from a job-off, but staging the consolidation sale may involve considerable expense. Spiegel had made a practice of staging consolidation sales in several areas of the country before they established their own outlet stores. They rented a huge auditorium and ran the sale for a number of weeks. They added inventory to the selection frequently to maintain interest in the sale. They used a system of highly publicized price reductions for each week of the sale.

A fourth option is establishing **outlet stores** designed to unload merchandise that cannot be sold in the original retail environment. Eddie Bauer sets up temporary outlet stores for a clearance period from January through March. Most retailers with outlet store divisions operate year around. They buy merchandise specifically for the outlets, as well as using these stores to dispose of distressed goods from their other retail divisions. The thriving manufacturers' outlet system was established based on the premise of disposing of unwanted manufacturer-owned inventory at wholesale prices. As a result of their success, some manufacturers have become highly vertically integrated and now sell more than over 50 percent of their merchandise through their own retail outlets.

A final option is to **carry over** merchandise to the next selling period (Levy & Howard, 1988). This might be acceptable for basic/staple goods, as some revenue may be recovered through carry over, however it is unsuitable for fashion/seasonal goods . Disadvantages include the necessity of storing the goods in a clean, secure area. Investing in goods of questionable value for an extended period of time is not good business practice.

Learning Activity 5.4

Strategic Pricing Fundamentals

1. What factors influence how much and when prices should be changed?

2. Collect a group of retailer "Sunday supplements," the advertising inserts commonly included in Sunday newspapers. Look for a statement of pricing policy in each, in relation to the time frame the advertised prices are in effect. Is the merchandise featured in the ads regular inventory, inventory purchased especially for the sale or distressed merchandise? What clues are given to customers as to the type of merchandise featured?

3. Does each supplement include a statement of a price-matching policy for merchandise offered by other retailers? Is a price-matching policy fair to consumers who do not ask for the lower price that might be available through price matching?

Components of Pricing Strategies

Many decisions must be made about how to price goods in relation to a firm's mission, image, and goals. To be effective, the pricing strategy a firm chooses to use must result in a mode of doing business consistent with the firm's other business strategies. The strategic components listed here include many of those pricing decisions. The particular combination of pricing components determines a particular firm's pricing strategy.

Table 5.8 is a taxonomy of pricing strategies to be discussed here. These pricing strategies are commonly used in consumer goods markets, particularly for textiles and apparel products. Each includes a different application of pricing components to express a unique communication to customers. The horizontal axis represents the names of different types of pricing strategies, along with the fundamental, strategic concept of each. The vertical axis of the taxonomy shows the components of pricing strategies. The interior

TABLE 5.8

Taxonomy of selected pricing strategies.

COMPONENTS OF STRATEGIES	PRICING STRATEGIES		
	Prestige Pricing	**Everyday-Low Pricing**	**High-Low Pricing**
Concept of strategy	*Quality/value/service image for people willing to pay "regular" price*	*Focus customers on value at their convenience*	*Periodic price promotions to stimulate customer traffic*
Market Price Position	Prices may be above competitors; appeal to customers desiring special service and/or quality/performance.	Price may be negotiable through price-matching policy	Pricing may focus on or match competitors' prices; prices change when competitors' prices change.
Price Lining	Likely to be used.	Can be used.	Likely to be used.
Price Endings	Even price endings used on first and premium prices; odd price endings on clearance prices.	Odd price endings will probably be used on all prices.	Odd price endings are very likely to be used during price promotion.
Role of First Price	Basis of additional markup for premium price and markdowns for clearance; promotional and below-market prices not used.	Most merchandise sold at first price with slightly below average markup; premium and promotional prices seldom used.	Basis of additional markup for comparison price and temporary markdowns; below-market prices may be used for sales promotion.
Role of Markdowns	Permanent markdowns used for inventory management at seasonal or semi-annual clearance.	Permanent markdowns used for inventory management at seasonal or semi-annual clearance.	Temporary markdowns used weekly to stimulate customer traffic; permanent markdowns for clearance.
Price Advertising	Institutional and image advertising promotes brands, fashion, quality, service, functional design.	Advertise value, convenience, and regular prices.	Constant advertising of temporary markdowns.

*Developed by Grace I. Kunz.

of the taxonomy describes the application of each pricing component in relation to each pricing strategy.

Market Price Position

Choices in market price position include above-market, at-market, and below-market. An **above-market price position** is usually

PRICING STRATEGIES		
Quick Markdown Pricing	**Penetration Pricing**	**Cost-Plus Pricing**
High value for bargain shoppers	*Establish value image and market share*	*Realize a specified markup from each product sold*
Prices are fixed in each time period; most merchandise sold at first price or less.	First price set slightly below competitors' on highly visible items; first price may increase after reputation is established.	Price is determined by multiplying unit cost by some "reasonable" markup.
Can be used.	Can be used.	Not likely to be used.
Odd price endings will probably be used on all prices.	Odd price endings will probably be used on all prices.	Even price endings are not possible.
Basis of additional markup and permanent markdowns; premium price establishes comparison price.	Most merchandise sold at first price with slightly lower than average markup; below-market prices used on highly visible items.	Price at which merchandise is sold; traditional level of markup.
Permanent scheduled markdowns administered throughout selling period.	Temporary markdowns to match competitors' prices; permanent markdowns for inventory management.	As desired; inventory value does not change with price.
Frequent advertising of percent off or may depend on word of mouth.	Advertise value.	As desired.

associated with products of high quality and/or performance, customers who are relatively insensitive to price and a strong customer service strategy. The above-market price is possible because customers get more than just the product and they value the associated product attributes and services.

At-market price position means the firm intends to offer products at prices similar to other firms in the same markets. Merchandisers may do frequent comparative price shopping to be sure prices are comparable on similar merchandise, and they adjust prices when they are out of line. The firm may guarantee any competitor's price for exactly the same item.

Below-market price position means the firm intends to sell goods for less than its competitors in the same markets. If the firm has the same product costs as its competitors, it must have lower operating expenses so it can survive on lower gross margin. This may be evident in self service/warehouse types of merchandise presentation.

Price Lining

Price lining is the practice of "offering merchandise at a limited number of price points that should reflect differences in merchandise quality" (Mason, Mayer, Ezell, 1984). **Price points** are the specified prices within a price line. Price lining simplifies the pricing scenario for customers, reducing concern about price and allowing customers to focus on selecting the desired product based on style, color, fit or coordination with a desired outfit. Price lining results in selling items of varying costs for the same price. Consequently, actual IMU might vary within the price line, but average markup is planned to achieve gross margin goals.

Price Endings

Consideration for price endings determines how prices are stated, i.e., $100.00; $99.99; $99.98; $99.95; $99.49; $99.00. Two outcomes are related to the way prices are stated: 1) What is the impact on customers' perceptions of price? 2) What is the impact on accuracy of accounting? Traditionally, odd-cents price endings have commonly been used based on the assumption that sales will be higher when odd price endings are used because the customer perceives the price to be lower. This assumption is unproved by research. Even-dollar pricing will not necessarily be a deterrent to sales. Regardless of this reality, odd-price endings are deeply ingrained in traditional pricing systems.

Customers have been trained by viewing prices to recognize odd price endings as representing lower priced or bargain goods. In apparel, better, bridge, and designer goods are more likely to be even-dollar priced, while low end, budget, and moderate goods are more likely to have odd-price endings. Upscale goods with even-dollar prices for regular prices are likely to have odd price endings used for promotional and clearance goods.

Role of First Price

Types of prices mentioned in previous discussions have included first price, premium price, comparative price, promotional price, and clearance price.

As previously defined, first price is the basis of determining subsequent prices. While customers may never see that first price may be the planning price, it is the basis for additional markups for premium or comparative price, for temporary markdowns for price promotion, and for permanent markdowns for clearance price. In these cases, first price may also represent a targeted average selling price. In other scenarios, first price may be what the customer perceives as "regular" price and may be the price at which most merchandise is sold.

Role of Markdowns

In the simplest of all apparel pricing environments, basic/staple goods would have one price, a regular price, and fashion/seasonal goods would have two prices, a regular price and a clearance price. The basic/staple goods have little styling change and would be stocked year around at the same price. Fashion/seasonal goods have demand for regular change in styling or according to the time of the year, so merchandisers must plan zero-to-zero inventories several times a year. Clearance prices are necessary to move out unwanted merchandise so new, fresh merchandise can be acquired and displayed.

Most of today's pricing strategies are more complex than the description above. There are basically three times reductions in price can be taken: pre-selling period, late selling period, and end of the selling period. Customers are perceived as being price sensitive and merchants find that sales increase when they advertise price reductions. Some retail firms advertise special prices several times a week, so often that some statistics show that department stores sell up to 80 percent of their merchandise at less than "regular" price.

From a merchandising perspective, there are three primary functions of markdowns: inventory management, sales promotion, and financial management. For inventory management, markdowns are intended to get rid of unwanted merchandise including, out-of-season goods, broken assortments, overstocks, and distressed merchandise. Clearing unwanted and unsalable goods makes room for new, fresh, exciting merchandise. Markdowns for inventory management are **permanent markdowns** and reflect decline in merchandise value both to the customer and the merchant.

Markdowns for sales promotion and financial management may be **temporary markdowns** for a specified period to motivate customers to buy more merchandise than they would at regular price. These are followed by markdown cancellations. The expectation is a price elasticity that will result in increased total revenue based on more units sold at a lower price.

Price Advertising

Firms may choose from many forms of advertising media, or can rely primarily on word-of-mouth advertising among customers. Among those that use advertising, they may or may not mention price. Firms wishing to focus customer attention on quality and service are unlikely to use price advertising. Instead, they use institutional or image types of advertising as a reminder of the firm's presence in the market. Firms that frequently use temporary markdowns *must* advertise so customers will know the timing available for the special prices. Firms that use selling period-based quick markdown schedules may or may not advertise their special values. Some rely entirely on customer knowledge of their strategies and word of mouth advertising between customers.

> ### *Learning Activity 5.5*
> **Components of Pricing Strategies**
>
> Three images of firms were mentioned earlier that might be supported by pricing strategies. They are: a) a purveyor of fine quality merchandise in a high service environment; b) a source of better-than-average quality/status merchandise at less than average price; c) a source of a wide variety of serviceable consumer goods available everyday at good value.
>
> Pick one of the images and describe how the components of pricing strategy relate to the the image you selected.

Types of Pricing Strategies

A **pricing strategy** is a particular combination of pricing components designed to appeal to a firm's target customers and contribute to achieving a firm's goals. Some firms have very clearly defined pricing strategies and practice them religiously; others use combinations of strategies or a combination of pricing tactics.

Prestige Pricing   This strategy is intended to reflect a quality/value/service image for people willing to pay "regular" price. Prestige pricing, as it is called here, is also known as status, psychological, or above-market pricing. Nordstrom is known nationally for its success with a prestige pricing strategy, although they would rather call it an EDFP (everyday-fair price) strategy. Von Maur, in the midwest, has also been successful with prestige pricing. Both Nordstrom and Von Maur use full-time, well-trained, well-paid sales associates. Prestige pricing is usually associated with an intensive customer service environment that includes personal selling services. Personal selling services may include wardrobe consultation, assisted product selection and fitting, notification of new merchandise, and personal thank-you notes for shopping. Firms may empower customer service associates to do anything to support the development of satisfied customers. Other services might include free gift wrap, home delivery, and interest-free credit cards. In these stores, merchandise presentation frequently involves spacious aisles, live music, particularly attractive visual merchandising, and large fitting rooms with telephones and beverage service.

Customers of firms that use prestige pricing are usually of two relatively distinct types: those that shop regular price and those that shop sales. Both groups of customers are essential for the success of this merchandising strategy. The regular-price customers value the services offered, as well as the quality, performance, and fashion offered by the merchandise. The sale customers are more price sensitive and value the merchandise, but cannot afford or do not choose to shop at regular price.

The clearance sales associated with prestige pricing are often highly celebrated events that occur only a few times a year. Sales are typified by hundreds of customers waiting for the doors to be opened on the mornings of the sale. Nearly every store employee may be engaged in the selling process, from president and CEO to secretaries. Clearance is essential to get rid of unwanted inventory to make space for new merchandise to sell at regular price. Clearance also generates good will with the sale customers and produces cash flow for investment in the new merchandise. (See Tables 5.9 and 5.10 for examples of prestige pricing by weeks of sale as viewed by customers.)

TABLE 5.9

Examples of pricing strategies for fashion/seasonal goods with a 10-week selling period as viewed by customer.

(Billed Cost—$50; First Price—$110; Markup on Retail—54.55%)

Selling Period	Prestige Price Strategy	Quick Markdown Strategy	High-Low Price Strategy	EDLP Strategy
Week 1	$140	$140	$140	$110
Week 2	$140	$130	$120	$110
Week 3	$140	$130	$100	$110
Week 4	$140	$110	$120	$110
Week 5	$140	$110	$ 90	$110
Week 6	$140	$110	$120	$110
Week 7	$140	$100	$ 80	$110
Week 8	$140	$100	$ 70	$110
Week 9	$ 70	$ 60	$ 70	$ 55
Week 10	$ 70	$ 50	$ 50	$ 55

TABLE 5.10

Examples of pricing strategies for basic/seasonal goods as viewed by customers.

(Billed Cost—$50; First Price—$100; Markup Based on Retail—50%)

Selling Period	Prestige Price Strategy	High-Low Price Strategy	EDLP Strategy
Week 1	$120	$120	$ 98
Week 2	$120	$100	$ 98
Week 3	$120	$100	$ 98
Week 4	$120	$120	$ 98
Week 5	$120	$120	$ 98
Week 6	$120	$120	$ 98
Week 7	$120	$ 95	$ 98
Week 8	$120	$ 95	$ 98
Week 9	$120	$ 95	$ 98
Week 10	$120	$110	$ 98
Week 11	$120	$110	$ 98
Week 12	$120	$110	$ 98
Week 13	$120	$ 90	$ 98
Week 14	$120	$ 90	$ 98
Week 15	$120	$ 90	$ 98
Week 16	$120	$110	$ 98
Week 17	$120	$110	$ 98
Week 18	$120	$110	$ 98
Week 19	$120	$ 85	$ 98
Week 20	$120	$ 85	$ 98

Everyday Low Pricing   This approach focuses the attention of customers on fair value at their convenience. Wal-Mart, Toys "R" Us, and The Home Depot have succeeded using everyday low price (EDLP). Its primary feature is absence of promotional pricing and the presence of a low "regular" price. Everyday low price requires control of both merchandise and operating costs so the firm can operate at slightly less than normal gross margin because up to 10 percent less than normal markup may be used (Reda, 1994). This pricing strategy invites customers to shop regularly at their convenience with the assurance that the price asked will be reasonable and fair. Firms that are successful with EDLP usually start with it and stay with it. Both Sears and Montgomery Ward tried, unsuccessfully, to change their businesses over to this strategy. It is a long and expensive process to retrain customers who have been accustomed to frequent price promotions (Reda, 1994). Everyday-low price flattens out fluctuations in sales and promotes partnerships with vendors. (See Tables 5.9 and 5.10 for examples of EDLP by weeks of sale as viewed by customers.)

High-Low Pricing   This is sometimes called promotional pricing. It involves periodic and sometimes very frequent temporary markdowns to stimulate customer traffic. Deception of consumers is a primary issue in the use of a high-low pricing strategy. Over the past 20 years, most U.S. department stores and some specialty stores have moved to high-low pricing in an effort to compete with discount and off-price stores. The common practice with high-low pricing is to establish a premium price as a comparison or reference price, then advertise the product at 20–50 percent off the comparative price, or just 40 percent off without stating the comparison price. This pricing practice might be deceptive, according to the *FTC Guides Against Deceptive Pricing*. Consumers are deceived if they assume the comparison price represents a product's intrinsic value and is thus a fair price, or if they assume the comparison price is the product's "regular" price. Other, more sophisticated consumers, might assume that the sale price is the regular price. In this case, the comparison price is the "penalty price paid only by those unable to wait even a short time for the retailer's frequent sale events" (Kaufmann, Smith, & Ortmeyer, 1994). (See Table 5.10 for examples of high-low pricing by weeks of sale as viewed by customers.)

Manufacturers may support retailers' high-low pricing by offering certain product lines at lower prices for sale during price promotions. Retailers pay less than regular price so the merchandise can be sold to customers for less than regular inventory at nearly full markup. Retail merchandisers may also pressure vendors for increased allocations of markdown discounts on purchase contracts. Some manufacturers do not allow their goods to be advertised at reduced prices during the main selling period.

Quick Markdown Pricing   This approach is designed to provide high value for the bargain shopper. Quick markdown is used for fashion and seasonal goods that have several selling periods per year. Merchandise may be upscale, first-quality goods; a mix of upscale, moderate, and budget goods; or a combination of first quality and distressed merchandise as presented by off-price retailers such as TJMaxx. It is common for prices to be reduced on a set time schedule. Customers that shop early in the the selling period find more complete assortments with a comparison price plus the current selling price on the ticket. As the selling period proceeds, multiple markdowns may appear on the ticket. Assortments become broken so, even though the price may be comparatively low, it will be difficult to find

CASE 5.2

Baby Superstore Grows Up

From Ratliff, D. (1996, February). *Discount Merchandiser*, pp. 22–24.

Instead of citing the numbers with the cold, objective eye of a statistician, the CFO of Baby Superstore recites these healthy numbers (4 million births annually in U.S. and for Baby Superstores) with undisguised excitement. Her 62-store chain with $300 million in annual sales, based in Greenville, SC, is taking its first steps toward becoming the first nationwide category killer for baby products. Taylor explains that the company's growth does not simply come from the birthrate, it comes from gaining market share. "We have less than 2 percent of the $20 billion baby industry . . . People are waiting until they are older to have children. This means they have more disposable income." This means today's parents are more able to make big-ticket purchases.

Baby Superstores average about 33,000 square feet with most new stores about 42,000 square feet. They carry products only for children from birth to about 4 years of age. Originally the target market included birth to 12 years of age but the firm has, over time, focused on babies.

Stores carry over 25,000 infant oriented SKUs. Sales from the assortment includes 48 percent furniture and accessories, 25 percent apparel, 17 percent baby bottles and related items, 8 percent toys, 3 percent shoes. In 1995, food-related items were added to the assortment.

The retailer is not promotion oriented and chooses to rely on consistently low prices. "We don't do much advertising," Taylor says. "We strive to have very low prices every day rather than having flyers that show our prices going up and down." The store likes to highlight service. "Our employees need baby products . . . customers come in who need help . . . With 30 to 40 strollers with prices all over the map, how do you know which to choose?" Customers need somebody who can explain different features and do it informatively.

Company employees are informed of new products through training sessions and an annual trade show at company headquarters where vendors introduce and explain how products work. Product demonstrations are a mainstay of the stores, with all employees taking turns to explain new products.

In addition to an array of recognizable brand names, Baby Superstores carry an assortment of private label items. Products carrying their rainbow-colored logo include clothing, baby wipes, shoes, bedding and automobile shades, accounting for about 7 percent of sales.

The private label goods generate approximately 40 percent gross margin compared to a storewide average of 29 percent. Sales per square foot averaged $204 in 1995 compared to $191 the previous year. The companies selling and administrative expenses are about 22 percent.

Baby Superstores plans to boost sales to $485 million in 1996, partly through opening 22 to 26 new stores. Targeted areas for new stores have 350,000 people within a 10 miles radius of the store.

---

companion pieces. (See Table 5.9 for an example of quick markdown pricing by weeks of sale as viewed by customers.)

Penetration Pricing   This strategy is designed to establish a value image in the mind of the customer while increasing market share. Wal-Mart is well known for using market penetration pricing strategies on high visibility items when entering new markets. The Arkansas Supreme Court overturned a lower-court decision ruling that Wal-Mart did not engage in illegal predatory pricing when one of its pharmacies sold products below cost. The court found that competition was thriving in the town despite Wal-

Mart's pricing strategy. "The maximum price for any item sold at Wal-Mart is set at the company's headquarters in Bentonville, Ark. The individual store managers may reduce prices to match or undercut competitors' prices without regard to the cost to Wal-Mart of individual items" (Lee, 1995, p B8).

Cost-Plus Pricing   This method makes it possible to realize a specified level of markup from each product offered for sale. Initial markup is based on cost, rather than retail; it is not necessary to use a retail method of inventory. There is a certain security in cost-plus pricing with the expectation that each product is initially expected to make an equal percentage contribution to gross margin. Conceptually, the process is simpler and requires less judgment in the pricing process but is not very strategic.

Other Pricing Strategies and Combinations of Pricing Strategies

Every retailer knows that the right pricing strategy can dramatically increase profits. Some apparel retailers have been successful with a single price strategy, i.e., "everything in the store for $10.99." These firms focus on an assortment of low-end and budget goods. Several firms have been successful using single prices with fashion goods in pre-teens and juniors (Corwin, 1990).

Some firms use EDLP on some merchandise while relying on high-low pricing on other merchandise to generate traffic (Reda, 1994). Many firms using prestige or EDLP have scheduled markdowns related to the rate of sale of merchandise. For example, the rule may stipulate a mandatory markdown if sales are two weeks behind plan (Carlson, 1983). The marked-down garments may be hung back on the rack with the regular-price merchandise as a bargain for regular shoppers.

Learning Activity 5.6

1. Read Case 5.2 very carefully. Construct a description of Baby Superstores pricing strategy using Table 5.8 as a model.

Summary

Market tradition continues to define pricing relationships between the manufacturing and retailing sectors despite the implementation of Quick Response business systems. Prices and pricing involve an intricate language related to interrelationships in the trade matrix. Key concepts include list price, first price, wholesale price, billed cost, gross margin, and adjusted gross margin. Common price changes in both the wholesale and retail sectors reflect differences in price elasticity throughout the selling cycle. Customers' perceptions of price may vary greatly from those of manufacturers and retailers.

A body of federal law beginning in the 1890s frames the legality of pricing practices. Resale Price Maintenance has been a point of particular contention over past 30 years. Deceptive retailer pricing has more recently become a legal issue.

Pricing strategies developed and applied by individual firms are the result of decisions made by executive management with input from the other constituencies of the firm. Merchandisers commonly select or develop products that can be sold within the firm's price range, at their price points, within their price lines. Pricing strategies are comprised of particular applications of six pricing components: market price position, price lining, price endings, role of first price, role of markdowns, and price advertising. To be effective, pricing strategies must uphold a firm's image, mission, and business goals.

Key Concepts

above-market price
additional markup
at-market price
below-market price
billed cost
cash discount
comparison price
contract dating
cost-plus pricing
distressed goods
everyday low pricing (EDLP)
first price
high-low pricing

initial markup
job-off price
list price
manufacturer's wholesale price
markdown
markdown cancellation
markup cancellation
penetration pricing
permanent markdown
predatory pricing
premium price
prestige pricing
price endings

price lining
price points
promotional price
quantity discount
quick markdown pricing
regular price
retail merchandise cost
seasonal discount
selling price
shipping terms
status/prestige pricing
temporary markdown
trade discount

Integrated Learning Activity 5.7

1. Review the company profile that you began developing with Integrated Learning Activity 3.6 and continued with Integrated Learning Activity 4.5.

2. Expand the Line Plan Summary to include descriptions for two of the following pricing strategies that are used by or could be appropriate for your store:
   • prestige price strategy
   • quick mark-down strategy

- high-low strategy
- every-day-low price strategy

3. Include in your description of each strategy:

   - role of first price
   - role of premium price
   - role of markdowns
   - number of price changes
   - timing of price changes
   - percent of each markup or markdown

4. Are the strategies consistent with the firms image? Are the strategies effective for the firm you have profiled? Are the strategies fair to customers?

5. Add columns to the previously developed merchandising calendars for your fashion/season and basic staple products (Learning Activities 4.5) related to pricing. Plan when and how much prices will change relative to each selling period when each pricing strategy is applied.

6. Are the strategies consistent with the firm's image? Are the strategies effective for the firm you have profiled? Are the strategies fair to customers?

7. Add columns to the previously developed merchandising calendars for your fashion/season and basic/staple products related to pricing (Learning Activity 5.4). Plan when and how much prices will change relative to each selling period when each pricing strategy is applied.

Recommended Resources

Agins, T. (1990, February 13). As retailers' sales crop up everywhere, regulators wonder if the price is right. *Wall Street Journal,* B1, B5.

Lee, L. (1995, January 10). Wal-Mart wins ruling on pricing policy. *Wall Street Journal,* B8.

Kaufmann, P. J., Smith, C., & Ortmeyer, G. K. (1994). Deception in retailer high-low pricing: A 'rule of reason' approach. *Journal of Retailing,* 70, (2), 115–138.

Manufacturers can refuse to sell to discounters, Supreme Court says. (1988, May 3). *The Daily Tribune,* B4.

Reda, S. (1994, October). Is E.D.L.P. coming up short? *Stores, 76* (10), 22–26.

References

Agins, T. (1990, February 13). As retailers' sales crop up everywhere, regulators wonder if the price is right. *Wall Street Journal,* B1, B5.

Barrett, P. M. (1991, February 27). Anti-discount policies of manufacturers are penalizing certain cut-price stores. *Wall Street Journal,* B1, B4.

Barrett, P. M. (1991, January 11). FTC's hard line on price fixing may foster discounts. *Wall Street Journal,* B1–B2.

Carlson, P. G. (1983, Spring). Fashion retailing: The sensitivity of rate of sale to markdown. *Journal of Retailing, 59* (1), 67–76.

Corwin, P. (1990, April). Finessing the one-price strategy. *Discount Merchandiser, 66–72.*

D'Aulnay, S. (1995, October 30). French facelifts. *Daily News Record,* p. 7.

Helsen, K., & Schmittlein, D. (1992). How does a product market's typical price-promotion pattern affect the timing of households' purchases? *Journal of Retailing, 68,* (3), 316–338.

Lal, R. (1990). Manufacturer trade deals and retail price promotions. *Journal of Marketing Research, 27,* 428–444.

Lattin, J., & Bucklin, R. (1989). Reference effects of price and promotion on brand choice behavior. *Journal of Marketing Research, 26,* 299–310.

Lee, L. (1995, January 10). Wal-Mart wins ruling on pricing policy. *Wall Street Journal,* B8.

Levy, W. K. (1994, November). Beware, the pricing genie is out of the bottle. *Retailing Issues Newsletter:* Arthur Andersen and Center for Retailing Studies, Texas A&M University.

Levy, W. K., & Howard, D. J. (1988). An experimental approach to planning the duration and size of markdowns. *International Journal of Retailing, 3* (2), 148–158.

Kaufmann, P. J., Smith, C., & Ortmeyer, G. K. (1994). Deception in retailer high-low pricing: A 'rule of reason' approach. *Journal of Retailing, 70,* (2), 115–138.

Kunz, G. I. (1995). Behavioral theory of the apparel firm: A beginning. *Clothing and Textiles Research Journal, 13*(4), 252–261.

Kunz, G. I., & Rupe, D. (1995). The status of merchandising technology, part 1: Merchandising technology definition and literature review. Unpublished manuscript. Iowa State University.

Manufacturers can refuse to sell to discounters, Supreme Court says. (1988, May 3). *The Daily Tribune,* B4.

Mason, B. J., Mayer, M. L., & Ezell, H. F. (1984). Foundations of retailing. Plano, TX: Business Publications, Inc.

Novak, V., & Pereira, J. (1995, May 5). Reebok and FTC settle price-fixing charges. *Wall Street Journal,* B1, B8.

Oretega, B. (1993, October 13). Wal-Mart loses a case on pricing. *Wall Street Journal,* A3.

Pashigian, B. P. (1988, December). Demand uncertainty and sales: A study of fashion and markdown pricing. *American Economic Review, 78,* 5, 936–953.

Pashigian, P. B., & Bowen, B. (1991, November). Why are products sold on sale? Explanations of pricing regularities. *The Quarterly Journal of Economics,* 1015–1038.

Ratliff, D. (1996, February). Baby superstore grows up. *Discount Merchandiser,* 22–24.

Reda, S. (1994, October). Is E.D.L.P. coming up short? *Stores, 76* (10), 22–26.

Rupe, K., & Kunz, G. I. (In Press). Building a financially meaningful language of merchandise assortments. *Clothing and Textiles Research Journal.*

Tellis, G. (1986, October). Beyond the many faces of price: An integration of pricing strategies. *Journal of Marketing Research, 50,* 146–160.

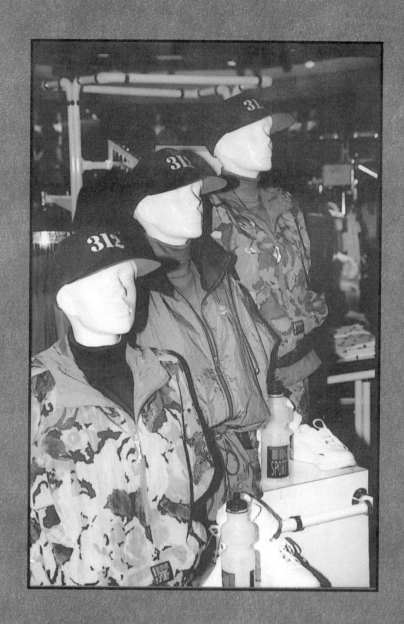

6

Planning and Controlling Merchandise Budgets

Learning Objectives

- Explore static vs. dynamic budgets.
- Examine components of merchandise budgets.
- Practice the mechanics of merchandise budgets.
- Explore the integrated relationships among the components of a merchandise budget.

Firms commonly generate numerous financial statements at the end of each quarter and fiscal year to assess the firm's financial position and establish goals for the coming year. These may include balance sheets, income statements, merchandising ratios, marketing ratios, operating ratios, and financial ratios. Of these, income statements (discussed in Chapter 3) with their corresponding ratios are most closely associated with merchandise planning processes. Merchandise budgets determine the levels of dollar investment in goods for a planning period in the merchandising cycle. Merchandise budgets are formulated within the context of a firm's business plan and goals for the planning period.

Components of Merchandise Budgets

Effective firms systematically make and evaluate plans related to all aspects of their businesses. They make marketing plans, operation plans, finance plans, merchandising plans, overall business plans, and annual goals. **Merchandising plans** primarily cover the planning of merchandise budgets, pricing, assortments, and deliveries. The income statement is a report of a firm's past performance. It provides one of many sources of information that might be used to modify a firm's strategic plans and set its annual productivity goals. A merchandise budget is designed to provide a foundation for implementing merchandising plans and to help the firm meet those goals. Merchandise budgets take different forms depending on the nature of the firm's business and its strategic priorities.

The retail merchandise budgets discussed here assume the firm uses the **retail method of accounting for inventory,** which means that value of inventory is determined by retail prices. So when merchandise price is permanently changed, the value of inventory is changed. For many products, the retail price is a better reflection of merchandise value than merchandise cost. Fashion/seasonal goods, for example, decline in value as the selling period progresses. Reduction in price can mean one of two things from the merchant's perspective: customers won't buy it at the original price because the price is too high or the merchandise needs to be cleared from inventory because of broken assortments or end of the selling period. In any case, the permanent price change is a conscious business decision on the part of the merchandiser with the purpose of increasing the rate of sale of the goods. The price reduction reflects a reduction in the retail value of the merchandise.

The merchandise budget discussed here is dynamic and forecast-based. Retail Merchandising Service Automation, Inc. (RMSA), a California-based consulting firm, uses a planning system that includes a dynamic merchandise budget similar to the one in Table 6.1. The budget is based on bottom-up, detailed sales and inventory forecasts for individual stores for each merchandise classification. With minor modifications this type of a budget could also be used as a merchandise plan for a manufacturer. The manufacturer would plan by classification but not plan for individual stores unless they had their own retail outlet operation. They might, however, plan by retail customer.

The budget is set up to allow immediate comparison, where appropriate, of actual figures for last year, plan for this year, actual figures for this year and percent change. The major elements of the budget relate to:

1. **Sales** at retail for the previous and current year for the same month
2. **Stock** at the beginning of each month and **stock/sales ratios**
3. **Reductions** compared to last year and **reductions as a percent of net sales**
4. **Planned purchases** and **merchandise on order** at retail and at cost
5. **Open-to-buy** at retail and at cost

As the dynamic plan is updated, it consistently shows history for the past two months and projected sales, inventory, and other information for the next ten months. Implementing this dynamic merchandise budget means the firm must have an integrated, computerized information technology system or a contract with a consulting service like RMSA to process the data. The more frequently the system can update the budget, the better merchandisers can plan. Most systems can update monthly; some can provide weekly figures, but only a few can update daily with the detailed information required for this budget.

Learning Activity 6.1

Dynamic Merchandise Budget

1. What is the fundamental purpose of a budget?
2. What is the fundamental purpose of a merchandise budget?
3. Why should a merchandise budget be dynamic as opposed to static?
4. What is required to make a budget forecast-based?

Mechanics of Merchandise Budgets

To better understand the conceptual relationships among the parts of a merchandise budget, a simplified merchandise budget with last year's actual sales for biking shorts at Mike's Bikes is presented in Company Profile 6.1, Mike's Bikes, Part 2. The elements are the same as for the dynamic budget in Table 6.1 but the comparative figures for each element are omitted to make the layout easier to interpret. A discussion of the thought process required to determine the numbers for each of the elements in the budget follows the company profile. All of the formulas and calculations in this section are presented in an outcomes type format, that is, the unknown concept being sought is listed first followed by the formula.

Planning Sales for a Classification by Store

Ultimately a sales plan comes down to past sales plus some percent increase or decrease. The forecasting process that determines the percent increase or decrease may include the following:

- sales for the previous year(s), same selling period.
- sales percentages by month or week of the selling period.

TABLE 6.1

Example of a merchandise budget.[1]

DYNAMIC, FORECAST-BASED MERCHANDISE BUDGET

Store _____ Merchandise Classification _____

Elements of Budget	Months and Weeks of Sale of the Merchandising Cycle					
	Feb 1–4	Mar 5–9	Apr 10–13	May 14–17	Jun 18–22	
Sales						
last year actual						
this year plan						
this year actual						
% change in actual						
Inventory First of Month						
last year actual						
this year plan						
this year actual						
Inventory/Sales Ratio						
this year plan						
this year actual						
Markdowns						
last year actual						
this year plan						
this year actual						
Purchases at Retail						
last year actual						
this year plan						
this year actual						
Purchases at Cost						
last year actual						
this year plan						
this year actual						
Initial Markup Percent						
last year actual						
this year plan						
On Order (Retail)						
On Order (Cost)						
Open-to-Buy (Retail)						
Open-to-Buy (Cost)						

[1]Based on a merchandise plan from Retail Merchandising Services Automation, Inc., Riverside, California.

Square Feet _____ Date _____

	Jul 23–26	Aug 27–30	Sep 31–35	Oct 36–39	Nov 40–43	Dec 44–48	Jan 49–52	Total or Average

COMPANY PROFILE 6.1

Mike's Bikes, Part 2

Merchandise Budget

The outlook for Mike's Bikes is bright. Biking is predicted to grow in popularity into the next century. Sales have increased about 5 percent every year except one and they have made a profit every year since the third year. A Sam's Club will open in the West Des Moines area during the coming year, but it is expected to have little impact on sales at Mike's Bikes.

Michelle and Kevin are active, visible members of local and regional biking clubs. The store regularly supports biking activities in the area and the state. They are active in the Chamber of Commerce and meet regularly with other entrepreneurs.

Kevin maintains an extensive database of current customers and uses direct mail as the primary form of advertising. He uses three mailings a year: early spring, pre-RAGBRAI, and holiday. Kevin estimates that RAGBRAI alone contributes 10 percent of sales.

The merchandise mix includes three categories: bikes (about 50 percent of sales) apparel (20 percent) and accessories (15 percent). In addition, bike service accounts for 15 percent.

They stock three types of bikes in both men's and women's styles: mountain bikes, road bikes, and hybrid bikes. They also have a few children's bikes.

Bikes have 6,200 square feet of space. Markup on bikes is 30 to 35 percent.

They carry four classifications of apparel. Biking shorts are 50 percent of apparel sales, with an average first price of $45. Shoes are 20 percent, shirts and jerseys 20 percent, and other, including gloves and outerwear, 10 percent. Apparel is crowded into 1,000 square feet of space. Markup on apparel is 50 percent to 60 percent.

Accessories include three classifications: helmets, water bottles and bags, and hardware accessories, such as computers to track distance, time, heart rate, etc. Initial markup on accessories is about 60 percent.

The service department assembles bikes for display, as well as assembles and repairs bikes for customers. The service department sells bike parts, tires, and wheels and has 2,000 square feet of space.

Markdowns are infrequent on bikes and they are used on apparel and accessories primarily to clear inventory. The only price promotion is on biking shorts in early July just prior to RAGBRAI. Reductions of inventory value because of theft and inventory damage is minimal, but they do provide employee discounts. An example of a Mike's Bikes merchandise budget follows.

TABLE 6.2

Mike's Bikes Merchandise Budget.

Classification Biking Shorts		Store Merle Hay		Square Ft 600		Selling Period 1		Year 1996
		Actual Dollars by Months and Weeks of Sale						
Elements of Budget	Feb 1–4	Mar 5–9	Apr 10–13	May 14–17	Jun 18–22	Jul 23–26	Aug 27–31	Total
Actual Sales		20,000	30,000	25,000	25,000	38,000	12,000	150,000
Actual FOM Stock		50,000	70,000	65,000	65,000	57,000	16,000	
Stock to Sales Ratios		2.5	2.3	2.6	2.6	1.5	1.3	
Actual Reductions			2,000	2,000	2,000	3,000	4,000	13,000
Merchandise Received	50,000	40,000	27,000	27,000	19,000			163,000
On Order at Retail	50,000	30,000	15,000	10,000				105,000
Open-to-Buy at Retail		10,000	12,000	17,000	19,000			58,000
Open-to-Buy at Cost		4,500	5,400	7,650	8,550			26,100
Initial Markup								55%

- recent trends in sales.
- changes inside the store, such as remodeling.
- factors outside the store, such as new competition.
- comparisons of productivity with competitors.
- trends in demographic and lifestyle priorities of target customers.
- planned marketing strategies for the selling period.
- short- and long-term goals of the firm.

Ultimately, the calculation of planned sales for a selling period for an ongoing business comes down to the following formula:

$$\textit{Planned sales for the selling period} =$$
$$\textit{past selling period sales} \times (1 + \% \textit{ change in sales})$$

Once the sales are planned and the other elements in the merchandise budget are determined, success of the selling period and the generation of the planned productivity figures is highly dependent on achieving the planned sales level. Planned sales necessarily becomes the **sales goal** for the selling period.

At Mike's Bikes, with last season's sales of $150,000 for biking shorts and a plan for a 5-percent increase as indicated in the company profile, planned sales for 1997 are as follows:

planned sales for the selling period	=	*past period sales*	×	*(1 + % change)*
$157,500	=	$150,000	×	(1 + 5%)

Sales can then be allocated to months and/or weeks of the selling period based on previous percent of sales per month or week, unless forecasts indicate that adjustments are necessary. Based on the 1996 merchandise budget, percent of sales for 1996 by month are as follows:

Percent Sales per Month		=	1996 Monthly Sales	÷	Sales for Selling Period	×	100
Mar	13.33%	=	$ 20,000	÷	$150,000	×	100
Apr	20.00%	=	30,000	÷	$150,000	×	100
May	16.67%	=	25,000	÷	$150,000	×	100
June	16.67%	=	25,000	÷	$150,000	×	100
July	25.33%	=	38,000	÷	$150,000	×	100
Aug	8.00%	=	12,000	÷	$150,000	×	100
Total	100%		$150,000				

Based on their sales forecast, Michelle and Kevin agreed to use the same sales percentages per month for 1997 as 1996. Planned sales by month for 1997 Selling Period 1 is as follows:

Monthly Planned Sales[1]		=	Planned Sales for Selling Period	×	Sales Percent per Month
Mar	$ 21,000	=	$157,500	×	13.33%
Apr	$ 31,500	=	$157,500	×	20.00%
May	$ 26,250	=	$157,500	×	16.67%
June	$ 26,250	=	$157,500	×	16.67%
July	$ 39,900	=	$157,500	×	25.33%
Aug	$ 12,600	=	$157,500	×	8.00%
Total	$157,500		$157,500		100%

[1]Planned sales are rounded to the nearest $25.

Planning Sales Based on Space Productivity

Space is a resource that must be used productively for a firm to succeed. For example, in New York City, value of real estate is assessed by the square foot. McDonald's restaurants there utilize vertical space, with street-level and seating both upstairs and down. Grocers allocate shelf space by the inch or centimeter and measure productivity of shelf space by the linear inch or centimeter. Catalog companies measure sales productivity by square inch of catalog space. Farmers measure productivity of space in bushels per acre; retailers measure productivity of space in sales per square foot. Retail display fixtures are evaluated based on how many dollars per square foot in sales a fixture should be able to generate.

The floor space allocated to a particular merchandise classification is expected to generate a planned number of dollars so the firm can meet its sales goals. The firm must balance sales productivity of the classification with the amount of space allocated to the classification. Merchandise categories differ greatly in **sales per square foot,** as indicated by industry averages. There are also wide ranges among specialty, department and discount stores. The ranges of sales per square foot in Table 6.3 span the store types.

Sales per square foot can be used as a zero-based or a bottom-up merchandise planning tool. **Zero-based budgeting** means no previous levels of sales or productivity are assumed. The budget begins with a blank sheet of paper. Bottom-up planning means plans are based on numbers generated at the store and classification level. Zero-based plans are sometimes more innovative than history-based plans; bottom-up plans are often regarded as more realistic than top-down plans. To set up a sales plan for a classification for a defined period based on sales per square foot, identify industry-wide annual sales per square foot generated by the classification and determine number of square feet allocated to the classification. Decide

TABLE 6.3

Ranges of sales per square foot by merchandise category.

Category or Classification	Sales per Square Foot	
	Low	High
women's and girl's apparel	$150	$460
men's and boy's apparel	$110	$400
women's accessories	$140	$415
footwear	$250	$450
cosmetics/health & beauty	$190	$345
sporting goods	$150	$280
home furnishings	$ 50	$170

if industry-wide averages should be adjusted based on sales forecasts. In a zero-based budget, planned sales could be determined based on sales per square foot as follows:

sales for the period = sales per week × weeks of sale

sales per week =
square feet for the class × (annual sales per square foot ÷ 52 weeks per year)

Planning sales based on the sale-per-square-foot method for Mike's Bikes requires referring back to Company Profile 3.1, Mike's Bikes, Part 1 (page 90), where annual sales are reported as $1,500,000 and total square feet in the store is 10,000. Thus, annual average sales per square foot is $150 ($1,500,000 annual sales ÷ 10,000 square feet). Apparel is 20 percent of sales ($300,000) and has 1,000 square feet of space. Thus, apparel sales are $300 per square foot ($300,000 in annual sales ÷ 1000 square feet). Remember that Mike's Bikes is closed in February, so annual sales is based on only 48 weeks of sale instead of the customary 52. Planned sales for biking shorts can then be calculated as follows:

sales for the period = sales per week × weeks of sale
$162,500 = $6,250 × 26 weeks

where:

sales per week =
square feet for the class × (annual sales per square foot ÷ 48 weeks per year)

$6,250 per week =
1,000 square feet × ($300 per square foot ÷ 48 weeks per year)

Planning sales based on space allocation is an alternate method to the percent increase or decrease method previously described. Both methods may be used for the same selling periods and the results can then be compared to evaluate the effectiveness of sales planning methods. Space productivity can also be used to *estimate* the sales of privately owned competitors or firms that do not reveal their financial status. Space productivity may also provide the basis of a business plan for an entrepreneur starting a new business.

Learning Activity 6.2

Planning sales

1. Before Mike's Bikes could implement the sales plan demonstrated in the previous discussion, it was announced that RAGBRAI would not be held in 1997. How might that affect the sales plan? Recalculate Mike's Bikes sales plan without RAGBRAI sales.

2. Calculate a sales plan for bikes at Mike's Bikes using the percentage-increase method and the sales-per-square-foot method. Use Company Profiles 3.1 and 6.1, Mike's Bikes, Parts 1 and 2 (pages 90 and 168), as a basis of your sales plan. Follow the series of steps demonstrated in the discussion of biking shorts. What are the advantages and disadvantages of each method?

Planning Reductions

Reductions are anything other than sales that reduce the value of inventory. When merchandise is sold, it is usually assumed that the value of inventory is reduced and new merchandise must be purchased to replace it so the firm can remain in business. When the value of merchandise is reduced by some means other than sales, merchandise must be purchased to replace the lost value or sales goals cannot be met. Reductions of inventory value by other means than sales is an implicit aspect of operating a manufacturing or retailing business. Therefore, reductions must be planned into merchandise budgets. Reductions take three forms: markdowns for purposes of sales promotion or inventory clearance, markdowns as employee discounts, and inventory shortage because of shoplifting, employee theft, damaged merchandise or record-keeping errors.

Reductions vary greatly by classification of merchandise. For example:

- cosmetics, books and drugs tend to be less than 5 percent of sales.
- costume jewelry about 10 percent of sales.
- men's suits may be a high as 20 percent of sales.
- women's dresses and shoes may be as high as 30 percent of sales.

- highly seasonal goods, such as holiday decorations, may be more than 30 percent of sales.

Since reductions tend to vary greatly by month during the selling period, it is common to plan total reductions for the selling period. Reductions are usually calculated as a percent of net sales. For purposes of planning reductions, a formula is:

$$\frac{percent}{reductions} = \frac{reductions \ for}{a \ selling \ period} \div \frac{net \ sales \ for}{same \ period} \times 100$$

The percent-reductions figure is included in the formula for planning merchandise to receive for the selling period.

For Mike's Bikes, as shown in the merchandise budget, reductions last year for biking shorts were $13,000.

$$\frac{percent}{reductions} = \frac{reductions \ for}{a \ selling \ period} \div \frac{net \ sales \ for}{same \ period} \times 100$$
$$8.67\% = \$13,000 \div \$150,000 \times 100$$

If the company could reduced its reductions, gross margin would increase because sales would be higher. Options for Mike's Bikes include decreasing employee discounts and trying to sell more merchandise at regular price. If present personnel and promotional policies continue, 8.67 percent may be a realistic reductions planning figure for Selling Period 1 for 1997.

To plan total reductions for the selling season do the following:

$$planned \ reductions = planned \ sales \times planned \ reduction \ percent$$
$$\$13,650 = 157,500 \times 8.67\%$$

To plan reductions by month for 1997, do the following:

Monthly Reduction Plan	=	Last Year's Monthly Reductions	÷	Last Year's Monthly Sales	×	This Year's Planned Sales
Mar	0	=	0	÷	20,000	×	21,000
Apr	$ 2,100	=	2,000	÷	30,000	×	31,500
May	$ 2,100	=	2,000	÷	25,000	×	26,250
Jun	$ 2,100	=	2,000	÷	25,000	×	26,250
Jul	$ 3,150	=	3,000	÷	38,000	×	39,900
Aug	$ 4,200	=	4,000	÷	12,000	×	12,600
Total	$13,650						

Planning the Amount of Merchandise to Receive

Planning the amount of merchandise to receive in order to achieve planned sales involves incorporating planned reductions. Since reductions reduce inventory value and revenue from sales, the amount of inventory available for sale must equal planned sales plus planned reductions. At Mike's Bikes, planned merchandise to receive for the selling period is calculated as follows:

$$planned\ merchandise\ to\ receive\ =\ planned\ sales\ +\ planned\ reductions$$
$$\$171{,}150\qquad\qquad =\quad \$157{,}500\quad +\quad \$13{,}650$$

In order to achieve the sales goal of $157,500 for biking shorts for the selling period, Mike's Bikes needs a total of $171,150 in inventory.

> ### *Learning Activity 6.3*
> #### Planning the amount of merchandise to receive for a selling period
>
> 1. Plan the annual amount of bikes to receive at Mike's Bikes. Assume the selling period is 48 weeks, since they are closed during the month of February. Use Company Profiles 3.1 and 6.1, Mike's Bikes, Parts 1 and 2, and Learning Activity 6.2, #2, as the basis of your thinking.
>
> 2. Big Bear, a well-established farm store, has decided to add flannel shirts to its product offerings for the fall selling period. The first price of the shirts is $30. Big Bear expects to devote about 36 square feet to display the shirts in each store. Big Bear expects the shirts to generate $95 per square foot during the fall selling period. Markdowns are expected to be 10 percent of sales. Determine how each of the following merchandise budget figures were calculated and write out the formula for each:
>
>   a) What is the sales goal for the sale of flannel shirts in each store? $3420
>   b) What is the total dollars in markdowns? $342
>   c) How much merchandise will Big Bear have to receive in each store in order to make their sales plan? $3762.
>   d) How many units of merchandise will have to be sold in each store? 126.
>
> 3. You are a children's wear merchandiser for Duber's, a small discount department store that specializes in interesting children's apparel at good value. The store's mission is to provide serviceable fashion goods at a low price. You are planning sales, reductions, and merchandise to receive for girl's tops. The economy is flat and sales are not expected to increase.
>
>   Last year's net sales for the store is $2,500,000. Children's apparel is about 20 percent of sales. Girl's apparel represents 40 percent of children's apparel and tops are 35 percent of girl's apparel. The four selling periods for girl's tops and the distribution of sales are as follows: spring (15%), summer (10%), back-to-school (60%) and holiday (15%). The selling periods are approximately equal

in length. The average first price is $10. Markdowns are 15 percent of sales and there is no inventory on hand.

Determine how the following merchandise budget figures were found and write out the formula:

a) Last year's children's sales? $500,000
b) Last year's girl's sales? $200,000
c) Last year's girl's tops sales? $70,000
d) Last year's spring tops sales? $10,500
e) Next year's planned spring tops sales? $10,500
f) Markdowns on planned spring tops? $1,575
g) Planned spring tops to receive to make the sales plan? $12,075
h) Total units of tops for spring? 1208
i) Sales goal for planned spring tops? $10,500

Planning Inventory and Purchases During the Selling Period

Planning and controlling inventory to support planned sales during specified periods should accomplish four things:

- fulfill sales goals
- avoid stockouts
- prevent overstocks
- minimize inventory investment (Lewison, 1994)

The means of accomplishing these goals is different depending on how and why products change. (Refer back to Figure 3.2, page 79.) The fashion/basic continuum relates to frequency of demand for changes in styling and the seasonal/staple continuum relates to changes associated with time of the year. When merchandise classifications are well defined by a manufacturer or retailer, the group of merchandise in the classification will fall into one of the four quadrants. Planning inventory and purchases for goods in each quadrant differs because of the nature of the merchandise in relation to customer demand. The following discussion begins with Quadrant 3, since at Mike's Bikes biking shorts are most logically regarded as fashion/seasonal goods with a relatively long selling period of 26 weeks. Inventory planning for basic/staple goods (Quadrant 1) and fashion/staple and basic/seasonal (Quadrants 2 and 4) follow.

Quadrant 3, Fashion/Seasonal Goods

Biking shorts at Mike's Bikes are more realistically regarded as fashion/seasonal goods that fall into Quadrant 3 of Figure 3.2. Fashion/seasonal goods experience frequent demand for change in styling and rate of sale because of the time of the year, thus the total selling period is 26 weeks or less. Defined weeks of sale for particular styles in a classification results in the need to plan zero-to-zero inventory for each selling period. The ideal condition is when inventory for the classification starts with no stock and ends with no stock. The **stock-to-sales ratio method** of planning inventory is most appropriate for fashion/seasonal goods (Mason, Mayer, & Ezell, 1984, 1994). The assumption is that the merchant should maintain a certain ratio of goods on hand to monthly sales (Lewison, 1994).

The formula for calculating a stock to sales ratio is as follows:

stock to sales ratio = total inventory for the period ÷ sales for the same period

A stock to sales ratio states the amount of inventory on hand to support a given amount of sales. A stock/sales ratio of 2 means that $6,000 of inventory was on hand to support $3,000 in sales. If ratios were very low for a month, it may indicate shortage of stock, too low planned sales or clearance for end-of-selling period; if ratios are very high, it may indicate too much inventory on hand or sales planned too high or that inventory is being built up in anticipation of a sales peak. The monthly stock-to-sales ratios are useful guides for planning necessary first-of-the-month (FOM) stock. To have merchandise available for sale on the first of the month, it must be received during the previous month.

For Mike's Bikes, the monthly stock-to-sales ratios are reported in the merchandise budget for 1996. For example, the stock-to-sales ratio for April was calculated as follows:

stock to sales ratio = total inventory for the period ÷ sales for the same period
    2.3   = $70,000   ÷ $ 30,000

The stock-to-sales ratios for biking shorts were similar, month by month, throughout the period until stock was allowed to decline in anticipation of the end of the selling period, when they wanted all inventory to be sold. When working with fashion/seasonal merchandise, each selling period ends by clearing inventory and marking down merchandise to stimulate sales. Notice that the stock-to-sales ratio for August is 1.3, which provides only enough merchandise to cover sales and reductions so ending inventory for the selling period is zero. The next selling period begins with all new merchandise.

Using the stock-to-sales ratio method of planning inventory, planned first of month (FOM) stock is determined by:

Planned FOM Stock[1]	=	Planned Sales	×	Stock-to-Sales Ratio
Feb	0	=	0	×	0
Mar	$52,500	=	21,000	×	2.5
Apr	$72,450	=	31,500	×	2.3
May	$68,250	=	26,250	×	2.6
Jun	$68,250	=	26,250	×	2.6
Jul	$59,850	=	39,900	×	1.5
Aug	$16,750	=	12,600	×	1.3

[1]Numbers are rounded to nearest $25.

Quadrant 1, Basic/Staple Goods

Products that fall into Quadrant 1 of Figure 3.2 are basic/staple goods that change little in styling over time and also change little related to the time of the year. New products are introduced infrequently. The length of the selling period ranges from 26 to 52 weeks a year. Planning inventory, then, is primarily a matter of determining the quantities of current goods required to maintain complete assortments throughout the selling period being planned. This type of merchandise lends itself to automated replenishment with computer-generated orders managed either by the vendor or the retailer. The periodic replenishment method (Donnellan, 1996) of planning inventory lends itself to merchandise that can be automatically replaced through computer generated orders.

The formula for periodic replenishment is:

maximum inventory = (lead time × rate of sale) + reserve stock

where

Maximum inventory is the amount of merchandise needed on hand during the period;

Lead time is a combination of 1) time between placing orders, and 2) time between placing and receiving the order;

Rate of sale is the retail value of units commonly sold during a reorder period; and

Reserve stock is additional stock kept on hand to prevent stockouts if sales exceed plan;

the formula is

2.3 × square root of (lead time × rate of sale) (Donnellan, 1996)

Periodic replenishment inventory planning assumes the rate of sale is relatively uniform throughout the selling period and that there is an ongoing need for similar merchandise in inventory. It is common to replenish basic/staple goods at least weekly, and sometimes daily. These strategies greatly reduce stockouts and increase sales. Reductions are infrequent and may be less than two percent of sales, since they are related primarily to employee discounts, damaged merchandise, and inventory shrinkage. Clearance is seldom required because the same styles, sizes, and colors are continuously included in the assortment. At Mike's Bikes, parts for bike repairs could be set up with a periodic replenishment system to keep parts continuously in stock with the lowest possible average inventory.

For purposes of comparing to the stock-to-sales ratio method of inventory planning, assume that biking shorts at Mike's Bikes had the characteristics of basic/staple goods, and were ordered every two weeks with two weeks between placing and receiving an order. Inventory would be calculated as follows:

maximum inventory = *(lead time* × *rate of sale) + reserve stock*
maximum inventory = *[(2 + 2)* × *($171,150 ÷ 24 weeks)]*
      + [2.3 × *square root of 4(4* × *$14,263)]*
maximum inventory = *(4* × *$14,263) + $549*
maximum inventory = *$57,601*

where

Four weeks lead time = (two weeks between placing orders + two weeks between placing the order and receiving the order);
$14,263 rate of sale = $171,150 merchandise to receive ÷ 12 reorder periods of two weeks each = the retail value of merchandise commonly sold during a reorder period; and
$549 reserve stock = 2.3 × square root of (4 lead time × $14,263 rate of sale)

If Mike's Bikes used the periodic replenishment method to calculate inventory, they would need to keep about $57,000 in biking shorts on hand during the selling period. An estimate of the number of units of biking shorts on hand can be determined by dividing maximum inventory by average first price:

number of units in inventory = maximum inventory ÷ average first price
      1,280 units   = $57, 601   ÷ $45

Quadrant 4, Basic/Seasonal and Quadrant 2, Fashion/Staple Goods

To produce more realistic results when stock turnover is high (more than six times a year) or relatively stable, basic/seasonal and fashion/staple goods (Quadrants 4 and 2 respectively in Figure 3.2) may be planned using the **percentage variation method.** Applying this method results in inventories that are closer to average than the other inventory planning methods (Berman & Evans, 1995). This method attempts to adjust stock levels in relation to actual variations in sales (Lewison, 1994). The formula is:

planned first-of-the-month stock = average inventory × 1/2 [1 + (planned sales for the month ÷ average monthly sales)]

Planned FOM Stock		=	Average Inventory	×	½ [1 +	(Planned Sales	÷	Average Monthly Sales)]
Mar	50,715	=	56,350	×	½ [1 +	21,000	÷	$26,250]
Apr	61,985	=	56,350	×	½ [1 +	31,500	÷	$26,250]
May	56,350	=	56,350	×	½ [1 +	26,250	÷	$26,250]
Jun	56,350	=	56,350	×	½ [1 +	26,250	÷	$26,250]
Jul	71,001	=	56,350	×	½ [1 +	39,900	÷	$26,250]
Aug	41,699	=	56,350	×	½ [1 +	12,600	÷	$26,250]

where:

average inventory is $56,350
average monthly sales = total monthly sales ÷ number of months

Planning inventory is clearly a challenging activity. The first step is to analyze the merchandise in terms of the nature of change (fashion, seasonal, basic, staple) and then choose the most appropriate method of planning inventory. The amount of inventory required for the first of each month depends on what assumptions are made about the needs for inventory; these assumptions differ for each method of calculation.

Learning Activity 6.4

Planning inventory

1. Assume that Mike's Bikes was able to work out QR partnerships with their biking shorts suppliers so they could reorder every week with a one-week lead time between order placement and delivery. Using the periodic replenishment system, calculate maximum inventory when placing orders every week with a one-week lead time. How does the maximum inventory on QR compare to maximum inventory with orders every two weeks with a two-week lead time?

2. What are the advantages and disadvantages of placing orders more frequently? What are the advantages and disadvantages of a shorter lead-time? What are the advantages and disadvantages of automating an ordering system?

3. Plan the maximum inventory for bikes using the periodic replenishment method. Use Company Profiles 3.1 and 6.1, Mike's Bikes, Part's 1 and 2, and Learning Activity 6.2, #2 and 6.3, #1, for necessary information. Is the periodic replenishment method appropriate for planning bike inventory? What other method might be used? Why?

Planning Open-to-Buy and Merchandise to Receive by Month

Open-to-buy is a means of controlling merchandise investment before and during a selling period. Dollar **open-to-buy** is the difference between planned merchandise to receive and merchandise on order:

dollar open-to-buy = planned merchandise to receive - merchandise on order

Calculation of total dollar open-to-buy for 1996 and planned total open-to-buy for 1997 for biking shorts for selling period 1, is as follows:

Selling Period 1, 1996 Actual		**Selling Period 1, Plan for 1997**	
actual sales	$150,000	planned sales	$157,500
+ actual reductions	$ 13,000	+ planned reductions	$ 13,650
= total merchandise to receive	$163,000	= planned merchandise to receive	$171,150
− actual merchandise on order	$105,000	− planned merchandise on order	$111,250
= actual open to buy at retail	$ 58,000	= planned open-to-buy at retail	$ 59,900

Open-to-buy during the selling period means money is available to provide flexibility to adjust the receipt of stock to the rate of sale. Open-to-buy is the planned purchase of yet-to-be determined merchandise, for instance, hot-selling or popular merchandise not included in initial orders. But if sales are not up to plan, open-to-buy may not be invested in merchandise at all.

Further monthly planning of open-to-buy refines the amount of stock available according to planned sales. First, a store determines planned merchandise to receive by month, followed by planned merchandise on-order and planned open-to-buy. The formula for calculating planned merchandise to receive by month is as follows:

planned merchandise to   = (planned EOM stock + planned sales + planned
receive by month   reductions) − planned FOM stock

where

end of month   = *first of the month (FOM) stock of the following month*
(EOM) stock

For example:

planned merchandise
to receive for April = (planned April EOM stock + planned April sales +
                      planned April reductions) − planned April FOM stock
      $29,400 = ($68,250 + $31,500 + $2,100) − $72,450

Last year, Mike's Bikes held a little more than one-third (35%) of total merchandise needed in open-to-buy. The rest was planned as merchandise on-order for delivery in specified months during the selling period. Proportion of merchandise on order is greater early in the selling period; proportion of open-to-buy is greater late in the selling period. Kevin would have merchandise on order for Selling Period #2 (August to January) during July and August, when no merchandise is on order or open-to-buy for Selling Period #1. Based on the merchandise plan so far for biking shorts:

Elements & Calculation	Feb	Mar	Apr	May	June	July	Aug	Total
EOM stock	52,500	72,500	68,250	68,250	59,850	16,750	0	
+ planned sales	0	21,000	31,500	26,250	26,250	39,900	12,600	$157,500
+ planned reductions	0	0	2,100	2,100	2,100	3,150	4,200	$ 13,650
= total merchandise needed	0	93,500	101,850	96,600	88,200	59,800	16,800	
− planned FOM stock	0	52,500	72,450	68,250	68,250	59,850[1]	16,750[1]	
= planned merchandise to receive	52,500	41,000	29,400	28,350	19,950	0	0	171,200[1]
− total merchandise on order	52,500	28,875	16,250	13,625	0	0	0	111,250
= planned open to buy at retail	0	12,125	13,150	14,725	19,950	0	0	59,950

[1]These discrepancies are the result of rounding error.

Planning Initial Markup

Initial markup is the difference between merchandise cost and first price. First price is a retailer's planning price and the basis of all price changes. Initial markup is part of the merchandise plan, but is closely associated with the income statement, specifically gross margin. The amount of money available for reductions, expenses, and profit is largely dependent on initial markup as the selling period progresses. For accounting purposes:

percent initial markup = (reductions + expenses + profit) ÷ (sales + reductions)

Merchandise purchased for and sold during the selling period being planned needs to have an average initial markup according to plan in order to make profitability goals. If the planned percent initial markup seems too high to be realistic, adjustments must be made in planned reductions, expenses or profits.

Mike's Bikes had an average initial markup on biking shorts of 55 percent on retail. To determine open-to-buy at cost for Selling Period #1, do the following:

planned open-to-buy at cost = open-to-buy at retail × (1 − percent markup on retail)
$26,950   = $59,900   ×   (1 − 55%)

Open-to-buy at cost is the actual dollar amount planned for spending at wholesale in the market. The same method can be used to calculate open-to-buy at cost for each month.

The completed merchandise budget for biking shorts based on the stock-to-sales ratio method of inventory planning is presented in Table 6.4. This provides guidelines for pricing strategy and developing merchandise assortments.

TABLE 6.4

Completed Merchandise Budget for Mike's Bikes.[1]

Classification Biking Shorts	Store Merle Hay		Square Ft 600		Selling Period 1			Year 1997
				Actual Dollars by Months and Weeks of Sale				
Elements of Budget	Feb 1–4	Mar 5–9	Apr 10–13	May 14–17	Jun 18–22	Jul 23–26	Aug 27–31	Total
Sales Last Year		20,000	30,000	25,000	25,000	38,000	12,000	150,000
Planned Sales		21,000	31,500	26,250	26,250	39,900	12,600	157,500
FOM Stock Last Year		50,000	70,000	65,000	65,000	57,000	16,000	
Planned FOM Stock		52,500	72,450	68,250	68,250	59,850	16,750	
Stock-to-Sales Ratio		2.5	2.3	2.6	2.6	1.5	1.3	
Reductions Last Year			2,000	2,000	2,000	3,000	4,000	13,000
Planned Reductions			2,100	2,100	2,100	3,150	4,200	13,650
Merchandise Received	50,000	40,000	27,000	27,000	19,000	0	0	163,000
Planned Merchandise Received	52,500	41,000	29,400	28,350	19,950	0	0	171,200
On Order at Retail	50,000	30,000	15,000	10,000				105,000
Planned On Order	52,500	28,875	15,000	9,350	0	0	0	105,725
Open-to-Buy at Retail		10,000	12,000	17,000	19,000	0	0	58,000
Planned Open-to-Buy at Retail	0	12,125	13,150	14,725	19,950	0	0	59,900
Open-to-Buy at Cost		4,500	5,400	7,650	8,550	0	0	26,100
Planned Open-to-Buy at Cost		5,450	5,925	6,625	8,975	0	0	26,975
Initial Markup								55%

[1]Numbers for plan are rounded to the nearest $25.

Summary

Firms often incorporate some sort of "management by objectives" philosophy into their business plans. This means that goals are set for business success. Short-term goals may relate to expectations for a merchandising cycle or a selling period within a merchandising cycle. Measurements of success often take the form of ratios that relate to the responsibilities of merchandising, marketing, operations, and finance. Merchandising success is reflected on the firm's income statement, particularly in relation to cost of merchandise sold and gross margin.

Planned percent gross margin is achieved through planning and controlling the merchandise budget, pricing, and assortments. Operating profit is determined by the relationship between gross margin and operating expenses. Operating expenses relate to the management of people and physical property and are primarily the responsibility of the operations constituency; gross margin is the result of acquisition and sale of goods and services, the primary responsibilities of merchandisers.

Merchandise budgets are tools for planning and controlling dollar investment in inventory. With today's information technology systems, it is possible for budgets to be forecast-based and dynamic. It is tempting to plan sales for the coming period based primarily on sales history, since it is comparatively easy to calculate percent increase or decrease. However, good forecasts are based on a wide range of variables that are chosen because their relevance to a particular firm's business environment. A dynamic budget is one that is updated frequently, preferably daily, to help identify the most recent historic trends. A dynamic budget assists with merchandise decisions before, during, and after a selling period.

A merchandise budget incorporates an integrated system of numbers representing dollars and merchandising ratios including sales, reductions, inventory, merchandise to receive, open-to-buy, and initial markup. Outcomes related to each part of the budget affects all other parts of the budget. The mathematics calculation of each budget component helps explain these interdependencies.

Key Concepts

additional markup	gross sales	open-to-buy
chargebacks	initial markup (IMU)	operating expense
cost of goods sold	inventory	operating profit
customer returns and allowances	merchandising plans	other income and expenses
gross margin	net profit	
	net sales	*continued*

percentage variation method of planning inventory	reductions	sales per square foot
	merchandise to receive	stock-to-sales ratio method of planning inventory
	retail method of inventory	
periodic replenishment method of planning inventory	sales	transfers
	sales goals	

Integrated Learning Activities 6.5

1. Review the company profile that you have developing based on Integrated Learning Activities 3.7, 4.6, and 5.8. Develop the following components of a merchandise budget.

   a) Identify and/or estimate annual sales for the total firm and the local store for last year.

   b) Estimate size of the local store and annual sales per square foot (based on and/or compared to industry averages).

   c) Estimate the number of square feet devoted to apparel and total sales of apparel annually.

   d) Using space productivity method, estimate annual and selling period sales for the basic/staple and fashion/seasonal classes for which you have developed merchandise calendars.

   e) Based on your company profile, what is a reasonable increase in sales to plan for the coming year? Develop a planned sales figure for each of your merchandise classes.

   f) Based on your merchandise classes and your pricing strategies, plan an average markdown rate for each of your merchandise classes. Calculate total merchandise to receive at retail for each selling period in order to achieve your sales goals.

2. Read Case 6.1 very carefully.

   g) Develop an income statement and associated financial ratios for Kmart based on the information presented in the case.

   h) Create a financial example of how "pushing more merchandise through the pipeline faster . . . pads slim profit margins."

   i) What merchandise budget-related ratios are presented in addition to those associated with the income statement. What is the meaning of these ratios in terms of well-being of the company?

   j) What guidance is provided in Case 6.1 in relation to developing a merchandise budget?

Recommended Resources

Allen, R. L. (1982, September). Planning a strategy for reordering goods. *Chain Store Age*, general merchandise edition, pp. 94–95.

Gable, M. & Topol, M. T. (1987, Fall). Planning practices of small-scale retailers. *American Journal of Small Business, 12*(2), 19–32.

CASE 6.1

Kmart's Stock Surge Masks A Weakness at the Core

From Strom, S. (1993, October 10). *The New York Times,* pp. C5.

The Kmart Corporation's stock has been on a roll lately. But despite the euphoria, some analysts are sounding a warning note: Kmart's main business—its 2,400 general discount stores—remains quite sick in spite of $1.66 billion in operating profits last year based on $24.15 billion in sales. The investor excitement over Kmart masks how difficult it may be to fix the discount operation, which has been losing ground to more nimble competitors like Wal-Mart and Target for the last 10 years.

Three years ago, Kmart embarked on an ambitious program to renovate its stores and increase the fashion appeal of its apparel but has had mixed results. The competition among Wal-Mart, Kmart and Target, which is owned by the Dayton Hudson Corporation, is getting tougher and tougher.

As a way of sidestepping head-on competition with Wal-Mart, Kmart has worked hard to increase apparel sales. In recent years, the retailer began emphasizing the fashion side of the clothing it sells, which clearly differentiates it from Wal-Mart. Still, Kmart's apparel sales have at best equaled last year's. No retailer has had much luck selling apparel this year. But analysts said they wondered whether Kmart would ever become the store of choice for apparel. Target is already perceived by consumers and analysts as the fashion provider among the three big discount chains, and Sears, while not a direct competitor, is making an all-out pitch to win over women to its new, spruced-up apparel.

The trick to making money by selling goods at low prices is pushing a lot of merchandise through the pipeline. The faster a discounter sells its inventory, the more it pads its slim profit margins.

Wal-Mart, whose savvy management of the flow of goods from manufacturers to consumers woke the retail industry to the value of computerized inventory systems, turns over its inventory about four and a half times a year. Target's turnover is a little more than four times an year while Kmart's is about three times. That helps to explain why Kmart is also in third place on sales per square foot, a key measure of performance. Wal-Mart's sales per square foot is $283, Target's is $209, and Kmart's is $143.

While Kmart has installed a new inventory system, suppliers and analysts say it uses its technology less effectively than the others do. Vendors have complained about merchandise sitting in distribution centers while stock is inadequate on the sales floors causing lost sales. One explanation of Kmart's inventory troubles is historical. All three of the big chains opened their first stores in 1962, but Kmart's big growth came much earlier, in the 1970s; Target and Wal-Mart did not expand dramatically until the 1980s. Because they were late bloomers, both Target and Wal-Mart were able to build their corporate cultures around more sophisticated, centralized inventory systems.

Kmart's overhead—what it spends on payroll, utilities, and other operating expenses, but not the cost of goods it sells—is much higher than Wal-Mart's. Analysts estimate that Kmart spends about 22.5 cents of every dollar of sales in its discount store on overhead, Wal-Mart spends about 17.3 cents, and Target about 21 cents. That means Wal-Mart can offer its customers lower prices on the same merchandise and still generate the same operating profit.

Because shoppers consider Target's merchandise and presentation more appealing than the other two big discounters, it does not have to be price competitive with the other two, analysts say. "Target can coexist profitably with Wal-Mart and grow. Kmart can't."

References

Berman, B. B., & Evans, J. R. (1995). *Retail management.* Englewood Cliffs, NJ: Prentice Hall.

Donnellan, J. (1996). *Merchandise buying and management.* New York: Fairchild.

Lewison, D. M. (1994). *Retailing* (5th edition). New York: Macmillan.

Retail Merchandising Services Automation, Inc. (1995). Retail intelligent forecasting: Merchandise planning for the future. Riverside, CA: Author.

CAP SLEEVE

LONG SLEEVE

FAR EASTERN SHIRT
BOXY CUT WITH MANDARIN COLLAR
AND SIDE SLITS AT HEM EDGE.
RECYCLED MAGAZINE BUTTONS WITH
BAR TAB CLOSURES.
• ANTIQUE PINSTRIPE SHIRTING
• CHAMBRAY   S M L
$70

FITTED TEE IN ECO WHITE
CREW NECK WITH SLIGHTLY TAPERED
BODY, "ECO WHITE" SCREENED LOGO
AT BACK NECKLINE, RECYCLED
COTTON JERSEY KNIT IN
ECO WHITE   S M L
CAP SLEEVE $24
LONG SLEEVE $28

SPAGHETTI STRAP SHORTS
SELF-FABRIC DRAWSTRING AT WAIST
WITH BABY BELT LOOPS, ON-SEAM
POCKETS, 5" INSEAM.
• ANTIQUE PINSTRIPE SHIRTING
• TEA-STAINED BIRDSEYE
• CHAMBRAY   S M L
$50

ND TRIMMINGS ARE MADE SAFELY, FREE OF HARMFUL CHEMICAL PROCESSES. TO PLACE AN ORDER OR FOR MORE INFORMATION CALL 800 409 7229

THE SHEATH POCKET DRESS
PRINCESS SEAM DETAILING WITH
SCOOP POCKETS AND LOW V-NECK.
BRASS ZIP BACK CLOSURE AND SLIT
VENT AT CENTER BACK HEM EDGE.
• HEMP   S M L
$100

CREW NECK T-SHIRT IN ECO WHITE
BOXY STYLE CUT WITH "ECO
WHITE" SCREENED LOGO ON
BACK SWEAT PATCH. RECYCLED
COTTON JERSEY KNIT IN
ECO WHITE   S M L
SHORT SLEEVE $24
LONG SLEEVE $28

MANDARIN WRAP JACKET
MANDARIN COLLAR. WRAP AROUND
SELF FABRIC TIE AT WAIST. CAN BE
WORN AS A DRESS OR JACKET.
RECYCLED MAGAZINE BUTTON WITH
LOOP CLOSURE.
• HEMP   S M L
$165

FRONT

BACK

7 Planning and Controlling Merchandise Assortments

Learning Objectives

- Examine a model of in-store shopping behavior in relation to stockouts.
- Learn a language of assortments.
- Introduce the concept of assortment diversity.
- Plan receipt of merchandise to optimize sales and inventory levels.

The newest form of Quick Response should be Customer Response (Lewis, 1996). **The Customer Response System** (CRS) means that merchandise assortments are truly customer-driven. Effective Customer Response is dependent on 1) determining what customers' want in advance, and 2) understanding customers' activities while they are the process of shopping, whether they are shopping in a retail store, via catalog or electronic media, and 3) planning assortments so the merchandise the customer wants is available when he or she wants it.

The challenge relative to assortments faced by manufacturers and retail merchandisers has some surprising similarities. Manufacturers compete in a global market where an overabundance of products can be sourced competitively in several countries; retailers, particularly in the U.S., face over-malled and over-stored markets where the greatest challenges include getting purposive customers into your store and having the merchandise they want while they are there. Balancing assortments at both the whole-sale and retail levels reduces stockouts. Some say that sales would double if stockouts were eliminated. As with many aspects of merchandising, manufacturers' problems with stockouts have not been addressed by research, so the focus of the following discussion is on the problem of stockouts in the retail sector.

In-Store Shopping Behavior

Sales increases of 10 to 50 percent resulting from introduction of Quick Response business systems (QR) are indicators of the magnitude of the retail stockout problem (Hunter, 1990; Nuttle, King, & Hunter 1992). Stockouts result from inadequate assortments of merchandise. Researchers have conducted hundreds of studies of consumer behavior but, until recently, the few studies of customer in-store shopping behavior have focused on grocery stores. Song and Kunz, in collaboration with a regional, up-scale, specialty retailer, conducted a 1996 study to examine customer reactions to stock-outs. The code name "Ramal" was used to protect the confidentiality of the retail collaborator. Ramal's product line includes career and dressy/casual wear for men and women. Ramal provided demographic and purchase information on a random sample of 250 credit card and 250 non-credit card customers for one year, one and a half years of sales and assortment data from multiple stores, and access to their customers for a survey.

Ramal has a unique customer group as defined by demographics. They are mostly white, middle aged, highly educated, married, and employed with high income. Average *family* income in the U.S. is about $40,000. For 41 percent of Ramal customers, the average individual income was between $100,000 and $200,000 per year, and 18 percent of the sample had annual income over $200,000. With regard to education, 34 percent had bachelors degrees and 38 percent had advanced degrees. The average annual apparel expenditure for *individuals* in the sample ($3,783) was more than twice the average annual expenditure of a *family* in the U.S. population ($1,710) (Bureau of the Census, 1994).

The model of in-store shopping behavior resulting from the Ramal research is based on Behavioral Theory of the Apparel Firm (BTAF/QR, see Chapter 2) (Kunz, 1995). See Figure 7.1. An important concept of BTAF is the interactive relationships among functional areas focused on the target market, thus the link to in-store shopping behavior. The dark box in Figure 7.1 indicates the relationship of the proposed in-store shopping behavior model to BTAF/QR.

Syntheses of previous research directly related to in-store shopping behavior resulted in the identification of four constructs that provide

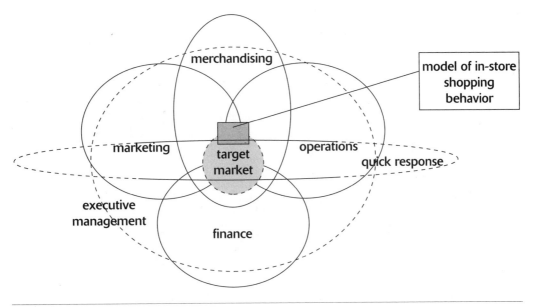

FIGURE 7.1

Interaction of the functional areas of specialization within an apparel firm selectively using Quick Response Systems combined with the Model of In-Store Shopping Behavior (Kunz & Song, 1996).

the structure of the in-store shopping behavior model: situational factors, shopping intentions, stock situations, and purchase decisions. See Figure 7.2.

Situational Factors

Situational factors is defined as all those factors particular to a time and place, excluding personal preferences and choice alternatives, that have a demonstrable and systematic effect on current behavior (Belk, 1975). Five situational factors that may influence an apparel shopper's in-store shopping behavior are identified in the model: demographics, store knowledge and loyalty, time available for shopping, type of shopping trip, and social surroundings.

For *situational factors/demographics,* previous research reported that the younger customers are, the more likely they are to buy something at the first store because it would take too much time to shop around (Meet the new competition, 1994). At the same time, customers over 65 years old may be more likely to shop at department stores for clothing because they believe department stores have better prices and selections than discount or specialty stores (Chowdhary, 1989).

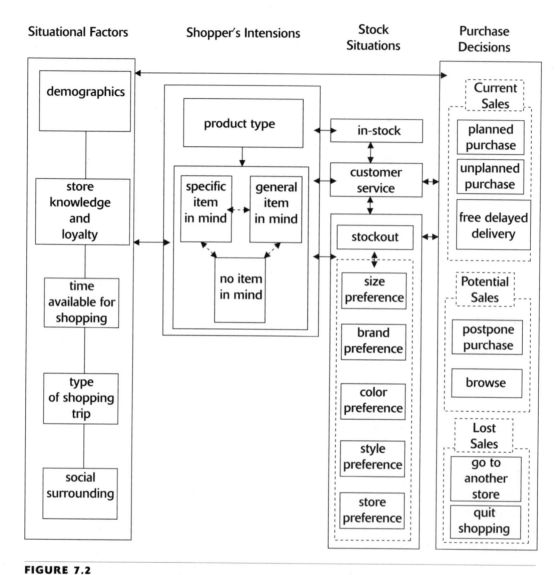

FIGURE 7.2

A model of apparel in-store shopping behavior (Kunz & Song, 1996).

For Ramal customers, age, education, income, level of clothing expenditure, gender, and possession of a Ramal credit card were all found to be significantly related to some aspect of in-store shopping behavior. Price was more likely to be an important consideration for the customers 18 to 34 years old and customers over 55. Females were more likely to be concerned about price than males. Strong relationships were found between holding a Ramal credit card and level of expenditure at Ramal.

In terms of reactions to stockouts, Ramal customers with higher levels of apparel expenditures were significantly more likely to postpone a purchase after experiencing a stockout than those with lower levels of clothing expenditure. A higher level of apparel expenditure may mean more shopping trips or more multiple purchases. Thus, the customer who spent more money for apparel may have had more chance to buy the stockout item on a later shopping trip or decided to buy another item instead.

Situational factors/store knowledge and loyalty refers to the information a customer has about a specific store's attributes and the perceived reliability of the store as a source of goods. Shopping trips and expenditures at Ramal were compared for three groups: the random sample of 250 credit card and non-credit card customers provided by Ramal and the survey sample of 95 credit card customers. See Table 7.1.

Customers with Ramal credit cards visited the store nearly twice as often, bought nearly twice as many items, and spent nearly three times as much money per year as non-Ramal credit card customers. Loyalty to Ramal was also exhibited in terms of product type: customers significantly preferred Ramal as a source for business suits, as compared to casual shirts. About 13 percent of customers answered that they only shopped in Ramal for business suits, while about two percent of customers answered that they only shopped in Ramal for casual shirts.

TABLE 7.1

Shopping patterns of the sample, credit card customers, and non-credit card customers based on Ramal sales records.*

	Credit Card Customers (N=250)	Non-Credit Card Customers (N=250)
Average number of items purchased per person per year	9.79	5.15
Average sales volume per person per year	$1,026.38	$383.81
Average frequency of visiting Ramal stores per person per year	3.82	2.02
Average number of items purchased per trip	2.56	2.55
Average expenditure per trip	$268.69	$190.00

*Kunz & Song (1996).

For *situational factors/time for shopping,* 30 percent of Ramal customers shopped every month and 52 percent shopped a few times a year. The average frequency of customers' shopping for their clothes was four times a year. There were no significant differences between males and females.

Situational factors/type of shopping trip is categorized as major shopping trip and fill-in shopping trip (Kahn & Schmittlein 1989, 1992; Kollet & Willett, 1967). A major shopping trip is an extended excursion for seasonal or annual needs. A fill-in shopping trip is a quick excursion for a current need. More unplanned purchases may be made during major shopping trips than fill-in trips. About 70 percent of Ramal customers engaged in major shopping trips to update their wardrobes.

Situational factors/social surroundings refers to how other people influence an individual's purchase behavior (Runyon & Stewart, 1987). Among Ramal customers, men were significantly more likely to shop with their spouse than women and women were significantly more likely to shop alone or with other family members than men. About half of respondents shopped with someone when they shopped for their clothes.

Learning Activity 7.1

Situational factors in relation to in-store shopping behavior

1. Think through the situational factors that influence in-store shopping behavior. How do your shopping experiences compare to the findings? What situational factors influence your parents, your grandparents, and your peers?

2. What situational factors might need to be included in a model of catalog shopping behavior? Electronic shopping behavior?

Shopper's Intentions

Shopper's intentions relate to the purpose of the shopping trip. Shopper's intentions were found to relate to product type and had three forms: specific item in mind, general item in mind, and no item in mind. Specific or general item in mind means the customer is **purposive:** He or she intends to make a purchase. *Specific item in mind* means the customer has a type of product and brand in mind; *general item in mind* means the customer has only the type of product in mind. *No item in mind* means the customer is **browsing** for pleasure or to collect information for future shopping trips. The three shopping intentions may interact. A customer who has no item in mind may recognize a need for a specific item or general item during the shopping trip. A customer who has a general or specific item in mind can lose purchase intention and move to no item in mind because of the stock situation or influence of other situational factors.

Jarboe and McDaniel (1987) reported that browsers in regional malls are more likely to be employed females. Females and customers over 55 years old may be more likely to regard shopping as fun. Ramal customers were much more likely to be purposive customers (89%) with a specific or general item in mind than browsers (11%). Males were significantly more likely to have a specific item in mind than females, and females were significantly more likely to have a general item in mind than males. About 84 percent of customers purchased multiple or coordinated items.

Stock Situations

Stock situations refer to the presence or absence of an item a customer wants to buy: in-stock or stockout. **In-stock** means the particular stock-keeping unit (SKU), defined by style, size, and color, is immediately available to buy. **Stockout** means the particular SKU is not immediately available to the customer. The stock situation is the point at which a shopper's intentions meet merchandising strategy. **Customer service** is any interaction between the customer and store personnel. It is a component in stock situation because customer service is required for a customer to make a purchase or to provide alternatives that might be available to compensate for a stockout. The components of the stockout element in the model are ordered in terms of the willingness of Ramal customers to adjust their preferences to make a purchase in spite of the stockout. The word preference was used because it suggests "the determining of choice by predisposition or partiality" (Kent, 1984, p. 38).

Ninety-three percent of Ramal customers experienced stockouts, 72 percent of these stockouts were because of size. (See Table 7.2.) Females were significantly more likely to experience stockouts because of size than males. Males were significantly more likely to experience stockouts because of other reasons (brand, style, and color) than females. Customers were significantly less flexible with regard to size of a business suits (94%) or casual shirts (87%) than any other response to stockouts. It follows then that a stockout because of size was most likely to result in a lost sale. Customers were more likely to change style or color than size and even more likely to change brand. Customers had a little more flexibility to change size in casual wear than business wear, even though most customers were not likely to change size when they encountered stockouts.

TABLE 7.2

Frequency of customer reactions to stockout for business suits and casual shirts.*

Reactions to stockouts	business suits			casual shirts		
	% less likely	% not sure	% more likely	% less likely	% not sure	% more likely
Change Size	93.55	5.38	1.06	87.31	7.35	06.31
Change Style	64.51	9.68	25.80	52.63	25.26	22.10
Change Color	59.14	10.75	30.11	50.52	25.26	42.10
Quit Shopping	55.91	16.13	27.96	60.00	16.84	23.14
Browse	41.93	13.98	44.09	28.42	16.84	54.94
Postpone	41.93	13.98	44.06	23.16	13.68	63.16
Change Brand	40.86	13.98	45.16	50.53	14.74	43.73
Delayed Delivery	30.11	8.60	61.29	03.16	2.11	94.74
Other Store	26.89	9.68	63.44	38.42	12.63	58.94

*Kunz & Song (1996).

Purchase Decisions

The purchase decisions construct is configured into three merchandising related elements: current sales, potential sales, and lost sales. **Current sales** occur when a customer makes a purchase and the store records the sale. Current sales could be recorded for planned purchases, unplanned purchases, and buying the item with free delayed delivery. The latter was a more acceptable option for casual wear than for business suits and more acceptable for women than for men (in the Ramal study the delay was specified as being within three days). For business suits, 61 percent of customers were likely to accept free delayed delivery of the stockout item, but 95 percent would accept free delayed delivery for casual shirts.

Potential sales exist if the customer postpones purchase or browses. Potential sales may result when a customer experiences a stockout. Store-loyal customers are more likely to change brands or products within the store, while brand-loyal customers were more likely to go to another store, resulting in a lost sale (Schary & Christopher, 1979). Non-loyal customers were more likely to buy available stock considering convenience, efficiency or economic factors. Ramal customers were significantly more likely to postpone purchase or browse when shopping for casual wear than business wear.

Lost sales result when a customer goes to a different store or quits shopping. Customers may perceive a less urgent need of a purchase of casual wear when they encounter stockout than business wear, for which customers would be more likely to go to another store for the same item. Higher income customers were significantly less likely to quit shopping for casual wear than business wear when they encountered stockouts.

Implications for Merchandising Strategy

Most Ramal customers were purposive shoppers, as is the trend nationwide. Customers are making fewer shopping trips, spending less time in each, but spending more money. They may make relatively few shopping trips per year, but make multiple purchases with a high-dollar expenditure per trip. Considering these customers' shopping patterns, several important implications for merchandising strategy are suggested from the Ramal research. The implications are as follows:

1. According to the results of this study, the most frequent reason for stockouts is the size a customer wants is not available. Furthermore, most customers do not want to change size when they encounter a stockout. It is unlikely, particularly for suits, that a garment of a different size will fit adequately. Thus, an appropriate range of sizes must be considered as a priority to reduce stockouts. Taylor (1970) pointed out the importance of size in assortment planning. He called it the least flexible assortment dimension. The findings of this study confirm his position. Both manufacturers and retailers of apparel need to set up sizing systems so that size is a customer-driven assortment dimension rather than a merchandiser- or production-determined dimension.

2. Offering free delayed delivery service to customers can result in eliminating lost sales and getting current sales. Offering fast replenishment of stockout items can change potential sales to current sales when the customer shops again for the stockout item. However, if replenishment is not made by the time the customer visits again, potential sales become lost sales. Walter and Grabner (1975) found that repeated stockouts increased the percentage of customers who would go to another store. Delayed delivery may help sustain store loyalty, thus justifying the cost of the service.

3. Considering customer service in relation to stockouts, if a salesperson knows a customer encounters a stockout, he or she can offer

the customer three options: 1) helping the customer find alternatives, resulting in current sales; 2) offering delayed delivery service, resulting in current sales; and 3) offering to call the customer when the item is restocked, resulting in a potential sales, thus, possibly avoiding a lost sale.

4. The trade press has reported the dressing down trend in professional apparel. Casual wear has become a more important category of business attire. The results in this study reported that Ramal customers tended to have less preference for Ramal as a source for casual wear than business wear. This can cause a critical loss of sales. Adjusting assortments to accommodate the business casual trend is a very difficult merchandising problem. However, free delayed delivery could help prevent lost sales in casual wear where the problem may be more prevalent because of diverse assortments.

5. A priority for Ramal should be persuading credit card customers to make more trips to Ramal each year to satisfy a larger proportion of their clothing needs. It is impossible to keep in stock all items customers might want and need. Therefore, careful merchandise planning and fast replenishment is essential.

To prevent stockouts and to support delayed delivery service and other stockout compensation policies, merchandisers need better merchandise planning and replenishment systems. Assortment planning systems remain archaic as compared to other retail and production technology. Inadequate assortment planning is the primary cause of stockouts. Effective resupply is dependent on accurate information, cooperation, and speed. Cooperation among a firm's five internal constituencies, as well as collaboration with external coalitions (suppliers) is required. The ability of the firm to achieve its goals may depend on how all constituencies interact, coordinate, and resolve conflicts among internal constituencies and external coalitions.

Learning Activity 7.2

Merchandising issues related to stockouts

1. What do stockouts have to do with planning, development, and presentation of product lines?

2. How can stockouts be prevented?

3. Are stockouts ever desirable?

4. Is it possible that a complete assortment is undesirable?

5. Is it possible to address the problem of stockouts because of size?

6. What are the implications of providing free three-day delivery service for stock-out items?

7. Based on these findings, what should be the particular concerns of merchandisers are they plan assortments?

Language of Assortment Planning

The foundation for planning assortments is the same as the foundation for planning budgets: classification analysis. A clear understanding of what categories of merchandise make up the merchandise mix and regular analysis of the classes and sub-classes within each keep the framework for the assortment current. At the same time, a well-planned pricing system strategically and consistently applied, supports the merchandise budget and assortment plan. An interactive merchandise budget and assortment plan provides the best opportunity to satisfy customers and optimize sales and financial productivity.

A balanced assortment is every merchandiser's goal. An assortment is balanced when it meets customers' needs and accomplishes the firm's goals with a minimum investment in inventory. It is nearly impossible to have completely balanced assortments but some assortments are more balanced than others. Assortment balance is the purpose of the processes of classification analysis discussed in Chapter 4, pricing strategies discussed in Chapter 5 and planning merchandise budgets discussed in Chapter 6. Another step in balancing assortments is more direct—assortment planning.

Assortment planning, the determination of the range of choices to be made available at a given time, is a primary merchandising function (Bohlinger, 1977; Glock & Kunz, 1995; Mason, Mayer, & Ezell, 1994; Risch, 1991). Assortment planning occurs at many different times and for a variety of purposes throughout the apparel business. For example, in apparel manufacturing, assortment planning is conducted by designers, merchandisers, and product managers during line planning and product development; by sales representatives as they communicate a line to potential buyers and write purchase orders for customers; and during cut order planning for production (Glock & Kunz, 1995). In the retail sector, assortment planning occurs when executive management determines merchandise categories, when retail buyers select product offerings, when merchandise controllers allocate goods to individual stores, when department managers merchandise the retail floor, and when visual merchandisers create displays and fill fixtures (Rupe & Kunz, In Press).

Measures of merchandising success may include adjusted gross margin, cash flow, finished goods turnover, percent gross margin, gross margin return on inventory, maintained markup, markdown percentage, materials cost, piece goods turn, sales per square foot, and/or sell-through. The success of a selling season, for both manufacturers and retailers, is often greatly dependent on effective assortment planning. An assortment plan, when used as a framework for line development, provides control over merchandise investment. However, until recently, there were no quantifiable guidelines for assortment planning that relate to potential financial outcomes.

Traditional Dimensions of Assortments

The most traditionally used terms for assortment dimensions are breadth and depth (Bohlinger, 1977; Brown & Davidson, 1953; Berman & Evans, 1995; Davidson & Doody, 1966; Dunne, Lusch, & Gable, 1995; Gillespie & Hecht, 1970; Mason, Mayer, & Ezell, 1994; Risch, 1991). Although the terms "breadth" and "depth" of assortment are widely used throughout the manufacturing and retailing sectors, the definitions of these terms that appear in merchandising and retailing textbooks are inconsistent and provide little quantitative meaning to merchandisers for planning profitable assortments. (See Table 7.3.) Each of these definitions offers a slightly different meaning, while none provides adequate quantitative measurement of breadth. Similar discrepancies exist for defining depth.

These traditional definitions are unidimensional in that they look at only one aspect of the assortment. For example, they may consider the number of SKUs or number of brands in an assortment, but never both dimensions at once. To get any meaningful understanding of an assortment using these terms, the merchandiser must compare one assortment plan to another using phrases such as "more broad than" or "less deep than," etc. The plan cannot be considered in isolation, but must always be accompanied by another frame of reference. This demonstrates the incongruous uses of the assortment dimension words of breadth and depth and indicates the lack of guidance available to merchandisers when carrying out assortment planning processes. (Rupe & Kunz, In Press). (Complete Learning Activity 7.3.)

Measurable Assortment Dimensions

Measurable assortment dimensions that can provide a basis for assortment planning include assortment factors, SKUs, volume and assortment variety.

TABLE 7.3

Examples of definitions found in the literature for assortment breadth and depth.[*]

Definitions for Assortment Breadth	Definitions for Assortment Depth
"characteristic of an individual assortment offering a large number of different categories" (Bohlinger, 1977, p. 369)	"characteristic of an inventory assortment offering limited versions of proved styles" (Bohlinger,1977, p. 368),
"description of the different categories available in a store" (Jernigan & Easterling, 1990, p. 548)	"description of quantity of each item available in the assortment" (Jernigan & Easterling, 1990, p. 548)
"the number of merchandise brands found in the line" (Dunne, Lusch, Gable, & Gerhardt, 1992, p. 475)	"average number of SKUs within each brand" (Dunne et al., 1992, p. 476)
"the number of product lines carried" (Clodfelter, 1993, p.361)	"number of choices offered within each brand" (Clodfelter, 1993, p. 362)
"refers to the number of different styles" (Rath, Peterson, Greensley, & Gill, 1994, p.487)	"how many pieces of each style carried" (Rath et al., 1994, p. 487)
"number of product lines" (Lewison, 1994, p. 423)	"number of product items within each product line" (Lewison, 1994, p. 423)
"refers to the number of distinct goods/service categories with which a retailer is involved (Berman & Evans, 1995, p. A63)[**]	"refers to the variety in any one goods/services category with which a retailer in involved" (Berman & Evans, 1995, p. A51)

[*]Rupe & Kunz.
[**]This definition is referred to as width of assortment.

Learning Activity 7.3

1. What is an assortment?

2. Think through the definitions of breadth and depth of assortments. How are the meanings similar and how are they different? What seems to be the fundamental meaning of breadth? What seems to be the fundamental meaning of depth?

3. Since these terms "broad" and "shallow," "narrow" and "deep" are widely used by the industry but vary greatly in meaning, how can you know the meaning in a particular instance of use?

4. Read carefully Company Profile 7.1, Mike's Bikes Part 3, Merchandise Assortments. It is used as the basis of examples throughout the rest of this chapter.

Assortment Factors

Assortment factors are dimensions that define characteristics of a product for purposes of identifying and describing it. Assortment factors for apparel are commonly style, size, and color. For example, these are

COMPANY PROFILE 7.1

Mike's Bikes Part 3, Merchandise Assortments

The target customers at Mike's Bikes are young and young-in-spirit individuals and families who have average to above average income and pursue biking as their primary form of recreation. Their fringe customers have similar demographics but pursue biking more casually. The majority of their customers are members of local bike clubs, know each other, as well as the other bike stores in the area. They tend to develop loyalty to the local bike store that best meets their needs.

The merchandise mix includes three categories: bikes (about 50 percent of sales); apparel (20%); and accessories (15%). In addition, bike service accounts for 15 percent of sales.

Mountain bikes are 70 percent of the bike business and the largest growth area. Road bikes are 10 percent of the business and sales are flat. Hybrid bikes, combinations of mountain, road and/or racing bikes, are 20 percent of the business and are also a growth area. Bikes are sold in three price ranges: low-end bikes are $250–$450; mid-range bikes are $500–$800; high-end and custom bikes are $900 and up. The average bike purchase is $700. They also carry some children's bikes. Bikes can be special ordered. Most of the inventory is stored on the sales floor.

They carry four classifications of apparel: biking shorts (50% of apparel sales); shoes (20%), shirts and jerseys (20%), and other including gloves and outerwear, (10%). Biking shorts (60% men's and 40% women's, with a price range of $25–$75 and an average first price of $45). The size ranges are small, medium, large, extra large and extra extra large. Apparel is crowded into 1,000 square feet of space. Markup on apparel is 50 to 60 percent.

Helmets are the most frequently ordered accessory purchase, ranging in price from $20 to $130. Water bottles and bags are next in frequency of purchase. Accessories have 800 square feet of space.

Vendor reps visit the store and help plan assortments. Kevin is very comfortable with the marketing aspects of the business, but is still working on the merchandising part. Many vendors leave catalogs so customers can special order merchandise. This means the store can stock a smaller variety of styles, sizes and colors. Even so, assortments are diverse, with only a few units stocked in each SKU. Ordering is done four to six months out; the goods are usually delivered in a single shipment. Branded merchandise is important, but there are few opportunities to re-order hot sellers.

appropriate assortment factors for biking shorts. Assortment factors for groceries might be brand, size (grams, ounces, or liters), and type (fresh, canned or frozen). Assortment factors for automobiles might be model, color, and accessories package. Assortment factors for shoes might be style, color, length, and width. (The term "might be" is used because firms use different systems for defining product characteristics.)

Stock-Keeping Unit

The combination of assortment factors embodied in a single product determines a **stock-keeping-unit (SKU).** A SKU is a unique piece of merchandise. A SKU is distinct from other similar merchandise because of its particular combination of assortment factors. For example, a baby's romper in pink, size small is a different SKU than the same style and size of romper in blue. The larger the number of SKUs in an assortment, the more difficult it is to keep all unique pieces of merchandise in stock.

Assortment Variety

Assortment variety can be determined by the total number of SKUs in the assortment. For example, an apparel assortment might include six styles, five sizes, and 12 colors for an assortment variety of 360 SKUs.

assortment variety = number of SKUs = numbers of assortment factors multiplied together

assortment variety =   360 SKUs   = 6 styles × 5 sizes × 12 colors

Reducing the number of SKUs means fewer unique pieces of merchandise to order, manufacture, ship, sort, stock, and display. It also means customers, either retail buyers if the firm is a manufacturer or ultimate consumers if the firm is a retailer, have a more limited selection to choose from. Identifying the appropriate level of variety is an on-going struggle.

Assortment variety is an indicator of the magnitude of the inventory management challenge. For example, it is conceivable that one retailer would have a merchandise mix with a variety of 20,000 SKUs; others might have a merchandise mix with 60,000 or 160,000 SKUs. Absence of any single SKU at a given moment can result in a stockout and a lost sale. The greater the variety, the greater the challenge of consistently having all planned merchandise in stock.

Assortment Volume

Assortment volume is the total number of units in an assortment. A **unit** is a single piece of merchandise. The number of units in an assortment may be determined by the merchandise budget, sales history, or a bottom-up merchandise plan. For example, if the merchandise budget specifies planned receiving at retail of $100,000 and if the merchandise class is sable coats or sports cars, the assortment volume could be one unit if the retail price of the product is $100,000 ($100,000 ÷ $100,000). With the same merchandise budget of $100,000 for T-shirts that will retail for $10, the assortment volume would be 10,000 units ($100,000 ÷ $10).

assortment volume		*planned receiving for a selling period*		*average retail price of a single unit*
	=		÷	
1	=	$100,000	÷	$100,000
10,000	=	$100,000	÷	$10

Assortment volume has to be matched to the level of demand. Assortment volume cannot be increased by ordering or manufacturing more products unless there is some sort of unsatisfied demand for the goods.

The purpose of the merchandise budget is to match merchandise investment to expected demand.

The merchandise budget (receiving at retail) for biking shorts for selling period #1 at Mike's Bikes (refer back to Table 6.4) is $171,200. Receiving at retail is planned sales plus reductions. According to Company Profile 7.1, biking shorts are 60 percent men's and 40 percent women's with an average first price of $45. The volume for women's biking shorts, then, can be determined by first calculating planned receiving of women's shorts. For example:

planned receiving of women's shorts	=	*receiving at retail*	×	*% women's shorts*
$68,400	=	$171,200	×	40%
volume of women's shorts	=	*planned receiving of women's shorts*	÷	*average retail price*
1522 units	=	$68,400	÷	$45

Learning Activity 7.4

1. Mike's Bikes tested adding in-line skates to their total merchandise assortment. They decided on planned sales of $10,000. With an average selling price of $195, what is the volume of the assortment? How many units are in the assortment?

2. What assortment factors do you think are relevant to in-line skates? Why? Given your assortment factors for in-line skates, what are the dimensions of a SKU?

Integration of Assortment Dimensions into Assortment Plans

Assortment plans can take a number of forms depending on a firm's priorities. Combinations of assortment dimensions can result in model stocks, assortment distribution, volume per assortment factor, and volume per SKU.

Model Stock

A **model stock** is a plan for a merchandise assortment according to assortment factors. The model stock identifies how many of each assortment factor should be included in the assortment, but it does not specifically identify what merchandise will fill out the merchandise plan. Determining the specific merchandise is a line development process. The model stock, in and of itself, is simply the number of each relevant assortment factor that is planned for the assortment. Assortment variety can be controlled via a model stock since the number of SKUs is controlled by the combination of assortment factors. A model stock for apparel commonly includes three assortment factors (style, size, and color) but does not always include three assortment factors. For example, a model stock for bras requires four assortment factors including two related to size: style, color, cup, and circumference. A model stock for bras may have five assortment factors if brand is regarded as an assortment factor. It is common for a department store assortment of bras to include over 50,000 SKUs. An assortment with that much variety is very difficult to manage. Examples for model stocks for different classifications are in Table 7.4.

The purpose of a model stock is to balance assortment factors relative to demand and to control the variety offered within a classification. Because of limited dollars available to invest in inventory and limited space for display or capacity for production, decisions have to be made about what combinations of assortment factors will best help the firm meet its goals. For example, when merchandisers go to market they may look at hundreds of styles of biking shorts; the inclination normally is to buy more than the nine styles, five sizes, and seven colors specified in the assortment plan, thus increasing the assortment variety. The model stock helps the merchandiser stay within the space available for merchandise display and within the merchandise budget. The merchandise budget and the model stock, of course, are based on projected customer demand.

Assortment Distribution

Assortment distribution is the allocation of volume across assortment factors at the classification level. It is an estimate of the relative rate of sale of each style size and color in the assortment. Assortment distribution determines the proportion of unit allocation to each assortment factor. The assortment must be distributed so available merchandise will meet customer demand. Assortment distribution usually takes place in the context of a model stock. See Table 7.5.

TABLE 7.4

Examples of model stock plans by merchandise classification with assortment variety stated as number of SKUs.

Classification	Model Stock	# of SKUs
Biking shorts	9 styles, 5 sizes, 7 colors	315
Junior jeans	8 styles, 5 sizes, 3 colors	120
Turtlenecks	1 style, 4 sizes, 12 colors	48
T-shirts	3 styles, 5 sizes, 9 colors	135
Bras	12 styles, 5 cup sizes, 6 circumference sizes, 5 colors	1800
Earrings	2 types, 50 styles, 5 colors	500
Skillets	4 brands, 7 styles, 3 sizes	84

TABLE 7.5

Example of a combination of model stock for women's biking shorts at Mike's Bikes with assortment distribution.

Assortment Factor		Assortment Factor		Assortment Factor	
Style	*Distribution*	*Size*	*Distribution*	*Color*	*Distribution*
1 — 6 panel	30%	1 — small	10%	1 — ebony	20%
2 — 4 panel	20%	2 — medium	25%	2 — color spliced	20%
3 — 6 panel PCL	15%	3 — large	40%	3 — fuchsia	13%
4 — 8 panel	10%	4 — extra large	15%	4 — plum	12%
5 — double duty	10%	5 — extra extra large	10%	5 — red	10%
6 — bib short	5%			6 — cobalt	8%
7 — short short	5%			7 — screaming yellow	6%
8 — bikeatard	3%			8 — navy	6%
9 — aerosuit	2%			9 — lime	5%
Total Volume	100%		100%		100%

The nine styles of women's biking shorts are distributed for a total 100 percent of women's shorts for selling period #1 based on forecasted customer preferences. The size distribution is allocated as a bell-shaped curve with the largest percentage in the center of the size range. Sales history and experience with customers in relation to stockouts and special orders should be the basis of size distribution. Colors are allocated based on fashion trends identified in the line plan. Note that each assortment factor must be planned relative to the total assortment volume.

Learning Activity 7.5

Measurable assortment dimensions

1. Refer back to Table 7.4. How many SKUs would be in the assortment if the merchandisers decided to carry only seven styles of junior jeans instead of eight? How many SKUs would there be if they carried four sizes instead of five? How many SKUs would there be if they carried two colors instead of three?

2. What would happen to the number of SKUs if they decided to carry three different lengths of junior jeans in addition to the five sizes? What are the advantages and disadvantages of carrying a greater variety in an assortment? What are the advantages and disadvantages of a smaller variety in an assortment?

3. Refer back to Learning Activity 7.4. Given the assortment factors you chose for in-line skates, create a model stock. Based on your model stock, how many SKUs are in the assortment? What is the variety of the assortment?

Volume Per Assortment Factor

An assortment distribution plan can be used to reveal volume per assortment factor. To determine units per style, per size, or per color for women's shorts, do the following:

volume per style, size, or color = units planned for the classification × percent allocation for the assortment factor

units for style #1	=	1522	×	30%
units for style #2	=	1522	×	20%
units for size #1	=	1522	×	10%
units for size #2	=	1522	×	25%
units for color #1	=	1522	×	20%
units for color #2	=	1522	×	20%

See Table 7.6. Notice that style #1 is 30 percent of the assortment, so Mike's Bikes will order 456 pieces of style #1. Style #1 had better be very popular with their customers. In contrast, style #9 is planned to be only two percent of the total classification, only 31 pieces. If this style is more popular than planned, stockouts and lost sales are likely.

Volume per SKU

To determine the number of units for each unique SKU in an assortment you can develop a volume-per-SKU plan, based on a combination of a

TABLE 7.6

Volume per assortment factor based on the model stock and assortment distribution in Table 7.5 and the volume based on the merchandise budget for women's biking shorts (1522 units).

Number	Style	Units per Style	Size	Units per Size	Color	Units per Color
1	30%	456	10%	152	20%	304
2	20%	304	25%	380	20%	304
3	15%	228	40%	609	13%	198
4	10%	152	15%	228	12%	183
5	10%	152	10%	152	10%	152
6	5%	76			8%	122
7	5%	76			6%	91
8	3%	46			6%	91
9	2%	31			5%	76
Total	100%	1521*	100%	1521*	100%	1521*

*rounding error

model stock, units per assortment factor, and an assortment distribution plan. It is calculated on a style-by-style basis; one table for each style. To calculate volume per SKU for styles in Table 7.6 (as demonstrated in Tables 7.7 and 7.8), do the following:

volume per SKU = *volume per style* × *% size* × *% color*

volume per SKU for Style #1 = volume for style #1 × % for size #1 × % for color #1
9 units = 456 × 10% × 20%

volume per SKU for Style #1 = volume for style #1 × % for size #1 × % for color #2
9 units = 456 × 10% × 20%

volume per SKU for Style #1 = volume for style #1 × % for size #1 × % for color #3
6 units = 456 × 10% × 13%

Each cell in each table represents a the number of units of a unique piece of merchandise. The percentage distribution plan demonstrated in Table 7.6 seems reasonable until the volume-per-SKU plan for style #9 is examined in Table 7.8. The volume-per-SKU plan is very insightful in terms of what kind of an assortment will be available to display on the sales floor. Some SKUs have none, one or a few units. A stockout can result in a lost sale and a lost customer.

TABLE 7.7

Volume per SKU for Style #1 based on 30% of total women's biking shorts, 456 units, with model stock and assortment distribution as indicated in Table 7.6.

Color	Size 1	Size 2	Size 3	Size 4	Size 5	Total
1	9	23	36	14	9	91
2	9	23	36	14	9	91
3	6	15	24	9	6	60
4	6	14	22	8	6	55
5	5	11	18	7	5	46
6	4	9	15	5	4	37
7	3	7	11	4	3	28
8	3	7	11	4	3	28
9	2	6	9	3	2	22
Total	47	115	182	68	46	458*

*rounding error

TABLE 7.8

Volume per SKU for Style #9 based on 2% of total women's biking shorts, 31 units, with model stock and assortment distribution as indicated in Table 7.6.

Color	Size 1	Size 2	Size 3	Size 4	Size 5	Total
1	1	2	3	1	1	8
2	1	2	3	1	1	8
3	0	1	2	1	0	4
4	0	1	2	1	0	4
5	0	1	1	0	0	2
6	0	1	1	0	0	2
7	0	0	1	0	0	1
8	0	0	1	0	0	1
9	0	0	1	0	0	1
Total	2	8	15	4	2	31

Learning Activity 7.6

1. As determined in Learning Activities 6.3, Big Bear has a merchandise budget that includes $3,420 in planned sales for flannel shirts, $342 in planned reductions, and $3,760 in planned merchandise to receive. The assortment includes two styles, two colors, and four sizes. First price on the shirts is $30. Big Bear expects to devote about 36 square feet to displaying the shirts in each store. Big Bear expects the shirts to generate $95 per square foot during the fall selling period. Markdowns are expected to be 10 percent of sales.

    How are the following numbers determined for the merchandise plan. Write the formula or explanation after the answer.

    a) What is the planned volume of the assortment? 126
    b) How many SKUs are in this assortment? 16
    c) What is the model stock? Two styles, two colors, four sizes
    d) How was volume-per-style determined in the following volume-per-assortment factor plan?
    e) Calculate volume-per-color and volume-per-size.

    Plan for Volume per Assortment Factor for Big Bear Flannel Shirts for Fall

#	Style	Volume per Style	Color	Volume per Color	Size	Volume per Size
1	60%	76	75%		10%	
2	40%	50	25%		20%	
3					40%	
4					30%	
Total		126 units		126 units		126 units

f) How was volume per SKU determined for Style #1?

g) Develop a volume per SKU plan for Style #2.

Volume-per-SKU for Style #1

Color	Size #1	Size #2	Size #3	Size #4	Total
#1	6	11	23	17	57
#2	2	4	8	6	19
Total	8	15	30*	23	76

*rounded down so total would equal 76

Volume-per-SKU for Style #2

Color	Size 1	Size 2	Size 3	Size 4	Total
1					
2					
Total					

2. Develop volume per SKU plans for biking shorts, Style #2 and Style #8 based on Table 7.6.

3. Considering your model stock of in-line skates (Learning Activity 7.5, #3), how would you distribute volume across assortment factors? Develop a volume-per-SKU plan to evaluate your assortment distribution.

The Concept of Assortment Diversity

The concept of assortment diversity (Rupe & Kunz, In Press) resulted from research using the Apparel Retail Model (ARM) (Nuttle, King, & Hunter, 1991), a computer simulation of the merchandising process. Included in ARM's capabilities is the capacity to perform rapid cost/benefit analysis of specific assortment situations. ARM allows the user to plan a merchandise assortment, a pricing strategy, and a delivery strategy. The computer program simulates customer demand and provides a financial analysis of the impact of the chosen strategies. ARM can be configured so that it can operate under the assumption that the merchandise is salable by planning assortments so there is one customer for each unit of merchandise. Consequently, it is possible to eliminate issues related to merchandise selection and customer shopping behavior and instead focus on outcomes related to the nature of the assortment. ARM tracks the prescribed assortment of merchandise, at the SKU level, throughout a selling period. The fundamental finding of the research was that *the more diverse the assortment, the lower the financial productivity* (Rupe & Kunz).

Assortment diversity is the range of relationships that can exist between assortment volume and assortment variety. Thus, assortment diversity is a combination of the total number of units in the assortment (assortment volume) and the number of SKUs in the same assortment (assortment variety). Assortment diversity, then, is measured by volume per SKU for the assortment (VSA). The VSA is the average number of units available per SKU. The actual number of units per SKU will depend on the assortment distribution plan. If the T-shirt assortment described in Table 7.4 were planned for 10,000 units, the VSA would be 74 (10,000 units ÷ *135 SKUs*).

assortment diversity	=	*volume per SKU for the assortment*		
volume per SKU for the assortment	=	*# of units*	÷	*# of SKUs*
74	=	10,000	÷	135

The VSA for the women's biking shorts is 4.83 (1522 units ÷ 315 SKUs).

The ARM simulation experiments revealed one reason why traditional definitions of assortment dimensions have been ineffective as assortment planning tools: They neglect to identify a relationship between assortment volume and assortment variety. Under the definitions of breadth and depth previously discussed, an assortment could not be defined without being compared to another assortment. They had to be vaguely defined as more broad, less shallow, more narrow, less deep, etc., than another assortment of comparison. Using the VSA, how diverse or focused an assortment is can be meaningfully described in and of itself:

- 100 units with 50 SKUs = VSA of 2 = more diverse
- 100 units with 20 SKUs = VSA of 5 = diverse
- 100 units with 10 SKUs = VSA of 10 = focused
- 100 units with 5 SKUs = VSA of 20 = more focused

The smaller the VSA, the more diverse the assortment; the larger the VSA, the more focused the assortment. Given the same number of units in the assortment, a smaller VSA indicates more variety in the assortment (more SKUs) and fewer items per SKU on the average. The larger the VSA, the less variety in the assortment (fewer SKUs) and the more items per SKU on the average.

The concept of assortment diversity adds the following to the assortment planning language:

- **assortment diversity** = the range of relationships that can exist between assortment volume and number of SKUs in an assortment
- **volume per SKU for an assortment (VSA)** = assortment volume divided by the total number of SKUs in the same assortment

The Relationship of VSA to Financial Productivity

The ARM simulation experiments also revealed that the nature of the assortment matters from the standpoint of financial productivity. Assortments, particularly with a VSA of less than 5, can be potentially detrimental to financial productivity simply because of the diversity of the assortment. Tables and graphs of VSA relative to percent gross margin (%GM) indicate that as VSA increases, the %GM increases. See Figure 7.3.

The graph shows that the lower the VSA, the lower the financial productivity; the higher the VSA, the greater the financial productivity, at least up to a point. The change in financial performance related to VSA is attributed primarily to lost sales in relation to stockouts. Figure 7.4 indicates that as an assortment has fewer units allocated per SKU on the average, the chances of not having the right SKUs for customers increase, therefore, stockouts increase. This is especially prevalent with a VSA of less than 2. As

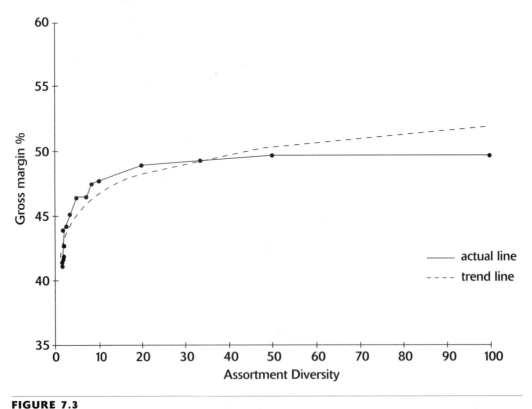

FIGURE 7.3

Graph of assortment diversity determined by VSA of 1 to 100 in relation to percent gross margin (%GM) (Rupe & Kunz).

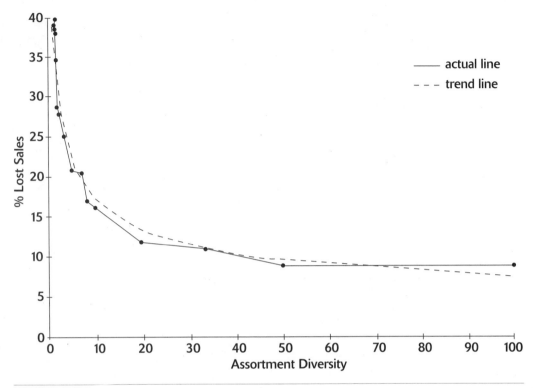

FIGURE 7.4

Graph of assortment diversity determined by VSA of 1 to 100 in relation to percent lost sales (%LS) (Rupe & Kunz).

fewer customers find what they are looking for, fewer purchases are made, leaving more merchandise unsold at the end of the selling period. In actual retail settings this merchandise must either be marked down from first price and sold at a lower selling price and/or jobbed off at the wholesale price or less (the latter was the option in the simulation sets). In either case merchandise is sold at lower than first price, resulting in less total revenue and lower financial performance. With low VSAs, what appears to be a merchandise shortage can result in more units being left at the end of the selling period.

The results were similar when financial outcomes from simulations based on the specialty and discount assortments were examined. (See Table 7.9.) For example, two specialty store assortments had VSAs of .81 (there were more SKUs than units in the assortment) and 2. As expected, the assortment with a VSA of 2 had better financial outcomes (that is, %GM) than the assortment with a VSA of .81. Similar results were

TABLE 7.9

Computer simulation inputs and outputs of analysis of specialty store and discount store assortments.

	VSA	Variety in SKUs	Volume in Units	% Gross Margin	% Lost Sales
Specialty Store	0.81	108	87	37.75	23.4
	2.00	40	80	42.93	12.0
Discount Store	3.30	80	264	32.60	4.0
	9.00	120	1080	32.67	0.8
	12.61	240	3026	32.99	0.6

obtained with the discount store's assortments. The three assortments had VSAs of 3.3, 9, and 12.61. (The assortment with the VSA of 12.61 had the highest VSA in the store data we examined.) As expected, the assortment with the VSA of 12.61 had a higher %GM. The assortment with an VSA of 3.3 exhibited the poorest %GM for the discount store assortments, while the assortment with VSA of 9 fell in the middle of the %GM performance range.

Because of the recent development of the assortment diversity concept, little is known about the diversity of "normal" store level assortments. If the store tier assortments reported in Table 7.9 are typical, VSAs would range below 15. Additional research is in progress to better understand store level assortments in relation to assortment diversity (Rupe & Kunz, In Press).

Learning Activity 7.7

VSA

1. How does volume-per-SKU for an assortment differ from volume per SKU?

2. Explain the logic behind the concept that as VSA is smaller, financial productivity is less.

3. If you have 1,000 units planned for an assortment distributed across 20 SKUs, what is the VSA for the assortment? How many units per SKU are in the assortment? What is the volume of the assortment? What is the variety of the assortment?

4. Why is an assortment with a lower VSA likely to have more stockouts?

Assortment Diversity Index

The Assortment Diversity Index (ADI) is a predictor of the impact of VSA on financial productivity. An index is "something that serves to guide, point out, or otherwise facilitate reference ... something that reveals or indicates" (*American Heritage Dictionary*, 1994). According to the simulation experiments, three ranges of VSAs were identified in relation to financial outcomes to form the basis of an ADI. The following words and definitions were developed to describe these segments (Rupe & Kunz, In Press):

- **diverse assortments**—assortments with few units allocated per SKU, 5 or less on the average for an individual store assortment. The reduction of VSA from 5 to 1 may result in more than a 5 percent reduction in gross margin.
- **transition assortments**—assortments with a moderate number of units allocated per SKU, between 6 and 10 on the average for an individual store assortment.
- **focused assortments**—assortments with many units allocated per SKU, usually 10 or more. The increase in VSA from 5 to 100 may improve gross margin by only about 3 percent.

Two of the VSA segments have been further refined. The diverse assortment is broken down into two areas: very diverse, with VSAs of 2 or below, and diverse with VSAs of 2 to 5. The focused assortment is broken down into three parts: focused with VSAs of above 10 to 20, very focused with VSAs of 20 to 50, and unaffected with VSAs above 50. Assortments with VSAs above 50 are so focused that they exhibited no impact on financial outcomes. (Review Figures 7.3 and 7.4.) To summarize, the six segments defined as parts of the Assortment Diversity Index (ADI) are as follows:

- **very diverse**—a VSA of 2 or less with a total impact on %GM of over 3%
- **diverse**—a VSA of 2.01–5 with a total impact on %GM of 2% to 3%.
- **transition**—a VSA of above 5.01–10 with a total impact on %GM of 1% to 2%.
- **focused**—a VSA of 10.01–20 with a total impact on %GM of 1% to 2%.
- **very focused**—a VSA of 20.01–50 with a total impact on %GM of less than 1%.
- **unaffected**—a VSA of 50.01–100 with an increase of %GM of 0%.

The key VSA points in the ADI are 2, 5, 10, 20, and 50. As VSA increases, the greatest change in financial productivity (%GM) occurs within very diverse assortments, those with a VSA of 2 or less. Within the diverse segment, VSAs of 2-5, sizable improvements in financial productivity are also realized as diversity decreases. Percent gross margins improved almost one percent per index point, e.g., an assortment with a VSA of 3 had a %GM about 1 percent greater than an assortment with a VSA of 2. With transition assortments, or those with VSAs of between 5 and 10, the rate of %GM increase is substantial. However, these changes were not as great as when VSAs were below 5, but greater than when VSAs were above 10.

As assortments became focused, VSAs of 10 to 20, the rate of increase in financial productivity is considerably less than for VSAs below 10. For the very focused segment, VSAs of 20-50, the rate of increase in financial productivity is very small; after 50, increases in financial productivity nearly disappeared. In general, as the VSAs increased to 50, the financial productivity increased. Conversely, as the VSAs decreased from 50, financial productivity decreased. The rate of change in financial productivity was noticeably greater when VSAs were less than five (Rupe & Kunz, In Press).

ARM simulation results indicate that the use of "volume per SKU for the assortment" (VSA) and the development of the concepts for an ADI have many potential uses. With further testing and refinement, the ADI may provide an indicator of the need for higher initial markup to compensate for stockouts and other selling problems that appear to particularly reduce the potential financial productivity of transition and diverse assortments. Many apparel retailers and manufacturers are attempting to offer an increasing number and variety of products to their customers (Fisher, Hammond, Obermeyer, and Raman, 1994). This implicitly means that assortments are becoming more diverse; consequently assortments are becoming more difficult to plan in a manner that satisfies both consumer demand and financial productivity. The ADI may be a tool that can help merchandisers solve these problems.

Learning Activity 7.8

Assortment Diversity Index

1. What is the purpose of an index like the ADI? How might a merchandiser use the ADI to plan more financially productive assortments?

2. What is the VSA for the assortment in Table 7.6? How does that VSA relate to the empty cells in the volume per SKU plan in Table 7.8? According to the VSA, what is the level of assortment diversity? What are the implications for financial productivity of the assortment?

3. What is the VSA and ADI of the assortment you created for in-line skates at Mike's Bikes? Based on the ADI, how much impact would you expect the diversity of the assortment have on financial productivity?

Integrated Merchandise Plans

Integrating company profiles, merchandise budgets, assortment dimensions, and assortment diversity into complete merchandise plans is a great merchandising challenge. Few merchandising technology systems have accomplished it. As with merchandise budgeting processes, the assortment planning process applied to a particular merchandise class is determined by demand for product change and change in the rate of sale:

- **basic/staple goods planned at SKU level**—basic stock or automated replenishment plan with an item replenishment system with a goal of continuous inventory throughout the merchandising cycle.
- **basic/seasonal and fashion staple goods planned at classification level**—model stock plan with assortment distribution with a goal of zero-to-zero inventory for the selling period; automated replenishment systems may be used.
- **fashion/seasonal goods planned at classification level**— model stock plan with assortment distribution with a goal of zero-to-zero inventory for the selling period.

Basic stock and automated replenishment systems were discussed in Chapter 6. A strategy for synthesizing the merchandise planning systems and practices discussed in Chapters 4, 5, 6, and 7 appears below. The key to good planning is on-going systematic analysis of past, present, and future opportunities.

Developing a Merchandise Plan for a Selling Period for a Classification at the Individual Store Tier

1. Develop a profile of the firm including its mission, goals, market positioning, target customers, product line, financial status, and current issues and trends.
2. Determine sales for the individual store if the firm is multi-stored and/or multi-tiered.
3. Evaluate the role of the classification in the product line and develop a forecast for the selling period for the individual store.
4. Determine the range of prices for the classification and an average first price.
5. Determine planned sales based on sales forecasts, sales history, and/or space productivity.
6. Determine planned markdowns based on sales history or industry averages for the classification.
7. Determine receiving at retail for the classification adequate to cover sales and markdowns.
8. Determine assortment volume.
9. Develop a model stock.
10. Distribute the assortment across the model stock.
11. Develop a volume-per-SKU plan.

12. Determine the VSA and rank of the plan according to the ADI.
13. Evaluate potential of plan in relation to stockouts.
14. Are changes needed in pricing, receiving at retail, model stock or assortment distribution?

Summary

Planning and controlling merchandise assortments is the least sophisticated area of merchandising. The magnitude of the retail stockout problem has had little study, but it is a serious problem in today's markets as shoppers spend less time shopping in fewer shopping trips. Competition for consumer dollars is so great that merchants must provide appropriate merchandise assortments to optimize sales from merchandise offerings.

Effective assortment planning is dependent on recognizing the interrelationships with the merchandise classification system, the pricing system, and the merchandise budget. The most effective plans are dynamic and interactive. Assortment plans are based on the measurable dimensions of volume, variety, and distribution. From those dimensions, model stocks, volume per assortment factor, and volume per SKU plans can be developed.

Volume per SKU for the assortment (VSA) is a means of measuring assortment diversity. The assortment diversity index (ADI) is an indicator of the impact of the assortment on potential financial productivity. Calculating assortment plans by hand is very labor intensive. Implementing computer-based merchandising plans is essential to improve the effectiveness of merchandise planning.

Key Concepts

assortment distribution
assortment diversity
assortment diversity index (ADI)
assortment factors
assortment planning
assortment variety
assortment volume
breadth
browsing customers

current sales
customer response system (CRS)
customer service
depth
in-stock
in-store shopping behavior
lost sales
model stock
potential sales

purposive customers
shoppers intentions
situational factors
stock-keeping unit
stockout
volume per assortment factor
volume per SKU
volume per SKU for the assortment (VSA)

Integrated Learning Activity 7.9

Integrated merchandise plans

1. According to Learning Activities 6.3, Dubers has a merchandise budget for girl's tops for the spring selling period that includes receiving 1,208 girl's tops for a total of $12,075 in merchandise in order to make their sales plan of $10,500. The sizes carried and distribution of sales by size for last spring were as follows: 6(8%), 7(25%), 8(40%), 10(20%), 12(5%), and 14(2%). You have observed a fashion trend toward wearing oversize tops. Since Duber's is the primary source for children's wear in this town, the store normally carries a diverse assortment. Markdowns are 15 percent of sales. You are developing an assortment plan with a model stock of eight styles, six colors, six sizes for girl's tops.

   a) Create a volume-per-assortment factor plan for tops.
   b) Create a volume-per-SKU plan for one style.
   c) What is the VSA and ADI of this assortment?
   d) How will the VSA impact potential stockouts?

Plan for Volume-per-Assortment Factor for Girl's Tops for Spring

#	Style	Units Per Style	Color	Units Per Color	Size	Units Per Size
1						
2						
3						
4						
5						
6						
7						
8						
total						

Volume per SKU Plan for Style #

Color	Size 1	Size 2	Size 3	Size 4	Size 5	Size 6	Total
1							
2							
3							
4							
5							
6							
Total							

2. Based on the merchandise budgets developed for Integrated Learning Activity 6.1, complete merchandise plans for the merchandise classes you have defined for 10-week and 20-week selling periods using Figure 7.5 as a guide. Make the class planned for 10 weeks have a VSA of less than 5 and the class planned for 20 weeks have a VSA of more than 10.

Recommended Resources

Lewis, R. (1996, May). Power to the consumer. In *DNR Infotracs,* a supplement to *Daily News Record.*

McConville, D. J. (1994, June 20). The casual corporation. *Industry Week,* pp. 12–17.

Shopping the big center. (1990). *Monitor, 20* (5), 13–22.

Taylor, C. G. (1970). *Merchandise Assortment Planning.* New York: Merchandising Division National Retail Merchants Association.

References

Anderson, P. E. (1982, Spring). Marketing, strategic planning and the theory of a firm. *Journal of Marketing, 46,* 15–26.

Belk, R. W. (1975). Situational variables and consumer behavior. *Journal of Consumer Research, 2,* 157–164.

Berman, B., & Evans, J. R. (1995). *Retail management: A strategic approach.* Englewood Cliffs, NJ: Prentice Hall.

Blackburn, J. D. (1991). The Quick-Response movement in the apparel industry: A case study in time-compressing supply chains. In J. D. Blackburn (Ed.), *Time-based competition: The next battleground in American manufacturing.* Homewood, IL: Irwin.

Bloch, P. H., & Ridgway, N. M., & Sherrell, D. L. (1989). Extending the concept of shopping: An investigation of browsing activity. *Journal of the Academy of Marketing Science, 17,* 13–21.

Bohlinger, M. (1977). *Merchandise buying: Principles and applications.* Dubuque, IA: Wm. C. Brown.

Brown, P., & Davidson, W. (1953). *Retailing principles and practices.* New York: Ronald Press.

Bureau of the Census. (1994). *Statistical abstract of the United States 1994* (114th ed.). Washington, DC: Author.

Chowdhary, U. (1989). Apparel shopping behavior of elderly men and women. *Perceptual and Motor Skills, 68,* 1183–1189.

Clodfelter, R. (1993). *Retail buying: From staples to fashions to fads.* Albany, NY: Delmar.

Cyert, R. (1988). *The economic theory of organization and the firm.* New York: Harvester-Wheatsheaf.

Cyert, R. M., & March, J. G. (1963). *A behavioral theory of the firm.* Englewood Cliffs, NJ: Prentice Hall.

Davidson, W., & Doody, A. (1966). *Retailing management.* New York: Ronald Press.

Dunne, P., Lusch, R., & Gable, M. (1995). *Retailing.* Cincinnati, OH: South-Western.

Dunne, P., Lusch, R., Gable, M., & Gerhardt, R. (1992). *Retailing.* Cincinnati, OH: South-Western.

Fisher, M. L., Hammond, J. H., Obermeyer, W. R., & Raman, A. (1994, May–June). Making supply meet demand in an uncertain world. *Harvard Business Review,* pp. 83–93.

Foxall, J. (1981). *Strategic marketing management.* New York: Halsted.

Gillespie, K., & Hecht, J. (1970). *Retail business management.* New York: McGraw-Hill.

Glock, R. E., & Kunz, G. I. (1995). *Apparel manufacturing: Sewn product analysis.* 2nd ed. Englewood Cliffs, NJ: Prentice Hall.

Hunter, A. (1990). *Quick response in apparel manufacturing: A survey of the American scene.* Manchester, England: The Textiles Institute.

Hunter, N., King, R., & Nuttle, H. (1991). Comparison of quick response and traditional retailing performance through stochastic simulation modeling (NCSIU-IE Technical Report #91-6). Raleigh, NC: North Carolina State University, Department of Industrial Engineering.

Jarboe, G. R., & McDaniel, C. D. (1987). A profile of browsers in regional shopping malls. *Journal of the Academy of Marketing Science, 15,* 46–53.

Jernigan, M., & Easterling, C. (1990). *Fashion merchandising and marketing.* New York: Macmillan.

Kahn, B. E., & Schmittlein, D. C. (1989). Shopping trip behavior: An empirical investigation. *Marketing Letters, 1*(1), 55–69.

Kahn, B. E., & Schmittlein, D. C. (1992). The relationship between purchase made on promotion and shopping trip behavior. *Journal of Retailing, 68*(3), 294–315.

Kahn, B. E., & Lehmann, D. (1991). Modeling choice among assortments. *Journal of Retailing, 67*(3), 274–299.

Kent, R. K. (1984). *Webster's New Word Dictionary of Synonyms.* New York: Simon & Schuster.

King, R. (February 2, 1994). [Personal telephone interview with co-developer of ARM program].

Kollat, D. T., & Willett, R. P. (February, 1967). Customer impulse purchasing behavior. *Journal of Marketing Research, 4,* 21–31.

Kunz, G. I. (1995). Behavioral theory of the apparel firm: A beginning. *Clothing and Textiles Research Journal, 13*(4), 252–261.

Kunz, G. I., & Song, J. (1996) Toward a model of in-store shopping behavior. Unpublished paper, Iowa State University.

Lewis, R. (1996, May). Power to the consumer. In *DNR Infotracs,* a supplement to *Daily News Record.*

Lewison, D. M. (1994). *Retailing.* Don Mills, Ontario: Macmillan College Publishing Co.

Mason, J. B., Mayor, M. L., & Ezell, H. F. (1994). *Retailing,* 5th ed. Burr Ridge, IL.: Irwin.

Meet the new competition: Emerging home shopping alternatives. (1994, February). *Stores,* pp. S3–S22.

Nuttle, H. L. W., King, R E., & Hunter, N . A. (1992). An apparel supply system for QR retailing. *Journal of the Textile Institute, 93*(3), 462–471.

Nuttle, H., King, R., & Hunter, N. (1991). A stochastic model of the apparel-retailing process for seasonal apparel. *Journal of the Textile Institute, 82*(2), 247–259.

Pfeffer, J., & Salancik, G. R. (1978). *The external control of organizations: A resource dependence perspective.* New York: Harper and Row.

Poindexter, M. (1991, January). *Apparel retail model version 2.0 operating manual* (Prepared for CRAFTM). Raleigh, NC: North Carolina State University.

Rath, P. M., Peterson, J., Greensley, P., & Gill, P. (1994). *Introduction to fashion merchandising*. Albany, NY: Delmar.

Risch, E. (1987). *Retail merchandising*. Columbus, OH: Merrill.

Risch, E. (1991). *Retail merchandising*. New York: Macmillan.

Runyon, K. E., & Stewart, D. W. (1987). *Consumer behavior*. Columbus, OH: Merrill.

Rupe, D. & Kunz, G. I. (In Press). Building a financially meaningful language of merchandise assortments. *Clothing and Textiles Research Journal*.

Schary, P. B., & Becker, B. W. (1978). The impact of stock-out on market share. *Journal of Business Logistics, 1*(1), 31–44.

Shopping the big centers. (1990). *Monitor, 20*(5), 13–22.

Taylor, C. G. (1970). *Merchandise Assortment Planning*. New York: Merchandising Division National Retail Merchants Association.

The American Heritage Dictionary. (1994). Boston, MA: Houghton Mifflin.

The true look. (1993). *Discount Merchandiser, 33*(6), 35–74.

Wagner, J. (1975). *Principles of operations research*. Englewood Cliffs, NJ: Prentice Hall.

Developing and Presenting Product Lines

8 Developing Product Lines

Learning Objectives

- Discuss the relationship between merchandise planning and line development.
- Examine line development through purchase of finished goods and product development.
- Examine issues in buyer/vendor negotiations.

Line development processes have become more diverse as Quick Response (QR) business systems have been implemented and industries have become more globalized. **Line development** is the process of determining the actual styles, sizes, and colors that will fill out the line plan (Glock & Kunz, 1995). In today's markets, line development is closely associated with sourcing. **Sourcing** is determining the most cost efficient vendor of materials, production, and/or finished goods at the specified quality and service level with delivery within an identified time frame. Both manufacturer and retailer merchandisers are commonly responsible for line development. Merchandisers are either responsible for sourcing or work closely with those who are responsible for sourcing.

Fundamental Methods of Line Development

In its purest form, a merchandise plan is a bunch of words and numbers. The words describe relevant socio-economic, cultural, environmental, fashion, and technological trends that impact a firm's target customers. The numbers reflect analysis of sales history, interpretation of trends, and forecast of future customer demand. They provide a dollar investment and quantitative framework for forecasting sales for specific merchandise classifications and time frames. The merchandise plan also guides variety and diversity of the line, but does not necessarily identify the actual merchandise that will be offered to customers.

Line development results in the determination of the actual styles, sizes, and colors customers will have the opportunity to examine, consider, and purchase. As shown in Figure 3.1 (pp. 66–67), the Taxonomy of Apparel Merchandising Systems (TAMS), line development is closely integrated with line planning and line presentation. The relationship is not linear; line planning does not necessarily come first, followed by line development and line presentation. Many activities among planning, development, and presentation may be simultaneous and, perhaps more important, interactive. Effective use of QR, 1) requires simultaneous and interactive processes to reduce the time required for merchandising decisions; and 2) moves the key decisions closer to the point of sale to the ultimate consumer. Simultaneous and interactive decisions through the use of multi-functional merchandising teams streamline the merchanding process and reduce redundancy.

Purchase of Finished Goods

Both manufacturer and retailer merchandisers may purchase finished goods. Manufacturers usually specialize in producing certain types of products. For example, an athletic shoe manufacturer is likely to offer socks, a jeans manufacturer may want to offer matching shirts, vests or jackets, but they may have neither the production capacity nor the expertise to do so. Merchandisers, then, may be charged with searching the market for appropriate finished goods to fill out the product line. The finished goods purchased from another manufacturer are sold at wholesale as if the shoe or jeans manufacturer had produced the items themselves.

Retail Organization for Line Development

Purchase of finished goods by retailer merchandisers is often regarded as the traditional form of retail line development. Merchandisers view and evaluate lines when presented by sales representatives that call on them in their stores or offices. Retail-merchandisers might also visit local, regional, national or international wholesale markets to view dozens or even hundreds of product lines that may be synthesized into the total retail product offering for a particular selling period. From a manufacturer's perspective, wholesale markets provide the opportunity to identify new prospects, service current customers, introduce new and modified products, enhance corporate image, test new products, improve corporate morale, gather competitor information, and sell merchandise (Kerin & Cron, 1987).

The merchandising division of a retail firm is usually charged with the responsibility for supplying merchandise to the firm's retail stores. The merchandisers responsible for this effort are usually called buyers. According to Figure 3.1, buyers of finished goods make line plans, develop line concepts, interact with sales representatives at wholesale line presentations, adopt styles to fill out the line plan, and determine delivery strategies for the goods. The process of choosing among thousands of potential styles at wholesale markets is challenging and can be confusing, expensive, and time consuming.

Buyers commonly purchase designer or brand name goods to fill out their line plans. They also may purchase private-label goods. **Private label** is "merchandise that bears a retailer's own name brand rather than that of a designer or manufacturer" (Jernigan & Easterling, 1990, p. 565). A retailer's private label may be the retailer's own name, another copyrighted name, or a designer with whom the retailer has an exclusive license for the use of the name. Private-label goods are acquired in many ways. Some manufacturers develop lines to be sold especially for private label. The retailer selects styles and specifies sizes and quantities and the manufacturer inserts the retailer's private label into already manufactured goods. Other times retailers are involved in the development of the products. Table 8.1 describes the trends in private-label goods as a portion of total retail assortments. According to the table, private label has increased as a proportion of total assortment for each of the merchandise categories. Women's and girl's apparel tends to have a slightly larger increase than men's and boy's. It is important to remember that these are averages. Private label, as a portion of total assortments, ranges from 0 to 100 percent of assortments.

Purchasing finished goods requires an individual who is organized, able to take risks, energetic, and capable of performing under pressure (Wickett, 1995). The life of a buyer is exciting, tedious, and stressful. Buyers commonly spend at least one week of every month attending wholesale

TABLE 8.1

The private-label percentage share of total retail assortments.*

Classification	1993	1994	1995
Men's tops	32%	32%	32%
Men's bottoms	23%	23%	25%
Boy's tops	30%	29%	35%
Boy's bottoms	30%	28%	32%
Women's tops	33%	35%	36%
Women's bottoms	31%	35%	36%
Girl's tops	29%	29%	33%
Girl's bottoms	29%	31%	36%

*Kurt Salmon Associates. (1996). *Soft goods outlook for 1996.* p. 6. Author.

markets in search of new merchandise and negotiating with vendors. While buyers may visit many exotic parts of the world, they may not be able to enjoy them. A buyer's time is fully consumed by the duties involved in line development. Then, after devoting much time and attention to merchandise selection, most buyers must then get the approval of his or her divisional merchandise manager for the finished goods selected.

In recent years, large retailers commonly use **matrix buying** to improve the effectiveness of its line-development processes. The merchandising group identifies its best and/or most dominant suppliers and creates a matrix of preferred vendors for each merchandise classification. In order to have a chance to show their product line to buyers, the vendor's name must be on the list. Matrix buying creates much greater interdependence between buyers and vendors. The buyer is limited by what the vendors in the matrix offer; and the vendor probably has a larger portion of the business committed to fewer retail customers. The scenario lends itself both to performing the line-development process outside the traditional wholesale market system and to engaging in joint product development.

Role of Manufacturer Sales Representatives

Part of the role of manufacturer merchandisers is to train sales representatives on how to present, assort, and sell a line. In Figure 3.1, this training session is called **wholesale line preview.** The training includes a summary of overall trends that influenced line development, how trends evolved into line concept, the nature of the merchandise plan, and how the merchandise groups and individual styles are expected to appeal to the target customer. Pricing strategies and assortments are reviewed with emphasis on key styles and colors to balance merchandise plans with sales. Merchandisers train the sales reps on how to plan assortments for their customers that will be consistent with sales forecasts for the selling period.

The **wholesale market** is an external line review, and is represented by the "wholesale" component in Line Presentation in Figure 3.1. Two-thirds or fewer of the styles in a line presented at wholesale may generate adequate purchase orders to justify putting products into production. This means that the retail buyers who placed orders for goods with low demand will not receive the goods or will have other merchandise substituted by the manufacturer. The wholesale market system is highly inefficient from a product development standpoint because it is common for nearly half of the product development effort to be wasted because of inadequate quantities ordered by retailers. On the other hand, the system provides an opportunity to test the acceptability of styles according to the retail buyers' perceptions of the ultimate consumers' wants and needs. Wholesale markets provide opportunities for new firms to display innovative product lines. Some become instant successes. Others are ignored and may never be heard from again.

Retail merchandisers/buyers are notorious among manufacturers for trying to engage in the product design process. They tell sales representatives they want a long sleeve or a short sleeve; put a collar on or take it off; change the fabric, etc. A classic example of buyer/vendor design conflict relates to a situation recently reported by a buyer regarding the design of little girls' velveteen holiday dresses. The manufacturer designed the dresses with short sleeves to control product costs. The velveteen fabric was very expensive compared to other fabrics being used for holiday dresses. Putting long sleeves on the dresses increased fabric costs by nearly two-thirds. The result would have been an increase in the wholesale price of $2 and an increase in suggested retail price of $4. The retail buyers were frustrated because they knew their customers wanted long sleeves on holiday dresses. The higher price might put off some customers, but the short sleeve would make most of the dresses unsalable. The manufacturer's concern about cost was interfering with the buyer's need to satisfy the holiday dress customer.

Professional manufacturers' sales representatives are invaluable resources for retail buyers, particularly inexperienced buyers. In a study to identify sources of information used by buyers to reduce the uncertainty of their buying decisions, manufacturers' representatives were identified as the most important source, followed by trade journals and top management (Shim & Kotsiopulos, 1991). Reps are storehouses of information about industry trends, competitors, and customers. Sales representatives are commonly required to purchase the sales samples that provide the visual and tactile aspects of showing a line. Manufacturer sales representatives are usually paid a commission based on how much merchandise they sell. In the short term, the more merchandise they sell the more money they make. In the long term, the more merchandise that successfully sells through at retail the better the relationship the sales rep will have with the buyer and the stronger the relationship between the two companies.

Learning Activity 8.1

Traditional forms of line development

1. In what way might a sales representative be a link between manufacturer and retailer merchandisers?

2. How does line development via purchase of finished goods relate to the merchandise budget and the assortment plan?

3. Read Case 8.1 very carefully. Identify three conflicts raised about the role of the buyer.

4. Propose a means by which the conflicts might be resolved.

CASE 8.1

Merchandisers at a Crossroads

From Chanil, D. (1996, July). *Discount Merchandiser,* p. 68+.

The alliance between retailers and suppliers is often described as a love/hate relationship, but both parties recently came to a decisive conclusion: Buyers are a notably frustrated lot.

A survey of 200 retailers and 158 suppliers, along with a panel discussion presented by the International Mass Retail Association, Discount Merchandiser, and Kurt Salmon Associates at the annual IMRA convention in May, found that buyers suffer from a high level of dissatisfaction with their jobs. Suppliers agreed that, from their dealings with retailers, buyers seem disappointed with their duties.

The study, called "Merchandising at a Crossroads" and sponsored by Dow Brands, also revealed that dealing with internal bureaucracy, too much paperwork, and inefficient use of time were the main reasons for this dissatisfaction. Almost two-thirds of the buyers surveyed agreed with the statement, "I often feel frustrated in my job," while nearly 80 percent of suppliers said they agree with this statement about buyers.

The level of frustration expressed in the survey comes as no surprise to Jim Philips, vice president of sales and distribution for Britannia, an apparel manufacturer. "There is more constant pressure on everybody," he said. "We are all in a survival mode."

Some of this emotion may stem from confusion regarding how much authority is actually wielded by the buyer. For Thomas Mueller, president and chief operating officer of Binney & Smith, a manufacturer of children's products, "the biggest surprise in the survey is that buyers believe they have authority, because that is not what we see at all." While most buyers (81%) claimed to have the authority to make purchasing decisions, few suppliers (32%) believe this to be true.

Often, buying decisions require approval from someone higher in the retail organization, which can work to undermine the authority of the buyer. However, one panelist believes that buyer autonomy may not be in the best interest of the retailer.

Robert K. Voss, senior vice president of merchandising for Sam's Club, said that although 90 percent of all buying decisions are made by the buyer, he believes that the buyer's authority should be limited. "That might surprise a few people, but all our retail businesses are trying to differentiate themselves," he said. "To do that, you have to have a certain set of disciplines that each company has to live within, and those disciplines—of SKU control, of quality, and so on—have to be checked every time a decision is made."

Too bad if this system of discipline frustrates the buyer, Voss concluded. "They always have been and they always will be [frustrated]."

Information Overload

Buyers and suppliers also agree on issues concerning information management—most importantly, they agree that improvement is needed. More than half of all buyers and suppliers think buyers receive too much information to process, while approximately two-thirds feel that buyers spend more time gathering than analyzing information.

The panel agreed with these findings as well. "There is not enough focus on selling merchandise through," Mueller said. "But there is an awful lot of focus on numbers. We get reams and reams of data, and not terribly actionable data at that."

"There is an overload of knowledge out there," seconded Voss. "It makes the buyer's job and the seller's job more frustrating because not only do we

Product Development as a Means of Line Development

Product development is the design and engineering of products to be serviceable, producible, salable, and profitable (Glock & Kunz, 1995). The line plan combined with the line concept provides the framework for product development. According to Figure 3.1, product development has three phases: pre-adoption, adoption, and post-adoption. The time frame

have more access to technology, but the suppliers have the same information as we do. When suppliers have the same information, they think they can make those buying decisions. They want to be the buyer."

When asked where retail companies should direct their efforts to make buyers more productive, more than half the buyers chose the addition of both support and store-level personnel. Not surprisingly, upper-level retail management was not as quick to agree to add to their overhead. "I'm not sure it's realistic in today's world of downsizing to say that we are going to add more people," said Steve Robinson, Pamida senior vice president and general merchandise manager. "The question is how to get more productivity out of the people we have."

Technology is the most practical solution, according to Robinson. "We need to figure out how to integrate technology much more effectively with the buyer's everyday life," he said. His goal is a system where "buyers can enter certain assumptions and hit a button and based on those assumptions decide if they can recommend a certain course of action."

Determining Risks

An area of disagreement between buyers and suppliers is the buyer's freedom to take calculated risks. About 70 percent of the buyers surveyed said they could make informed yet risky decisions, while a mere 13 percent of the suppliers felt the buyers had the authority to do so. Further, only 32 percent of the buyers and 16 percent of the suppliers agreed that buyers are rewarded for creativity and initiative.

"One of the things that surprised me in the survey is the option that risk is not rewarded," Robinson said. "Over the past year, every merchant with the best performance—the one we thought most highly of— was the one who introduced the most new products

aggressively. And it's not just new products; sometimes it involves trying whole new strategies, new ways of doing business."

"Mass merchants can't always take risks because they are difficult to execute," added Philips, "it comes down to a key word, 'calculated risks.' I don't think there are too many people here who have said to their buyer, 'Hey, nice job on the buy you made. It wasn't successful, but really nice job on taking a risk.' Risks have to be long-term and they have to be calculated."

A reason that more risks are not taken, according to Mueller, is that "the buyer has become almost a tenured position. We've all seen buyers who have difficulty getting dressed by themselves, and yet there they are, year after year. That sends a signal to everybody else that there is no need to take a risk, you can have a nice long career by just doing the same-old same-old."

Voss addressed a basic dichotomy in how buyers' decisions are made. "To me, a great buyer generally has to be kind of a maverick or a guerrilla, and sometimes mavericks and guerrillas don't go hand-in-hand with people who analyze data. What you need is a process whereby when the maverick wants to select an item, he can trust that someone will analyze the data and say, "OK, Mr. Maverick, before you do that, let me know where you might go with this."

Can retailers and suppliers work to effect changes? The survey's conclusion offered the following advice to the industry: RE-THINK the current buying and merchandising model to streamline the process and add clarity and authority to the role. RETOOL the merchandising team to increase productivity, improve access and accuracy of information, and REWARD buyers and suppliers to include true measures of productivity and educated risk-taking.

and actual sequence of events related to product development may differ considerably from one firm to another and from one product line to another. Through application of CAD systems and modification of processes, product development time from concept to consumer has been reduced from 56 weeks in 1982 (American Apparel Manufacturers Association, 1982) to 26 weeks in 1997, and some are trying to reduce it further.

The process of product development involves planning, creating, copying, modifying, sampling, costing, testing, reviewing, adopting, and rejecting (Glock & Kunz, 1995). Some steps may take weeks, while others may take only a few hours. But a small time investment makes a process no less important. The execution of the process differs depending on whether the products will be wholesaled and how they will be retailed.

Product Development by a Manufacturer for Wholesale Distribution

Product development for wholesale distribution represents traditional processes where the timeline for product development is determined by merchandising and marketing calendars. Sales samples must be prepared in time for wholesale line preview and presentation at seasonal wholesale markets. Sales samples are not made until the pre-adoption and adoption phases of product development have been completed. Other deadlines are backed up and planned forward from the timing of wholesale markets.

The amount of time required for product development is a central issue in QR. For example, at Wrangler, 18 cross-functional teams were challenged with reengineering 18 major processes. As a result, they reduced product development times by almost 75 percent (Black, 1995). Improvements of this sort impact pre-adoption, adoption, and post-adoption product development. Review these phases in Figure 3.1.

The **pre-adoption phase** of product development focuses on analysis, creativity, and the formation of product groups with commonalties such as piece goods, design features or trim. The nature of the groups that are created depends on how the manufacturer defines its business. If it is a coordinates house, merchandise groups might consist of jackets, skirts, pants, blouses, and perhaps accessories. If it is a separates house, merchandise groups might include short-sleeve tops, knit tops, dressy blouses, and shirts. New designs are created, design specifications developed, first patterns are made, design samples are sewn, materials are evaluated and cost estimates are made. Designs may be modified and sampled several times before a design is finalized and presented for line adoption.

If a firm planned for 60 styles in their line, historically, up to 200 new designs might have been created—the "best" of which were adopted and became styles in the line. Less than two-thirds of the 60 styles were likely to represent over 90 percent of the sales for the selling period. Recent modifications of product development processes have focused on providing more focus and more effective trend analysis to reduce costs and time required for product development. Depending on where in the world materials will be purchased, materials sourcing often occurs simultaneously with pre-adoption product development. In order to have goods on hand for production, orders often have to be placed early in the product development process.

The purpose of **line adoption** is to determine which designs will become the styles to fill out the line plan, the styles for which sales and catalog samples will be made, and the styles that will go forward into post-adoption product development. Line adoption forces designers and merchandisers to articulate their reasons for their line plans, line concepts, and proposed designs. They must persuade the decision makers that their proposed line is well founded, salable, and potentially profitable.

The purpose of **post-adoption product development** is to perfect styling and fit and engineer perfect production patterns. Adapting fit to the target customer is very important as garment shapes must be adapted to the body shapes of different ethnic groups (Giddings & Boles, 1990). Merchandisers must ensure quality and performance of materials and develop detailed style specifications, including descriptions of assembly methods. Detailed costs are developed and patterns are graded in preparation for the development of markers. Post-adoption product development will proceed immediately for styles for which forecasts are very certain. Other styles will not move into the post-adoption product development phase until after sales potential is confirmed at wholesale markets. A manufacturer may or may not have its own factories, but in any case production planning often proceeds simultaneously with post-adoption product development.

Learning Activity 8.2

Stages of product development

1. If a manufacturer is forward vertically integrated by having its own retail stores, how would the product development process be different than product development for wholesale distribution?

2. If a manufacturer is backward vertically integrated by having its own materials production, how might the product development process differ?

3. Read Case 8.2 very carefully. Why did Tommy Hilfiger drop the Collection? What is the role of line development in the decision?

Product Development by a Retailer

Retail product development is "the process of creating research-based private-label merchandise manufactured or sourced by a retailer for its exclusive sale to an identified target market" (Wickett, 1995, p. 59). Many retailers have assumed responsibility for product development by creating

CASE 8.2

Hilfiger Drops Higher-Priced Collection

From Socha, M., & Williams, S. (1996, August 12). *Daily News Record,* pp. 4, 31.

New York—Last week's firings at Tommy Hilfiger Corp., soft-pedaled by the company, were in fact part of a major decision by the designer to drop his flashy, higher priced Collection, the featured attraction at his recent spring '97 runway show here.

In total, eight people were let go, including vice-president and creative director Reed Krakoff, who was also head designer of Hilfiger's Collection division.

"I've changed my philosophy on the Collection," an uncharacteristically rueful Hilfiger explained Friday. "We are not going to develop that business to the extent that was originally planned."

The designer stated that it was a "bottom-line" decision as a public company not to invest millions of dollars to develop a collection that was projected to generate perhaps $500,000 annually. Hilfiger's company is expected to top $600 million in sales this year.

"It is such a small business and potentially highly unprofitable, it's not as important to me," he stressed. "It just doesn't make sense. When you add in sales, showroom, advertising, production, etc., it becomes a very expensive proposition."

Hilfiger said that the company geared up in the last five months to launch a full-fledged Collection division of vivid rock-star-worthy suits and funky sportswear. Hilfiger debuted his Collection concept at his fall '96 runway show last February and has since outfitted several rock acts, including Nancy Boy and Metallica. Collection, however, will not become a part of retail assortments.

Owing to late deliveries of his mainstream sportswear samples, Hilfiger's runway presentation on July 25 was largely devoted to Collection—"It was 95 percent collection and 5 percent sportswear, whereas it should have been 50–50. My company should stand for what it is."

Looking ahead, Hilfiger said he plans to continue offering more exclusive, higher-priced items, but only as an adjunct to his sportswear line. The higher-priced items will likely now be denoted by a crest label rather than a flag label. There will be no separate showroom, sale force, advertising or design teams. "I don't need a team of seven plus one to design a tiny collection." In total, the design staff consists of 63 people.

their own product development divisions. These groups often work closely with and/or report to the merchandising division. Based on a case study of such a retailer, Gaskill (1992) proposed a model of retail product development. See Figure 8.1. The components of Gaskill's model are similar to some of those identified in Figure 3.1. Gaskill's trend analysis, concept evolvement, fabrication selection, palette selection, fabric design, and silhouette and style directions are included in Line Concept in TAMS. Gaskill's prototype construction and analysis is part of Pre-adoption Product Development in TAMS.

Gaskill's line presentation is part of Internal Line Presentation in TAMS and results in Line Adoption. Line presentation is described as presentation of the line by the product developers to the merchandisers. Interaction of product development with merchandising is also implied in Gaskill's inter-

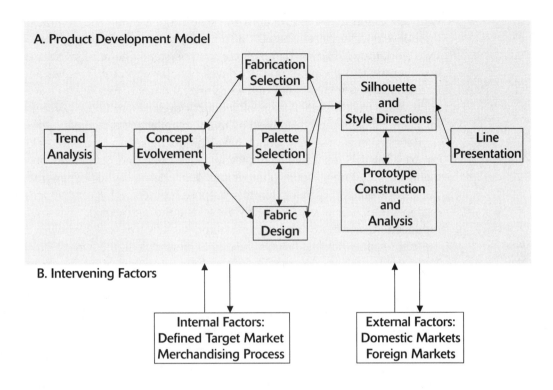

FIGURE 8.1

Model of retail product development from Gaskill (1992).

vening factors where the merchandising process is recognized as an internal factor related to the product development process.

Interestingly, Gaskill's model does not include any indicators of post-adoption product development. Historically, retail product development groups do not always include people trained as designers or have pattern-making technology available. Therefore, technical aspects of patternmaking for sample development may have been lacking in the retail firm. Many retail product developers have relied on their production contractors for developing of samples for the desired styles.

Retail product developers commonly have been responsible for private-label goods where style development depends on **knockoffs** of competitors' lines or other higher-priced merchandise. Finished goods purchased at retail by the product developers were often supplied to contractors along with fabric and a few instructions for style modification. The contractor then developed a pattern based on the ready-to-wear garment or from a style block they already had in their computer system. The resulting sample was then sent to the retail product developers for approval. Samples and instructions were mailed back and forth several times before the style was approved. The knockoff system of product development is still common for many retailers and is also used by many manufacturers, as well.

Retailers engaging in product development have no need for sales samples but they may need samples for advertising and promotion photographs. Catalogers need photographs for catalog layout. They may use design or style samples for this purpose, consequently catalog presentation does not always perfectly represent the garment as it is mass produced. Color is a very import factor. Usually the color shown in the photograph has by far the best sales potential. If the wrong color is chosen for the catalog picture, the style may not sell at all. Decisions are also made about catalog layout and catalog copy by merchandisers or catalog specialists.

The current trend in retail product development is to develop product-development divisions complete with designers and CAD systems of all kinds, including patternmaking. The Gap is regarded as a model of product development strategy. The Gap sells only its own designs and restocks its stores every six weeks throughout the year. Under this system, core products (basic goods) are stocked continuously with only occasional modifications in style and color. At the same time, the selling period for fashion goods is six weeks. Every six weeks new merchandise replaces goods from the last selling period (Schultz, 1997). The product line includes everything from underwear to casual professional apparel. The Gap corporation also includes Banana Republic at upper-moderate price points and Old Navy at lower-moderate price points, each appealing to different target markets. Jeans at Banana Republic might retail at $55, while jeans at Old Navy retail at $22. Each has its own product development group.

The Gap product development team has grown from 10 to 80 designers in just a decade. The challenge to the designers is to interpret European fashions for the average American consumer. The product development team receives assistance with the color palette from a fashion consultant. They also travel to European fabric and fashion shows looking for inspiration. Members of the team take extensive notes and collect samples. Design ideas are copied, developed, and modified to suit The Gap's customer. The team also decides which styles will be continued, dropped, or modified, and what new styles will be introduced (Schultz, 1997).

Line adoption occurs four times a year at The Gap when Chief Executive Millard Drexler and a group of merchandising executives fly from the headquarters in San Francisco to New York to evaluate the proposed line. They decide what will be offered at retail eight months later. The 1997 fall show, for instance, consisted of over 1,000 samples of men's, women's, and children's apparel, which were displayed in a room arranged like a Gap store. The product development team works on the line for 10 weeks. Their presentation includes the line concept (theme) and an overview of the line plan, for example, the change in the number of styles and colors offered. Individual designs are critiqued by the executive group; some are dropped, others modified. Endorsement by The Gap executives means the styles are prepared for production (Schultz, 1997).

Other retailers are imitating The Gap's success. Federated Department stores has a design/product development team of more than 400. Others are signing exclusive licensing deals with well-known designers. Retailers are trying to increase the uniqueness of their assortments by doing their own product development, which often translates into private-label goods. Private label used to be thought of as "bargain" merchandise; now it is regarded as exclusive brand name merchandise. JCPenney's Arizona line is a classic example. Sears has developed Canyon River Blues to counter the success of Arizona. Other retailers are following The Gap's premise that image and customer demand are dependent on the goods' design (Berner, 1997).

A retailer vertically integrated into product development is providing some of its own manufacturing services. A reality of retailers taking on the complete product development process is that they must bear the cost of design, sourcing, and inventory. Retailers bear the risk of bad sales forecasts and being over- or under-inventoried. They also have to find ways to dispose of unsalable merchandise. Under traditional product development systems that included wholesale markets, manufacturers shared these risks.

Another result of this trend is that demand by retailers for product development expertise has driven up designer salaries. Base salaries for design directors have risen 30 percent to $250,000. Demand for graduates with product development expertise is high. Retailers are hiring both creative and technical designers away from apparel manufacturing firms (Berner, 1997).

Retailers are also experiencing conflicts between their merchandisers who set budgets and their designers, who develop products. As predicted by (BTAF) in Chapter 1, constituencies develop conflicts because of differing in responsibilities and priorities. Joint-product development teams may be the answer.

> ### *Learning Activity 8.3*
> **Retailer apparel product development**
> 1. What are the primary advantages of a retailer engaging in its own product development?
> 2. What are the primary disadvantages of a retailer engaging in its own product development?

Joint Product Development

Joint product development is a key component of merchandising in a QR environment. **Joint product development** means that retailer merchandisers are working with manufacturer merchandisers and designers to develop the line concept, to establish line direction, and to develop products. The goal of the retailer may be to buy the finished goods produced by the manufacturer. However, by having the retailer's early input in the product development process, the manufacturer can reduce the number of unsalable styles that are developed under traditional product development systems, hence saving both time and money. The manufacturer benefits from the retailer's experience in directly serving the target customer. The line developed by the manufacturer more closely reflects the retailer's interpretation of the customer's needs.

As with traditional product development, joint product development also includes pre-adoption, adoption, and post-adoption product development, but the need for the wholesale market is eliminated. The breadth of perspective provided by the combination of both retailer and manufacturer merchandisers provides an excellent foundation for line analysis and the development of new styles. The proximity of the retailer merchandisers to their customers and the retail sales history is otherwise unavailable to the manufacturer retailers.

Integrating the manufacturer's and retailer's perspective into pre-adoption product development should reduce the number of inappropriate designs and improve the development of successful ones. But the methods used in pre-adoption processes may differ. For example, design development may be based primarily on computer-generated images and product specifications, rather than on design samples. Sampling to test patterns may be delayed until after designs are approved for the line. By reducing the number of samples required, time and money is saved since samples are often made in another part of the world.

Under joint product development, line adoption may focus more on developing the retailer's line plan than on choosing styles for the line. Most of the style decisions have been made before line adoption. No sales samples, and possibly no photo samples, are necessary since the wholesale market process has been eliminated. Styles with certain sales forecasts can go immediately into post-adoption product development and then into mass production. Firms may decide to test more risky styles with short production runs. A few days, well-positioned on a retail selling floor, is regarded as an excellent predictor of sales potential.

Post-adoption product development needs to be closely integrated with production planning. A short production run for style testing should serve as a test of style specifications, assembly methods, and plant layout. Considerable redundancy may exist between post-adoption product development and production planning under traditional product development systems. A multi-functional product development team may be able to eliminate those redundancies.

Learning Activity 8.4

Joint product development

1. From the perspective of Behavioral Theory of the Apparel Firm in a Quick Response Business System (Chapter 2), what kind of problems are likely to develop during an effort to do joint product development?

2. Saving what resource provides the primary motivation for engaging in joint product development?

Negotiating with Vendors

Both manufacturer and retailer merchandisers, whether engaging in acquisition of finished goods or product development, are often responsible for negotiating contracts with their vendors. To be effective, they must understand wholesale price structures and how these interrelate with retail price structures. Retail price structures were discussed in Chapter 5; Table 5.3. It is reproduced here as Table 8.2 to examine the wholesale price structures portion of the pricing relationship.

Manufacturer's Wholesale Price Structures

Market tradition has established and perpetuated a series of discounts in relation to list price that determine how much a retailer pays for apparel at wholesale. List price is the *base price for wholesale price structures.* It is the suggested retail price used in manufacturer/wholesaler catalogs and price sheets. It is also the manufacturer's estimate of the value of the product to the ultimate consumer. List price is useful to retail merchandisers because it

TABLE 8.2

Relationships among pricing factors as viewed by manufacturers, retailers, and consumers.

Manufacturer Pricing		Retailer Pricing		Retail Customer's View of Pricing	
		premium price	**$110**	**regular price**	**$110**
list price	**$105**[1]				
quantity/seasonal discounts	−5%	additional markup	+10%		
reduced list price	**$100**	**first price**	**$100**[5]		
		planned average markdown	−20%	special sale	−27%
		planned average selling price	**$ 80**	**bargain price**	**$ 80**
trade discount	−50%	initial markup	−50%	great sale	−55%
wholesale price	**$ 50**	**planned cost**	**$ 50**	**clearance price**	**$ 49.50**[10]
advertising/markdown discounts	−10%	advertising/markdown discounts	−10%		
billed cost	$ 45	billed cost	$ 45		
production cost	−$ 32				
$ gross margin	**$ 13**	**$ gross margin**	**$ 35**[6]		
% gross margin	**28.89%**[2]	**% gross margin**	**43.75%**[7]		
cash discount on billed cost	−8%	cash discount on billed cost	−8%		
reduced billed cost	$ 41.40[3]	reduced billed cost	$ 41.40[3]		
reimbursed shipping expense	+$ 2	shipping expense	+$ 2		
amount received	$ 43.40	amount remitted	$ 43.40		
other expenses	−$ 2	other expenses	+$ 3		
production cost	−$ 32	net cost of goods	$ 46.40		
$ adjusted gross margin	**$ 9.40**	**$ adjusted gross margin**	**$ 33.60**[8]		
% adjusted gross margin	**21.66%**[4]	**% adjusted gross margin**	**42%**[9]		

[1]price changes in wholesale sector are based on list price or reduced list price
[2][(billed cost − production cost) / billed cost] × 100
[3]billed cost − cash discount
[4][amount received − (production cost + other expense) / amount received] × 100
[5]all price changes in the retail sector are based on first price
[6]planned average selling price − billed cost
[7][(planned average selling price − billed cost) / planned average selling price] × 100
[8]planned average selling price − net cost of goods
[9][(planned average selling price − net cost of goods) / planned average selling price] × 100
[10]regular price − great sale percent

allows comparison of the style and quality of the product to the price lines and price points included in merchandise plans. Table 8.3 examines factors that might impact the determination of the manufacturer's wholesale price and the amount actually received for goods.

List price is the suggested retail price because **resale price maintenance** is illegal in the United States. The Consumer Goods Pricing Act of 1975 terminated the right of manufacturers to control the retail prices of their products. Resale price maintenance is also known as vertical price fixing and fair trade. Manufacturers may seek to fix prices to protect the firm's quality image and to prevent retailers from using well-known brand names to draw customers into promotional sales. Resale price maintenance is regarded as anti-competitive and thus it is illegal for manufacturers to require that retailers sell their products at a particular price.

Discounts on List Price

The Robinson-Patman Act, 1936, prohibits manufacturers from discrimination in price to purchasers of products of "like quality" if the effect of such discrimination is to injure competition. This law seeks to prevent large, influential retailers from using their market power to obtain discounts that are not justified by cost savings. In other words, discounts allowed to retail buyers must be justifiable in terms of economies to the manufacturer. Proportional promotional allowances must be available to all customers related to economies of scale. In light of this legal scenario, three types of discounts may be applied to list price to determine a manufacturer's wholesale price: seasonal discount, quantity discount, and trade discount.

TABLE 8.3

Determining manufacturers' wholesale prices.

	list price
—	seasonal & quantity discounts
=	reduced list price
—	trade discount
=	wholesale price (billed cost)
—	cash discounts
—	other discounts
=	reduced merchandise cost
+	transportation costs
=	remittance from retail customer

A **seasonal discount** is a reduction from list price that relates time of purchase to the stage of the selling period. A manufacturer may offer pre-selling period, late selling period, and end-of-the-selling-period discounts. A **pre-selling period discount** may be allowed when the retail merchandiser commits to merchandise well ahead of the traditional buying period. This allows the manufacturer to spread production for a fashion/seasonal line over a longer time period, hence easing production schedules, while still being assured that the merchandise being produced is sold. With flexible production systems, the early selling period discount teamed with early delivery may allow style testing prior to delivery of the most salable merchandise.

The pre-selling period discount may also be offered in combination with a requirement for early payment for the goods. Traditional payment terms frequently allow retailers to pay for merchandise several weeks or even months after the merchandise has been produced and shipped. This means the manufacturer may be paying interest on loans used to purchase materials and cover production expenses for the line over a prolonged period of time, which greatly increases merchandise costs. The pre-selling period discount, then, can provide financially justifiable benefits to both retailer and manufacturer.

A **late-selling-period discount** might be used to extend production and the sale of items where the manufacturer had already invested in materials. It can also help clear finished goods still in stock. An **end-of-selling-period discount** is used to clear the manufacturer's inventory of finished goods and distressed merchandise at the close of the selling period. **Distressed goods** owned by the manufacturer might include design samples, sales samples, experimental goods, production test runs, production overruns, second-quality goods, and retailer returns.

A **quantity discount** is used to provide incentive for retail merchandisers to make large or multiple purchases. Large orders usually provide manufacturers with the benefits of economy of scale. Production systems require considerable investment in non-variable costs such as buildings and utilities, as well as set-up costs for producing particular products. Increasing the quantity sold from a given production set-up allows distribution of non-variable costs over more finished goods. The result is lower average production costs for all goods produced. The application of seasonal and quantity discounts results in a **reduced list price,** which becomes the foundation of the trade discount.

A **trade discount** is a reduction from list price or reduced list price. Sometimes a trade discount is granted to a firm who performs some marketing or distribution function. A trade discount to a wholesaler may be 30 percent at the same time the trade discount to a retailer is 50 percent. The amount of trade discount is proportional to the perceived services to be rendered. A wholesaler may assemble merchandise assortments to offer to small retailers who lack the skill or the resources to travel to markets to develop the assortments on their own. Thus, the service provided to a manufacturer by a wholesaler translates to getting finished goods into the hands of retailers. Wholesalers provide a substitute mechanism for the apparel wholesale market system in which most manufacturers and retailers participate.

The trade discount offered directly to retailers is higher than that for wholesalers because the retailer will sell the goods to the ultimate consumer. Ownership of merchandise must be transferred to the ultimate consumer before the distribution system is complete. The ultimate consumer bears all the production and distribution costs. Manufacturers sell goods by the group, dozen, pre-pack or shipping container. Retailers sell goods to consumers, for the most part, one piece at a time, a very expensive process. If retailers did not buy goods at wholesale to sell in their stores, then manufacturers would have to invest in catalogs, electronic shopping or retail stores to get their goods to ultimate consumers. Some form of retailing is an essential aspect of merchandise distribution.

A trade discount to a retailer tends to be roughly comparable to initial markup in the retail sector. Trade discounts to apparel retailers have traditionally been 50 percent. Now, with retail markups more in the 60 percent range, list prices are proportionally higher, as are trade discounts. Applying the trade discount to list price or reduced list price results in the wholesale price and billed cost reported on an invoice. However, the billed cost is not necessarily what the retailer will pay for the merchandise. The final payment is dependent on invoice payment terms and on discounts and allowances on the wholesale price.

Invoice Payment Terms

Invoice payment terms determine when and how much of the billed cost will be paid by the retailer. Most sales of finished goods to retailers are made on credit and the retailer pays for the goods after they have been received in the retail store, perhaps even after they have been sold to the ultimate consumer. Three common types of invoice payment terms are cash discounts, contract dating, and shipping terms.

A **cash discount** is a reduction in billed cost as incentive to pay the invoice by the time specified by contract dating. Common terms for women's wear are eight percent cash discount on billed cost in 10 days of receipt of invoice, with total billed cost due in 30 days. Cash discounts for men's wear have commonly been two percent.

Contract dating determines when a cash discount can be taken and when an invoice is due to be paid. Unauthorized extension of the time period in which cash discounts can be taken is a common source of conflict between retailers and vendors. Vendors frequently complain about retailers waiting 60, 90 or even 120 days before paying bills and then taking discounts anyway. Sears recently announced that its standard terms for all products would be no less than 60 days instead of the traditional 30. This practice metes particular hardships on small manufacturers who depend on prompt payment of invoices to maintain cash flow.

Invoice due dates may be specified as COD, DOI, ROG, or EOM. **COD** (cash on delivery) means the merchandise must be paid for in full in cash or certified check when delivered or the goods will be returned to the vendor. COD terms are only used when the buyer has a poor credit rating or no credit rating, as might be the case with a new firm. Retailers that are involved in bankruptcy proceedings (Chapter 11) may be required by vendors to pay COD. **DOI** (date on invoice) is regarded as normal or ordinary dating. *DOI is assumed when no other terms are stated.*

ROG (receipt of goods) dating means the cash discounts and due dates relate to the date the goods are received by the store or distribution center. Receipt of goods dating may be appropriate when goods are being shipped from foreign ports. Because of shipping delays, an invoice may be received well ahead of the merchandise. With DOI dating on foreign-made goods, the bill might have to be paid before the merchandise is received and quantity and quality can be verified.

EOM (end of month) dating means discounts and due dates are calculated from the end of the month when the invoice is dated rather than the invoice date itself. Other forms of dating that might be negotiated include the following: **extra** dating, or extending credit for an additional period; **advanced** dating, or setting the invoice due date at some future time; **anticipation,** or allowing a discount for paying the invoice early; and **loading** to adjust billed cost so the same discount rate will be applied to all invoices. Clearly invoice payment terms can have a profound impact on merchandise costs. See Table 8.4 for examples of invoice payment and shipping terms as they might appear on an invoice.

Shipping Terms

Shipping terms determine who bears the transportation costs and when the buyer takes title/ownership of the merchandise. **FOB** (free on board) origin or factory means ownership is transferred when goods are loaded on a transporting vehicle and the buyer bears the shipping costs. FOB distribution center or FOB store means ownership is transferred when the goods are delivered at their destination and the vendor bears the freight

TABLE 8.4

Examples of invoice payment and shipping terms.

COD	No discounts are allowed; merchandise must be paid for in cash or by certified check when delivered.
3/10, n/30, FOB factory	Three-percent discount allowed if bill is paid within 10 days of date on invoice; otherwise n/30 (net 30) means total billed cost is due within 30 days of date on invoice; retailer pays the freight; ownership is transferred when goods are loaded on the truck at the factory.
8/10 EOM, FOB store	Eight-percent discount allowed within 10 days of the end of the month in which the invoice is received (n/30 is implied, meaning 30 days from end of the month); manufacturer pays freight costs and ownership is not transferred until goods reach the store.
6/10 ROG, FAS	Six-percent discount allowed within 10 days of receipt of goods (n/30 days from receipt of goods [ROG] is implied); manufacturer pays for delivery of goods to the dock or airport where ownership is transferred and the remainder of freight costs are born by the retailer.
2/10, n/60 CIF	Two-percent discount on billed cost if paid within 10 days of date of the invoice; otherwise n/60 (net 60) means total billed cost is due within 60 days from date of the invoice; CIF means ownership is transferred as soon as merchandise is shipped; billed cost includes merchandise cost, insurance, and freight, hence the term CIF.

costs. **CIF** (cost, insurance, freight) means the billed cost includes merchandise cost, insurance, and freight. All are due to the vendor according to other contract terms. **FAS** (free alongside the ship) means the vendor will pay for transportation of goods to the dock where the ownership is transferred to buyer. All shipping costs are borne by the buyer.

Other Contract Terms

Numerous other contract terms may be negotiated by either the manufacturer or retailer. Manufacturers may specify minimum-order quantities. Assortments may be confined to pre-packs prescribed by the manufacturer that contain a set combination of styles, sizes, and colors. Manufacturers may require a minimum of retail display area in terms of number of square feet and may supply special fixtures (for a fee) and point-of-purchase displays. Manufacturers may also provide free or co-op advertising, offers of free goods, and/or "push" or prize money for sales contests for

CASE 8.3

Negotiating With Your Vendors

From Lenser, J. (1996, June). *Catalog Age*, pp. 89–90.

A wise merchant once advised me that margin is the difference between what I am willing to pay for a product and what my customer is willing to pay; if the margin is not sufficient, I have only myself to blame for paying too much. Too many buyers compromise their judgment and end up overpaying by first looking at the cost of a product, then applying a margin formula and deciding if the customer will pay the resulting retail price.

Instead, you need to first look at a promising product through the eyes of the customer and decide the appropriate retail price. Next you apply your margin formula to the retail price in order to determine an acceptable cost. Only then should you look at the wholesale price to see if it would allow you to meet the goal.

If the answer is no, you have two options: Walk away, or negotiate for an appropriate price.

Successful Negotiation

Negotiating for price is a fundamental part of the buyer's responsibility. Successful negotiation requires a positive attitude, adequate time or priority, appropriate role definition between the buyer and the purchasing staff, and excellent negotiation skills.

Some buyers find negotiation to be distasteful and an impediment to their relations with suppliers. While this may be true of "confrontational" negotiation, where one party is a loser and the other a winner, it should not be the case when working with merchandise vendors. Negotiation with vendors must be a cooperative process in which both parties search for a win-win solution.

Because the negotiating process requires a full discussion of all issues, you will rarely be successful negotiating at a merchandise show where there are frequent interruptions, little privacy, the need to "keep moving" and, perhaps, only a product rep who is not empowered to modify price of terms on behalf of the vendor. You're better off negotiating, sampling, and ordering in subsequent weeks, even if it means doing so by phone.

The merchant should have primary responsibility for selecting products and negotiating the initial price and terms. Frequently, however, the merchant shares this responsibility with the purchasing staff, which can compromise the process in favor of the vendor.

For one thing, by the time the staff has decided to pursue a purchase, the vendor is likely to perceive a strong commitment to the product and a reduced likelihood that they will "walk away." For another, the staff may know less about the vendor's financial objective and costs than the lead merchant does. Finally, the purchase staff is less likely to have the personal relationship with the vendor that facilitates understanding, trust, and partnership.

The Fundamental Skills

Negotiation has developed into such a sophisticated art form that you should invest in formal training. In the meantime, here are several basic concepts:

Be willing to walk away. Keep in mind that the vendor is almost always more eager to sell than you are to buy and is therefore motivated to seek acceptable terms. You lose this edge if you show any degree of commitment to the product. This is why you need to spell out to the vendor that you both must agree to the price and the terms before you'll even consider the product.

Know the product. Don't assume that the asking price bears any relation to what the product costs the vendor. To properly assess the fairness of the vendor's asking price and his flexibility in negotiating , ask about the product's country of origin, manufacturing minimums, lead times, methods of shipment, packaging, quality control, royalties, licenses, and anything else of relevance you can think of.

Know the vendor. Again, to understand avenues for negotiation, learn as much about the vendor as possible, including sales commissions, inventory levels, capitalization, credit line, and whether you would be a big account or a small one.

Take your time. To avoid being hurried into paying a higher price than you can afford, you must allow yourself time for give and take.

Aim high. Request a price and terms that are much better than what you realistically expect to achieve. This leaves room for compromise.

Remember that money has many forms. While you may need to ask the vendor to lower the price, it is more likely that you will negotiate around the price through discounts, terms, and related benefits to you or the vendor.

Points of Negotiation

The crux of win-win negotiation is finding a combination of terms that has high value to both you and the vendor: You try to give concessions that cost you little but are valuable to the vendor, and vice versa. Here are several methods many catalogers have used, and several ways to implement each of them. Any one could impact the true cost of the product.

Reduce the vendor's expense in order to justify price reductions or discounts.

- Guarantee a purchase volume so that the vendor can negotiate volume discounts for materials or production.
- Place orders sufficiently early to allow the vendor to produce and ship the goods (particularly from Asia) at the lowest cost.
- Order case packs to save the vendor labor and materials and eliminate fancy retail-display packaging.
- Accept delivery directly from overseas rather than through the vendor's warehouse.
- Agree not to return damaged or defective product unless such problems exceed an agreed-to percentage.

Finance your vendor in exchange for a discount.

- Pay in less than 30 days to receive a discount—perhaps a 2 percent discount for payment within 10 days.
- Pay prior to shipment.
- Accept early delivery, saving the vendor storage expense and allowing it to borrow against a receivable.

Require the vendor to share the financial risk, protecting your long-term margin.

- Secure the right to return unsold inventory for credit, perhaps paying only a restocking fee.
- Request that the vendor provide "markdown dollars" to reserve your planned margin should you need to sell the product at a reduced price.
- Agree that there will be no price increase on the product for a set period, at least for the life of the catalog, but preferably for the typical life cycle of similar products.

Have the vendor finance your business.

- Receive extended net payment terms; net 30 days may be normal, but 60 days, 90 days or more is frequently available for the asking.
- Participate in a "dating program" that allows you to pay at the end of the selling season.

- Accept inventory on consignment, eliminating your investing in product and the need to liquidate unsold goods.
- Request the vendor to drop ship your orders, which not only has the benefits of inventory on consignment but can also save on fulfillment costs.

Have the vendor enhance the product value and, in turn, retail price and margin.

- Persuade the vendor to give you a total or catalog exclusive.
- Have the vendor create a private-label product with your brand name.
- Work with the vendor to add special features, such as packaging or companion items that can add substantial value at minimal cost.

Reduce your secondary merchandise costs.

- Request that the vendor pay for insurance and freight to your distribution center.
- Ensure that the individual product cartons supplied by the vendor can be used as the shipping cartons, minimizing your pick and pack costs.
- Require the vendor to mark products or include any necessary information such as bar codes, safety warnings or instructions that will save you expense or increase your efficiency.

Secure advertising support from the vendor.

- Request an advertising allowance of at least 10 percent (the industry norm).
- Ask for an advertising fee based on the size and location of the catalog space given to the product and on the catalog's circulation.
- Request an initial placement fee to offset all or a portion of the catalog photography, copywriting, and film costs associated with the product.
- Ask for support materials such as transparencies to save you photography costs, or printed promotional material that can be mailed or used as package inserts.

As the pressures on the bottom line increase, many catalog executives cut advertising or expenses, rather than address what is their single greatest expenditure, the product they sell. Yet every point of additional margin achieved is a point that goes straight to the bottom line. And it's certainly more pleasant to negotiate your way into an additional point of margin than it is to lay off staff and enforce other reductions in order to cut a point of expenses.

sales associates. Retailers may negotiate markdown allowances for merchandise unsalable at first price, guarantees of refunds on damaged or defective goods, and guarantees of shipping dates or discounts on late shipments.

The manufacturer's wholesale price must cover a great variety of identified costs, as well as only vaguely defined costs associated with the manufacture of goods and the transfer of ownership of the merchandise. Establishing a wholesale price that is at once adequate to cover expenses, produce a profit, and regarded as reasonable by the retail buyer is clearly a challenge.

Learning Activity 8.5

Manufacturer pricing

1. Why might contract terms impact list price? Merchandise cost?

2. Why is a retail merchandiser concerned about contract terms?

3. Read Case 8.3 very carefully. What are fundamental negotiation strategies? What skills are required to be a successful negotiator? What kind of experiences do you need in order to be an effective negotiator?

Summary

Line development provides the means of filling out a line plan. Common methods of line development for apparel are buying finished goods and engaging in product development. Both manufacturer and retailer merchandisers may buy finished goods to develop a line. Retailers may exclusively purchase finished goods while manufacturers are more likely to supplement the product development process by purchasing finished goods.

Sales representatives provide key linkages between manufacturer and retailer merchandisers. Manufacturer merchandisers train sales representatives on how to sell a line; retailer merchandisers use the knowledge and skills of sales representatives in developing their retail product lines.

Product development evolves in a series of phases. Who is responsible for what depends on the relationships among materials vendors, apparel manufacturers and/or contractors, and retailers involved. Retailers engaged in product development have probably had more effective forecasting processes than manufacturers doing product development. Today, there is a strong trend toward retailers assuming more and more of the product development responsibilities.

Acquisition of materials and finished goods for line development requires merchandisers to negotiate contracts with vendors. Key points in contract negotiations include contract terms and delivery systems.

CASE 8.4

Solving the Special-Size Puzzle

From Reda, S. (1996, June). *Stores,* pp. 22–24.

While department stores may be doing a better job these days of catering to large-size and petite shoppers, a recent survey makes clear that it's no time for anyone to be resting on their laurels.

The survey, conducted by Kurt Salmon Associates, reveals that large-size and petite shoppers are highly dissatisfied with product availability, fashion/styling, and brand offerings across all retail tiers. A resounding 84 percent of large-size customers and 62 percent of petites feel that fashion/styling selection is less in their size than any other. When asked if the choice of brand names is too limited in their size, 70 percent of large-size customers and 48 percent of petites agreed.

"Just because you make a large-size dress doesn't mean you satisfy this customer," say Mara Urshel, president of brand development for August Max Woman and Petite Sophisticates. "There are fit, quality and fabric issues that must be addressed," says Urshel. "We've confronted these factors, and I think we've conquered them."

The KSA survey underscores, however, how far Urshel and others have to go. Of the 2,700 women interviewed, 33 percent said they were large size, while 19 percent described themselves as petite; 48 percent were misses/junior customers. Although more than half of all women classified themselves as special-size customers, 78 percent of large-size and 49 percent of petites said they felt stores favored misses/junior customers. The survey showed that 57 percent of large-size consumers and 45 percent of petites have difficulty finding stores that carry their size.

Inconsistencies in apparel sizing add to the high level of dissatisfaction. Three-quarters of special-size women say there is wide variation in fit among brands, and more than half have found that fit is inconsistent within brands.

Another issue concerns limitations on fabric choices. "Because the yield is less when you're laying patterns in sizes 14 to 24, the price per item jumps dramatically to cover the cost of the fabric," explains Urshel. "Typically, retailers and manufacturers have traded down in fabric to meet desirable retail prices, but doing so compromises quality."

Mary Duffy, executive director of special sizes for the Ford Modeling Agency and a frequent speaker on apparel retailing for large size women, say the future of the business rests on standardized sizing. "I've grown accustomed to taking my tape measure to determine whether or not they'll fit," says Duffy. "In some cases, the same size varies by a matter of inches," "Fifty-two percent of American women are 5'4" or under, and 37 percent wear size 16 or above," she says. "Yet 95 percent of floor space, mannequins, promotional effort and marketing is devoted to the average-size consumer. Tell me if I'm doing the math wrong, but in my book that doesn't add up."

"When a large-size shopper walks past misses sportswear and sees a bunch of new looks in pastels, then walks into her department and sees everything looks cheap and cheerful, she gets upset—and rightly so," says Wendy Banks, president of Banks strategic Marketing and New Business Consultancy. "For years she's been asking for the same looks and the same quality as the misses shoppers, but there are a lot of folks who still haven't listened."

Special–Size Customers

Petite		Large–size	
Sizes	*Percentage*	*Sizes*	*Percentage*
2 or smaller	2.1	9–10	0.8
3–4	7.1	11–12	2.5
5–6	13.2	13–14	5.7
7–8	15.4	15–16	14.3
9–10	14.1	18	20.2
11–12	17.9	20	15.7
13–14	12.4	22	12.0
15–16	7.0	24+	20.6
16+	2.3		

Key Concepts

buyer
cash discount
contract dating
distressed goods
joint product development
knock-off
line adoption
line development
list price
matrix buying

post-adoption product
  development
pre-adoption product
  development
private label
product development
product development for
  wholesale distribution
purchase of finished goods
quantity discount

resale price maintenance
retailer product
  development
seasonal discount
shipping terms
trade discount
wholesale line preview
wholesale market
wholesale price structures

Integrated Learning Activity 8.6

Using merchandise planning and line development to satisfy customers

1. Read Case 8.4 carefully. What is the nature of the problem that prevents merchandisers from offering goods in an adequate range of sizes to satisfy a wide range of customers?

2. What issues must be resolved in order to solve the sizing problem?

Recommended Resources

Berner, R. (1997, March 13). Now the hot designers on Seventh Avenue work for Macy's, Sears. *Wall Street Journal,* B1; B13.

Gaskill, L. R. (1992, Summer). Toward a model of retail product development: A case study analysis. *Clothing and Textiles Research Journal, 10*(4), 17–24.

Schultz, L. (1997, March 13). How Gap's own design shop keeps its imitators hustling. *Wall Street Journal,* B1; B13.

Glock, R. E., & Kunz, G. I. (1997). *Angelica's uniform business.* Ames, IA: Iowa State University Media Resources Center (videotape).

Shim, S., & Kotsiopulos, A. (1991, Summer). Information-seeking patterns of retail apparel buyers. *Clothing and Textiles Research Journal. 10*(1), 20–30.

References

American Apparel Manufacturers Association Technical Advisory Committee (1982). *Fashion apparel manufacturing.* Arlington, VA: Author.

Berner, R. (1997, March 13). Now the hot designers on Seventh Avenue work for Macy's, Sears. *Wall Street Journal,* B1; B13.

Black, S. S. (1995, July). AAMA touts globalization. *Bobbin,* 36(11), 22–24.

Gaskill, L. R. (1992, Summer). Toward a model of retail product development: A case study analysis. *Clothing and Textiles Research Journal, 10*(4), 17–24.

Giddings, V. L., & Boles, J. F. (1990, Spring). Comparison of anthropometry of black males and white males with implications for pants fit. *Clothing and Textiles Research Journal. 8*(3) 25–28.

Glock, R. E., & Kunz, G. I. (1995). *Apparel manufacturing: Sewn product analysis.* Englewood Cliffs, NJ: Prentice Hall.

Jernigan, M. H. , & Easterling, C. R. (1990). *Fashion merchandising and marketing.* New York: Macmillian.

Kerin, R. A., & Cron, W. L. (1987, July). Assessing trade show functions and performance: An exploratory study. *Journal of Marketing, 51.* pp. 87–94.

Schultz, L. (1997, March 13). How Gap's own design shop keeps its imitators hustling. *Wall Street Journal,* B1; B13.

Shim, S., & Kotsiopulos, A. (1991, Summer). Information-seeking patterns of retail apparel buyers. *Clothing and Textiles Research Journal. 10*(1), 20–30.

Wickett, J. L. (1995). Apparel retail product development: Model testing and expansion. Master's thesis, Iowa State University.

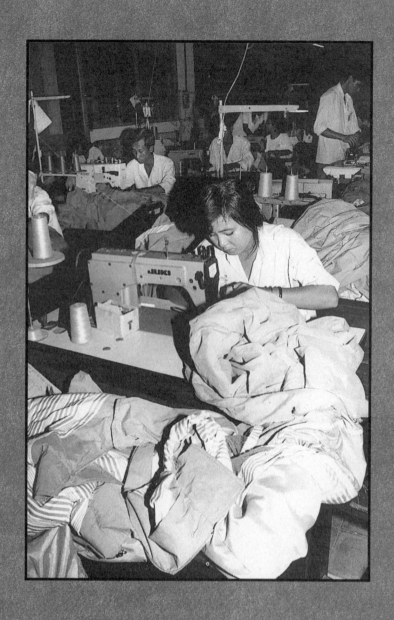

9

Global Sourcing

Learning Objectives

- Examine the concepts of globalization.
- Explore U.S. textiles and apparel sourcing from major suppliers.
- Discuss the sourcing process.
- Examine labor and exploitation issues.

Merchandising decisions frequently include not only what, how much, and when merchandise should be acquired, but also where. At any given time, a major apparel company like The Limited or Liz Claiborne is probably sourcing materials, production, and/or finished goods in more than 40 countries. **Sourcing** is determining the most cost efficient vendor of materials, production, and/or finished goods at the specified quality and service level with delivery within an identified time frame. Sourcing may be domestic or foreign and thus may result in imports. Most of the more than 200 countries in the world export textiles and apparel to the United States. At the same time other markets around the world offer huge potential for export of U.S.-made goods. Sourcing finished goods, materials or production is closely associated with and may be a part of the merchandiser's responsibilities.

The Concept of Globalization

Imagine if you will, the requisite label of origin in the year 2095 after we have colonized other planets in our solar system. Just as we now say "Made in America" or "Made in Sri Lanka," chances are the label of 2095 may say "Made on the Planet Earth" to distinguish the products made on the third planet from the sun (Made on the Planet Earth, 1995).

Globalization may be simple compared to solarization! To say something is **global** means it relates to or includes the whole earth. To globalize is to organize or establish worldwide. From a business standpoint, the term **globalization** is associated with viewing multiple sites in the world as markets and/or sources for producing or acquiring merchandise. Global firms use advanced communication and transportation technology to simultaneously coordinate manufacturing and distribution in multiple locations (Bonacich, Cheng, Chinchilla, Hamilton, & Ong, 1994). Power of global firms may transcend and sometimes overwhelm the power of political states. Some global firms command more capital and economic power than entire countries.

Successful global competitors are characterized by less bureaucracy and more communication. Vertical control and hierarchy of command are being replaced by more horizontal, peer-oriented relationships across borders and boundaries (Kanter, 1994). As with Quick Response (QR) business systems, the greatest challenge to global firms is "developing new organizational capabilities and managerial mindsets" (Kanter, 1994, p. 232). Agile production for QR is inherently global production, whereas mass production is merely international, i.e., between countries (Goldman, Nagel, & Preiss 1995).

But not only large firms are impacted by globalization. Small firms are both suppliers and buyers in the global market. Many textiles and apparel industry participants believe that globalization favors large firms because of capitalization requirements, economies of scale, breadth of product lines, and sophistication of technology and communications systems. At the same time, globalization factors that favor smaller firms include flexibility, ability to serve niche markets, focus, unique and differentiated products, and higher margin products (Made on planet earth, 1995). More disperse locations of production units have resulted in using more functional, smaller scale, and less expensive production equipment (Goldman, Nagel and Preiss, 1995). The reality of the global market and world trade in textiles and apparel is so pervasive that it is impossible to be an apparel manufacturer or retailer without participating in it.

Regulation of Trade

Countries have always felt the need to regulate commerce between countries, often to protect domestic industries. Until recently, the primary source of textiles and apparel trade regulation was the **General Agreement on Tariffs and Trade (GATT)** operating along with the **Multi-Fiber Arrangement (M-FA).** Through extended negotiations of the Uruguay Round, GATT has now been replaced by the **World Trade Organization (WTO).** The fundamental purpose of GATT and WTO, its successor, is to increase international trade by reducing trade barriers, which include tariffs, taxes on goods that are imported or exported, and quotas. The U.S. now uses the **Harmonized System of Tariffs** to tax imports of all kinds of products, including textiles and apparel.

The M-FA is operated as a system of quotas for textiles and apparel based on bilateral agreements among 50 or so member countries. These countries are the world's largest producers of textiles and apparel. The M-FA was designed to protect the textile and apparel industries in developed countries from excessive imports from low-wage developing countries. Since the M-FA violates the fundamental purpose of GATT—to promote free trade—the WTO includes a phaseout of M-FA bilateral agreements over a period of 10 years, beginning in 1992. The result is intended to be freer trade of textiles and apparel throughout the world.

During the time the GATT was being renegotiated, the U.S./Canadian Free Trade Agreement (1988) came into being, followed in 1994 by the North American Free Trade Agreement (NAFTA). The development of these trade agreements, along with the dissolution of the Soviet Union and the formation of the European Union (EU), have reformed world order. The result is three major trading blocs: The Americas, Europe, and Asia/Pacific Rim. While trade may be more free *within* each of these trading areas, trade is not necessarily freer *among* the trading areas (Marlin-Bennett, 1994). As an indicator or the economic power of these trading blocs, Table 9.1 reports their populations, retail sales, and sales per capita.

TABLE 9.1

Population and total retail sales in world markets.

Continent/Trading Bloc	1994 Population (millions)	1994 Retail Sales (millions $)	1994 Sales per Capita ($)
Americas			
North America	290.0	$2,385.2	$8,226
Latin America	340.6	226.7	666
Europe			
Western Europe	357.8	1,971.0	5,509
Eastern Europe	192.0	154.0	802
Asia			
Asia/Pacific Rim	1,669.6	2,030.1	1,216
Australia	21.3	96.2	4,516
Total	2,871.3	6,853.2	
Rest of World	2,862.8		
World Total	5,734.1		

*Source: Management Ventures, Inc. as published in *Discount Merchandiser,* May, 1996, pp. 78–79.

CASE 9.1

Wal-Mart Puts on Pajamas, Lies Down in King-Size Mess

From the *Des Moines Register.* (1997, March 16), p. 2G.
Originally published in the *Miami Herald.*

The case of the Cuban pajamas, already at the vortex of a burgeoning trade dispute between the United State and Canada, has also produced a palace revolt with the management ranks of mega-retailer Wal-Mart.

The incident began more than a week ago, when Wal-Mart Canada pulled Cuban-made sleepwear from its stores, apparently in the mistaken belief that selling them violated the Helms-Burton Act. Helms-Burton, passed last year, forbids companies anywhere in the world from "trafficking" in property confiscated from U.S. citizens or companies by the Castro regime after it took power in 1959. However, the law has sparked global outrage, with the United States' trading partners charging it violates their sovereignty.

As it turns out, the pajamas may not have violated Helms-Burton. However, they likely violated the embargo-tightening Cuban Democracy Act of 1992, which prohibits foreign subsidiaries for U.S. companies from buying or selling most Cuban goods. When Wal-Mart Canada pulled the Cuban pajamas off its shelves, it sparked widespread protests in that country. And Canadian officials said the move violated a Canadian law, the Foreign Extraterritorial Measures Act,

which is designed to prevent other countries from extending their laws into Canada.

Thursday, Wal-Mart Canada relented—executives faced potential fines of up to $1 million Canadian and up to five years in prison—and said it would start stocking the pajamas again. Wal-Mart has 136 stores in Canada, with a commanding 45 percent share of the discount merchandise market. But its actions drew the ire of Wal-Mart Stores, the Bentonville, Ark. parent, which had ordered its Canadian subsidiary to abide by U.S. laws.

"Wal-Mart Canada made a decision to return that stock to the shelves," said Wal-Mart spokesman Dale Ingram. "They did that in conflict with the directive from Wal-Mart Stores Inc. We had asked them to follow any applicable U.S. law."

As a result, Wal-Mart, United States' largest retailer, finds itself in conflict with Washington, Ottawa, and its own rebellious division. Although the company has been cooperating with the U.S. Office of Foreign Assets control since the incident first erupted, it will nonetheless be held accountable for Wal-Mart Canada's actions.

The pajamas "must be a pretty funky little creation," said Washington lawyer Robert Muse, who has closely followed the Helms-Burton Act. "But the legal issues involved in this case are quite serious."

International trade agreements are only a few of the laws that impact opportunities for importing and exporting goods. Case 9.1 provides an example of complexities that can develop as a result of international sourcing and operation of a transnational corporation like Wal-Mart.

Learning Activity 9.1

Complexities of international business activity

1. Read Case 9.1 very carefully. What is the problem from Wal-Mart Stores' perspective?

2. What is the problem from Wal-Mart Canada's perspective?

3. What is the problem from the U.S. government's perspective?

4. What is the problem from the Canadian government's perspective?

5. How could this problem have been avoided?

The Americas

In Table 9.1, the combination of North America (Canada and U.S.) and Latin America (Mexico, Central and South America, and West Indies) represents The Americas trading bloc. Table 9.2 lists the countries in each area. The population of the U.S. consumes nearly half of world production for most products (Stone, 1994). According to sales per capita, the North American segment of The Americas trading bloc has considerably more spending power than the Latin American segment, but Latin America has a larger and more rapidly growing population, as well as a grand supply of low-cost labor. With favorable trade regulations and the implementation of QR, U.S. apparel firms are sourcing increasingly in Latin America.

Before NAFTA in 1992, the Caribbean Basin Initiative (CBI) in 1987 and the Special Regime (SR) in 1988, were already in place providing incentive for doing business within The Americas. CBI affects a combination of countries located in Central America and the West Indies. CBI took advantage of a special provision in the U.S. tariff schedules (Item 807 or Chapter 9802) that allowed products to be designed and cut in the U.S., exported, sewn in a foreign country, and then imported with tariffs assessed only on value added. Value added was determined primarily by labor costs for sewing. Item 807, as it has been commonly known since 1965, allowed manufacturers to take advantage of low labor costs in foreign countries, particularly those in close proximity to the U.S. CBI also

TABLE 9.2

Countries in Americas trading area.

Central America	North America	South America	West Indies
Belize	Canada	Argentina	Antigua
Costa Rica	Mexico	Bolivia	The Bahamas
El Salvador	United States	Brazil	Barbados
Guatemala		Chile	Cuba
Honduras		Colombia	Dominican Republic
Nicaragua		Ecuador	Grenada
Panama		Galapagos Islands	Guadeloupe
		Guyana	Haiti
		Paraguay	Jamaica
		Peru	Martinique
		Suriname	Puerto Rico
		Uruguay	Trinidad and Tobago
		Venezuela	Virgin Islands

provided guaranteed access levels (GALS) to U.S. markets as a part of what is known as 807A. GALS eliminated the problem of quota limitations on U.S. imports from specified countries. Mexico was not included in CBI so the Special Regime (SR) was developed to provide Mexico with access to the U.S. market similar to CBI. By 1990, 10 percent of U.S. apparel imports were via 807, 807A, and SR.

Eighty percent of trade between Canada and the U.S. was already unrestricted prior to the U.S./Canadian Free Trade Agreement (Wall & Dickerson, 1989). The trade restrictions in place, however, included automobiles, textiles, and apparel. Some U.S. firms like Ford Motor Company built production plants in Canada because tariffs were prohibitive for exporting to Canada. In general, Canada's wages and costs of living are higher than the U.S. (Millstein, 1993). When the tariffs were eliminated by the free trade agreement, these plants were closed to take advantage of lower labor costs in the U.S. Textiles and apparel between U.S. and Canada were restricted by tariffs and also by quotas from the M-FA. Thus, the impact of the free trade agreement on textiles and apparel was not immediate because of provisions for phasing out of the quota restrictions between the two countries over a 10-year period.

The U.S./Canadian Free Trade Agreement also has a "fabric forward" rule of origin clause. This means that in order to qualify for free trade, apparel must be made from fabric manufactured in the U.S. or Canada. Canada has long imported high-quality fabrics from Europe, tariff free. Garments made from these fabrics do not qualify for free trade with the U.S. because of the rule of origin clause.

Negotiation of NAFTA, including U.S., Canada, and Mexico, was concluded in 1992 with implementation beginning in 1994. Formulation of NAFTA was extremely controversial (Ellis, 1992) and its impact continues in this vein. It is very clear that many U.S. apparel companies are producing in Mexico. An executive of a major U.S. jeans producer claims that each pair of jeans produced in Mexico costs $1 less than the same jean produced in the U.S. The result is millions in total annual savings that can be passed on to ultimate consumers. These companies use the same technology, production processes, and quality standards and run their plants in Mexico in the same manner as they run plants in the U.S.

NAFTA also has a rule of origin clause but it is "yarn forward" rather than "fabric forward." This means that all yarn manufacturing, fabric manufacturing, and garment manufacturing processes must take place in Mexico, U.S., or Canada (Antoshak, 1992). Since little textile manufacturing takes place in either Canada or Mexico, the rule of origin clause strongly favors the U.S. textile industry.

Benefits of NAFTA include the following: 1) The ability to cut parts in Mexico. Under the Special Regime, as with 807 and 807A, firms had to export cut parts in order to benefit from reduced tariff on imported finished goods; 2) The ability to do stone-washing, pressing, and other finishing operations in Mexico. Under the Special Regime, as with 807 and 807A, finishing operations were not allowed to be included in value added. Thus, these operations had to performed in the U.S. after the goods were sewn in Mexico or a CBI country; 3) Under NAFTA, firms can both import goods and sell directly to Mexico from Mexican operations. Mexican customers can have access to the same products that are being exported to the U.S.; 4) Much less paper work is required under NAFTA than under the Special Regime (DeWitt, 1995). The issue now is extending NAFTA to CBI and other Central and South American Countries (Black & Cedrone, 1995). Chile has been identified as the first country that could be added because of its political and economic stability.

Since the early 1970s, when employment in the U.S. textiles and apparel industry peaked, total employment has declined by one-third, from 2.4 million to 1.6 million in 1995 (Good, 1997). However, textile and apparel output have not declined in similar proportion. Because of improvements in technology, particularly in textile production, the U.S. industry remains globally competitive (Cline, 1990).

Many U.S. companies have new priorities relative to exports. At a recent American Apparel Manufacturers Association (AAMA) Annual Meeting, 81 percent of executives attending reported that their firms were selling internationally (Black, 1995). A group of U.S. women's fashion apparel firms have developed export connections in United Kingdom (U.K.), Germany, and Kuwait. Successful development of export markets is dependent on strategic marketing and great persistence (Abend, 1996, August). Case 9.2 describes the efforts of one U.S. fashion firm that is entering European markets.

Europe

Western Europe and Eastern Europe provide a scenario in some ways similar to United States and Mexico. Western Europe includes many of the most developed countries of the world. Eastern Europe includes some of the least developed as it emerges from communist rule at least in part as a result of the demise of the Soviet Union. (See Table 9.3 for a listing of countries in each region.) Western Europe has long sought to create economic, if not political, unity. The European Economic Community (EEC), also known as the Common Market, was formed in 1952 followed by the European Free Trade Association (EFTA) in 1960. The EEC has evolved

CASE 9.2

U.S. Firms Exporting to Europe

From Abend, J. (1996, August). Sigrid Olsen on a roll. *Bobbin*, p. 76.

Sigrid Olsen doesn't manufacture in New York. The New York, NY-based women's casual sportswear house that does about $50 million, produces primarily offshore, with factories in Hong Kong, Taiwan, Israel, Greece, and Bulgaria. It makes a small portion of its lines in the U.S. and Canada, and sells mostly in the States.

Why, then, did the company take part in Fashion Exports/New York (FE/NY) at the Düsseldorf, Germany, Igedo Exhibition, and subsequently, a London, England, trade mission this past March? Because it is keen to break into Europe.

Sigrid Olsen's president and CEO, Edward Jones III, explains: "The whole purpose of the trip was to scout the market and see if what was happening in the United States, in terms of sportswear, was happening in Europe in general. And what I learned by talking to a number of retail buyers and potential agents and distributors was, the movement of the market and the way it was changing for us in the States was almost a carbon copy of Europe."

That's good for his type of multi-product sportswear, which encompasses lots of knits and sweaters and different lifestyles items, including T-shirts, with retail prices that range from $18 to $85. What's not so good, he explains, is having to bring the merchandise into the U.S. from his multi-country sourcing network and then ship it to Europe. As Jones puts it: "The prices would be so high that I wouldn't be able to accomplish what I'm out to accomplish."

Jones' strategy, as a part of his plan to enter the European marketplace, it to be able to offer the same products globally at prices that are as consistent as possible with those in the U.S. by bringing the goods in directly.

As a result of his participation in the London trade mission program, the CEO already is set up in the U.K. Jones says, "The embassy staff in London was incredible. They did such a great job of organizing things that in two days I had 17 appointments. I had four of the best retailers and then a number of potential agents and distributors. I could never have done it without it being organized the way it was."

By the time Jones got to London from Germany, he was "75 percent sure" that he wanted to go through a distributor, not an agent. He selected one—out of five possibilities—that he met at the embassy, who is starting distribution for all of the U.K. for holiday. The firm will do shows in Ireland, Scotland, Manchester, and London. Jones notes, "They have already written some orders."

From the trip the CEO found that, "There's an amazing amount of similarity between the U.S. and Europe in regard to value. It's just as important throughout Europe as it is for us."

Learning Activity 9.2

Textile and apparel trade and the Americas

1. Make a list of the primary trade regulations that are currently in effect that affect the Americas.

2. Why is trade regulated?

3. How do exports affect the economy of a country?

4. How do imports affect the economy of a country?

5. Why is NAFTA so controversial?

into a 12-nation group known both as the EC (European Community) and EU (European Union). Numerous other countries in both Western and Eastern Europe are seeking to join. EFTA includes five northern European countries, as well as Switzerland and Austria.

TABLE 9.3

Members of European Union (EU) and European Free Trade Association (EFTA) and developing countries of Eastern Europe.

European Union	European Free Trade Association	Eastern European Countries with Preferential Access to European Union
Belgium	Austria	Czech Republic
Denmark	Finland	Hungary
England	Iceland	Poland
France	Liechtenstein	Slovak Republic
Germany	Norway	*Other Eastern European Countries*
Ireland	Sweden	*Active in Textiles and Apparel*
Italy	Switzerland	Belarus
Luxembourg		Bulgaria
Netherlands		Romania
Portugal		Russia
Scotland		Turkey
Spain		

In spite of these unification efforts, the European economy and European competitiveness "passed through a deep trough" in the late 1970s and early 1980s. The combined profits of Europe's 100 largest corporations was zero. Unemployment, especially among the young, was very high. Growth in productivity had lagged behind wage increases. Social costs (health care, unemployment and disability compensation, education, etc.) were twice that of either Canada or the U.S. (Stone, 1994). It was very apparent changes had to be made to revitalize European business. The effort became focused once again on attempting to create a unified Western Europe.

In 1993, EU and EFTA joined to form the European Economic Area (EEA). Accomplishments include development of common product standards and reduction of trade barriers among countries to a so called "single-document" structure. Truck drivers previously had to carry more than 35 documents to be processed when going from one country to another. Nationalistic policies within countries had created internal monopolies in services, particularly in telecommunications. These monopolies were in a position to continue to charge their customers for the inefficiencies that had become common in their operations. Monopolies are now being abandoned in favor of competition. Government procurement has also now been opened up to all countries in the group instead of being confined to within individual countries. It is now possible to access the whole Western European market and take advantage of economies of scale (Stone 1994).

CASE 9.3

Italy's Best Fabrics Come to the U.S.

From Gallagher, J. (1997, March 20). *Daily News Record,* p. 8.

New York—Trumpeting in the latest important textiles and fabric trends from Italy is next week's biannual presentation of Texitalia at the Hotel Inter-Continental, March 25–27, 1997. Following the major European fabric shows, Texitalia is a prime opportunity for Italian mills to present and U.S. buyers to view the best and brightest of this year's textile collections.

As the only show in the U.S. where American companies can view a full assortment of high-quality European fabrics, Texitalia is fast becoming a significant venue for American buyers. Joined under the banner of "European Textile Selection," major exhibitors from leading textile producers from Italy, France, Spain, Austria, and now Portugal, which plans its first appearance at the March show, offer buyers a second opportunity to see Europe's hottest trends.

Only the finest selection of textiles and accessories is exhibited at the show, which is primarily aimed at the bridge to designer markets.

An important aspect of Texitalia is it offers only the most popular and important themes and products introduced at the European shows, resulting in a smaller and more focused presentation. Anne Marie Staniski, product director for Men's Inc. (part of Federated's Merchandising Division), concurred, "Texitalia gives us a perfect opportunity to round out our collection once we have reviewed our fabric selections from Prato Expo and Moda In." Staniski added "It's a very easy show to work because it is so organized."

A designer from DKNY Jeans noted Texitalia provides a valuable service for U.S. buyers: "The presentation and direction are very nice, very well-done," she commented, adding it is a great show format because the major mills are represented, allowing attendees to see everything in one high-grade venue. She feels a

Negotiations continue as other European countries apply to become a part of EEA. The EEA potentially could control up to 40 percent of world trade, including some of the highest income countries in the world. Western Europe is not yet completely united with Eastern Europe as a trading bloc, but economic power would be clearly increased if they were.

Among the European countries, Germany and Italy have assumed unique roles in the global textiles and apparel industry. Germany is a global leader in the development and export of textile-and-apparel production machinery. Italy is the leading exporter of upscale, fashion forward, apparel and shoes, with the U.S. as its primary customer. Production of high-value garments tends to be spatially concentrated around sources of high-quality fabrics produced in Europe. Demands of sophisticated Italian consumers and the Italian fashion sense perpetuated by brands like Giorgio Armani, Gianni Versace, Valentino, and others have solidified Italian dominance in the high-value market (Appelbaum, Smith, & Christerson, 1994). Case 9.3 describes efforts of European textile producers to market fabrics in the U.S.

Asia

The Asia/Pacific Rim trading bloc clearly represents the largest segment of the world population and great variety of levels of economic development.

more intimate show like Texitalia is ultimately an easier way to work with vendors.

Liz Heusman, fabric buyer for Oscar de la Renta, has attended Texitalia for the last five years and agrees it is a "nice recap" of the European show and style themes. "I think it's great, because when you go to the big shows you can get overwhelmed. It's nice to be able to come back, refocus and review."

Heusman also stressed Texitalia is a great benefit for buyers who cannot make it to Europe, allowing them to see the significant trends emerging, as well as meet with officials of Italy's major mills.

Representatives of Italian mills also praise Texitalia as a valuable tool to their trade. Raul Mazza, president of Mazza USA, represents mills at Texitalia and has attended the show "since the beginning." Mazza, who currently represents four mills, noted "Texitalia is good for business." He believes the show is crucial for his clients, both as a follow-up to customers courted in Europe as well as to meet potential new clients.

Richard Hunte, president of Hunte Associates, which represents several leading Italian suppliers, agreed with Mazza on the growing influence of Texitalia. "Each season we see more visitors and a higher quality of visitor." He stressed the fabrics exhibited are of the finest quality "from bridge to designer to haute couture." Hunte added Texitalia is beneficial to the participating mills: "Every season they are introduced to new clients," he said.

As Italy's textile industry prospers, the integral role played by Texitalia continues to grow. The show thrives on inspiration and innovation, bringing Italy's top fabric producers and stylists to the doorstep of America's leading buyers and designers.

Learning Activity 9.3

Trade in Europe

1. What are similarities between the European and the American trading areas?

2. What are differences between the European and the American trading areas?

3. What are the advantages to U.S. designers of having a European fabric show in the U.S.?

4. What are the advantages to European fabric firms of showing fabrics in the U.S.?

5. How might merchandisers of budget and moderate priced apparel benefit from Texitalia?

Asia is often described in sections that relate to geographic location. Southeast Asia includes both mainland and island countries. Members of the Association of Southeast Asian Nations (ASEAN), formed in 1977, include Brunei, Indonesia, Malaysia, Philippines, and Singapore. These countries have dominated textile and apparel trade from this region of the world because of investment by Japan, Hong Kong, Taiwan, and Korea (Dickerson, 1995).

Countries involved in textiles and apparel in East Asia include Hong Kong, Korea, Taiwan, China, and Japan. Hong Kong, Korea, and Taiwan became known as the "Big Three" apparel exporters dominating world trade. In the early 1970s trade was opened between the U.S. and China. By the late 1980s, China became the largest apparel exporter in the world. Recent visits to China confirmed the expectation that China intends to become a recognized manufacturer of high-quality garments (Fralix, 1996, August). Countries in each area of Asia are summarized in Table 9.4.

Japan aggressively entered textiles and apparel markets following World War II and became a dominant force in the 1950s. Beginning in the 1970s Japan experienced a huge influx of imports of textile fibers, fabrics, and apparel. Imports have continued to grow and Japan now has a $13.8 billion trade deficit. The Japanese response to the import competition is a strategy of globalization, quality improvements, and technology to expand in overseas markets. Japanese manufacturing has gradually moved to China, Southeast Asia, and to some extent Europe. Japanese efforts have focused on long-term vision: How to improve the product and quality and reduce costs. The development of ultra-fine, microfiber polyester yarns is one example of the outcomes of this effort. Japan has assumed technical leadership of the global textiles and apparel industry (Good, 1997). Case 9.4 describes opportunities that Japanese and other global retailers have taken to expand into Asian markets.

TABLE 9.4

Countries located in different areas of Asia involved in the global trade of textiles and apparel.

East Asia	South Asia	Southeast Asia
China	Afghanistan	*Mainland Countries*
Hong Kong	Bangladesh	Kampuchea (Cambodia)
Korea	Bhutan	Laos
Japan	India	Myanmar (Burma)
Taiwan	Nepal	Thailand
	Pakistan	Vietnam
	Sri Lanka	Western Malaysia
		Island Countries
		Brunei
		Eastern Malaysia
		Indonesia
		Malaysia
		Philippines
		Singapore

CASE 9.4

The Asian Opportunity for Retailers

From Treadgold, A. (1995, December). *Discount Merchandiser,* pp. 33–34.

"Considering that China has a potential market of 1.2 billion customers, this may be the most exciting consumer revolution the world has ever seen," stated one of Hong Kong's leading retail property development companies during last year's International Council of Shopping Centres' Retail Asia Conference. Fueled by similar visions, many of the world's leading retailers are moving quickly to establish a presence in China. In fact, during the last 18 months, there have been few days when a proposed market entry joint venture agreement has not been announced.

Prominent among this development rush are:

- Yaohan, one of Japan's largest department store and food retailers, which moved its corporate headquarters from Japan to Hong Kong—slated, of course to become part of China after 1997. Its visionary chairman's ambition is to see 1,000 Yaohan supermarkets trading in China, the first of which are already open.
- Park 'n Shop and Wellcome, two Hong Kong-based food retailers with parent companies that already hold an extensive presence across Asia, and that opened stores in China in the last year.
- Luxury branded goods retailers, such as UK-based Gieves & Hawkes, Dunhill and Burberry, with joint-venture arrangements to sell their merchandise in Chinese department stores.
- Leading international retailers that already operate extensive international store networks, some of which have been among the first to establish a foothold in China. Benetton, for example, reportedly plans to open 300 stores.
- Fast-food concerns, an area where foreign investment was first permitted, enabling operators such as McDonald's, KFC and Pizza Hut to establish themselves.
- Carrefour, France's leading hypermarket retailer, which already has a significant presence in Southeast Asia, has signed a joint venture agreement to operate a hypermarket in the Shanghai region. (A hypermarket is a shopping center all in one store.)

This run into China, following the government's decision in mid-1992 to "accelerate the development of the tertiary sector," is easily explained by such headline-grabbing facts as a 1.2 billion-plus population; 60 million consumers with annual incomes greater than $1,000 (U.S.), and 32 cities with populations greater than 1 million. The unprecedented path of political and economic reform down which China is now hurtling may lead to the creation of the largest consumer market that the world has ever seen.

If all of this sounds too good to be true, that's because it probably is. Although the reform process may appear today to be irreversible, the one certainty in China's recent and ancient history is that nothing is certain. Any prospective investor in retailing in China would be well-advised to remember that the country is at the extreme end of the risk-reward spectrum. That is to say, the potential rewards are fabulous, but so too are the risks.

Patience and a calm temperament, not to mention extremely good political connections, are essential in a country where in many of the major cities economic growth is far outstripping the development of a modern legal and physical infrastructure. McDonald's found this out the hard way when it was required by the Chinese authorities to relocate its central Beijing outlet—the world's largest and possibly busiest McDonald's—to make way for a newer and still larger development.

A retailer making entry into China needs to remember some basic rules of the road. First, there is no such thing as the Chinese market, just as there is really no such thing as the U.S. or European market. In China, however, enormous economic and physical diversity makes this maxim even more valid. The only sensible way to enter China is with a strategy focused very specifically on a city or a province. Second, a new entrant is almost certain to need a joint-venture partner. Going it alone is unlikely to be a realistic option. There is simply too much to learn and too much that can go wrong. Third, this is a market for the long term. There are certainly some very attractive short-term profit opportunities but any retailer must understand that the complexities of the country and of the legal environment mean that most so-called overnight

continued

success stories are, in fact, the result of many years' hard work and long-term planning.

The first wave of foreign investment into Chinese retailing comprised mostly the international luxury-branded retailers and the very up-market, mainly Japanese-owned, department store groups, taking advantage of a proportionately very small but extremely affluent consumer group hungry for Western brands. It is characteristic of the Asian markets that, as wealth becomes more evenly distributed, a huge opportunity emerges for mass retailers offering high-quality goods at prices which, although expensive in local terms, are far less than those in the upscale department stores.

For this reason alone, it seems inconceivable that the U.S. discount department store operators should not seek to imitate their closest European counterparts, the hypermarket retailers, by moving into China. However, the benefits to be gained from being a "first mover" into the mass consumption part of the Chinese market are probably less compelling than elsewhere. It may, therefore, be prudent to wait a while for the market to mature at least a little for wealth distribution to even out somewhat.

In the meantime, other Asian countries offer potentially interesting opportunities for mass retailers. These are the so-called Little Dragons, whose economies are among the fastest growing in the world. Thailand is one such market. According to World

Bank forecasts, Thailand will be the seventh-largest economy in the world by the year 2020.

Taiwan is quite different. Urban Taiwan is already highly developed, sophisticated, and affluent. Foreign retailers are so ubiquitous that they really don't seem foreign at all. But any foreign entrant into Taiwan will come up against very powerful trading companies that no longer exist in the U.S., but which remain a pillar of the business and political environment in Taiwan and elsewhere in Asia.

Although the Indonesian Government has recently reaffirmed its ban on foreign investment in retailing, this will not stop a great many more foreign retailers from entering, lured by the attraction of close to 190 million consumers, a rapid economic growth rate, and a fast-emerging middle class with discretionary spending power. Kmart is one such company, scheduled to open in Jakarta within the next two years.

In summary, China, Thailand, Taiwan, Indonesia, and other countries in the Asia Pacific region are together exerting a powerful appeal for many foreign retailers based on their startling rates of economic growth and their modernization into affluent, sophisticated, and vibrant consumer markets. But any prospective entrant must understand the complexities of these markets and the difficulties of doing business in them. So the message is: Be bold, but beware.

Learning Activity 9.4

Opportunities in Asia

1. Read Case 9.4 very carefully. What factors frame successful entrance of retailers into Asian Markets?

2. What is the relationship between development of retail markets in Asia and the use of Asian firms as sources of textiles and apparel?

Globalization of Apparel Sourcing

About half of apparel sold in the U.S. is now imported. This means that about half of apparel is produced by firms in the U.S. and the other half is imported from firms in dozens of countries around the world.

Today, companies are operating increasingly in an interconnected world. Global competitors are learning to develop and manufacture products that can be introduced and marketed simultaneously in many countries. And in so doing, they find themselves sourcing materials, components, and technology from sites and suppliers worldwide. . . . Moreover, computer to computer communication, generally called e-mail, is increasing at a rate of 10 percent per month in the United States. . . . Entry level management positions are being filled by a computer literate group of young people—setting the course for our electronic future (Anderson & Todaro, 1995).

Historically, firms have used networks of personal contacts and printed directories of suppliers and trade associations to identify potential sources of materials and production. Determining the appropriate sources meant numerous phone calls and trips to production sites to examine capabilities. Some companies, including Mast Industries (a subsidiary of The Limited) and JCPenney, have gained the competitive edge by developing their own electronic sourcing systems. Specifications, costing, and distribution forms were the first sourcing information to be communicated electronically (Anderson & Todaro, 1995). Rapid increases in reasonably priced microcomputer capability has made electronic sourcing a reality. Numerous online sourcing databases are being developed. A National Sourcing Data Base, housed at Textiles and Clothing Technology Corporation [TC]^2, is being developed. The goal is to provide access to multiple sourcing data bases with a single electronic contact.

The development of sourcing networks will allow materials and production sourcing to become an integrated aspect of product development. For example, firms developing new fabrics in several different countries might be accessed via the Internet as the product development process evolves. Materials orders can be placed and delivery dates negotiated. Sourcing of production might include electronic displays of plant layouts, production statistics, and capacity availability. Sourcing activity by U.S.-based firms, for the most part, results in imports into the U.S.

Most of the textiles and apparel imported into the U.S. is sourced by U.S. apparel manufacturers and retailers. Table 9.5 provides numerous ways to think about trends in quantities of U.S. apparel imports. The table summarizes imports from the 28 countries that were the largest exporters of textiles and apparel to the U.S. since 1993. Data are reported in square meter equivalents (SME), in dollar value, by percent change 1995 to 1996, and in dollars per square meter equivalent. The impressions garnered from each of these measures differ considerably. Unless the figures are examined closely, they can be very misleading.

TABLE 9.5

U.S. imports of apparel by region from the largest exporting countries ranked by
percent change (1995-to 1996) in millions of SME (square meter equivalents) and
dollars; dollars per SME by country for 1996.

Countries	1993 SME	1993 $	1994 SME	1994 $
North America				
Mexico	321	$1,127	482	$1,594
Canada				
Central America & West Indies				
Haiti	49	$ 92	16	$ 29
Honduras	153	$ 506	213	$ 645
El Salvador	98	$ 251	162	$ 398
Guatemala			161	$ 591
Dominican Republic	488	$1,410	546	$1,572
Costa Rica	241	$ 653	265	$ 685
Jamaica	158	$ 389	199	$ 454
Other CBI Countries	186	$ 610	187	$ 646
Europe				
Italy	40	$ 684	52	$ 813
Africa				
Egypt				
South & Southwest Asia				
Sri Lanka	237	$ 805	254	$ 832
United Arab Emirates				
Bangladesh	355	$ 741	430	$ 896
India	232	$ 890	265	$1,179
Pakistan	124	$ 357	145	$ 437
Turkey	106	$ 368	151	$ 517
Southeast Asia				
Indonesia	260	$ 978	281	$1,025
Thailand	228	$ 824	234	$ 897
Macao				
Philippines	393	$1,262	411	$1,351
Malaysia	140	$ 609	147	$ 637
Singapore	116	$ 517	96	$ 470
East Asia				
China	935	$3,449	934	$3,859
Japan				
Taiwan	652	$2,197	651	$2,154
Hong Kong	772	$3,776	864	$4,205
Korea	428	$1,884	410	$1,841
All Other Countries	833	$3,836	1004	$4,190
Total Imports	7,545	$28,215	8,421	$31,386

Source: American Apparel Manufacturers Association, Apparel Import Digest.

	1995			1996		% Change 95–96		$/SME
SME	$		SME	$		SME	$	1996
774	$2,566		1,099	$3,560		42%	39%	$ 3.24
123	$ 770		140	$ 947		14%	23%	$ 6.76
47	$ 72		56	$ 98		19%	36%	$ 1.75
329	$ 918		527	$1,220		60%	33%	$ 2.31
239	$ 582		287	$ 721		20%	24%	$ 2.51
185	$ 682		203	$ 796		10%	17%	$ 3.92
632	$1,733		653	$1,753		3%	1%	$ 2.68
297	$ 757		266	$ 704		−10%	−7%	$ 2.65
225	$ 531		201	$ 505		−11%	−5%	$ 2.51
209	$ 737		66	$ 213		18%	29%	$ 3.23
53	$ 967		58	$1,149		9%	19%	$19.81
85	$ 234		87	$ 255		2%	9%	$ 2.93
281	$ 928		285	$1,007		1%	9%	$ 3.53
67	$ 190		70	$ 202		5%	6%	$ 2.89
519	$1,067		529	$1,125		2%	5%	$ 2.13
265	$1,158		301	$1,187		14%	3%	$ 3.94
154	$ 550		161	$ 561		5%	2%	$ 3.48
178	$ 630		150	$ 579		−16%	−8%	$ 3.86
310	$1,183		330	$1,326		6%	12%	$ 4.02
244	$1,037		239	$1,049		−2%	1%	$ 4.39
155	$ 757		155	$ 760		0%	0%	$ 4.90
465	$1,540		441	$1,503		−5%	−2%	$ 3.41
152	$ 675		137	$ 648		−10%	−4%	$ 4.73
84	$ 424		71	$ 326		−15%	−23%	$ 4.59
862	$3,518		863	$3,769		0%	7%	$ 4.37
5	$ 52		5	$ 52		0%	0%	$10.40
598	$2,049		574	$1,974		−4%	−4%	$ 3.44
821	$4,189		760	$3,861		−7%	−8%	$ 5.08
343	$1,622		287	$1,381		−16%	−15%	$ 4.81
859	$3,529		815	$3,616				
9,255	$34,651		9,659	$36,390		4.37%	5.02%	$ 3.77

Square Meter Equivalents and Dollar Values

The amount of fabric required to make a garment or a group of garments is measured in square meter equivalents (SME) for purposes of determining quantities of apparel that are exported and imported. The number of square meters required for a garment can vary from a small fraction of a square meter if the garment is a bikini bathing suit or a baby's shirt, to several square meters if the garment is a pair of work-wear coveralls. The wholesale price or merchandise cost is used as a measure of quantity traded in dollars. Thus, if the firms in a country are primarily engaged in the manufacture of better lingerie, the measure of square meter equivalents may be relatively low compared to the dollar value of garments exported.

Comparing the quantities of SMEs exported year to year helps establish the trend. Comparing quantities in dollars provides another trend. For example, for Mexico, both SMEs and dollar values increased substantially every year; Korea had declines in both SMEs and dollar values every year; Italy had small increases in SMEs, but substantial increases in dollar values.

Percent Change in Imports

At the top of Table 9.5 are countries with the fastest-growing rates of exports to the U.S.; those with the greatest decline are at the bottom. Mexico had the largest percentage increase (43 percent in SMEs; 39 percent in dollar values) from 1995 to 1996. Mexico was already established as a major U.S. supplier before NAFTA. Exports to the U.S. from Mexico have tripled since NAFTA. A variety of products are being sourced in Mexico from lingerie to men's suits to jeans.

Canada, whose exports to the U.S. are also rapidly increasing, addresses a much more upscale market involving men's and women's upper moderate and better sportswear and outdoor wear. Some Canadian firms have been very successful in securing U.S. market share.

About half the Central American and Island countries of the West Indies are experiencing rapid increases in exports to the U.S.; others have stabilized or have had significant decreases. Most CBI countries benefit from the 807 (9802) provisions in the tariff schedules and proximity to the U.S. market for Quick Response. Haiti, Honduras and El Salvador had the biggest increases. Haiti's increase in dollar values is nearly double their increase in SMEs; Honduras had increases in dollar values that were nearly double the increases in SMEs; for El Salvador, the percentage increases in SMEs and dollars were nearly equal. Jamaica and Costa Rica both experienced percentage decreases in SMEs and in dollars. Africa is one of the least developed parts of the world from an apparel sourcing standpoint, but Egypt is now making noticeable contributions to U.S. apparel imports.

In general, the textiles and apparel industry in Western European countries, with the exception of Italy, has experienced extreme downsizing in both numbers of employees and overall sales. Labor costs have risen and productivity has not kept up with the rest of the world (Cline, 1990). Italy alone has been successful in continuing to grow market share by focusing on an upscale market. Italy is the only European country that falls within the top 28 exporters to the U.S. High labor costs are commonly blamed for low rates of imports from other European countries. Nevertheless design, fashion, and quality are still desirable attributes of European-made products.

Asian countries are broken into three groups in Table 9.5. The first group of South and Southwest Asian countries has lower levels of market share; the second group is Southeast Asian, where ASEAN (Association of Southeast Asian Nations) has contributed to the development of some of the fastest-growing economies in the world (Dickerson, 1995), and the third group is Eastern Asian where Asian textile and apparel trade with the U.S. was first established. The so-called Big Four in Far East Asia until recently dominated U.S. apparel imports. With the exception of Bangladesh and United Arab Emirates, South and Southwest Asia sell more upscale products than Mexico, CBI, and Egypt. Sri Lanka, Bangladesh, India, and Pakistan all had increased exports to the U.S. in 1996. In Southwest Asia, United Arab Emirates had increases, but Turkey suffered a decline in exports in 1996 after a series of aggressive annual increases.

Among the ASEAN countries, the least developed—Indonesia—still shows a rapid increase in apparel exports, while Singapore, the most economically developed, shows a marked decline. The ASEAN countries organized for economic development and had rapid growth in the apparel industry during the 1980s. But labor rates have increased in some areas, thus prompting low-cost producers to move to other parts of the world.

In 1992, the "Big Four" East Asian Countries (China, Taiwan, Hong Kong, and Korea) had 48.4 percent of the dollar value of the U.S. apparel import market (Glock & Kunz, 1995); in 1996, the Big Four have 30.2 percent of the U.S. market. This may be the most significant indicator of the shift in U.S. sourcing structure. Of the Big Four, China is the only country that had an increase in 1996; the others all declined in both SMEs and dollars. Korea has suffered the greatest loss of market share, with a decline of 15 percent in 1996. Korean apparel firms are trying to reposition and upscale their products to be more fashion oriented and to adjust to their increasing production costs. Japan's exports to the U.S. are small compared to other East Asian Countries but high in dollar value.

Dollars Per Square Meter

The dollars per square meter in Table 9.5 provides an understanding of the relationship between the dollar value of the shipments and the quantity measured in square meter equivalents. In Table 9.5, dollars per square meter ranges from a low of $1.75 per square meter (Haiti) to a high of $19.81 per square meter (Italy). Central America, West Indies, and Egypt average primarily in the two-dollar range; Mexico and some of the South and Southeast Asian countries average in the three-dollar range; two of the Big Four East Asian countries are in the four-dollar range, while Hong Kong averages in the five-dollar range. Canada is the only country in the six-dollar range; Japan exports a relatively small quantity in the ten-dollar range, and Italy tops the dollars per SME at nearly $20. Honduras generates a few more dollars for exports to the U.S. than Italy, but processes nearly 10 times as much fabric to do it.

> ### *Learning Activity 9.5*
>
> **Trends in U.S. apparel sourcing**
>
> 1. Create another set of columns for Table 9.5 entitled "U.S. Market Share". Calculate market share for each country represented in Table 9.5. in SME and dollar values for 1996. Determine the percent market share for each country by using the following formulas: 1) SME for each country divided by total SMEs imported into U.S. times 100; and 2) dollar value for each country divided by total dollar value imported into U.S. times 100.
>
> 2. What country has the largest market share of the U.S. market? What part of the world has the greatest portion of the U.S. market? What other new information about U.S. apparel imports does market share information provide?
>
> 3. Does knowledge of market share change your perspective of U.S. apparel imports? How?

The Sourcing Process

Two firms are the key ingredients in an apparel sourcing relationship: the sourcing company, which may be a manufacturer or a retailer, and the contracting company, which may be located domestically or anywhere in the world. The sourcing company decides what, when, and where the goods are to be acquired; the contracting company provides the merchandise. If goods are being sourced in a foreign country it is common for an agent to act as an intermediary between the sourcing company and potential contractors. The agent is often native to the contractor's country and is knowledgeable about the companies, their products, production capacities, and quality levels. The agent is paid a commission for services that may be five percent of the cost of the goods produced. As sourcing companies become well established in foreign countries, they sometimes establish their own offices or even a subsidiary that takes over the duties of the agent. Sourcing takes two basic forms: Full Package Sourcing (FPS), and Cut, Make, Trim (CMT) sourcing.

Full Package Sourcing

Full Package Sourcing (FPS) means the contractor provides everything required to make the garment. The contractor purchases materials, develops samples, makes garments, and ships first-quality goods to the sourcing company. Under FPS no fabric or findings are owned by the sourcing company, these are sourced and purchased by the contractor. Full package sourcing is facilitated by having materials of appropriate type and quality locally available. Import fees for materials may be included in costs if materials have to be sourced from another country.

The contractor may also make and perfect all the patterns and samples. It is fairly common for contractors to subcontract the sewing portion of manufacturing. For example, when the full package contractor is Hong Kong-based, product development activities including materials sourcing and patternmaking may take place in Hong Kong while garment assembly is subcontracted to firms in China or Indonesia, where labor costs are lower.

The sourcing company places detailed orders that include product specifications, quality standards, assortments, quantities, and shipping dates. Contract terms may specify that no seconds are to be shipped by the contractor. The sourcing company backs order commitments by an irrevocable letter of credit. When finished goods are shipped and order requirements are satisfied, payment is made automatically from the sourcing company's bank to the contractor's bank. Production and quota reservations are often needed six months in advance of production. Quota rent is determined by market conditions and can vary greatly by time and country. The time required for transit and customs processing is likely to be 60 days.

FPS is well established in Hong Kong, Korea and Taiwan where U.S. department stores have long standing relationships with contractors. Many Caribbean Basin contractors are now receiving pressure to provide FPS. Business ethics have become a primary concern for firms collaborating in the apparel manufacturing process. Some have attempted to standardize operating relationships by establishing standards of conduct for sourcing relationships. Table 9.6 reports standards of conduct for business partners of Nordstrom.

TABLE 9.6

Standards of conduct for business partners.*

1. Legal Requirements: Nordstrom expects all of its partners to comply with applicable laws and regulations of the United States and those of the respective country of manufacture or exportation. All products must be accurately labeled and clearly identified as to their country of origin.

2. Health and Safety Requirements: Nordstrom seeks partners who provide safe and healthy work environments for their workers, including adequate facilities and protections from exposure to hazardous conditions or materials.

3. Employment Practices: Nordstrom firmly believes people are entitled to equal opportunity in employment. Although the company recognizes cultural differences exist, Nordstrom pursues business partners who do not discriminate and who demonstrate respect for the dignity of all people.

4. Environmental Standards: Partners must demonstrate a regard for the environment, as well as compliance with local environmental laws. Further, Nordstrom seeks partners who demonstrate a commitment to progressive environmental practices and to preserving the Earth's resources.

5. Documentation and Inspection: Nordstrom intends to monitor compliance with our Partnership Guidelines and to undertake on-site inspection of partners' facilities. Nordstrom will review and may terminate its relationship with any partner found to in violation of the Partnership Guidelines.

Based on Spector, R., & McCarthy, P. D. (1995). *The Nordstrom Way.* New York: Wiley, pp. 219–220.

Cut, Make, Trim (CMT)

With cut, make, trim sourcing (CMT), the sourcing company is responsible for product development, including development of designs, patterns and product specifications, and sourcing of materials. The primary contribution of the contractor is sewing. The materials are purchased by the sourcing company and may or may not be cut into garments parts when they are delivered to the contractor. No fabrics are owned by the contractor. In some countries, findings are included in the contractor's price. Second-quality garments may be shipped along with those of first quality depending on the purchase agreement.

CMT is common in the Caribbean Basin and in countries where apparel production is just being established. For 807/Chapter 9802 production, CMT is appropriate because assembly is all that is allowed with duty assessed on value added. Freight costs vary by point of departure and point of entry. Other variable costs borne by sourcing companies might include broker's fees, inland freight, bank charges, and insurance. The latter may be about 18 percent of merchandise cost.

> ### *Learning Activity 9.6*
> **Full package and cut, make, trim sourcing**
> 1. What is the difference between FPS and CMT?
> 2. Why might a sourcing firm prefer FPS?
> 3. Why might a sourcing firm prefer CMT?

Sourcing Decisions

Sourcing proceeds in several stages with different requirements of the sourcing company and the contractor at each stage. In Chapter 8, Line Development, we looked at terms related to negotiating contracts with vendors. Those terms are certainly part of sourcing language since contracts are an essential outcome of sourcing. In addition, however, there is the language of the sourcing process related to product descriptions, international trade regulation, transportation systems, and contracts. Table 9.7 itemizes some of the terminology used in sourcing.

Choosing a Country or Countries

Contractors in one or more countries might be necessary in order for the sourcing company to provide adequate quantities of a particular style or merchandise group. Contractors in particular countries tend to be specialized in certain types of products: knits or wovens; top-or bottom-weight fabrics; budget, moderate, or better price ranges; and simple or complex assembly methods. Thus, the type of product desired (jeans, jackets, sweaters, shirts, etc.) is a primary criteria in determining likely countries for sourcing.

A second consideration also relates to type of product, that is, whether it is a basic or fashion good. Type of styling, quantity required and lead-time are often related to whether goods are basic or fashion. Basic goods often require larger quantities and lead-time may be less of a factor. Fashion goods may be more complex in design and construction and require smaller quantities and shorter lead-times. Fashion goods may also have a greater likelihood of change in quantity desired, which would have to be written into the garment purchase agreement (GPA).

Type of fabrication is another determining factor. Availability of materials varies greatly by country. Some countries have little domestic materials production, thus all fabrics and findings must be imported. Others have

TABLE 9.7

Definition of terms for a merchandising language for sourcing.*

Product Description	Trade Regulation
Assists—an item or service supplied free of charge (or at reduced cost) to a contractor (e.g. rivets, buttons).	**Certificate of Origin**—a document that certifies that the goods referred to were manufactured in a specific country.
audit—methodical quality and/or quantity examination applying pre-established company guidelines.	**clearing a shipment**—process involving Customs to validate duty rates and ensure quota is available for goods subject to quota restriction.
care label—a label sewn into a garment showing the care instructions and plant identification code; may also contain product code, fiber content, size, country of origin, etc.	**Customs house broker**—an agent in a port who facilitates Customs clearing on behalf of a company; a person or a firm licensed by the Treasury Department to prepare and file Customs entries, arrange payment of duties due, take steps to release goods from Customs, and represent clients in Customs matters.
carton tag—coded tags attached to cartons of finished garments identifying contents.	
counter sample—a copy of the prototype garment made by the contractor.	**duty classification**—one element of a system for applying taxes related to importing goods.
Development Package—basis of counter sample and costing; sketch and fabric descriptions or prototype and swatches along with sample size specifications and size range.	**duty**—a tax levied on articles of foreign manufacture imported into a country.
fabric testing—series of lab tests to identify a fabric's characteristics (shrinkage, tear strength, fading, water absorption, etc.) so that appropriate care instructions can be determined and to ensure standards are met.	**port of entry**—a port having Customs authorities and designated as a place for the entry and clearance of vessels and goods; major ports include Oakland, Los Angeles, New York City, and Miami.
Pattern Check Run (PCR)—production of samples to ensure all aspects of construction and sizing have been clearly communicated and can be properly executed by the contractor.	**quota rent**—purchase of quota from a firm that has excess quota for import of a specific classification of goods from a specific country; cost depends on market demand at a particular time.
Technical Package—product specifications supplementing the GPA detailing construction, measurement, patterns, and markers.	**Style Sheet**—describes products to Customs for establishment of duty rates and quota classifications; requires merchandiser input to describe garment's construction and fabric.
	U.S. Customs Service—agency responsible for establishment of duty rates and quota classification.

*Based on the *Levi Strauss sourcing manual*.

Transportation	Contract Terminology
airway bill of lading (AWB)—a written receipt given by an air carrier for goods accepted for transporation.	**CMPQ**—cut, make, pack, and quota.
	CMQ—CMT and quota.
	CMT—cut, make, trim.

airway bill of lading (AWB)—a written receipt given by an air carrier for goods accepted for transporation.

bill of lading (B/L)—a written receipt given by a carrier for goods accepted for transportation.

brokers delivery order—instructions issued by a Customs house broker to an inland carrier to move cargo that has been cleared through U.S. Customs from the dock, to the port of entry, to a specified location.

conference carriers—an organization of ocean carriers that fixes rates and sailing times.

freight forwarder—an agent who facilitates the movement of goods from Customs to inland transportation.

freight on board (FOB)—the cost of the goods up to the time they are shipped.

on the water or shipping report—a report notifying merchandisers that products are being shipped.

Preliminary Inspection Certificate (PIC)—authorizes shipment of goods when they have passed a final audit at the offshore contractor; required by the bank to release funds to pay the contractor.

ship date—the date a Bill of Lading is signed and the goods are physically in transit.

CMPQ—cut, make, pack, and quota.

CMQ—CMT and quota.

CMT—cut, make, trim.

contractor evaluation—a procedure to evaluate a potential contractor's ability to meet standards of quality, cost, delivery reliability, and financial stability.

consignee—one to whom goods are shipped or consigned.

cost and freight (C&F)—seller includes price of the merchandise and freight charge in the price to the buyer.

cost, insurance, freight (CIF)—seller includes cost of merchandise, insurance and freight charge in price.

Fabric Booking Confirmation—letter of intent used to block or book fabric for use by specified contractors when a merchandiser requires a unique fabric for use by several contractors (e.g. for coordinates).

Garment Purchase Agreement (GPA)—legal contract to purchase a stated quantity of goods, at a certain price, within specified dates, and on stated terms and conditions.

landed cost—the cost of goods up to the time they are delivered to the distribution center of the buyer.

letter of credit—written document issued by a bank at the request of a buyer authorizing a seller to claim payment in accordance with certain terms and conditions; may or may not be irrevocable or transferable.

production activity report (PAR)—a status report summarizing contractor production activity for use by merchandisers.

well-developed textile industries. Availability of appropriate materials can significantly reduce costs, and timelines. Fiber content is an important factor, because it is a determinant of the quota category of the finished goods. Garment finishing requirements (e.g., stonewashing, bleaching, garment dying) may be other determining criteria. Consideration must also be given to whether estimated landed costs are appropriate to planned list or first price and allowable costs and quota availability.

Choosing a Contractor or Contractor(s)

Sourcing companies provide agents in selected countries with a development package. A **development package** may be as simple as a sketch and fabric description with size specifications and size range, or a fully developed prototype with fabric swatches, size specifications, and size ranges. A development package is the outcome of pre-adoption product development and the line adoption process. Packages may be sent simultaneously to several countries and several contractors in each country. The contractors prepare **counter samples** and costs as a basis for a bid on the contract. Based on the counter samples and the bids, the agent recommends the best contractor(s). Buyers representing the sourcing company then usually visit the contractors to evaluate facilities, working conditions, production capacity, etc.

The sourcing company evaluates samples, costs, and information from plant visits. **Garment Purchase Agreement(s) (GPAs)** are drawn up with the desired contractor(s). GPAs are legal contracts among the sourcing company, the contractor, and the agent. A **Letter of Credit** to the contractor is opened for the value of the order. This Letter of Credit specifies the ship date and other requirements indicated in the GPA.

Prepare for Production

A detailed **technical package** is prepared by the sourcing company, including materials and findings specifications, graded size specifications, pattern check run requirements, assembly and quality inspections specifications, labeling and ticketing, packing specs, lab dips for fabrics, etc. Technical packages are the result of the post-adoption product development process. For goods that will be sold at wholesale, sales samples and swatches must be completed immediately—and they need to be a good representation of the finished goods.

Pattern Check Runs (PCR) are samples that help ensure all aspects of construction and sizing have been clearly communicated and can be properly executed by the contractor. Sometimes the production of sales samples serves as a PCR. PCRs are done for each new combination of fabric, style, and contractor. Production fabric is also tested to ensure quality and performance of finished goods and to determine final care instructions. Approval of a final production garment test using the approved materials, findings, assists, patterns, and assembly methods results in a release to cut order, then production begins.

Production

Quality Assurance inspections usually take place during and following production. In-line inspections evaluate the quality of sewing operations and materials. Quality audits of finished goods are also conducted. When the goods pass inspection, a **Preliminary Inspection Certificate** (PIC) is issued by the sourcing company. The PIC authorizes shipment of the goods to the sourcing company. The contractor presents the PIC and the Bill of Lading to the bank for payment based on the letter of credit. The **Bill of Lading** is a written receipt from the carrier that the goods have been received for shipment.

Customs

Merchandise arrives at **port of entry,** where Customs authorities will examine **style sheets** and **certificates of origin** in relation to duty rates and quota availability. If there is some question about the style sheets, the merchandise itself may be inspected. Inspection can result in days or weeks of delay in making goods available for sale. **Customs House Brokers** are often used to facilitate the process.

Labor Availability and Cost

Production costs are a major consideration in making sourcing decisions. Retail buyers believe foreign sources provide better quality for the price than domestic sources (Sternquist, Tolbert, & Davis, (1989). A comparison of cost from selected countries in dollars for each standard allowed hour (SAH) of production time is shown in Table 9.8. A SAH is an expression of a production standard that "reflects the normal time required to complete one operation or cycle using a specified method that will produce the expected quality" (Glock & Kunz, 1995, p. 297). By using SAHs for the table, it is possible to compare the cost of one hour of the same operations in multiple countries.

The first three listings illustrate the high costs of manufacturing in developed countries. Germany's rates are nearly double those in the U.S. and

TABLE 9.8

Today's apparel manufacturing costs in dollars per standard allowed hours (SAH).*

Country	$/SAH
Germany	31.41
U.S.	16.56
U.K.	13.82
Hong Kong	12.67
Hungary	10.22
Costa Rica	7.74
Thailand	7.63
Russia	6.31
Mexico	6.00
China	5.09

*Kurt Salmon Associates; does not include freight and import duty.

U.K. Hong Kong is close to U.K. The comparison then moves to less developed countries. It is apparent that production costs can vary markedly depending on the part of the world where sourcing occurs.

Issues of Exploitation

Exploitation of labor in developing countries by the apparel industry has had higher visibility than other industries, but it is by no means unique. Exploitation, in this sense, is to make unethical use of for one's own advantage; to make a profit from the labor of others without giving just return. Exploitation often occurs when the opportunity is available. Levi Strauss is a company that is making a comprehensive effort to improve business ethics. Their ethics statement encompasses decision making and relationships in all aspects of the business. (See Table 9.9.) Applying these business ethics in a domestic market is challenging; applying them in the global market is extremely complex. Other manufacturers and retailers including Wal-Mart (Ramey, 1993), have established policies intended to prevent exploitation of labor.

Each country in the world has a unique mix of customs, laws, values, and ways of doing business (Nichols, 1993). What is regarded as exploitation in one part of the world is standard practice in another. Most countries have laws and regulations regarding exploitation of labor, particularly child labor. For example, it is fairly common for age 14 to be the minimum age for employment. Major differences, however, lie in the effectiveness of enforcing the law, in the cultural standards and expectations relative to employment, and in the socio-economic conditions under which people live. Case 9.5 describes efforts in one country to provide "fair" employment.

TABLE 9.9

Levi's ethical aspirations.*

New Behaviors: Management must exemplify "directness, openness to influence, commitment to the success of others, and willingness to acknowledge our own contribution to problems."

Diversity: Levi's "values a diverse workforce (age, sex, ethnic group, etc.) at all levels of the organization. . . . Differing points of view will be sought; diversity will be valued and honestly rewarded, not suppressed."

Recognition: Levi's will "provide greater recognition—both financial and psychological—for individuals and teams that contribute to our success. . . . Those who create and innovate and those who continually support day-to-day business requirements."

Ethical Management Practices: Management should epitomize "the stated standards of ethical behavior. We must provide clarity about our expectations and must enforce these standards throughout the corporation."

Communications: Management must be "clear about company, unit, and individual goals and performance. People must know what is expected of them and receive timely, honest feedback. . . ."

Empowerment: Management must "increase the authority and responsibility of those closest to our products and customer. By actively pushing the responsibility, trust, and recognition into the organization, we can harness and release the capabilities of all our people."

*Reproduced from Mitchell, R. (1994, August 1). Managing by values. *Business Week,* pp. 46–52.

Exploitation of labor is not confined to developing countries (Headden, 1993). Every developed country has "pockets" of apparel sweatshops often made up of immigrants and illegal aliens. The U.S. fast-food industry has been charged with the exploitation of teenagers because of long hours and unsafe conditions with inadequate training. The newly developed telemarketing system may be another "sweatshop" in the making. Some parts of the retail sector might also be challenged as exploiting its sales force with unreasonable hours and low pay although the working conditions may be better than in apparel manufacturing. Resolution of the exploitation problem is incredibly complex from economic, social, and cultural perspectives.

The apparel industry combines some of the most sophisticated product development, production, communication, and transportation technologies in some of the least developed countries of the world (Bonacich, et al, 1994). The primary activity that takes place in the least developed countries is garment assembly. Sewing continues to be a labor-intensive activity that does not require formal education. In apparel, contracting or licensing tends to be the method by which foreign labor is acquired. The result is little long-term commitment to the to the contracting firms or the locations. The scenario is ripe for exploitation of labor by local management and remotely by global corporations. The electronic industry also has assembly

CASE 9.5

Kids Trade Sweatshops for School

From *The Des Moines Register*. (1996, November 2), p 7A.

At 13, Rina Begum is a veteran seamstress who recently worked 10-hour days in a sweatshop [in Dhaka, Bangladesh] for $16 a month, stitching clothes destined for the discount chains of the United States. Now, she's going to school for the first time in her life, under an agreement by Bangladesh's garment industry to end child labor by October 31, 1996.

"I always wanted to go to school, but two years ago my parents sent me to work for money," said Rina in her classroom, a tin shed in a poor Dhaka neighborhood where she studies with a dozen other young ex-laborers.

Threatened with an international boycott of their products, garment manufacturers signed an accord last year with the International Labor Organization and UNICEF to end child labor in Bangladesh's highest earning export industry. Under the accord, the industry cannot employ children younger than 14.

Revenue from U.S.

Bangladesh earns $2.4 billion a year on garments, 66 percent of the country's export earnings. Nearly half the revenue comes from the United States. After the agreement was reached to end child labor, a joint survey by UNICEF and the ILO—both U.N. organizations—and Bangladesh's manufacturers found more

than 10,000 children in the garment industry, most of them girls under 14. By Thursday's deadline, about 3,000 of the workers were estimated to have reached the age of 14 and could stay at work. Of the 7,000 others, nearly 4,000 already have been enrolled in 180 schools across Bangladesh.

Two-thirds of the 1,171 garment factories surveyed in mid-October were found to have no child workers, the ILO's Dhaka office said. The others planned to dismiss their child workers in November, when education arrangements were to be ready. The accord said no child worker could be fired unless the child had a place in school.

Monthly Stipend

In the schools, run by voluntary agencies, each child gets a monthly stipend of $7 to compensate for lost wages. The children also learn wage earning skills such as handicrafts. Some, like Rina Begum supplement the stipend with after-school work. But that doesn't come close to her previous $16 a month, a pretty good salary in a country where the average monthly wage for an adult industrial worker is $23. The drop in income has hurt many families.

Aklima, another 13 year old who lost her job, has three brothers and sisters—all too young to work. Her mother is a widow, and until six months ago, the family depended on Aklima's $23 per month.

taking place in the world's least developed countries. In electronics, however, assembly tends to take place in subsidiaries of the trans-national corporation (TNC). A subsidiary means considerable investment by the TNC and longer commitment to the area (Bonacich et al, 1994).

In 1980, The United Nations reported that women, half the world's population, did two-thirds of the world's work, earned one-tenth of the world's income, and owned one-one hundredth of the world's property. In spite of many changes in world politics, women remain victims of abuse and discrimination (War against women, 1994). Employees in the least developed countries tend to be young women, often in their first and perhaps only opportunity for regular employment. Unemployment and poverty rates tend to be very high. Parents often need their children to work so the family can have basic necessities. Deciding on a "fair" employment policy under these conditions is extremely difficult. Case 9.6 reports

CASE 9.6
Who's Making the Clothes?

From Dowling, M. (1996, October 15). *Catalog Age,* p. 6.

Although there's plenty of pressure to keep apparel manufacturing costs down, the discovery of modern-day sweatshop conditions in garment factories [in the United States] has stunned both consumers and marketers. The problem has touched many, including upscale women's apparel cataloger/retailer Talbots. Two sub-contractors manufacturing Talbots merchandise were cited for Labor Department violations in the past year, says spokeswoman Margery Brandfon.

Unfortunately, it's not easy to control who's making your clothing or under what conditions. Most apparel suppliers farm out manufacturing to subcontractors, which may in turn send the work to other subcontractors without the marketer knowing—until there's a problem. As Brandfon says, "The labor problem is not with the supplier—it's further down the {manufacturing} chain."

In November 1995, the Labor Department notified Talbots that a subcontractor for supplier David Brooks was cited for a technical infraction involving

overtime. "The situation had already been resolved, so it was an informational call, not an active notice," Brandfon says. But when another subcontractor of David Brooks was cited for unpaid overtime in May, Talbots took action.

In June, the Hingham, MA-based company announced that its suppliers must work with Los Angeles-based independent garment auditing firm Cal Safety Compliance Corp. to monitor subcontracts. As of August, all merchandise received by Talbots had to be accompanied by a certificate stating that it was made under the subcontractor monitoring program. All of Talbots' top suppliers have so far agreed to comply.

What's more, Talbots and several other catalogers—including Frederick's of Hollywood, JCPenney, J. Crew, Lands' End, and Spiegel—have endorsed the National Retail Federation's Statement of Principles on Supplier Legal Compliance, which warns that "appropriate action" will be taken if a factory used by a supplier has committed legal violations. Actions may include refusing shipments, terminating the relationship with the supplier or taking legal action in the event of labor violations.

---

the choices being made by the apparel industry to resolve exploitation related issues in one country.

Learning Activity 9.7
Labor issues

1. What are the central issues of labor exploitation?
2. What makes a labor policy "fair"?
3. Give an example of applying one culture's standards in another culture. Why might this be a problem?
4. What is a "fair" wage in a developing country?

Summary

The textiles and apparel business is one of the most globalized businesses, involving most of the more than 200 countries in the world. World trade is regulated by a multitude of laws and trade regulations. Recent agreements have defined three major textile and apparel trade areas: The Americas, Asia, and Europe.

East Asia for many years dominated apparel trade. The countries that are now showing marked increases in the share of U.S. imports are Dominican Republic, Mexico, Costa Rica, Honduras, El Salvador, and Guatemala. All are trading areas favored by U.S. trade legislation including NAFTA, CBI (Caribbean Basin Initiative), Special Regime and the so-called "807" provisions in the Harmonized Commodity Code.

Two major methods of sourcing apparel are full package sourcing (FPS) and cut, make, trim (CMT). Firms in East Asia are known for FPS, while CMT is still predominant in Caribbean Basin and Mexico. Labor exploitation in apparel production is an ongoing problem that must be addressed by the sourcing firms involved.

Key Concepts

Americas trading bloc

Asian/Pacific Rim trading bloc

assist

Association of Southeast Asian Nations (ASEAN)

audit

bill of lading

business ethics

Caribbean Basin Initiative (CBI)

certificate of origin

counter sample

customs house broker

cut, make, trim sourcing (CMT)

duty classification

European trading bloc

European Union

full-package sourcing (FPS)

Garment Purchase Agreement (GPA)

General Agreement on Tariffs and Trade (GATT)

global

globalization

Harmonized System of Tariffs

Item 807/Chapter 9802

labor exploitation

landed cost

letter of credit

Multi-Fiber Arrangement (M-FA)

North American Free Trade Agreement (NAFTA)

pattern check run (PCR)

port of entry

Preliminary Inspection Certificate (PIC)

quota rent

ship date

sourcing

square meter equivalents (SME)

style sheet

technical package

U.S. Customs Service

U.S./Canadian Free Trade Agreement

World Trade Organization (WTO)

Integrated Learning Activity 9.8

Sourcing decisions

1. Read Case 9.7 very carefully. What are the principal factors that must be considered in making sourcing decisions?

2. Rank the factors according to their level of importance.

3. What criteria determine the ranking of sourcing factors?

CASE 9.7

Third World Sourcing: Cheap but Tricky

From Ostroff, J. (1996, April). *Daily News Record,* pg. 2.

On paper, it's a no brainer. But in reality, sourcing in Third Word countries can be risky business. Today's best deals on imported apparel are in Bangladesh, the world's lowest-cost producer. The country's 26¢-per-hour average wage for textile workers is the lowest for any major producing nation, and apparel wages are even lower than that.

A few years hence, Vietnam is expected to surpass its Asian neighbor as the place for rock-bottom prices. Sir Lanka, China, Indonesia, and the Philippines also appear attractive for apparel and textile sourcing, with average hourly wages estimated at less than $1.

However, analysts and consultants who specialize in foreign sourcing warn that importers and retailers who follow this sourcing mantra could literally and figuratively lose their shirts. A raft of critical factors—from plant productivity and order lead times to quota status and logistics—are more important than mere dollar-per-dozen production costs, sourcing specialists caution.

All these underdeveloped Asian countries share common problems: political and economic instability and questionable infrastructures. All of these factors must be figured into the sourcing equation, according to Michael Eads, an international trade analyst. That's especially true as free trade opens up closer to home countries as low-cost alternatives to the faraway Asian nations, although many of these Western hemisphere countries also have human-rights and economic problems.

"It's one thing for a company to go into a country to extract gold or diamonds, since the regime in power generally will be friendly because you're bringing in money," said Eads, whose Washington-based firm, International Business-Government Counselors, advises companies on sourcing. "But apparel and textile production are very labor-intensive and make inviting targets for [attacks by some foreign governments and labor organizers] as being tools of repressive capitalists," he said. Eads noted that in some small African and Asian countries workers are alienated · and their lives are threatened for taking wages from Western firms.

Production prices alone play minor roles in determining the best sourcing options, said Julia K. Hughes,

chairman of the U.S. Association of Importers of Textiles and Apparel. "Our industry is global, but is based more on quality, availability, and delivery schedules than on prices."

Hughes said in making sourcing decisions, firms also weigh a nation's political stability and the potential for bad publicity for manufacturing in countries with questionable human-rights records. China is a case in point—one that encapsulates all of the fears and opportunities confronting companies that import, or contemplate setting up production facilities there. China's apparel plants and textiles facilities are among the world's most advanced. With 25 percent of the world's population, analysts say Chinese makers can produce apparel and textiles to match any price.

Yet, its unsettled political and economic situation, coupled with the uncertainty about whether the U.S. will renew its Most Favored Nation trade status each year, has sent many U.S. importers scurrying elsewhere to source. Compounding the problem, in July the U.S. is changing its origin rule so that the country where the apparel is assembled confers origin, not where the fabric is cut.

"This is unmitigated disaster for many of us," said one importer who requested anonymity. The importer said that long-established sourcing programs with China, Hong Kong, Singapore, Malaysia, and other nations will be rendered obsolete in a wink. Consequently, many importers now are trying to find new places that have the capacity to handle large orders.

But quota limits often present another problem. A retailer may have the perfect source for producing a hot item, only to find that tight U.S. controls render these plans moot. Another nation can fill the order, though at price points that force the firm to gamble whether consumers will shell out an extra $5 for a blouse.

"What does it mean if Korea has 50 percent of the world's quota for an item, if the production costs now are so high that your profit" is problematical, said Clinton Stack, president, International Development Systems, a Washington-based textile-trade consulting firm.

To Claude Barfield, trade specialist and resident scholar with the American Enterprise Institute, a Washington think tank, quotas skew importers' sourcing decisions, profits, and prices.

continued

"The entire apparel business is screwed up by anti-consumer quotas doled out to countries, rather than global limits that would allow importers to make their sourcing decisions based on economics rather than quota availability," Barfield said.

Perhaps, but this picture will change within a few years to the importer's benefit, counters Robert Antoshak, president of Trade Resources, of Alexandria, Va., which advises domestic makers.

"Within three years, with quota growth as the Multi-fiber Arrangement is phased out, there will be so much quota available that it will exceed [importers] needs and will be irrelevant," Antoshak said. Quota will be totally eliminated for World Trade Organization member nations on Jan. 1, 2005, as agreed to under the GATT accords.

Stack, though, believes that quotas will continue to skew importer's apparel and textile sourcing plans for years, possibly beyond 2005.

"The quota-growth argument totally ignores the fact that importers make sourcing decisions based on individual countries," he said. He said Antoshak's "growth-on-growth" argument is invalid, since in many of these countries the growth rate will remain small even through 2005.

Stack added that many importers fret that quotas will be extended beyond 2005 due to political pressures from U.S. textile and apparel makers. Some analysts contend that arguments over quota/origin rules and sourcing nations' stability overlook other vital factors that determine where importers will source.

"With a low-growth retail environment and increasing pressure on prices, retailers will be squeezing [apparel] suppliers for every nickel," Antoshak said. "Retailers wouldn't be doing programs in the Middle East or Bangladesh unless they were driven by price pressures that will continue."

Meanwhile, Peter Harding, a New York-based vice president with consulting firm Kurt Salmon Associates, contends sourcing decisions are being driven not only by profit margins or quotas per se. "Lead times are becoming crucial as the apparel business becomes more focused on narrowed selling seasons and quick deliveries, which allow retailers to make decisions as close to the sales date as possible," said Harding.

Jeffrey Sands, apparel practice national director with KPMG, New York, adds that flexibility in sourcing has become key. "Retailers from Wal-Mart to Bergdorf's are insisting on quick turnarounds to help them correctly forecast color, style, and size" Sands said. [Stores] are also demanding that deliveries be made to their stores, rather than filling warehouses with a season's worth of apparel."

Logically, then, importers should be flocking to Mexico and the Caribbean Basin nations, given their proximity to the U.S. and relatively low wage rates. This has occurred in recent years, with many U.S. makers setting up production facilities in these nations, mostly using U.S. fabrics.

But analysts point out the close-to-home syndrome does not negate distant sourcing. In a nutshell, they argue retailers and importers will source anywhere in the world for commodity apparel that isn't particularly sensitive to time or fashion trends, and will stay as close to home—even manufacturing in the U. S. for higher priced apparel. "I think we will see companies like Liz [Claiborne] sourcing in the U.S., Mexico or the CBI where they can transmit a buy for 100 pairs of slacks, rather than go to the Far East and waiting months for an order," Sands said.

Moreover, he and other analysts point out the sourcing decisions could be further slanted to the Americas should the U.S. expand the 807 program, giving apparel assembled in Mexico and the CBI using foreign-fabrics quota and duty breaks.

"You could find a lot more sourcing from the CBI if these nations could directly import Chinese-cut fabric for assembly there." Stack said. "But this overlooks two factors that could affect sourcing decision: wages in the CBI will rise, reducing their cost advantages versus Far East production." Secondly, with higher productivity in some Asian countries and their ability to do full-package, hanger ready programs, goods can be in Seattle within a week. It's not like you have to wait for favorable winds and sail around the Cape to New Amsterdam."

Recommended Resources

DeWitt, J. W. (1995, February). Home away from home. *Apparel Industry Magazine, 56*(2), 42–44.

Nichols, M. (1993, January–February). Third-world families at work: Child labor or child care? *Harvard Business Review,* 12–23.

Jones, S. H., & Anderton, G. (1995, January). Shaping strategic alliances in Mexico. *Bobbin, 36*(9), 70–76.

Des Marteau, K. (1995, December). U.S. contractors seek survival solutions. *Bobbin, 37*(4), 16–18.

Fralix, M. T. (1996, August). Into the Far East: A perspective on quality, globalization & fried goose. *Bobbin,* 37(21), 80–84.

Staff Report. (1996, April). Look before you leap. *Bobbin,* 37(8), 71–74.

References

Abend, J. (1995). U.S. firms excel in export. *Bobbin, 37*(21), pp. 70, 74, 78.

Anderson, L. J., & Todaro, M. (1995, May). Sourcing in the year 2000. *Bobbin,* pp. 74–80.

Antoshak, R. P. (1992, August). NAFTA rule of origin: A help or hindrance? *ATI,* pp. 46–49.

Appelbaum, R. P., Smith, D., & Christerson, B. (1994). Commodity chains and industrial restructuring in the Pacific Rim: Garment trade and manufacturing. In Gereffi, G., & Korzeniewicz. *Commodity chains and global capitalism.* Westport, CT: Greenwood Press.

Bernard, H. (1987, January). Vertical ventures. *Apparel Industry Magazine,* pp. 56–58.

Black, S. S. (1995, July). AAMA touts globalization. *Bobbin, 36*(11), 22, 24.

Black, S. S., & Cedrone, L. (1995, July). Americas focus on trade opportunities. *Bobbin, 36*(11), 74–79.

Bonacich, E., Cheng, L., Chinchilla, N., Hamilton, N., & Ong, P. (1994). Global production: The apparel industry in the Pacific rim. Philadelphia: Temple University Press.

Cline, W. R. (1990). The future of world trade in textiles and apparel (rev. ed.). Washington DC: Institute for International Economics.

DeWitt, J. W. (1995, February). NAFTA: One year later. *Apparel Industry Magazine, 56*(2), 34.

Dickerson, K. G. (1995). *Textiles and apparel in the global economy* (2nd ed.). Englewood Cliffs, NJ: Merrill.

Dickerson, K. G. (1988, Spring). The textile sector as a special GATT case. *Clothing and Textiles Research Journal,* pp. 17–25.

Ellis, K. (1992, October). The great North American free trade debate. Reprinted from *Chicago Apparel News.*

Forney, J. C., Rosen, D. M., & Orzechowski, J. M. (1990, Spring). Domestic versus overseas apparel production: Dialogue with San Francisco-based manufacturers. *Clothing and Textiles Research Journal,* pp. 39–44.

Fralix, M. T. (1996, August). Into the Far East: A perspective on quality, globalization & fried goose. *Bobbin,* 37(21), 80–84.

Glock, R., & Kunz, G. I. (1995). *Apparel manufacturing: sewn product analysis.* Englewood Cliffs, NJ: Prentice Hall.

Goldman, S. L., Nagel, R. N., & Preiss, K. (1995). *Agile competitors and virtual organizations: Strategies for enriching the customer.* New York: Van Nostrand Reinhold.

Good, M. L. (1997, January 30). The U.S. textile industry outlook: Competitive and technology challenge. Remarks at The 5th Annual National Textile Center Forum, Murtle Beach, SC.

Headden, S. (1993, November 22). Made in the U.S.A. *U.S. News and World Report,* pp. 48–55.

Jacobs, B. A. (1996, June). New U.S. rules create global anxiety. *Bobbin,* 37(10), 15–18.

Kanter, R. M. (1994). Afterword: What "thinking globally" really means. In *Global Strategies.* Boston, MA: Harvard Business School Press.

Levi Strauss and Company sourcing manual.

Made on Planet Earth (1996). *DNR*

Marlin-Bennett, R. (1994, Winter). Camouflaged trade restrictions in the 1990s: Trends in international trade policy. *Futures Research Quarterly,* 61–77.

Milstein, A. G. (1993, September). U.S. manufacturers bringing home the Canadian bacon. *Bobbin,* pp. 100–104.

Mitchell, R. (1994, August 1). Managing by values. *Business Week,* pp. 46–52.

Munk, N. (1994, January). The Levi straddle. *Forbes,* pp. 44–45.

Nichols, M. (1993, January–February). Third-world families at work: Child labor or child care? *Harvard Business Review,* 12–23.

Planning and implementing an apparel sourcing strategy. 1986 report of the Technical Advisory Committee of the American Apparel Manufacturers Association, pp. 1–3; 37; 39–41.

Ramey, J. (1993, June 10). Wal-Mart sets sourcing rules to monitor labor conditions. *Women's Wear Daily,* p. 14.

Sternquist, B., Tolbert, S., & Davis, B. (1989, Summer). Imported apparel: Retail buyers reasons for foreign procurement. *Clothing and Textiles Research Journal,* pp. 35–40.

Stone, N. (1994). The globalization of Europe: An interview with Wisse Dekker. In *Global strategies.* Boston, MA: Harvard Business School Press.

Wall, M., & Dickerson, K. (1989, Winter). Free trade between Canada and the United States: Implications for textiles and clothing. *Clothing and Textiles Research Journal,* pp. 1–10.

War against women. (1994, March 28). *U.S. News and World Report,* pp. 42–56.

10 Presenting Product Lines

Learning Objectives

- Examine concepts of merchandise presentation.
- Discuss merchandise replenishment and its impact on merchandise presentation.
- Explore multiple delivery strategies in relation to productivity.

The line plan establishes merchandise budgets and assortment plans for a specified time period. Line development through the purchase of finished goods and/or product development determines the actual merchandise, styles, sizes, and colors that will be offered. Line presentation may occur internally within a firm, at wholesale, and/or at retail, depending on the product line and a particular firm's strategies. Merchandise presentation includes processes required to evaluate the line and make it visible and salable (Glock & Kunz, 1995).

Concepts of Merchandise Presentation

Merchandise presentation is stereotypically associated with retail merchandise display, which may actually be the last commercial presentation of the merchandise. If the goods are purchased from a retail display by the ultimate consumer, the next time the goods are presented may be in the consumer's home or on the consumer's body. The final time the goods are offered for sale may be at the ultimate consumer's yard sale or, if the merchandise is donated to charity, it may be displayed for sale at a thrift store.

Merchandise, however, is presented for evaluation many times before it reaches the retail selling process. The presentations prior to the retail display determine what will be offered by retailers. TAMS, Figure 3.1 identifies three components of merchandise presentation: internal, wholesale, and retail. **Merchandise presentation** is a fundamental part of the merchandising process intended to enhance sales by offering products for consideration in a consciously designed environment that positively affects attitudes and behaviors toward the products and the presenter(s) (Yan, 1996).

Offering Merchandise for Consideration

Offering merchandise for consideration leads to **line evaluation.** Merchandise lines are evaluated internally by executives in both manufacturing and retailing firms, by retail buyers at wholesale, and by ultimate consumers at retail. Executive reviews are a form of evaluation that is used often in the line planning and development process to assess progress and appropriateness of decisions. Executive reviews of merchandising processes, particularly for line adoption, commonly involve comprehensive presentation of line plans, line concepts, and pre-adoption product development. These presentations commonly include persuasive visualization of the line through the use of story boards, videos, live models, and/or runway fashion shows. In addition, persuasive rhetoric by the presenter iterates the line's features in terms of the wants, desires, and needs of the target market, the firm's market positioning, and the actions of its competitors. Merchandise budgets and assortment plans are also summarized and pricing strategies are discussed, including allowable merchandise costs. Estimates of the production costs of new designs are presented, along with quality and performance of materials and assembly methods.

The presentation to sales representatives, often called a **line preview,** is sometimes the most elaborate internal merchandise presentation for manufacturers. Merchandisers and designers are challenged to persuade sales representatives (reps) to sell the line the way it was conceived and approved by executives. How they communicate assortment plans is particularly important. Purchases of materials and commitments for production capacity often have to be made before purchase orders are received. Since sales representatives frequently plan assortments for retail buyers, the reps have a profound opportunity to influence how much of what gets ordered. The effectiveness of the line preview may determine the success of the wholesale selling period.

JCPenney Company has a very special form of internal line review. Merchandisers/buyers at the JCPenney headquarters periodically present lines via CD-ROM to merchandisers at individual JCPenney stores. The goods are usually presented on live models and the merchandisers discuss the merits of merchandise groups and each style including retail price and planned percent initial markup. Store merchandisers place orders based on the relationship between the merchandise presented, their current inventory, and what they see as local trends, wants, and needs of their local customers. (Read Case 10.1 and do Learning Activity 10.1 here.)

Consciously Designed Environments

Merchandise presentation takes place in environments that are manipulated to provide the desired impression. "The environment is the multisensory setting that surrounds and interacts with the product" (Fiore & Kimle, 1997, pp. 10–11). The aesthetic experience associated with merchandise presentation enhances participants' perception of the products by providing pleasure and/or satisfaction. Both utilitarian and aesthetic benefits of products are usually featured. **Utilitarian benefits,** including comfort, protection, quality, social acceptance, status, efficiency, and value, provide social or economic gain (Fiore & Kimle, 1997). Line plans, merchandise budgets, assortment plans, materials specifications, and product specifications provide cognitive assessment of utilitarian benefits.

Aesthetic benefits, including sensual pleasure, beauty, aroused emotion, creative expression, and identity, result in pleasure or satisfaction (Fiore & Kimle, 1997). Of the different forms of line presentation, a fashion show may be the most effective in providing aesthetic benefits because it is a multi-sensory experience. All the human senses may be stimulated, including visual, tactile, kinesthetic, olfactory, auditory, and gustatory. Aesthetic benefits are magnified by multi-sensory merchandise presentation (Fiore & Kimle, 1997; Yan, 1996). A complete aesthetic experience can create a positive influence on executives, sales representatives, customers, and sales.

What is commonly called **display or visual merchandising** in the retail sector is more successful when it is regarded as multi-sensory merchandising. The senses easily targeted in a retail store are visual, tactile, auditory, and olfactory, that is, sight, touch, sound, and smell. The combination of the sensory and cognitive perceptions defines a customer's image of the store.

CASE 10.1

Lifting Store Sales: Rx From Vendors

From Feitelberg, R. (1995, October). *Women's Wear Daily*, p. 34.

With consumers still showing no great inclination to crowd the stores these days, legwear manufacturers feel there are a number of strategies retailers could use to get more out of their legwear business. Interviewed last week, several vendors were quick to offer their suggestions, such as greater support of best-selling brands, improved customer service, and hosiery outposts. Some acknowledged their ideas were basic, but still useful and often overlooked in the general angst of the current retail clime.

Consumers can forget they need socks, and retailers need to remind them, according to Kevin Angliss, vice president of marketing for Auburn Hosiery Mills, which produces licensed Wilson, Coke, and Converse socks.

"Part of the big problem is that some retailers do not cross-merchandise. Outposting hosiery in other departments such as sportswear with coordinating apparel would increase impulse sales," he said. "Wal-Mart does it and it increases volume."

When the outpost is simply for display, he said, it is helpful to place small signs indicating where the displayed merchandise can be purchased in the store, he said. With store traffic down in most retailers, it is essential to put new looks front and center as much as possible, he said.

"Sometimes hosiery is the most forgotten category even though it's profitable," Angliss added. Consumers are not likely to purchase anything they have to hunt for, contended Mark Heirbaum, president of DML Marketing, which produces and distributes Legale, as well as the licensed Kenneth Cole legwear. Therefore, retailers should improve merchandising and maintain neatly organized hosiery departments.

"It won't get people out of their homes and into shopping malls, but it will help," he said. "Merchandising is more difficult. We have [vendor employed] merchandisers in the stores every month, but that's not enough."

Retailers should support best-selling brands by allotting more space, Heirbaum added. Retailers should clean out leftover merchandise from previous seasons to keep current with emerging fashion trends such as sport-influenced looks, according to Karen Bell, president for K. Bell, Culver City, Calif. The firm, which makes socks and tights, is expanding into sheers for the first time this spring.

"This is going to be a year for fashion, not for basics. Stores need to be pared down on basics to make a fashion statement," she said. "They can't be afraid to get behind merchandise that's selling by offering it in volume." Bell also said retailers should give manufacturers more lead time, which would help eliminate out-of-stock items.

Mitch Brown, legwear manager for Pennaco Hosiery, also pointed to the necessity of maintaining

Retail chain organizations often control images created by retail display through the use of planograms. **Planograms** are the result of space management technology first developed for grocery stores. Sears has been a leader in developing merchandise planning technology for general merchandise that "take the buyer's recommended assortment and customize it right down to the specific store, complete with printed planogram" (Sears. . . . , 1990, p. 62). Sears now has two systems: MAPS for general merchandise, and SAMS for apparel. Sears markets the planogram software under the name Spaceman. Before Spaceman, Sears did planograms by manually setting up the displays, photographing them, and sending the pictures to each store. The process was time consuming and expensive.

stocks for their core brands. He further stressed the importance of in-store training through round robins where several vendors teach sales associates about the benefits of each product.

"It requires increased costs and travel for the manufacturer, but a trained salesperson sells more product," Brown said. To create more interest in the category among consumers, stores should offer new products on a regular basis, he said.

Michele Siegel, national sales manager for American Essential, which produces its own socks, as well as licensed Calvin Klein socks, said improving customer service is essential to better business.

"Salespeople need to be more friendly to make shopping more inviting. Shoppers want to know they can find what they need with a good level of service," she said. "That's what department stores need to focus on." Siegel also said that several retailers should improve lighting to make the product look more attractive to consumers.

Meeting with key retailers to discuss ways to improve the business is valuable to both parties, said Pat McNellis, national sales director for the Kayser-Roth Corp. Representatives from several of the store's divisions, such as systems operations, buying, accounting, and receiving should be present to offer their input to correct any problems. McNellis said she also supports the idea of allocating more retail floor space to best-selling brands and offering more new products.

"Retailers should be asking manufacturers where the business is headed and supporting it by changing models and offering point-of-sale information," she said. "They should tailor the trend information to their own businesses."

Robert Sussman, executive vice president for ETC Inc., which produces licensed Evan-Picone socks, agreed that newness is key. Many retailers use the same vendor structure, but they should try new products in a variety of price points, he said. "They have to do something creative, whether it's boxed socks or multipacks," he said. "To get to the consumer, the need to make it sizzle—change displays to make it new and exciting and not just the same old thing."

Learning Activity 10.1

Read Case 10.1 very carefully

1. Identify principles of merchandise presentation reflected in the recommendations offered by marketing executives employed by hosiery vendors.

2. According the Roger's theory of diffusion of innovation (introduced in Chapter 2), the innovators of change might be regarded as the vendor's marketing executives, while the implementors would be retail merchandisers. How might this impact success of innovation in merchandise presentation? What suggestions can you make for improving success of innovation?

Now a computer generates planograms based on the assortments planned for each store. Plans can be electronically transmitted to stores, reducing both costs and time. Case 10.2 itemizes some of the other decision-making factors related to consciously designed retail environments.

CASE 10.2

The Art of Store Layout

From Dyches, B. (1996, January). *WWD Specialty Stores/ A Business Newsletter.*

Did you know over 80 percent of all people move to the right when entering a store: According to human behavior researchers, this has to do with the orientations of the brain. So, why do so many retailers place low-profit, low turning items or their cash-wrap in this so-called oceanfront real estate area instead of prime merchandise? Mostly it's because so little is understood about retail space layout and how to maximize your investment. Yet, with a basic understanding of predictable customer behavior, you'll gain an edge in any retail climate.

The Control Zone

Your store's entrance area is where you turn customers on enough for them to either come in or turn back to the street. So what does it take? Give 'em some space. Primarily, a customer needs enough room not to feel crowded. Avoid placing merchandise all the way up to your lease line—customers associate this tactic with discounters. Leaving open an area between 60 and 80 square feet is appropriate for a 2,000 square-foot store.

Focus

Here your feature or focal display should be the first thing your customers see. It should always be trimmed neatly and with some frequency—every week or two.

The Right Direction

Your store's front third is the most critical sales area. If you don't keep the customer's interest here,

then you've most likely lost them. The front right wall should contain your expensive and most complete groupings. Keep the psychology of layout in mind here —it is easier to go from high to low prices than the other way around. Most stores tend to place merchandise along the walls with a corresponding aisleway that is parallel. The problem here is that the merchandise is not perpendicular with the customer's line of eyesight. Angle merchandise to the entrance so customers will see and be drawn to key merchandise assortments.

Service Areas

The most important decision here is where to place your cash-wrap. The center is convenient because of the control it affords the retailer. A centrally placed cash-wrap also helps to promote the desired circular traffic pattern. Otherwise, its location will vary depending upon space size and the number of employees. Dressing rooms should be placed in convenient, but not prime, real estate locations. Back corners or the rear right wall often work best.

Must Haves and Resources

Merchandise display and product evaluation are key elements in every store's layout. First capture the customer's attention with creative and stimulating displays; then give them enough room to touch, try on, and evaluate the merchandise. Have you allowed for sufficient movement at this critical time? The effective use of your square footage is indeed a critical area that all retailers need to master. Otherwise, with rents being what they are today, you pay dearly for space not fully utilized.

Learning Activity 10.2

Consciously designed environments

1. What utilitarian benefits are derived from following the guidelines provided in Case 10.2?

2. What aesthetic benefits are derived from following the guidelines provided in Case 10.2?

3. From your observation of retail store layout and displays, what utilitarian benefits are most likely to be neglected?

4. From your observation of retail store layout and displays, what aesthetic benefits are most likely to be neglected?

Sales Enhancement

The fundamental purpose of merchandise presentation is **sales enhancement** and, thus, contribution to the success of the firm. From the first evaluation of line concept, the purpose is to create a line that will be highly desired by customers. Each additional evaluation has the same goal—to enhance sales. Selecting merchandise desired by customers, of course, is a key component of salability. The risk of selecting unsalable merchandise is reduced by using effective forecasting techniques, market research, and positioning strategies. Acquiring the right amount of merchandise at the right time, and replenishing assortments with the right amount of merchandise at the right time, are two of merchandise presentation's greatest challenges.

CASE 10.3

Fashion First When it Comes to Space in Midwest

From Sharoff, R. (1996, August 19). *Daily News Record,* p. 72.

As real-estate costs continue to climb, Midwest men's wear retailers say sales per square foot are only one factor when deciding what goes where on the selling floor. Others that are important to a greater or lesser degree are minimum-square footage levels set by key vendors and the display requirement of different categories. Also important for most stores is being perceived as a "headquarters" store—a place where men can take care of all their wardrobe needs.

In general, fashion merchandise is perceived as a category that requires more space than classifications in order to maximize sales. "With fashion goods, you want to show them in a lifestyle setting with the right props, and fixtures, and that takes more space than basics," said David Zant, men's senior vice-president at Cincinnati-based Mercantile Stores.

Wally Naymon, owner of Kilgore Trout in Cleveland suburb of Beachwood, added: "With basic merchandise you can do it in several colors and stack it high and it looks fine. But fashion merchandise takes more space and also more thought about the location of the space. You want people to know you're in the fashion business."

The demands of vendors are also playing an increasingly important role in determining the amount and location of space. The Big Three sportswear collections—Tommy Hilfiger, Polo and Nautica—have certain minimum requirements in both areas. Most stores say that, given the returns, it's not a problem.

According to Stuart Goldblatt, men's senior vice-president of Carson Pirie Scott in Milwaukee, "The Big Three do a great job of putting a lot of units into a fairly small space while still maintaining a fashion presentation. One of their secrets is making the walls work. Overall, it's a great package—you get a good assortment of core merchandise and regular deliveries of fresh goods, and the productivity and margins are there."

At Mercantile, Zant said, collection sportswear and dress shirts and neckwear are all picking up more space while clothing is declining. "We're getting a betting return on investment with those areas, so when we expand or build new stores, those are the areas that get more space, "he said. He added that space for the Big Three has doubled or more in many cases. "In the past those lines would have gotten anywhere from 500 to 800 square feet a piece," he said. "But in our new and renovated store they're getting 1,000 to 1,800 square feet and it will probably go higher in the future. We recently opened a 3,000-square-foot Hilfiger megashop in one store."

Zant added, however that it is still important to offer customers a full selection. "Just because one category is performing well doesn't mean you can cut

continued

everything else back and just sell that one category. A store still needs a full presentation on the floor."

Goldblatt said that Carson first looks at increasing capacity before automatically giving more space to top-performing areas. "You can add spinners on counters or replace four-ways with cube units or tables, all of which give you more capacity without changing the basic makeup of the floor."

Goldblatt continued, "Outerwear is a category that is productive about three months of the year. It's important to be able to downsize that business during the rest of the year."

At Kilgore Trout, Naymon said outerwear is an example of a marginal category that he still has to carry in order to offer a balanced assortment. "My customer drives from heated garage to heated garage and outerwear just isn't that important to them. Fashion outerwear sells, but not much else."

While clothing is not picking up space, Naymon said space with the category is shifting. "Opening price is no longer a factor for us. Better clothing is getting more space."

At Hubert White in Minneapolis, owner Bob White said clothing currently leads the store in terms of productivity for several reason. The key one is that Hubert White is primarily a clothing store. But also important is that clothing is a category that can be merchandised vertically and does not require elaborate displays. "We do a lot with vertical racks with suits, but that's not really possible with sportswear or with furnishings. Both of those require more space. They need to be right in front of the customer."

Learning Activity 10.3

1. According to "Fashion First . . .", what are the fundamental principles guiding the allocation of space?

2. What are the productivity measures of space allocation?

3. Can these principles of space allocation and productivity measures be applied to other merchandise categories and classifications?

Merchandise Replenishment

Merchandise replenishment systems are key factors in merchandise presentation. They determine what merchandise is available for customers to buy at any particular point in time. Complete assortments prevent stockouts and thus increase sales. **Quick Response (QR) replenishment systems** provide competitive advantages and they are a pull-through, instead of the traditional push-through system (Blackburn, 1991; Glock & Kunz, 1995). In the traditional retail environment, there was little opportunity to adjust merchandise assortments offered during a selling period because of lengthy lead times. Retailers ordered and received most merchandise ahead of the selling period (Hunter, King, Nuttle, & Wilson, 1993; Taylor, 1970). Only one or two shipments were delivered during the selling period. The remaining inventory not delivered as part of the initial shipment was sent in weeks predetermined by merchandise plans. No demand re-estimation was employed during the selling period. QR multiple delivery strategies solve this problem by frequently re-estimating customer preferences based on up-to-date POS data (Nuttle, King, & Hunter, 1991). Production capability and merchandise offered is adjusted to respond to customer demand based on POS information and style testing (Glock & Kunz, 1995).

Multiple delivery strategies are one means of merchandise replenishment. Multiple delivery strategies employ an initial delivery followed by a series of reorders to accommodate customer needs and preferences and to adjust for merchandise planning errors ("Measuring the impact," 1991; Nuttle, King, & Hunter, 1991; Setren, 1993). Replenishing merchandise by reordering best sellers during the selling period may increase the store's profit (Troxell, 1976) and reduce merchandisers' plan errors (King & Poindexter, 1991). Plan errors include assortment error and volume error. **Assortment error** represents differences in distribution of assortment factors (usually style, size, and color for apparel) between planned and actual demand; **volume error** represents a difference between the actual demand volume and the planned volume. Both errors can be reduced by re-estimating customer demand after evaluating POS feedback. Merchandisers may revise the original plan and replenish with merchandise that customers want (King & Poindexter, 1991). Table 10.1 provides a set of terms required for understanding multiple delivery strategies and merchandise replenishment.

TABLE 10.1

Terms for multiple delivery strategies and merchandise replenishment.

- **assortment error**—difference in distribution of assortment factors between planned and actual demand.
- **average inventory**—the average number of units in stock during the selling period (Poindexter, 1991).
- **demand re-estimation**—recalculation of sales forecasts based on POS data.
- **frequency of additional deliveries (FAD)**—the number of additional deliveries in a selling period.
- **gross margin return on inventory (GMROI)**—the financial ratio that shows the relationship between the gross margin in dollars and the average inventory investment.
- **initial order**—a request to receive merchandise not previously stocked.
- **lead time**—the time between placing the initial order or reorder(s) and receiving the merchandise on the retail sales floor.
- **merchandise replenishment**—the process of planning and placing reorders, as well as handling, shipping, receiving, distributing if necessary, and displaying merchandise.

TABLE 10.1 (continued)

Terms for multiple delivery strategies and merchandise replenishment.

- **multiple delivery**—using more than one shipment of a given merchandise assortment based on an initial order and reorder(s).
- **order**—a request to receive merchandise.
- **performance measures**—the indicators that help a firm judge the efficiency and effectiveness of their strategies.
- **Quick Response (QR) merchandise replenishment**—a customer-driven process of planning and placing reorders, as well as handling, shipping, receiving, distributing if necessary, and displaying merchandise with the shortest possible lead time.

- **reorder**—a request to replenish merchandise previously stocked.
- **single delivery**—shipment of 100 percent of a given merchandise assortment based on an initial order.
- **stock turnover**—the number of times the average stock is sold within a given period of time.
- **stockout**—the particular SKU desired by the customer is not immediately available (Kunz & Song, 1996).
- **volume error**—difference between the quantity planned and actual sales.
- **volume per SKU for the initial delivery (VSID)**—the number of units allocated on the average for each SKU in the initial delivery.

Merchandise Replenishment Model

In academic literature, there have been few descriptions of the process of merchandise replenishment. Hughes (1994) indicated that merchandise replenishment is the process of moving stock from suppliers to the retail sales floor. Setren (1993) indicated that the merchandise replenishment process involves purchase order creation, approval, vendor receiving, and shipping, as well as retailer receiving and processing. For purposes of this textbook, **merchandise replenishment** is defined as the process of planning and placing reorders, as well as handling, shipping, receiving, distributing if necessary, and displaying merchandise. A model of the merchandise replenishment process is presented in Figure 10.1.

Placing the Initial Order

The **initial order** may be based on basic stock, model stock, or automated stock plans depending of the type of merchandise being planned. The quantity of the initial order should be sufficient to meet sales until a reorder can be placed and received (Taylor, 1970) if additional merchandise is desired. Retailers may place small initial orders for a variety of merchandise to observe customer reactions. Preferred products can then be reordered in larger quantities to reduce plan errors.

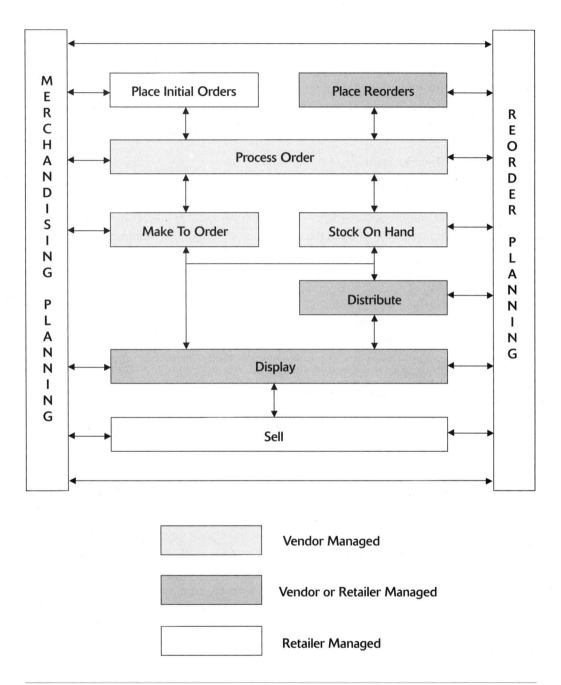

FIGURE 10.1

A model of merchandise replenishment process (Lin, 1996, p. 18).

Initial delivery refers to part or all of the initial order shipped to an individual store at the beginning of the selling period. Traditionally, initial delivery has been determined as a percentage of total inventory (Nuttle, King & Hunter, 1991). The initial delivery usually consists of the styles and/or sizes and colors that the manufacturer put into production first.

Reorder Planning

Reorder planning is as important as original merchandise planning (Allen, 1982). This happens when an initial order is placed and part or all of the initial order is sold. Its objectives involve correcting errors between merchandise plans and actual customer demand (Donnellan, 1996; Nuttle, King & Hunter, 1991; Troxell, 1976), as well as keeping complete assortments during the selling period and minimizing residual inventory at the end of the selling period (Taylor, 1970). These objectives are accomplished by regularly monitoring inventory positions; carefully comparing actual sales against merchandise plans; identifying best-selling styles, colors, and sizes (Taylor, 1970); accurately re-estimating customer demand; and incorporating these re-estimations into reorders (Donnellan, 1996; Nuttle, King, & Hunter, 1991; Troxell, 1976).

Many factors affect reorder planning:

1) The length of the selling period limits the number of reorders (Hunter, 1990). Merchandise with short selling periods is usually more difficult to plan.
2) Merchandise with considerable fluctuation in the rate of sale during a selling period needs more time and effort to plan (Troxell, 1976). The rate of sale is determined by analyzing past sales performance and predicting new trends (Allen, 1982).
3) The frequency of updating information affects the ease and accuracy in analyzing customer preferences and determining the quantities of reorders (Allen, 1982). Daily updates of purchase orders, sales records, merchandise transfers, returns from customers, returns to vendors, order cancellations, and price changes are necessary for re-estimating customer demand and adjusting merchandise plans.
4) Lead time for delivery of merchandise depends on the geographic location of vendors, the overall demand of the specified item among competing retailers, and the vendor's perception of the importance of the retailer among the vendor's customers (Bhat, 1985). Lengthy lead time forces retailers to reorder merchandise when a full inventory still exists (Berman & Evans, 1995).

5) The firm's expected customer service level determines the quantity of safety stock (Bohlinger, 1977). Safety stock is the amount of merchandise required to be on hand to prevent stockouts. Maintaining safety stock may overcome uncertainty in demand and/or supply of merchandise (Lewison, 1991).

6) Large purchases may have quantity discounts and thus reduce per-unit costs. Smaller orders may increase the cost per unit, but reduce inventory carrying costs (Berman & Evans, 1995).

Placing the Reorder

Reorders can be created by retailers or suppliers. Reorders generated by suppliers may be prepared and shipped with or without retail merchandiser review and modifications (Buzzell & Ortmeyer, 1995; Gray, 1993). Traditionally, most reorders are created by retailers (Setren, 1993).

Reorders are preferably placed only after actual sales have given sufficient indication of the quantity customers are likely to buy (Taylor, 1970). Reorders are usually placed with current suppliers for previously purchased goods under terms and conditions specified by the initial order (Allen, 1982; Lewison, 1991). Reorders can be placed via mail, telephone, electronic transmission, or computer-to-computer transmission (Lambert & Stock, 1993).

Order Processing

Order processing includes entering the order, checking the customer's credit, assembling, packing, invoicing, and arranging to ship (Buzzell & Ortmeyer, 1995; Lambert & Stock, 1993). Suppliers are responsible for this process.

Make to Order/Stock on hand

Purchase orders may be assembled from stock on hand or by production if not currently in inventory (Glock & Kunz, 1995; Lambert & Stock, 1993). Producing products after receiving the purchase orders is sometimes called make-to-order. From the manufacturers' perspectives, the goal of make-to-order is to have zero inventory at both the beginning and end of the selling period (Glock & Kunz, 1995). Traditionally, basic and staple goods are assembled from stock on hand (Glock & Kunz, 1995; Taylor, 1970); fashion and seasonal goods are often make-to-order (Glock & Kunz, 1995).

Distribution

Distribution is the process of receiving, sorting, storing, allocating, picking, and shipping merchandise. Receiving may take place in the individual store or distribution centers or both. **Receiving** consists of checking and marking merchandise. The checking activities involve comparing the supplier's invoice and a shipment's physical contents against the original purchase order, inspecting the incoming shipment for defects, and recording any disagreement (Buzzell & Ortmeyer, 1995; Lewison, 1994). **Marking** is the process of affixing or tagging the individual items with a price and other identifying information for stocking, controlling, and selling (Lewison, 1991).

The methods for receiving merchandise include direct store delivery, distribution center delivery, and cross-docking (Lewison, 1994). **Direct store delivery** means that merchandise is received directly in the individual stores. This is the quickest way to move merchandise to individual stores, since merchandise is never stored in a distribution center (Gray, 1993). **Distribution center delivery** means that merchandise is first received in distribution centers and then shipped to individual stores after it is sorted and allocated. The time merchandise is stored in distribution centers depends on distribution plans and real sales data. Receiving merchandise at a distribution center permits retailers to adjust the allocation of merchandise based on sales during the time between preparing an order and its receipt (Buzzell & Ortmeyer, 1995). **Cross-docking** means that "merchandise is received, sorted, and routed directly from receiving to shipping without spending any time in storage" (Lewison, 1994, p. G-4). The distribution center becomes a sorting area instead of a holding area (Lalonde, 1994).

Displaying

Displaying is the process of making merchandise available for purchase by the customer. Displaying takes place in the individual store and involves moving merchandise to the sales floor for presentation, or to the stock rooms for storage (Lewison, 1994). For reordered merchandise, merchandisers may use the same sales displays designed for original orders.

Selling

Selling is the process of changing ownership of merchandise from the retailer to the ultimate customer. POS data provide information for merchandisers to identify the characteristics of fast sellers, to invest more money on up-trending categories, to manage down-trending categories to minimize markdowns (Setren, 1993), and to make decisions on reorders and new product introductions (Kunz & Rupe, 1995).

The model (Fig. 10.1) delineates the merchandise replenishment process, interactions among elements and possible interactions among retailers and suppliers. It shows that all the elements of the merchandise replenishment process are interdependent. Any change or result in one element impacts the others. Merchandise planning and reorder planning play dominant roles in merchandise replenishment. Those making those plans receive information from both inside and outside the model, coordinate information into the respective reorder plans, and provide guidelines for ongoing interaction.

CASE 10.4
Levi's Perfects Custom Fit

From Schmidt, J. (1996, August). *Computerworld Retail Journal,* p. R7.

Imagine purchasing your entire wardrobe from a store that has zero inventory. Levi Strauss & Co., for one, sees that as a distinct possibility. The company already offers women the opportunity to order custom-fit, mass-produced blue jeans. It hopes to extend the approach to other lines.

Levi's Personal Pair Program is the brainchild of Sung Park, founder of Custom Clothing Technology Corp. The idea originated on a trip to Hong Kong where Park purchased custom-fit business suits. With no knowledge of the clothing industry, he thought why not expand the concept to other lines of clothes. Independent research zeroed in on blue jeans as a good candidate.

Park quickly struck a partnership with Levi's, which acquired Custom Clothing Technology in Newton, Mass., late last year.

The custom jeans process begins when a salesclerk inputs the customer's measurements into a handheld computer or PC networked to the store's backoffice server. A prototype jean is recommended by a Microsoft Visual Basic built program for the initial fitting. Any feedback about the fit is fed back into the computer, and another prototype is suggested. The process continues until a perfect fit, leg style, and fabric finish are found. A bar code is assigned to each order to trace its progress.

Each night Levi's remote Lotus Development Corp. Notes server dials every store's backoffice server via modem and batches together all orders. The orders are then transferred via modem to the factory's computer. The next morning, new orders displayed at the factory are assigned a particular pattern number, and from there, the manufacturing process begins.

The system was initially rolled out last year to more than 55 Levi's stores in North America. Additional stores will be brought online this year in North America and Europe.

"Initial sales and customer feedback has been a rousing success," said Bethe Palmer, director of retail operations at Custom Clothing.

Before year's end, Levi's expects to extend the program to women's khakis and men's jeans.

Palmer said she is aware of only one other mass-produced custom product, from a shoe manufacturer.

Alison Malkin, an apparel analyst at Dillon Read & Co., in New York, sees the custom approach spreading into other lines of clothing but not in the near term. "Everyone seems to be waiting to see if it is an economical thing to do," she said.

Learning Activity 10.4

Merchandise replenishment processes

1. Read Case 10.4 carefully. Are there component parts of Levi's Custom Fit merchandise replenishment process?

2. How do the components in Levi's Custom Fit relate to the components of the merchandise replenishment model in Figure 10.1? What is the same and what is different?

Merchandise Replenishment in Relation to BTAF/QR

The Merchandise Replenishment Model is based on the following assumptions of Behavioral Theory of the Apparel Firm with a Quick Response construct (BTAF/QR) discussed in Chapter 2. According to BTAF/QR, an apparel firm consists of six constituencies: Quick Response, merchandising, operations, marketing, finance, and executive management. Satisfying target customer desires and needs within the limitations of the firm is the central focus of decision making among the six constituencies. Both merchandising and operations constituencies take major responsibilities for replenishing merchandise to satisfy customer demand, all while considering the firm's limitations. Merchandisers plan, develop, and present product lines to satisfy customer demand. Operations personnel manage human resources, physical facilities, equipment, and inventories to maximize the efficiency and profitability of operations.

The dark box in Figure 10.2 indicates the relationship between the model of the merchandise replenishment process and BTAF/QR. The box overlaps the merchandising and operations constituencies because they co-operate both with each other and with external coalitions regarding mer-

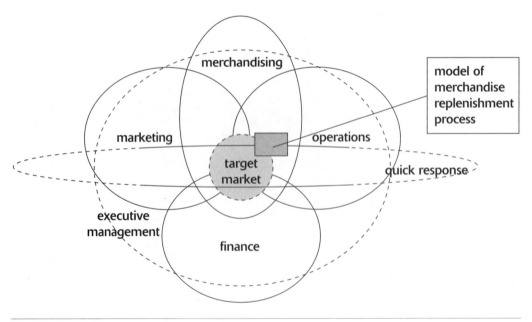

FIGURE 10.2

The proposed model of merchandise replenishment process in relation to Behavioral Theory of the Apparel Firm operating with Quick Response systems (BTAF/QR) (Lin, 1996, p. 51).

chandise replenishment. The box overlaps the target market because POS data are the source of information for predicting future demand and determining the SKUs and quantities to reorder. Only part of the box overlaps the QR constituency because not all firms use the QR concepts to replenish merchandise or may not use them for all merchandise. Some firms may still use traditional methods. The model provides a framework for developing and testing research questions related to merchandise replenishment and developing merchandise replenishment technology.

Merchandise Replenishment Technology

In QR, time is regarded as a firm's primary competitive resource (Blackburn, 1991). Shortening the cycle time of the entire soft-goods production and distribution process helps textile, apparel, and retail firms to acquire competitive advantages. Quick decisions made closer to the time of sale in response to actual customer demand can be more accurate and, consequently, more profitable (Blackburn, 1991; Hunter, 1990).

The process of converting raw materials into apparel includes both a product flow from the suppliers to the retailers and an information flow from the retailers to the suppliers (Blackburn, 1991) See Figure 10.3. Product flows forward from textile producers to customers in value-added processes. Information flows backward from customers to apparel and textile manufacturers by using electronic data interchange (EDI) (Blackburn, 1991).

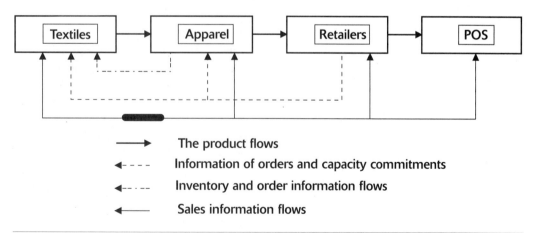

FIGURE 10.3

Product and information flows in the apparel chain (Blackburn, 1991).

Conventional approaches to shorten the cycle time of the entire apparel chain from fiber production to the retail sales floor emphasize **speeding product flows** through the pipeline. QR strategies pay attention to speeding not only product flows, but also information flows (Blackburn, 1991; "Quick response technologies," 1991). The methods used to speed both flows include changing operating procedures, using technology, and developing cooperative partnerships (Blackburn, 1991; Glock & Kunz, 1995; Hammond, 1993).

In terms of changing operating procedures, Buzzell and Ortmeyer (1995) identified four key issues: 1) using information technology to automate manual activities; 2) eliminating redundancies in operating procedures; 3) reassigning tasks for maximum apparel chain efficiency; and 4) reducing or eliminating control steps in operating procedures.

The benefits of using technology include improving the response time of transmitting customer preferences back to all members of the apparel chain (Blackburn, 1991; "EDI," 1991); reducing the amount of paper work and data entry for both vendors and retailers; improving the efficiency of creating, communicating, and tracking purchase orders (Gilman, 1989; "Measuring the impact," 1991); and increasing the efficiency and effectiveness of merchandising, producing, and distributing (Buzzell & Ortmeyer, 1995; Hammond, 1993; Rupe & Kunz, in press).

EDI, bar coding and scanning are the most common QR technologies used to support time-based competition. EDI is computer-to-computer communication that uses the direct computer-to-computer exchange of business information between vendors and customers in a standard electronic format without any human intervention (Baker, 1991, "Quick response technologies," 1991). The information exchanged by computers may include product catalogs, product planning schedules, sales, purchase orders, advance ship notices, invoices, functional acknowledgment, and capacity commitments (Blackburn, 1991; Gordon, 1993; Gray, 1993; "Quick response technologies," 1991).

Bar coding, used in conjunction with scanning devices, facilitate merchandise tracking and inventory control at the SKU level by automatically capturing all relevant information for each product. (Hammond, 1993; Gilman, 1989, "Measuring the impact," 1991). Universal product code (UPC) and shipping container marking (SCM) are the two important bar coding systems for retail firms. UPC is the dominant bar coding system used at POS (Hammond, 1993, "Quick response technologies," 1991). This is a 12-digit merchandise code that includes a five-digit vendor number, a five-digit merchandise number, and leading and trailing digits. This code is scanned and translated by an optical scanning device at POS when a customer makes a purchase (Hammond, 1993). POS information helps firms analyze customer preferences, forecast sales trends, make future decisions on reorders and new product introductions, manage inventory, and speed customer flow at checkout (Rupe & Kunz, in press).

SCM increases the speed and accuracy of merchandise distribution processes (Hammond, 1993). SCM supplied by the manufacturer provides information on vendors, orders, destinations, and carton numbers for each shipping carton. This information allows containers to be received, verified, and sent to the sales floor without being opened (Hammond, 1993; "Quick response technologies," 1991). By pre-ticketing merchandise with UPC and cartons with SCM, retailers may reduce the labor force handling merchandise and accelerate the flow of merchandise through the distribution center (Gilman, 1989). With the use of SCM, shipments may flow constantly and consistently and merchandise may be re-stocked directly from the manufacturer to the sales floor (Setren, 1993).

Multiple Delivery Strategies in Relation to Merchandise Planning

Merchandise planning, along with appropriate delivery strategies, are major tools for achieving balanced assortments to satisfy customer needs and desires. Previous research (Hunter, King & Nuttle, 1992; Nuttle, King, & Hunter, 1991) indicated that frequently re-estimating customer demand and replenishing merchandise is one way to increase stock turnover and reduce stockouts. Lin (1996) identified two performance measures and quantitative guidelines for developing delivery strategies in fashion and seasonal goods with two selling periods. Tables 10.2 and 10.3 provide examples of how multiple deliveries might be timed for 10- and 20-week selling periods. The last delivery in the 10-week selling period is in week 7; and the last delivery in the 20-week week selling period is in week 14. Assuming the merchandise plan includes zero-to-zero inventory, ending deliveries in weeks 7 and 14 allows time to sell as much of the remaining inventory as possible before the merchandise is replaced with fresh goods.

Measures of Performance in Relation to Multiple Delivery Strategies

Lin (1996) evaluated the performance of multiple delivery strategies in relation to volume per stock keeping unit for an assortment (VSA). He introduced the concept of volume per SKU for initial delivery (VSID) as a

TABLE 10.2

Examples of timing additional deliveries for a 10-week selling period.*

Frequency of additional deliveries	Weeks in the selling period					
	2	3	4	5	6	7
1			X			
2		X				X
3	X		X			X
4	X	X		X		X
5	X	X	X	X		X
6	X	X	X	X	X	X

*Lin (1996).

TABLE 10.3

Examples of timing additional deliveries for a 20-week selling period.*

Frequency of additional deliveries	weeks in the selling period												
	2	3	4	5	6	7	8	9	10	11	12	13	14
1						X							
2						X							X
3			X					X					X
4		X			X				X				X
5	X			X			X			X			X
6	X		X		X		X			X			X
7	X		X		X		X		X		X		X
8	X	X	X		X		X		X		X		X
9	X	X	X	X	X		X		X		X		X
10	X	X	X	X	X	X	X		X		X		X
11	X	X	X	X	X	X	X	X	X		X		X
12	X	X	X	X	X	X	X	X	X	X	X		X
13	X	X	X	X	X	X	X	X	X	X	X	X	X

*Lin (1996).

companion concept with VSA. He generated data using the Apparel Retail Model (ARM) computer simulation and examined performance for two selling periods, 10 weeks and 20 weeks. Lin used Anova and least significant difference (LSD) multiple comparisons (two statistical techniques) to identify two performance factors based on nine performance measures generated by ARM for both selling periods. The performance factors and their respective performance measures are defined in Table 10.4.

The first factor was labeled **revenue and service (RS).** The measures in the RS factor were influenced primarily by reduced percent total stock-

TABLE 10.4

Definitions of performance measures.*

1. Revenue and Service (RS)

Percent total stockouts	=	the amount of total stockouts divided by total inventory.
Percent lost sales	=	the amount of total lost sales divided by total inventory.
Gross margin	=	total revenue (or net sales) minus total cost of goods.
Total revenue	=	sales revenue plus job off revenue.

2. Inventory and Profitability (IP)

Average inventory	=	the average number of units in stock within a specified selling period.
Percent jobbed off	=	residual inventory at the end of the selling period divided by total inventory.
Percent gross margin	=	total revenue minus total cost of goods divided by total revenue.
Percent adjusted gross margin	=	gross margin minus distribution and inventory carrying costs divided by total revenue.
Gross margin return on inventory	=	gross margin dollars divided by the average dollar investment in inventory.

*Lin (1996).

outs. Reduced stockouts led to decreased percent lost sales and increased gross margin and total revenue because more customers got merchandise they wanted. Revenues increased because of improved in-stock position. Based on RS measures, the fewer the stockouts, the higher the revenues.

The second factor developed by Lin (1996) is composed of five measures: percent jobbed off, percent gross margin, percent adjusted gross margin, gross margin return on inventory (GMROI), and average inventory. This factor was called **inventory and profitability (IP).** The components of the IP factor reflected reduced average inventory, resulting in decreased percent jobbed off as well as increased percent gross margin, percent adjusted gross margin, and GMROI because less merchandise was stocked on the average while the same merchandise or more was sold during the selling period. Reduced average inventory was the major reason for the improved performance in IP.

In order to understand the influence of considering both factors at the same time for different strategy combinations, Lin created a third performance measure named **overall performance (OP).** The scores of OP for selected strategy combinations were determined by totalling the scores of RS and IP since both factors had a similar percentage of variances. The results indicated that when RS and IP factors were considered together, multiple delivery strategies were useful only for the 20-week selling period.

For a selling period of 10 weeks or less, multiple delivery strategies did not improve OP.

Guidelines for Applying Multiple Delivery Strategies

Lin (1996) developed some quantitative guidelines that may be used for plotting delivery strategies. Merchandisers may identify the volume per SKU for the assortment (VSA) and its selling period, select performance measures based on the firm's positioning, and then refer to the following guidelines as a basis of appropriate delivery strategies. They may also use the guidelines to negotiate the frequency of tabulating inventory and provide information to the merchandisers so better reorder strategies can be used.

1) In relation to volume per SKU for the assortment (VSA):
    - When the assortment is more diverse (VSA = 2) or diverse (VSA = 5), multiple delivery strategies can improve revenue and service (RS).
    - When the assortment is diverse (VSA = 5 or below), multiple delivery strategies are unlikely to improve inventory and profitability (IP) or overall performance (OP).
    - When the assortment is focused (VSA = 10 or greater), the best chance exists for using multiple delivery strategies to improve assortment performance as compared to single delivery.
2) In relation to volume per SKU for the initial delivery (VSID):
    - The higher the VSID the fewer additional deliveries required to get better performance than single delivery.
    - When VSID is low, assortment performance for IP can be improved.
    - When VSID is low or high (close to VSA), assortment performance for RS and OP cannot be improved.
3) In relation to the length of selling period:
    - Multiple delivery strategies do not improve OP for a 10-week selling period.
    - Multiple delivery strategies are likely to improve OP for a 20-week selling period.

However, the results of this study were based on specified simulation scenarios and data; additional research is needed to verify findings by using real-world data and different scenarios.

The Value of Product Velocity

Product velocity is the speed with which a product passes through the industry matrix. The measure of product velocity is average inventory during a selling period. Gilreath, Reeve & Whalen Jr. (1995, March) explained the product velocity advantage, focusing on gross margin return on inventory (GMROI) as the measure of productivity. Their example compared Hare (the QR company) and Tortoise (the traditional company). Table 10.5 itemizes their logic.

The scenario begins with a comparison of Tortoise and Hare where the two firms have generated identical total revenue (TR), merchandise cost (MC), gross margin (GM), and percent gross margin (%GM). Tortoise has an average inventory (AI) of $240,000. At the same time, Hare, through use of QR business systems that include smaller initial deliveries and more frequent smaller shipments for merchandise replenishment, has an average inventory of $100,000. Consequently, Tortoise's inventory turnover is 2.5, meaning the average quantity of stock on hand during the selling period was sold two and a half times. Hare, with a much lower average inventory, has inventory turnover of 6.0.

inventory turnover = merchandise cost / average inventory
(Tortoise) 2.5 = $600,000 / $240,000
(Hare) 6 = $600,000 / $100,000

TABLE 10.5

Time is Money, the Concept of Product Velocity.*

	Tortoise	Hare	Formula
Total revenue (TR)	$1,000,000	$1,000,000	
Merchandise cost (MC)	$600,000	$600,000	
Gross margin (GM)	$400,000	$400,000	TR-MC
Percent Gross margin (%GM)	40%	40%	(GM/TR)×100
Average inventory (AI)	$240,000	$100,000	
Inventory Turns	2.5	6.0	MC/AI
Gross Margin Return on Inventory (GMROI %)	167%	400%	(GM/AI)×100
Inventory Carrying Costs (ICC)	$48,000	$20,000	AI × 20%
Profit	$50,000	$50,000	(5% × TR)
Potential Profit		$78,000	(P + ICC Savings)

*Based on Gilreath, T. L., Reeve, J. M., & Whalen Jr., C. E. (1995, March). "Time is money: Understanding the product velocity advantage." *Bobbin,* pp. 50–55.

In this scenario, Tortoise has gross margin return on inventory (GM-ROI) (gross margin ÷ average inventory) of 167 percent. Gross margin was 167 percent of average inventory for Tortoise. At the same time, Hare had GMROI of 400 percent. The realized gross margin was four times as great as average inventory investment.

gross margin						
return on inventory	=	*(gross margin*	÷	*average inventory)*	×	*100*
(Tortoise) 167%	=	($400,000	÷	$240,000)	×	100
(Hare) 400%	=	($400,000	÷	$100,000)	×	100

Level of average inventory is a primary determinant of inventory carrying costs, including interest, storage, and insurance. Tortoise has carrying costs of $48,000, while Hare has carrying costs of $20,000. In this example, carrying costs are 20 percent of average inventory. Since Hare has much lower average inventory, carrying costs are also much less.

inventory carrying costs	=	*average inventory*	×	*20%*
(Tortoise) $48,000	=	$240,000	×	20%
(Hare) $20,000	=	$100,000	×	20%

Savings in carrying costs translate directly to the bottom line. If the profit generated is five percent of total revenue given merchandise cost and gross margin, then potential profit with QR is profit plus inventory carrying cost savings. Inventory carrying cost savings is the reduction in ICC related to the reduction in average inventory. Potential profit is profit plus ICC savings.

profit	=	*total revenue* × 5%
$50,000	=	$1,000,000 × 5%
potential profit	=	*profit* + *inventory carrying cost savings*
(Tortoise) $50,000	=	$50,000 + ($48,000 − $48,000)
(Hare) $78,000	=	$50,000 + ($48,000 − $20,000)

Thus Hare experiences a 56 percent increase in potential profits ($78,000 − $50,000 ÷ $50,000) based solely on savings in inventory carrying costs because of lower average inventory using QR systems.

Product Velocity at Mike's Bikes

By using a combination of information from Mike's Bikes Income Statement, Table 3.7, and Mike's Bikes Merchandise Budget, Table 6.4, the

Tortoise and Hare product velocity concepts can be applied to biking shorts. See Table 10.6.

The scenario begins with a comparison of traditional (Traditional) and Quick Response (QR) business systems where the two scenarios have generated identical total revenue (TR), merchandise cost (MC), gross margin (GM), and percent gross margin (%GM). As indicated in the Chapter 6 (for example) for biking shorts, Mike's Bikes' traditional business system has an average inventory (AI) of $56,350. Through the use of QR, including smaller initial deliveries and more frequent, smaller shipments for merchandise replenishment, they might achieve an average inventory of $35,000. According to the merchandise budget, planned merchandise received is $171,200, with an initial markup of 55 percent. Consequently, merchandise cost is $77,040 (planned merchandise received − initial markup). Under Traditional inventory, turnover is 1.4 (merchandise cost ÷ average inventory), meaning the average quantity of stock on hand during the selling period was sold not quite one and one-half times. QR, with a lower average inventory, has an inventory turnover of 2.2.

$$
\begin{array}{lcrcl}
\textit{merchandise cost} & = & \textit{planned merchandise received} & - & \textit{initial markup} \\
\$77,040 & = & \$171,200 & - & 55\% \\
\textit{inventory turnover} & = & \textit{merchandise cost} & \div & \textit{average inventory} \\
\text{(Traditional) } 1.4 & = & \$77,040 & \div & \$56,350 \\
\text{(QR)} \quad 2.2 & = & \$77,040 & \div & \$35,000 \\
\end{array}
$$

Traditional has gross margin return on inventory (GMROI) (gross margin / average inventory) of 143 percent. At the same time, QR had GMROI of 230 percent. The realized gross margin with QR was nearly two- and one-half times as great as average inventory investment.

$$
\begin{array}{llcrccc}
\textit{gross margin} & & & & & & \\
\textit{return on inventory} & = & \textit{(gross margin} & \div & \textit{average inventory)} & \times & 100 \\
\text{(Traditional) } 143\% & = & (\$80,460 & \div & \$56,350) & \times & 100 \\
\text{(QR)} \quad 230\% & = & (\$80,460 & \div & \$35,000) & \times & 100 \\
\end{array}
$$

As with the Tortoise and Hare example, the level of average inventory is a primary determinant of inventory carrying costs. Using the assumption that carrying costs are 20 percent of average inventory, Traditional has carrying costs of $11,270, while QR has carrying costs of $7,000. Since QR has lower average inventory, carrying costs for QR are less than Traditional.

$$
\begin{array}{llll}
\textit{carrying costs} & = & \textit{average inventory} & \times \ \textit{20\%} \\
\text{(Traditional) } \$11{,}270 & = & \$56{,}350 & \times \ 20\% \\
\text{(QR)} \quad \$7{,}000 & = & \$35{,}000 & \times \ 20\%
\end{array}
$$

As indicated in the Income Statement (Table 3.7), profit generated at Mike's Bikes is three percent of total revenue. Planned sales (total revenue) according to Table 6.4 is $157,500. Potential profit with QR is profit plus savings in inventory carrying cost.

$$
\begin{array}{llll}
\textit{profit} & = & \textit{total revenue} & \times \ \textit{\% profit} \\
\$4{,}725 & = & \$157{,}500 & \times \quad 3\%
\end{array}
$$

$$
\begin{array}{llll}
\textit{savings in inventory carrying costs} & = & \textit{Traditional carrying costs} - \textit{QR carrying costs} \\
\$4{,}270 & = & \$11{,}270 \qquad - \qquad \$7{,}000
\end{array}
$$

$$
\begin{array}{llll}
\textit{potential profit with QR} & = & \textit{profit} & + & \textit{savings in inventory carrying cost} \\
\$8{,}995 & = & \$4{,}725 & + & \$4{,}270
\end{array}
$$

Thus QR experiences a 90.4 percent increase in potential profits (QR potential profit − Traditional profit ÷ Traditional profit).

TABLE 10.6

Product velocity at Mike's Bikes.

	Traditional	QR	Formula
Total revenue (TR)	$157,500	$157,500	planned sales in Table 6.4
Merchandise cost (MC)	$77,040	$77,040	planned merchandise received − initial markup
Gross margin (GM)	$80,460	$80,460	TR-MC
Percent Gross margin (%GM)	51%	51%	(GM÷TR)×100
Average inventory (AI)	$56,350	$35,000	
Inventory Turns	1.4	2.2	MC÷AI
Gross Margin Return on Inventory (GMROI %)	143%	230%	(GM÷AI)×100
Inventory Carrying Costs (ICC)	$11,270	$7,000	AI × 20%
Profit (P)	$4,725	$4,725	profit = (3% × TR)
Potential Profit with QR		$8,995	PP = P + ICC Savings

Learning Activity 10.5

Multiple delivery strategies and product velocity

1. How do multiple delivery strategies increase product velocity?

2. According to Lin's research, what is the primary determinant of measures of inventory and profitability (IP)?

3. According to Lin's research, what is the primary determinant of measures of revenue and service (RS)?

4. Using your previous Learning Activities related to Mike's Bikes and Mike's Bikes Income Statement, examine how much profits might be increased by using QR systems for bikes.

Summary

Merchandise presentation includes processes required to evaluate the line and make it visible and salable. In Chapter 3 TAMS, Figure 3.1, identifies three components of merchandise presentation: internal, wholesale, and retail. **Merchandise presentation** is a fundamental part of the merchandising process intended to enhance sales by offering products for consideration in a consciously designed environment that positively affects attitudes and behaviors toward the products and the presenter(s) (Yan, 1996).

The fundamental purpose of merchandise presentation is sales enhancement and, thus, contribution to the success of the firm. Merchandise presentation takes place in environments that are manipulated to provide the desired impression. The aesthetic experience associated with merchandise presentation enhances participants' perception of the products by providing pleasure and/or satisfaction. From the first evaluation of line concept the purpose is to create a line that will be highly desired by customers.

A multiple delivery strategy means an initial delivery and several additional deliveries based on re-estimation of POS data (Nuttle, King, & Hunter, 1991; Hunter, King, & Nuttle, 1992). The purpose of developing multiple delivery strategies is to help retailers order in smaller quantities on a more frequent basis to reduce inventory investment, stockouts, markdowns, and to improve salability. The primary decision elements of multiple delivery strategies involve the number of deliveries, the quantity of each delivery, and the timing of additional deliveries. The advantage compared to single delivery is that customer preferences can be more accurately accommodated. The disadvantages are increased costs of merchandise order processing, handling, and transportation. Multiple delivery strategies have been extensively applied to basic and staple goods. The research and practical execution of multiple delivery strategies on seasonal and fashion goods is limited.

Integrated Learning Activity 10.6

1. Read Case 10.5 carefully. How is the Flexsteel's furniture business different than Levi's Personal Pair jeans business in terms of line development? How is it similar?

2. How is Flexsteel's furniture business different than Levi's jeans business in terms of line presentation? How is it similar?

3. Refer back to Figure 3.1. How might the processes of pre-adoption, adoption and post-adoption product development differ for furniture as compared to apparel?

4. How could QR systems be applied to furniture?

Key Concepts

aesthetic benefits

assortment error

display

displaying

distributing

gross margin return on inventory (GMROI)

initial delivery

initial order

inventory and profitability (IP)

line evaluation

line preview

make to order

merchandise presentation

merchandise replenishment

multiple delivery strategies

order processing

overall performance (OP)

placing reorders

planograms

product velocity

Quick Response replenishment systems

reorder planning

revenue and service (RS)

sales enhancement

selling

stock on hand

utilitarian benefits

visual merchandising

volume error

Recommended Resources

Allen, R. L. (1982, August). Planned assortments: Buying what sells. *Chain Store Age, General Merchandise Edition,* pp. 90, 95.

Allen, R. L. (1982, September). Plan a strategy for reordering goods. *Chain Store Age, General Merchandise Edition,* pp. 94–95.

Buzzell, R. D., & Ortmeyer, G. (1995). Channel partnerships streamline distribution. *Sloan Management Review, 36*(3), 85–96.

Gilreath, T. L., Reeve, J. M., & Whalen Jr., C. E. (1995, March). Time is money: Understanding the product velocity advantage. *Bobbin,* pp. 50–55.

Lalonde, B. J. (1994, January). Distribution inventory: More speed, less cost. *Chain Store Age Executive,* pp. 18MH–20MH.

Sears' Maps' customized assortments. (1990, October). *Chain Store Age Executive,* pp. 62–69.

CASE 10.5

Flexsteel Finds Niches in Embattled Industry

From Wiley, D. (1995, February 4). *Des Moines Sunday Register,* pp. 4S–5S.

Deep in the heart of the Flexsteel plant, Tom Baldwin pulls a customer order slip from a newly upholstered creamy-white leather loveseat. It's bound for the largest furniture retailer in Detroit. He checks a pricey floral tapestry sofa. It's headed to Luxemburg, Wis., a small town east of Green Bay. A plain blue sofa with basic padding sitting on the conveyer belt next to these two beauty queens will be shipped to Edwards Air Force Base. "We're one of the largest suppliers of upholstered furniture to the U.S. government," said Baldwin, a company spokesman. Despite the inviting look of these comfy sofas rolling off the manufacturing lines, this is no time for Flexsteel Industries Inc. officials to lounge.

Sales Up, Profit Down

The Dubuque, Iowa-based furniture manufacturer, one the 10 largest in the country, finds itself in a business paradox: The company had record sales during fiscal year 1995, but posted sharp drops in profitability. That this decline in profits is an industry-wide trend is little comfort, Flexsteel officials say.

"It's been a very tough year," said Baldwin. The first quarter of the new fiscal year looked even gloomier. Sales were down from last year's first quarter. There appears to be several reasons for the slump. Rising interest rates in early 1995 meant it costs more for consumers to finance furniture purchases.

Raw material price increases for fabric, wood, and foam padding "have risen far beyond what could be passed on to the consumer," said Baldwin. Topping off the profit picture, is the competitive market for scarce consumer dollars. "We are a very deferrable item. A $699 sofa in 1989 is probably selling for $699 or less today," Graham said. "Manufacturers have had to squeeze the fat out of their processes. The entire supply chain has to be extremely efficient to be profitable."

Furniture trends used to hit the East and West coasts and take a year or two to hit the Midwest. "Today, that is no longer true," he said. "The consumer is much more cognizant of color, design, and what they want. We're a fashion-oriented business, and we're having to react to changes of consumer lifestyle much quicker."

To capture that ever-changing market, Flexsteel has been helping its gallery dealers with special programs and offers 400 of its 1,000 fabrics choices exclusively to those galleries. Video design catalogs allow customer to custom-order a sofa in a particular fabric and see ahead of time what it will look like. Those are important selling tools for a company that gets 50 percent of its business from custom orders.

Flexsteel responds to what's hot in the retail furniture world right now: wingback chairs, leather goods, "motion furniture" and furniture covered in a collage look of fabrics or designs. "Leather is just out of this world. In residential sales, leather is more than 20 percent of our volume. I'd see it hitting 25 percent in the next three to four years."

Buyers want more casual, softer furniture to fit in a relaxed, homey lifestyle look. Dual purpose furniture, like motion furniture and sleepers, has become very important and takes away from our sofa sales." Flexsteel officials say they've tried to position themselves for the future through diversification of products and tightening up supply and production costs.

Since 1984, Flexsteel has helped retailers with a gallery program to arrange its furniture attractively on a sales floor, hoping to attract buyers. "Studies show the customers will stop at five stores before they buy, and their first stop will only be 8 to 10 minutes. It had better be good if you want them to come back."

References

Allen, R. L. (1982, August). Planned assortments: Buying what sells. *Chain Store Age, General Merchandise Edition,* pp. 90, 95.

Allen, R. L. (1982, September). Plan a strategy for reordering goods. *Chain Store Age, General Merchandise Edition,* pp. 94–95.

Baker, C. (1991, April). EDI in business. *Accountancy,* pp. 121–124.

Berman, B., & Evans, J. R. (1995). *Retail management: A strategic approach* (6th ed.). Englewood Cliffs, NJ: Prentice-Hall.

Bhat, R. R. (1985). *Managing the demand for fashion items* (2nd ed.). Ann Arbor: University of Michigan.

Blackburn, J. D. (1991). The Quick-Response movement in the apparel industry: A case study in time-compressing supply chains. In J. D. Blackburn (Ed.), *Time-based competition: The next battleground in American manufacturing.* Homewood, IL: Irwin.

Bohlinger, M. S. (1977). *Merchandise buying: Principles and applications.* Dubuque, IA: Wm. C. Brown.

Buzzell, R. D., & Ortmeyer, G. (1995). Channel partnerships streamline distribution. *Sloan Management Review, 36*(3), 85–96.

Donnellan, J. (1996). *Merchandise buying and management.* New York: Fairchild.

EDI and quick response: Easy money. (1991, March). *Chain Store Age Executive,* p. 20B.

Fiore, A. M., & Kimle, P. A. (1997). *Understanding aesthetics for the merchandising and design professional.* New York: Fairchild.

Gilman, A. L. (1989, May). Assessing quick response benefits. *Chain Store Age Executive,* p. 314.

Gilreath, T. L., Reeve, J. M., & Whalen Jr., C. E. (1995, March). Time is money: Understanding the product velocity advantage. *Bobbin,* pp. 50–55.

Glock, R. E., & Kunz, G. I. (1995). *Apparel manufacturing: Sewn products analysis* (2nd ed.). Englewood Cliffs, NJ: Prentice-Hall.

Gordon, P. (1993). Rapid replenishment. *Proceedings of the Quick Response 93 Conference,* 197–204.

Gray, S. B. (1993). Foundation for quick response strategies: A retail point-of view. *Proceedings of the Quick Response 93 Conference,* 41–56.

Hammond, J. H. (1993). Quick response in retail/manufacturing channels. In S. P. Bradley, J. A. Hausman, & R. L. Nolan (Eds.), *Globalization, technology, and competition: The fusion of computers and telecommunications in the 1990s.* Boston, MA: Harvard Business School Press.

Hughes, S. (1994). How to build and maintain a management team to manage stock replenishment. *Quick Response 1994 Conference Proceedings,* 55–66.

Hunter, A. (1990). *Quick response in apparel manufacturing: A survey of the American scene.* Manchester, England: The Textiles Institute.

Hunter, N. A., King, R. E., Nuttle, H. L., & Wilson, J. R. (1993, February). The apparel pipeline modeling project at North Carolina State University (paper presented at the 4th Annual Academic Apparel Research, Raleigh, NC).

Hunter, N. A., King, R., & Nuttle, H. (1991). *Comparison of quick response and traditional retailing performance through stochastic simulation modeling* (NCSIU-IE Technical Report # 91-6). Raleigh: North Carolina State University, Department of Industrial Engineering.

King, R., & Poindexter, M. (1991, September). *A simulation model for retail buying* (NCSU-IE Technical Report # 90-9). Raleigh: North Carolina State University.

Kunz, G. I. (1995). Behavioral theory of the apparel firm: A beginning. *Clothing and textiles Research Journal, 13*(4), 252–261.

Kunz, G. I., & Rupe, D. (1995). *The status of merchandising technology, part 1: Definition of merchandising technology and literature review.* Unpublished manuscript, Iowa State University.

Kunz, G. I., & Song, J. (1996). *The influence of stockouts on in-store shopping behavior.* Unpublished manuscript, Iowa State University.

Lalonde, B. J. (1994, January). Distribution inventory: More speed, less cost. *Chain Store Age Executive,* pp. 18MH–20MH.

Lambert, D. M., & Stock, J. R. (1993). *Strategic Logistics Management* (3rd ed.). New York: Richard D. Irwin.

Lewison, D. M. (1991). *Retailing* (4th ed.). New York: Macmillan.

Lewison, D. M. (1994). *Retailing* (5th ed.). New York: Macmillan.

Lin, Tiing-Sheng. (1996). The effectiveness of multiple delivery strategies in relation to retail apparel assortments. Masters thesis, Iowa State University.

Measuring the impact: Quick response and the bottom line. (1991, March). *Chain Store Age Executive,* pp. 8B–9B.

Nuttle, H., King, R., & Hunter, N. (1991). A stochastic model of apparel retailing process for seasonal apparel. *Journal of the Textile Institute, 82*(2), 247–259.

Quick response technologies. (1991, March). *Chain Store Age Executive,* pp. 6B–7B.

Rupe, D., & Kunz, G. I. (in press). Building a financially meaningful language of merchandise assortments. *Clothing and Textiles Research Journal.*

Sears' Maps' customized assortments. (1990, October). *Chain Store Age Executive,* pp. 62–69.

Setren, M. (1993). Changing measures of performance. *Proceedings of the Quick Response 93 Conference,* 253–260.

Taylor, C. G. (1970). *Merchandising assortment planning: The key to retailing profit.* New York: Merchandising Division National Retail Merchants Associations.

Troxell, M. D. (1976). *Fashion merchandising* (2nd ed.). New York: McGraw-Hill.

Yan, Xinlu. (1996). Effect of environmental fragrancing on customers' attitude and purchase intention toward apparel product and aesthetic experience. Master's thesis, Iowa State University.

11 Customer/Vendor Relationships

Learning Objectives

- Examine the concept of customer service in the customer/vendor relationship.
- Discuss the role of personal selling service in customer service.
- Examine the components of an effective personal selling process.

A customer/vendor relationship exists any time materials or finished goods change ownership. The vendor is selling the product and the customer is buying. Some types of customer service are provided and expected along with the transaction. The concept of strategic partnering between vendors and their customers was introduced in Chapter 2 as a component of Quick Response business systems. Partnering fosters interdependence and on-going business relationships. Retailers have a problem trying to foster a similar interdependence with ultimate consumers. Customer loyalty is sought in the retail sector, but retail customers seem to exhibit less and less of it. In response, many retailers are returning to more intensive forms of customer service to stimulate sales.

The Concept of Customer Service

Customer service has become a key competitive strategy for both manufacturers and retailers. Global competition for manufacturers, over-storing for retailers, and intensive price competition have driven firms to find productive ways to draw and retain customers (Gaskill & Kunz, 1991). Davidow and Uttal (1989), management consultants and authors of *Total*

Customer Service, state that "good old-fashioned service, plus newer, more innovative ways of winning and keeping customers, may be the ultimate competitive weapon in the 1990s."

Customers have the ultimate power—the power to reject. Consequently, customers have become a primary focus in modern business environments (Goldfarb, 1989). From a vendor's perspective, "the key is getting closer to our customers and making it easier for them to do business with us" (Anton, 1996, p. 4). Retailers equate effective customer service with the willingness of customers to pay more for products, the opportunity for repeat business, lower advertising costs due to positive word-of-mouth advertising (Lele, 1987), and subsequent increases in bottom-line profits (Zemke, 1986). From the retail buyer/merchandiser's perspective, good customer service helps get merchandise into the hands of customers, the people for whom it is planned, developed, and presented.

Customer needs, whether in a business-to-business relationship or business-to-ultimate consumer relationship, seem to be relatively simple: responsiveness, promptness, knowledgeable people, accuracy, and accessibility. When customers are lost, shortcomings in customer service are the cause 75 percent of the time; dissatisfaction with products 13 percent of the time, and other reasons 12 percent of the time (Anton, 1996).

Levels of Customer Service

Components of customer service offered by manufacturing and retailing firms vary greatly. When firms are involved in QR partnerships, technology plays a key role in the type and quality of customer service. Technology is also a key player in retailer customer service, particularly in relation to visual merchandising, inventory management, and database management. "Customer-oriented information technology can empower an employee to manage successful interactions with customers . . . One of the most important attributes driving customer satisfaction is the availability of accurate information on a timely basis" (Anton, 1996, p. 5). Many components of customer service are dependent on information.

Table 11.1 demonstrates the components of four different levels of retail customer service. While most of the components are applicable to many different types of retail operations, the components related to fitting rooms are unique to apparel. The components include the role of sales associates, training sales associates, assistance with merchandise selection, operation of fitting rooms, alteration services, packaging and wrapping services, methods of payment, merchandise return, and other amenities, including availability of parking (Berman & Evans, 1995; Lewison, 1994;

Spector & McCarthy, 1995). An individual firm may use any combination of these components, depending on its overall business strategy.

Self Service

Self service means just what it says: customers provide their own selling service. The retailer records the sales, and may provide minimal display. Or the merchandise may simply be set out on the sales floor in shipping boxes. Customers roam about looking for what they want to buy. They depend on labels or printing directly on packing cartons for product information. When customers find something, they carry it to the checkout; or if the product is too large, they rip a ticket off the box and take it to the check out, where they pay for the product, probably in cash. Customers then figure out how to get the merchandise home. Warehouse markets and wholesale clubs probably are closest things to self service environments, although many accept credit cards.

Limited Service

Limited service combines some aspects of self-service and full-service environments. Limited service usually requires customers to self select merchandise, although greeters are frequently available at the door to direct customers to appropriate areas. Visual merchandising techniques may be used to help customers find and choose appropriate merchandise. Labels and hang tags are the primary source of product information, although stores may post comparisons of product features. Credit card services and liberal exchange policies are likely to be in place, but the trend is toward more limited return policies. According to the National Retail Federation, returns averaged 12 percent of sales at department stores in 1995 and 8.6 percent of sales at specialty stores. Delivery, alterations, and gift wrap may even be available in limited-service environments for a fee. Most super stores and discount stores, many department stores, and some specialty stores provide some combination of limited customer service.

Full Service

Full service incorporates a personal selling service into the customer service environment along with other amenities such as free gift wrap, alterations, delivery, and convenient parking. Knowledgeable sales associates may keep personal selling books to assist customers in both wardrobe development and with purchases for friends and family. Stores make a considerable investment selecting, training, and updating sales associates, who are a primary source of product information. Full-service stores display less merchandise on the sales floor since ensembles may be developed for personal

TABLE 11.1

Levels of retail customer service.

	Self Service	Limited Service
Store Hours	May be limited	Long hours including evenings and weekends
Parking	Free parking	Free parking
Checkout Facilities	Centralized	Centralized or decentralized
Role of Associates	Greet & thank customers, checkout, clean, count, reprice, fill racks	Greet & thank customers, checkout, fill shelves and racks, clean, count, reprice, may assist customers within department
Training of Associates	Trained on purchase, return, and exchange	Trained on purchase, return, and exchange; may have basic sales training
Customer Information	Signs, hang tags, and labels	Greeter, signs, hang tags, and labels
Merchandise Selection	Customer finds and chooses items from self-service displays	Customer finds and chooses items/may have some assistance from sales associate
Fitting Rooms	Merchandise is counted in and out of fitting room; customer returns merchandise to racks	Merchandise is counted in and out of fitting room; may have some assistance from sales associate; sales associate returns merchandise to racks
Alterations	None available	May be available for a fee
Packaging/Wrapping	Customer provides own bag	Bags or boxes provided
Methods of Payment	Cash only	Cash or credit cards accepted
Delivery Service	Customer carries or arranges delivery	May be available for a fee
Merchandise Return	No exchange/no refund or exchange only in limited time with sales receipt	Exchange or refund on charge purchases; delayed refund on cash purchase
Other Amenities		

Full Service	Premier Service
May meet in customer's home	Location and time at customer's convenience.
Adjacent parking ramp	Valet parking available
Decentralized	Decentralized
Greet, assist, checkout, and thank customers in department; other activities if time allows; maintain customer contact book	Empowered associates assist customers in any way possible; generate sales in any department; maintain customer book; send personal letters/thank you notes
Trained on purchase, return, and exchange; selling strategies, product information	Extensive training on cash register, wardrobe analysis, multiple sales strategies, fashion trends, fit, and satisfying customers
Sales associates, signs, hang tags, and labels	Concierge's desk, sales associates, signs, hang tags, and labels
Customer is assisted with merchandise selection if desired; may use personal shoppers; customers may be called when new merchandise comes in	Assisted merchandise selection and personal selling service by appointment, personal consultant presents entire ensembles after wardrobe analysis; merchandise may be charged and mailed to customer for approval
Fitting room is larger so sales associate can assist customer with dressing and additional merchandise; sales associate may gather and return merchandise to inventory	Spacious fitting room equipped with telephones as well as food and beverage service; sales associate gathers merchandise, assists customer, and returns merchandise to inventory
Available free or for a fee	Available free
Signature bags and boxes, free gift wrap	Signature bags and boxes, free gift wrap
Cash or credit cards accepted	Cash or credit cards accepted
Merchandise delivery for a fee	Free merchandise pick up or delivery
Exchange or refund on any purchase	Exchange or refund on any product, any time
Comfortable waiting areas for shoppers' companions	Child care and entertainment for shoppers' companions

presentation to individual customers. The sales floor may include a pianist to contribute to a relaxed, comfortable ambiance. Specialty stores are more likely than department stores to provide full customer service.

Premier Customer Service

Premier customer service involves intensive interaction with customers; indeed, there are few limits on what sellers can do to satisfy customers. The first priority of the company is to satisfy customers. As such, sales associates are empowered to do whatever it takes to reach that end, and are, in fact, rewarded for unusual customer service efforts. Numerous amenities accompany customer service, including entertainment for shopping companions; food, drink, telephones, e-mail, computers, and television sets in dressing rooms; availability of travel consultants; and on-the-spot alterations, delivery, shipping, and gift wrapping services. Sales associates are usually full-time, commissioned, professional employees who may make $60,000+ annually. They culture their relationship with their customers with personal calls and thank-you notes to keep them abreast of purchasing opportunities and to show appreciation for patronage. Only a few upscale stores offer premier customer service, Nordstrom probably being the most notable.

Role of Personal Selling Services

Emphasis on personal selling and knowledgeable sales people remains a critical competitive component of customer service for the nation's top firms (Farnsworth, 1990). Employees who provide **personal selling services** play major roles in a firm's merchandising efforts:

- Sellers are the most direct means by which the firm communicates with their customers. They facilitate the exchange process by providing information and matching product offerings to customers' needs.
- The quality, ability, and cooperation of sellers have a major influence on how customers perceive a firm.
- In the retail sector, sellers increase sales by turning browsers into shoppers and by building long-term relationships with customers.
- Sellers have direct responsibility for executing most aspects of customer service: the speed of transactions, handling complaints, and providing security (adapted from Ghosh, 1990).

Poorly trained and unmotivated personal service employees affect business through alienation of customers, frequent mistakes in processing, lack of initiative, and low productivity. Some studies suggest it takes 12 positive experiences with customers to rectify one bad experience (Cathcart, 1988). Davidow and Uttal (1989) claim that, "by far the largest costs that outstanding service saves are those of replacing lost customers."

Recognizing the need for good personal service is easy; developing, executing, and evaluating an effective personal-service system in a firm is time consuming, frustrating, and potentially expensive. However, for many firms, the benefits of personal service outweigh the costs. Establishing and maintaining excellent customer service requires commitment that permeates the entire organization. Case 11.1, Keys to Customer Service at Nordstrom, personifies the level of on-going investment required to provide excellence in customer service and, in particular, personal selling services.

CASE 11.1
Keys to Customer Service at Nordstrom

From Spector, R., & McCarthy, P. D. (1995). *The Nordstrom Way* pp. 129–130. New York: Wiley.

The Nordstrom culture sets employees free. The company believes that people will work hard when they are given the freedom to do their job the way they think it should be done, and when they can treat customers the way they like to be treated. Nordstrom believes that too many rules, regulations, paperwork, and strict channels of communication erode employee incentive. Without those shackles, Nordstrom people can operate like entrepreneurial shopkeepers.

- Nordstrom is informally organized as an "inverted pyramid," with the top positions occupied by the customers and the salespeople, and the bottom position filled by the co-chairmen. Every tier of the pyramid supports the sales staff.
- Empowering the people on the sales floor with the freedom to accept returned merchandise is the most obvious illustration of the Nordstrom culture because it directly impacts the public.
- The unconditional money-back guarantee is designed for the 98 percent of customers who are honest.
- Nordstrom tears down barriers. Salespeople are free to sell merchandise to their customers in any department throughout the store. This promotes continuity in the relationship between the salesperson and the customer.

- Like everyone at Nordstrom, department managers begin their career as salespeople to learn what's required to take care of the customer. This sends the signal that management values the role of salesperson.
- Managers are encouraged to have a feeling of ownership about their department. They are responsible for hiring, training, coaching, nurturing, and evaluating their sales team, and are expected to spend some of their time on the selling floor, interacting with the customers and the selling staff.
- Buying at Nordstrom is decentralized, which means that buyers in each region are given the freedom to acquire merchandise that reflects local lifestyles and tastes. Because buyers are responsible for just a few stores, they can afford to take a chance on a unique item without fear of jeopardizing the bottom line.
- Empowerment for getting the right merchandise in the store begins not in the buying office, but on the floor—at the point of sale. Nordstom encourages entrepreneurial salespeople to provide input to their manager and buyer on fashion direction, styles, quantities, sizes, and colors.
- Employee compensation is based on sales commissions. The Nordstrom brothers felt that the best way to attract and retain self-starters was by paying them according to their ability.

continued

CASE 11.1 (continued)

- An employee profit-sharing retirement plan inspires motivation and encourages loyalty. Because contributions are made to the plan directly from the company's net earnings, employees have an incentive to be productive and cost conscious.
- Goal-setting is essential to the culture. Employees at every level are perpetually striving to meet or surpass personal, departmental, store, and regional goals for the day, month, and year. Peer pressure and personal commitment push competitive employees toward constantly higher goals.
- Employees have access to sales figures from all departments and stores in the chain, so they can compare their performances.
- Outstanding sales performances are rewarded with prizes and praise, as are good ideas and suggestions.
- Top salespeople are encouraged to help others with sales techniques and building a customer base.

Learning Activity 11.1

Concepts of customer service and personal selling service

1. What is the relationship between planning, developing, and presenting product lines and customer service?

2. Identify two stores that you frequent and, using the components of customer service identified in Table 11.1, would you classify them as self service, limited service, full service or premier service?

3. Based on Case 11.1, what are the fundamental leadership principles underlying the Nordstrom customer service strategy?

4. How do the Nordstrom principles relate to the Behavioral Theory of the Apparel Firm presented in Chapter 1?

Why Customers Buy

Customers, whether materials buyers for manufacturers, finished goods buyers for retailers or ultimate consumers shopping retail stores, catalogs or the Internet, do not buy merchandise; *they buy what the merchandise will do for them*:

- Materials buyers/merchandisers are concerned about appearance, serviceability, handling, minimums, and price.
- Retail buyers/merchandisers are concerned about suitability to fashion trends, styling, color, sizing, quantity discounts, markdown money, delivery dates, gross margin potential, and contract terms.
- Ultimate consumers are concerned about wardrobe coordination, fit, styling, color, durability, and care.

Customers are looking for something to meet their needs and desires. They may be seeking some of the following:

1. To *gain* time, prestige, health, professional advancement, the feeling of personal worth, a better life.
2. To *be* professional, hospitable, influential, efficient, kind, an outstanding merchant, a good parent, recognized as an important person.
3. To *achieve* their own goals, expression of themselves, balanced assortments, their sales goals, satisfaction of curiosity, acquisition of things, emulation of others.
4. To *save* time, money, energy, work, personal embarrassment.

The success of the interaction between the seller and the buyer may determine the success of the transaction. Factors that inhibit customer contact and create sales resistance include the following:

- *Fear* of being pushed or being pushy. Potential customers in both wholesale and retail markets may avoid direct contact with sellers because they fear being talked into buying something that is not consistent with their needs and wants. Sellers who are sensitive to this fear may hesitate to make customer contact because they do not want to be perceived as being pushy. Refining the seller's skills can overcome this problem and benefit both the buyer and the seller.
- *Uncertainty* related to benefits and features of products/services. Customers who are uncertain of their product knowledge need help to make an appropriate choice. When sellers also are inadequately informed about how products can meet customers' needs, potential customer satisfaction is lost. Well-trained sellers know their products and can match products to the potential customer's desires.
- *Doubt* about the ability to make a wise purchase or about the ability to sell. Potential customers may have difficulty making decisions or lack confidence in their ability to make the right decisions. Effective sellers find ways to build confidence in the buyer. However, when sellers are inadequately trained, they may lack the professional confidence required to assist the potential customer with decision making.

The seller's greatest challenge is to identify the potential customer's needs and wants and to show how he or she will benefit from purchasing of the seller's products and/or services. Both buyers and sellers benefit by a complete understanding of the selling process.

The Personal Selling Process

Understanding the fundamentals of selling is useful for both sellers and the buyers. Basic expectations of sellers are similar regardless of product type or stage in the trade matrix. Sellers, whether selling industrial sewing machines, automobiles, buttons, life insurance, fabrics, budget lingerie, or designer apparel, are expected to generate business. Selling is a percentage business; the more potential customers approached, the more sales that are made. But sales may be improved even more by effective selling processes. Effective selling processes improve the well-being of both the buyer and the seller. Fundamentally, their are seven stages in the selling process: prospecting, approaching, determining needs, presenting merchandise, handling objections, closing the sale, and follow-up.

Prospecting

Prospecting includes two phases, personal preparation, including developing product knowledge, and evaluating potential customers:

Personal Preparation

Personal preparation includes appearance, improving selling practices, improving product knowledge, reviewing merchandise and being relaxed, poised, and confident. Appropriate appearance means dressing in a manner appropriate to the business. For example, in recent years both Levi Strauss and the Lee Company have encouraged their employees to wear the products their company sells when representing the company. Consequently, their employees appear at national meetings wearing jeans and chambray shirts while other attendees are wearing suits and ties. Retail employees are also encouraged to wear apparel consistent with the products they are selling, i.e., in sporting goods departments, sellers wear active sportswear; in career wear departments, sellers wear career wear. Employees also must be sensitive to the "audience of the day." If a special presentation will occur involving a person or company known to be conservative or traditional, pulling the navy blue suit out of the closet is probably an appropriate move.

On-going improvement of selling practices is essential. Some companies develop sales presentations that sellers memorize in order to present a complete, effective selling process every time. However, an accomplished seller knows that carbon-copy sales presentations are not appropriate for every customer. Many of the components are the same, but the strategy is adapted to the individual needs of each customer. Effective sellers constantly hone their skills and look for new ideas about how to help their customers better understand the benefits of their products and how they match their needs.

Effective sellers continually try to learn more about their products and their competitor's products. Knowledge needs to go beyond a superficial listing of the product features. Understanding alternate designs, manufacturing processes, global sources, performance, and quality provide the seller with an arsenal of information that can be used to satisfy customer needs. Retail sales associates always need time to become acquainted with new merchandise and newly arranged sales floors. Knowing what, how much, and where merchandise is located is essential for good customer service. With this type of preparation, the seller can be relaxed, poised, and confident in his or her ability to do the job.

Categories of Product Knowledge

Well prepared sellers need to be well informed on a broad variety of topics, such as general market trends in relation to the products for which they are responsible, as well as current assortments and company policies. Being a well-informed seller means making a constant effort to gather, evaluate, and improve product knowledge.

Information from the global market
What are cutting-edge technology, new designs, fashions, fads, and best sellers?
What are the characteristics of competing brands and price lines?
What is available at competing outlets?
What are their assortments and their prices?

Information related to the current selling period
What styles, sizes, and colors are available in house?
Where is the merchandise located or how can it be acquired?
How do prices and pricing policies compare with competitors?
What is the desirability and availability of coordinating or companion products?
What are the features and benefits of the products?
What are the options in relation to stockouts?
What are the firm's return and exchange policies?

Sellers gather information by regularly reading the trade press and daily newspapers. Attending trade shows where products are shown at wholesale provides a broad perspective on the totality of what is available in the market. Since many sellers do not have the opportunity to attend trade shows, buyers, designers, and merchandisers often provide training related to fashion trend assortment strategies and product performance attributes. Catalogs and detailed product information provided by vendors may contain the most detailed product descriptions available. Since it is time consuming to study all of this information, it requires extra effort on the part of sellers to make time to absorb this information.

Evaluating Potential Customers

Sellers in the wholesale area are challenged to perpetuate the loyalty of current customers and, at the same time, find new customers. Sellers in the retail area, for the most part, are challenged to sell merchandise to the customers that come in the door. But the information they need to gather is quite similar:

- Is there a want or need that can be satisfied?
- Is there an ability to pay?
- Who has the authority to buy?
- Are the needs consistent with the merchandise?

Characteristics of past customers are often used as a guide for determining potential future customers. Sellers at wholesale often look for centers of influence that can be drawn upon by networking. Sellers at retail in full- and premier-service organizations also may use networking to identify new customers.

Greeting and Approaching Customers

Effective sellers have the ability to make and maintain customer contact. Making customer contact may take the form of a phone call or e-mail for an appointment, a personal visit to an office, or greeting a customer on a retail sales floor. Maintaining customer contact may require another phone call or e-mail to deliver a sales pitch, a personal visit to present a product, or engaging in conversation with the customer. In the world of selling, usually many more customer contacts are made than sales. Maintaining the contact so product benefits can be discussed is a key to selling.

In a retail setting, it is common courtesy to contact a customer immediately upon entering the store. Some firms set a standard for making a greeting less than 30 seconds after a customer enters. Greeting customers is commonly regarded as a welcome to the store and as a shop-lifting deterrent. The friendliness and sincerity of the greeting establishes the shopping atmosphere for the customer. The greeting is particularly important if the seller is already engaged with another customer. "Hi, I'll be with you in a minute. If you are looking for holiday dresses, they are to the right in the back." The greeting should be natural and appropriate to the personality of the seller.

Making contact is as easy as greeting the customer by saying "Hello," but maintaining contact is an art form. It may be useful to observe the customer to learn as much as possible before approaching him or her. A brief observation might reveal how hurried the customer is and whether he is shopping for himself or someone else. If the customer is part of a group, the seller might be able to determine which person is the shopper, what type of goods they are looking for, and which person is the decision-maker.

There are three common techniques for approaching customers for the first time. The **merchandise approach** is used when the shopper seems to be viewing specific merchandise. The greeting usually includes a casual "Hello" and a comment about the merchandise like, "These just came in yesterday. Aren't they terrific?" The **personal, informal or social approach** is used if the customer approaches the seller or if the customer appears to be browsing. The greeting might be a positive statement such as simply "Hi," or may include a comment on the weather, business, merchandise, customer's clothing, or customer's children. For a **service approach,** avoid the standard "Can I help you?" because of the easy "No thank you, I am just looking" response, unless the customer obviously needs help. Maintaining a pleasant, professional attitude is essential.

Determining Customers' Needs and Wants

It is essential to determine the potential customer's needs and wants in order to know what merchandise to show and how to show it. It may be helpful to distinguish between needs and wants. **Needs** might be described as practical or functional desire; **wants** may be described as emotional desire. Since most consumption is by U.S. citizens above the poverty level, the majority of purchases are motivated by emotional desire although they may be justified by functional need. Strategies to determine customer needs and wants include:

- determine what type of product/service the customer is seeking.
- ask questions related to intended use.
- listen carefully to what the customer says.
- briefly summarize the customer's needs and wants.
- ask questions to narrow the selection, if necessary.

Ask questions to determine the customer's needs and wants. To question does not mean to interrogate. Questions should be non-threatening and should encourage dialogue between the seller and the customer. Phrase questions so they cannot be answered by a simple "yes" or "no." Open-ended questions confirm your interest in the customers well being and encourage the customer to talk about their needs. Open-ended questions begin with "what," "why," "how," or "tell me" and encourage the customer to elaborate when responding. The seller can quickly determine how purposive the customer is and how defined he or she is in identifying the desired product. The seller can also help the customer to define a product available in the current assortment that will suit his or her needs. Examples of open- and closed-ended questions related to customer's needs and wants include:

closed—Is this the product you are looking for?
open—What type of product are you looking for?

closed—Is this within your price range?
open—What is the price range that you would consider?

closed—Do you like this color?
open—What colors might you consider?

closed—Do you have anything in your wardrobe that will go with this?
open—What will you be wearing this with?

closed—Will you need more than a dozen?
open—What are your volume requirements?

Questioning moves the seller toward a sale. Careful listening keeps the seller on track. Listening is the key to determining customer needs and wants. Most people do not listen effectively. Distractions are many. It takes concentrated effort to keep the seller's mind tuned to what the customer is saying. Listening improves if eye contact is maintained. Sellers must also be alert to a customer's body language for signals related to product priorities.

After questioning and listening, the seller then must decide on the appropriate action. The preferred option is taking the customer to the merchandise of primary interest and providing selection assistance. Options also include pursuing additional conversation or backing off and letting the customer browse or self-select merchandise. The seller maintains contact with the customer by checking in regularly to see if assistance is needed. The appropriate strategy is determined by the method most likely to meet the needs and wants expressed by the customer.

Presenting the Merchandise/Providing Selection Assistance

Providing **merchandise selection assistance** requires showing the merchandise and discussing its benefits and features. If possible, show more than one item that would seem to satisfy the customer. This might include similar items in different colors or at different prices. Be careful not to prejudge how much the customer will spend or to assume the customer will want to buy the lowest-priced item. Point out features at different price points. Be sure to discuss why one costs more than another.

Show the merchandise that will appeal to the customer based on the customer needs analysis. Be sure that the merchandise selected meets the needs of the customer. Have the customer examine the merchandise. Explain the benefits of the merchandise and the price of the product in relation to its benefits. Discuss the features of the produce that provide those benefits.

A seller might also include compatible or coordinating items in the presentation. This provides an opportunity for comparing attributes and possibly a multiple sale. However, presenting too many choices may be confusing. Enhance decision making by helping the customer state preferences and remove items from view that the customer rejects.

Always handle the merchandise in a way that shows the merchandise is special. Treat items with pride. Involve the customer with the merchandise. Encourage him or her to examine the product, hold it, try it out, or, if appropriate, try it on. This promotes ownership for the customer. Talk about the merchandise. Tell about its features and benefits. To present merchandise effectively the seller must relate his or her knowledge of the products/services to the needs and wants of the customer.

Merchandise Features and Benefits

Customers buy merchandise for the benefits it provides, not the features related to the product. **Product features** are characteristics of the product. **Product benefits** are statements of what the product will do to or for the customer. Benefits relate directly to customer needs and wants, while product features are the sources of the benefits. See Table 11.2 for examples of product features and benefits. Features and benefits are usually described on hang tags, labels or packaging materials, or in catalog

TABLE 11.2

Applying product knowledge by distinguishing between features and benefits.

Examples of Product Features	Corresponding Product Benefits
1. The appearance, style, or design of the product	1. Good taste, beauty, fashion
2. Brand name of product or manufacturer	2. Quality, reputation, snob appeal, dependability
3. Materials from which the product is made	3. Easy care, durability, superiority
4. How product is made	4. Beauty, workmanship, durability, safety
5. What can be expected of the product in use	5. Economical, convenient, enjoyable, efficient
6. How the product is used	6. Versatility, reliability, cost effectiveness
7. How to take care of the product	7. Easy care, economical
8. History and background of the product	8. Intrigue, uniqueness
9. How the product compares with competing brands	9. Advantages, disadvantages, similarities, differences

copy. By showing merchandise to the customer, customer needs can be better defined.

Handling Objections

Sellers should anticipate **customers objections;** they may occur at any time during the sale. From a seller's perspective, objections are indications of interest by the customer, a way of learning more about customer's needs and wants, something blocking the way of closing the sale, and should not be taken personally. Objections may be caused by:

- the seller showing merchandise that is not well matched to the customer's needs and wants.
- customer not recognizing benefits of the merchandise.
- the seller showing merchandise not within the customer's price range.

Sellers can use objections to better understand the customer's viewpoint. Careful listening is as important when dealing with objections as when trying to determine a customer's needs and wants. Acknowledge the customer's objections without agreeing or disagreeing. "I see." "I understand." "I appreciate what you are saying." The seller must try to identify core issues related to the objections. Restating the objections to test the core issues can provide an opportunity to better understand the customer's perspective and to determine what else the customer needs to know. When dealing with price objections, emphasize value by reviewing benefits and how they relate to the customer's needs and wants. Compare features of lower-priced products and talk about investment.

It is important to respond to the customer's objections honestly and sincerely by relating objections to the merchandise benefits. Be attuned to non-verbal signals. It may be necessary to suggest different merchandise than was originally shown. Restating benefits and features related to core issues helps to reassure the customer that the product is suitable.

Closing the Sale

The purpose of **closing the sale** is to get the customer to agree to buy the product. It is the seller's responsibility to help the customer make a buying decision. There are definite signals or signs of interest by the customer indicating it is time to close:

- closely inspecting merchandise
- asking questions about details
- asking questions about delivery

- smiling
- nodding
- a big sigh

When the customer provides the signals, it is the seller's job to ask for the sale. A number of different closing strategies may be appropriate given the specific situation:

- Direct close—"Does this product serve your needs?" "Are you ready to make this purchase?"
- Take it for granted close—"I'll ring this up."
- Method of payment close—"Would you like this on your JCPenney charge?"
- Companion merchandise close—"We have shoes and a belt that are perfect with this suit."
- Delivery/service close—"We can deliver this tomorrow. Shall I call the tailor?"
- Summing up close—"This sleeping bag is good for 30 below zero, it is waterproof, and it is 20 percent off the regular price." "Your ad will explain your products and be seen by 1,000 people who attend the trade show."
- Last-chance close—"This is the last day of the sale." "This model is being discontinued."
- Choice close—"Would you prefer the green or the blue? Or perhaps both?" "Would you prefer a full-page of a half-page ad?"
- Gentle persuasion close—"Why don't you take it with you. It will save you the time of returning to buy it. If you decide it doesn't meet your needs, with our return policy, you can always return it."
- Come back close—used when it is obvious that customer is not going to buy on this visit; if possible, set a specific time to return.

It is important for the seller not to be afraid to ask for the sale. Not every customer will buy, but more will if they are asked for the sale.

Alternate Selling

If it is not possible to close the sale, the seller's first priority is to show interest and concern that it is not possible to meet the customer's needs. Discuss options of how the customer might be able to receive the merchandise he or she desires. Try to determine if other merchandise might meet the customer's needs or wants. Suggesting competing sources where the seller knows the desired merchandise is likely to be in stock is the sincerest form of customer service. It proves the seller has the customer's best interest at heart and might generate customer loyalty based on giving up a sale.

Enlarging the Sale

The ability to expand a sale with companion products or other merchandise can result in greater satisfaction for the customer and a substantial increase in sales overall. Customers may be also willing to buy a larger quantity of the original product. This process is sometimes called suggestion, suggestive, or add-on selling and may occur in any part of the selling process. **Suggestion selling** can save the customer time in shopping for coordinating or related items in the future and/or help the customer to select related accessories.

A seller should suggest additional merchandise to every customer. Even a customer in a great hurry may listen to suggestions for future merchandise while the sale is being processed. Effective suggestion selling should add to the customer's enjoyment of the original purchase, add to the functionality or use of the first purchase, add another product that meets the customer's needs, or plant an idea for a future purchase.

Suggestion selling should fit the person, the time, and the situation. Avoid closed-ended questions just as in the approach and greeting phase, e.g., "Would you like to look at a scarf to go with this blouse?" "No." Use positive statements about the merchandise. "Look at these scarves; they are the perfect accent for this blouse." When the customer agrees to buy the scarf, continue. "The other item to complete this look are these earrings. . ." Don't stop with one item; keep playing the percentages. Continue suggesting merchandise until customer is satisfied with the total purchase.

There are eight categories of multiple sale merchandise: 1) more of the same item; 2) compatible merchandise (see previous discussion); 3) merchandise the customer needs; 4) fashion, fad, trend merchandise; 5) best sellers; 6) new merchandise, 7) price promotional, clearance or special purchase merchandise; and 8) selected, "surprise" merchandise that the seller wants everyone to see no matter what. The seller should be creatively prepared to use the method or methods most suited to a particular customer and situation.

Follow-Up

The purpose of the follow-up is to solve any problems related to the sale and to develop and maintain good customer relations. Follow-up begins during the processing of the current sale. Collecting personal information about the customer and his or her family to develop a listing for a personal sales book might be part of the process. Ask the customer if he or she would like to be called when new or special merchandise arrives.

It is common to use the customer's name whenever possible to personalize the process. Throughout the sale, be friendly, courteous, efficient, and show genuine interest in the customer. Knowing and using correct procedures makes processing the sale comfortable for the customer. State pleasure in having the opportunity to serve the customer. Offer to add the customer to a mailing list so he or she will receive notices of special events. It might be appropriate to ask for suggestions of other prospects the seller might contact at the customer's recommendation. Thank the customer for shopping and invite a return to the store. The first contact outside the current sale might be a hand-written note thanking the customer for their patronage.

Handling Merchandise Returns

Merchandise return policies are important factors in determining a customer's choice of vendors. When retail buyers/merchandisers negotiate purchase contracts, terms related to refunds or discounts for markdowns of unsold merchandise need to be a part of the discussion. When retail customers experience bad service related to merchandise returns, they often do not complain to the retailer, they simply do not come back. They are also much more likely to tell their friends about their frustrating experience than about a satisfactory one. Each happy customer will tell five people about their experience; each unhappy customer will tell nine. More than 90 percent of unhappy customers won't be back (Anton, 1996). JCPenney says it costs six times as much to get a new customer as it does to keep an existing customer. It is common for more than two-thirds of a company's business to come from existing customers.

It is the seller's job to handle merchandise returns according to the company policy. Remember that great majority of customers are honest, fair, and reasonable and their returns of merchandise are legitimate and justifiable. It is not the seller's job to judge the customer, but to process the return. A smile and a good attitude are essential. Use the process to chat with the customer about the merchandise, their needs, and to do suggestion selling.

Dealing with Difficult/Unhappy Customers

Regardless of the quality of the selling process, sometimes customers are difficult or unreasonable and sometimes they are justifiably unhappy. Keeping in mind that most customers are satisfied helps put difficult customers in the proper perspective. The unhappy customer tends to direct his or her anger and frustration at the person who is available, in even though this person is unlikely to be the cause of the problem. Therefore the representative of the seller must not take the customer's dissatisfaction personally. It is essential for the individual dealing with the complaint to remain calm and objective. The following sequence will facilitate processing a complaint:

- Listen, let the customer unload
- Empathize, show concern, let the customer know you care
- Ask open-ended questions
- Restate the facts
- Avoid offering excuses or placing blame on someone else
- Offer options
- Agree on a solution
- Take action
- Follow up

In this simple list form, it looks like dealing with a frustrated customer should be very straightforward. It seldom is, but if the person handling the complaint is well informed about company procedures and can remain calm, they stand a good chance of successfully resolving the situation.

Learning Activity 11.2

Practicing effective selling

Form the class into groups. Identify a retailer each group will represent. Use coats or books or other things in the room as merchandise to mock up a display. Each person in each group will play one of three roles: customer, seller, and critic. Customers will exit then return to be greeted by the seller. The customer and seller will engage in conversation related to the selling process. The critic will stand by, observe, and take notes on the interaction. When the selling process is completed, the three people will sit down and discuss the interaction. The critic will report observations and the group will discuss how to improve the process. Then the three people will rotate roles and repeat the process.

Improving the Customer/Vendor Relationship

Most manufacturers and retailers are striving to improve customer service. Some are continually striving to improve customer service. Even Nordstrom, which is recognized as one of the most outstanding customer service companies in the world, has improving customer service as its primary goal (Spector & McCarthy, 1995). For some firms, improving customer service means changing corporate structures, organizational priorities, and management strategies. For many firms, it means a major cultural change. Corporate culture change often means changing the way people think and act—no small task. "The single most visible factor that distinguishes major cultural changes that succeed from those that fail is competent leadership at the top" (Kotter & Heskett, 1992, p. 84).

There are distinct differences between leadership and management. **Management** embodies budgeting, organizing, and controlling. **Leadership** embodies empowerment: directing, motivating, and inspiring (Adair-Heeley, 1991; Kotter & Heskett, 1992). How an organization's leaders believe things should be done drives a firm's culture (Schneider, 1994). Table 11.3 compares aspects of management and leadership. Management results in predictable outcomes; leadership results in adaptability to current conditions and progress to the future.

TABLE 11.3

The difference between management and leadership.

Management	Leadership
Planning and Budgeting—establishing detailed steps and timetables for achieving needed results then allocating the resources necessary to make that happen.	*Establishing Direction*—developing a vision for the future, often the distant future, and strategies for producing the changes needed to achieve that vision.
Organizing and Staffing—establishing some structure for accomplishing plan requirements, staffing that structure, delegating responsibility and authority for carrying out the plan, providing policies and procedures to help guide people, and creating methods or systems to monitor implementation.	*Aligning People*—communicating the direction by words and deeds to all those whose cooperation may be needed; influencing the creation of teams and a coalition that understand the vision and strategies and accept their validity.
Controlling and Problem Solving—monitoring results vs. planning in some detail, identifying deviations, and then planning and organizing to solve these problems.	*Motivating and Inspiring*—energizing people to overcome major political, bureaucratic, and resource barriers to change by satisfying very basic, but often unfulfilled, human needs.
Outcome—Produces a degree of predictability and order, and has the potential of consistently producing key results expected by various stakeholders (e.g., for the customer, always being on time; for stockholders, being on budget).	*Outcome*—Produces change, often to a dramatic degree, and has the potential of producing extremely useful change (e.g., new products that customers want, new approaches to labor relations that help make a firm more competitive).

Source: Kotter and Heskett, page 99.

Implementation of Quick Response (QR) business systems embodies improvements in customer service because QR permeates the customer/ vendor relationship. Implementation of QR, in most cases, requires a change in corporate culture. Firms operating in a leadership environment are more adaptable to change than those operating in a management environment. (See Table 11.4.) **Adaptive corporate cultures** are able to be **agile,** i.e., "capable of operating profitably in a competitive environment of continually, and unpredictably, changing customer opportunities" (Goldman, Nagel, and Preiss, 1995, p.3). Agile companies must go beyond being customer-centered to being centered on the customer-perceived value of products (Goldman, Nagel and Preiss, 1995).

The behaviors itemized by Kotter and Heskett (1992) in Table 11.3 and 11.4 epitomize the leadership/management behaviors that support the Behavioral Theory of the Apparel firm with Quick Response business systems (BTAF/QR) discussed in Chapters 1 and 2. Merchandising as a constituency is dependent on teamwork and successful interactions within and among constituencies to support planning, development, and presentation of product lines. The assumption of a **marketing concept** means the ability of a firm to meet its goals is partially dependent on satisfying the needs and wants of external coalitions that are exchange partners, particularly their customers (Houston, 1986). The marketing concept, as a philos-

TABLE 11.4

Adaptive vs. unadaptive corporate cultures.

	Adaptive Corporate Culture	Unadaptive Corporate Culture
Core Values	Most managers care deeply about customers, stockholders, and employees. They also strongly value people and processes that can create useful change (e.g., leadership up and down the management hierarchy).	Most managers care mainly about themselves, their immediate work group, or some product (or technoogy) associated with that work group. They value the orderly and risk-reducing management process much more than leadership initiatives.
Common Behavior	Managers pay close attention to all their constituencies, especially customers, and initiate change when needed to serve their legitimate interests, even if that entails taking some risks.	Managers tend to behave in a somewhat insular, political, and bureaucratic manner. As a result, they do not change their strategies quickly to adjust to or take advantage of changes in their business environments.

Source: Kotter & Heskett, 1992, p. 143.

ophy of the firm, is implicit to the firm with leadership structures and adaptive cultures. The marketing concept reflects a mode of operation for the firm that directs the agendas and activities of individual constituencies. Seeing the marketing concept as a standard mode of operation is essential for firms that wish to improve customer/vendor relationships. Merchandisers cannot plan, develop and present product lines without the support of all of a firm's constituencies.

CASE 11.2

Evolution of Off-Pricers:
A Changing Retail Environment Demands Survival Tactics

From Ratliff, D. (1996, March). *Discount Merchandiser,* pp. 22, 23, 30.

In a retail world fostering a Darwinian survival of the fittest, off-price retailers are evolving. Battling for market share in an industry where only strong, adaptable companies will survive, unchanging off-pricers are clearly in danger of becoming extinct.

Off-price retail chains have existed for at least 20 years. These companies made their reputations by offering well-known department store brands at 20 to 60 percent less through a variety of different buying [merchandising] techniques. Tactics like scooping up irregular goods, buying out of season, and the avoidance of typical department store subsidies like co-op [advertising] and markdown money, allowed off-pricers to merit their moniker. Together, companies such as T.J. Maxx, Marshalls, Burlington Coat Factory, Stein Mart, Ross Stores, and Filene's Basement sold an estimated $15 billion worth of apparel in 1995.

"When they entered the market they really came on strong," says Howard Eilenberg, retail analyst for Johnson Redbook Service. "Off-pricers are selling branded goods at prices that were lower than the department stores. There were clear reasons for their existence and growth."

Much of the future of the off-price retail segment will be defined by the yet-to-be determined strategy of the T.J. Maxx/Marshalls merger. The combined stores sales of $6.5 billion is more than four times the size of Burlington Coat Factory, with approximately $1.6 billion in sales. T.J. Maxx rang up profit increases for 18 consecutive years until last year. Some industry analysts say the successful run of off-pricers, as a whole, may be winding down.

The apparent waning of the heyday of off-pricers is due to several factors. The retail environment from which the format arose has changed dramatically. In recent years, department stores have consolidated, gaining more buying clout and paring-down operating costs.

"The survivors of the department-store shakeout are able to meet prices," Eilenberg says. "An off-pricer can no longer say the merchandise is 25 percent off department store prices. With the price difference gone, customers will go to department stores. "They know the assortments are fresh and full. Customers know that off-pricers have only a couple of sizes and colors and they're lacking in ambiance."

Off-pricers' positioning is also hurt by an overabundance of apparel manufacturing, which leads to more promotions at department stores and specialty shops. Manufacturers looking to make up for weak unit sales compensate by offering markdown money to department stores for promotions, observers say.

At the same time, discounters such as Kmart and Wal-Mart are upgrading their apparel merchandise mix. Concurrently, spending on hardgoods such as computers and home furnishings is increasing while unit apparel sales stagnate.

"The tug of war for that middle-income apparel consumer is significant," says Thomas Tashjian of Montgomery Securities. "The consumer is being pulled in all sorts of directions. The off-pricer that only use price as its advantage has had its advantage subdued because of all the competition in the marketplace."

continued

Not all observers are ringing the death knell for off-price retailers, however. Bryant points to TJX's purchase as a significant improvement for the industry as a whole. The company will close between 100 to 150 of the most unprofitable Marshalls stores, alleviating some of the over capacity of the industry.

He also gives TJX an advantage over its competition. "TJX can now increase buying power and leverage fixed expenses as it nearly doubles sales volume in two years while simultaneously eliminating its largest competitor," Bryant says. This will be particularly helpful during the buying process. "They not only doubled their buying power, but they also eliminated their number one buying competitor. If you need to move large amounts of merchandise, this company is now far and away the choice. The economies of scale should be significant with the merchandise supply line, central operations, and advertising.

Bryant theorizes that the apparel industry is likely to lower sales expectations and inventory levels as it adjusts to the realities of apparel deflation. "The apparel industry is waking up to the fact that there is an oversupply problem, and that a lot of the selling that they're engaged in is profitless selling," he says. "Since everyone recognizes it's a problem, people are implementing more conservative sales budgets leading to fewer markdowns leading to greater profitability."

Bryant adds that there will be a reduction in the level of department store sales promotions as manufacturers reduce the unsustainably high levels of markdown money they are currently doling out. "This should help restore the pricing differential traditionally enjoyed by off-pricers," he says.

Learning Activity 11.3

Customer/Vendor relationships: Evolution of off-pricers

1. Based on Case 11.2, what aspects of customer/vendor relationships at the wholesale level are shaping the retail sector?

2. What aspects of customer/vendor relationships at the retail level are shaping the retail sector?

3. What aspects of customer/vendor relationships identified in items #1 and #2 are likely to be under the control of merchandisers?

4. Would the merchandisers in the off-price industry appear to prefer executive leaders or managers? Why?

5. Do the off-price firms need to be operating with adaptive or non-adaptive corporate cultures? Why?

Summary

Merchandisers play a primary role in customer/vendor relationships throughout the textiles and apparel trade matrix. Merchandisers are frequently responsible for buying and/or sourcing materials for apparel manufacturers, training sales representatives on how to present product lines, buying and/or sourcing finished goods for retailers, and training retail sellers in product knowledge and presentation strategies. Merchandisers negotiate merchandise contracts and follow-up based on satisfactory or unsatisfactory results. Merchandisers are both sold to and sell.

Without appropriate customer service, the planning, development, and presentation of product lines can be a frustrating exercise. In the manufacturing sector, sales representatives are commonly part of the marketing constituency. In the retail sector, sales associates are commonly part of the operations constituency. Cooperative interaction, flexibility, and teamwork are essential for successfully executing the merchandising strategy.

Firms are increasingly recognizing opportunities for customizing product lines and services to customers needs. Today's technology makes it possible to operate very large firms in ways that will serve hundreds, thousands, maybe even millions of unique markets. The evolution of QR business systems into time-based competition, partnerships, and agility has just begun.

Key Concepts

adaptive corporate culture
agile
alternate selling
approaching a customer
Behavioral Theory of the Apparel Firm (BTAF)
closed-ended question
closing the sale
customer needs
customer service
customer wants

customer's objections
follow-up
greeting a customer
leadership
limited service
marketing concept
management
merchandise approach
merchandise selection assistance
open-ended question

personal/informal/social approach
personal selling service
premier service
product benefits
product features
prospecting
self service
service approach
suggestion selling

Integrated Learning Activity 11.4

Improving customer service with secret shoppers

1. Purposes of the project:
   - Gain knowledge of the selling process as it impacts on personal service.
   - Experience the selling process from the customer's viewpoint by secretly shopping at local retail establishments.
   - Evaluate the selling concepts in the retail environment through retailer and educational interaction.
   - Experience retail management functions by making suggestions for improving the effectiveness of personal service.

2. Develop a personal selling service evaluation instrument to be used by secret shoppers. Topics to be addressed include:

- Store appearance (stock, display, cleanliness).
- Staff (grooming, friendliness, knowledge).
- Selling process (approach and greeting, identification of customer wants and needs, merchandise demonstration and handling, objection handling, suggestion selling, closing the sale, and follow-up).
- Overall service (efficiency, interest, product knowledge, availability, and responsiveness)
- Overall impression of the store.
- Activity level at the time of shopping.

3. Each student will secretly shop three different stores acting as a customer. Immediately following the shopping experience, the student will record his or her observations on the secret shopper instrument before shopping another store.

4. Discuss each student's secret shopping experience in class. Identify similarities and differences and things that are most consistently problems.

5. Identify management actions that might improve customer service.

Recommended Resources

Anton, J. (1996). *Customer relationship management.* Upper Saddle River, NJ: Prentice Hall.

Gaskill, L. R., & Kunz, G. I. (1991, Summer). Commitment to customer service: An interactive learning strategy. *Journal of Home Economics 83*:2, 29–32.

Goldman, S. L., Nagel, R. N., & Preiss, K. (1995). *Agile competitors and virtual organizations: Strategies for enriching the customer.* New York: Van Nostrand Reinhold.

Spector, R., & McCarthy. (1995). *The Nordstrom way.* New York: Wiley.

Customer Service training manuals for major retailers.

References

Adair-Heeley, C. B. (1991). *The human side of just-in-time.* New York: American Management Association.

Anton, J. (1996). *Customer relationship management.* Upper Saddle River, NJ: Prentice Hall.

Berman, B. B., & Evans, J. R. (1995). *Retail management.* Englewood Cliffs, NJ: Prentice Hall.

Cathcart, J. (1988). Winning customer service. *Management Solutions*, p. 33.

Davidow, W. H., & Uttal, B. (1989). Coming: The customer service decade. *Across the Board 26*, 33–37

Farnsworth, S. (1990). Peter Glenn: Consumer with bad service. *Daily News Record 20*:245, 32.

Gaskill, L. R., & Kunz, G. I. (1991, Summer). Commitment to customer service: An interactive learning strategy. *Journal of Home Economics 83*:2, 29–32.

Goldfarb, M. (1989). Developing a customer focus. *Business Quarterly*, p. 54.

Goldman, S. L., Nagel, R. N., & Preiss, K. (1995). *Agile competitors and virtual organizations: Strategies for enriching the customer.* New York: Van Nostrand Reinhold.

Ghosh, A. (1990). *Retail Management*. Chicago: Dryden Press.

Kotter, J. P., & Heskett, J. L. (1992). *Corporate culture and performance*. New York: The Free Press.

Lele, M. M. (1987). *The Customer is key*. New York: Wiley.

Lewison, D. M. (1994). *Retailing* (5th edition). New York: Macmillan.

Schneider, W. E. (1994). *The reengineering alternative*. New York: Irwin.

Spector, R., & McCarthy. (1995). *The Nordstrom way*. New York: Wiley.

Zemke, R. (1986). Contract! Training employees to meet the public. *Training 23*:8, 41–45.

Career Opportunities

Chapter 12 Merchandising-Related Career Development

Merchandising-Related Career Development

Learning Objectives
- Explore career development theory.
- Examine job titles, career development levels, and areas of specialization via a Taxonomy of Merchandising Careers.
- Discuss methods of career advancement.
- Examine means for selecting an employer.

Careers have been an important subject of inquiry from sociological, psychological, and organizational perspectives since the 1920s, with a concentration of publications in the 1970s. Several researchers have summarized and evaluated research related to careers including Glaser, Ed. (1968), *Organizational Careers: A Sourcebook for Theory*; Minor (1992), *Career development: Theories and Models*; Hall (1976), *Careers in Organizations*; Stevens-Long (1979), *Adult Life: Developmental Processes*; and Van Maanen, Ed. (1977), *Organizational Careers: Some New Perspectives*. More academic attention has been paid to apparel merchandising careers related to the retail sector than the manufacturing sector, although the strong trends toward vertical integration have blended the two in many firms over the last 10 years.

The Concept of Career Development

For purposes of this discussion, **career** is defined as the individually perceived sequence of attitudes and behaviors associated with work-related experiences and activities over the span of the person's life (Hall, 1976). Research regarding careers has had two dominant themes: career choice and career development. **Career choice** is the process of selecting an area of specialization as a focus of one's work. Holland's *Making Vocational Choices: A Theory of Careers* (1973) is a prime example of the culmination of vocational research focusing on career choice. Holland developed a classification for personality interest styles that includes realistic, investigative, artistic, social, enterprising, and conventional. He then identified occupations that correspond to the interest styles and developed a "self-directed search" to determine appropriate occupations according to one's personality. Career-choice research tends to focus attention on the young adult. This approach seems to assume that career choice is made only once during early adulthood—not a very realistic expectation in today's job market.

Futurists see today's college students making at least three major specialization changes during their total working career. The rapid increase in the use of information technology is expected to make some jobs and career paths completely disappear, while new, currently unknown career opportunities will emerge. Thus, in today's job market, making a career choice during young adulthood is merely a place to begin; that choice will not necessarily fulfill one's entire worklife.

Career development is the lifelong process of examining the possibilities for work-related experiences and activities and deciding, with awareness, what one wishes to do with one's life (*"Born Free:" A world of options,* 1978). It is part of the development of the adult as an evolving, growing human being. Career-development research has identified stages of development and associated those stages with the age range at which each occurs. The concepts for the stages, age classification and terminology differ with each researcher. For example, Erikson's (1959) stages of development are childhood (0–15), identity (15–25), intimacy (25–35), generativity (35–65), and ego integrity (65+). Super (1957) identified stages of development that are more career specific: growth (0–15), exploration (15–25), establishment (25–45), maintenance (45–65), and decline (65+). More recently, Super and Ginzberg have contributed the idea that career development and even career choices, are the result of a process rather than a point-in-time event (Minor, 1992).

"A significant limitation of all developmental career theories, as well as almost all other career theories, is that the supporting research has been done [almost] exclusively on men" (Minor, 1992, p. 13). Some of the findings have been generalized to women, however, but sometimes inappropriately. In fact, some research related to women's careers suggests that career development for women is considerably different than for men.

Three inter-related **realms** tend to dominate adult life in the western world: marriage, family, and employment. Men are often stereotypically regarded as being more "serious" about their employment, meaning they are more likely to give their career priority over their other life roles. Karelius (1982) found that men tend to be **"life-structure modifiers,"** while women regard changes in their lives as "rebirth of individual potential." For example, a change in a man's career, such as a geographic job transfer, has traditionally been accompanied by the movement of his family to the new location. This provides modification of his job environment, but continuity in his family life. His wife, if employed, would probably resign from her job and find another in the new location. This frequently involves starting over at entry level and retraining for new responsibilities. Karelius found this **"rebirth of potential"** to be a common occurrence in the lives of females, thus slowing career development.

Because traditional western family-structure places males in the role of the bread-winners and females as homemakers, men have not often had to choose among spouse, parent, and career. Many women, however, do have to make that choice. Women continue to experience more role conflict than men. A recent survey revealed that men in top management tend to have wives who are full-time homemakers; women in top management tend to be single. Numerous other studies have demonstrated that women in two income households are still responsible for the vast majority of home and childcare. Consequently, in order to give adequate attention to their career, many women giveup or postpone marriage and/or childbearing until their careers are well established.

Learning Activity 12.1

Career development perspectives of males and females

1. What might it mean to say that men are "life-structure modifiers"? Think of some examples from your experience of how men's life structures have been modified in the process of career development?

2. What might it mean to say that women regard career changes as "rebirth of individual potential"? Think of some examples.

3. The research on which the concepts of "life-structure modifiers" and "rebirth of individual potential" were based was completed in 1982. Are these concepts still appropriately applied to career development of men and women? What changes have occurred that might moderate the application of these concepts?

Career Development in Relation to the Firm

Dalton, Thompson, and Price (1977), recognizing the importance of organizational constraints, combined career stage/life cycle theory with **organizational theory.** In their model, career growth is a dynamic process that is the result of the interaction of three primary forces: the job(s) assigned the individual in the organization; the interaction of the individual with others inside and outside the organization; and the personal development of the individual in this setting(s). This approach to career development recognizes the importance of the environment in which one works and its relationship to career growth and success. A research study involving 2,500 engineers found a "negative correlation after age 35 between age and performance rating" (p. 20). The researchers found poor performance was often blamed on obsolescence, and so recommended continuing education or additional coursework. However, data analysis revealed that high performers were no more likely to have taken continuing education courses than low performers (Dalton, Thompson, and Price, 1977).

Thus, Dalton, et al., embarked on another study to try to identify how high performers differ from low performers. This time they interviewed 550 professionally trained employees, including 155 scientists, 268 engineers, 52 accountants, and 75 university professors. When they looked at the time employed relative to performance rating, they found that high performers who were early in their careers were performing different functions than high performers who were in the middle of their careers. Both these groups had different responsibilities from high performers whose careers were near completion.

The Dalton, et al., model identifies four distinct **stages of career development** of professionally trained persons based on the dynamic interaction of three primary forces: primary relationship with fellow workers, central activities of a job, and psychological orientation to the firm. (See Table 12.1.) The four stages might be best identified by the primary relationships to fellow workers (apprentice, colleague, mentor, and sponsor) with corresponding developments of central activities and psychological orientation. Dalton, et al., found that, "it was the individuals who were moving successfully through these stages who had high performance ratings. Conversely, individuals who remained in the early stages were likely to be low-rated" (p. 22). Their research also pointed out there may be some faulty assumptions on the part of firms and educators about the relationship between career growth and education; continuing education courses are not a "quick fix" to make an individual more productive. An individual's productivity is much more complex than that.

Apparel manufacturing and retailing firms provide environments for career development for more than two million employees in the United States. Apparel-related businesses have unique characteristics because of the intense focus on product change (Kunz, 1987). It is in the firm's environment that each employee takes advantage of opportunities, experiences

TABLE 12.1

Stages of successful career development.*

Career Stage	Performance Functions		
	Primary Relationship with Fellow Workers	**Central Activities of a Job**	**Psychological Orientation to the Firm**
Stage 1 entry level	apprentice	helping, learning, and following directions	dependence
Stage 2 middle management	colleague	being an independent contributor	independence
Stage 3 senior management	mentor	training	assuming responsibility for others
Stage 4 executive leadership	sponsor	shaping the direction of the organization	exercising power

*Based on Dalton, Thompson, and Price (1977).

frustrations, and makes career decisions. Examining the career development available to apparel firm managers and executives helps one understand career opportunities and operation of apparel businesses.

Learning Activity 12.2

Career growth and success

1. Examine Table 12.1. Paraphrase the words in each cell of the table. Do your interpretations of each concept make sense together?

2. Look the words "apprentice," "colleague," "mentor," and "sponsor" in several dictionaries. Do these words mean what you thought they did? What dictionary definitions are appropriate to this model?

3. As a college graduate, would you expect to enter a merchandising career in Stage 1 of the Dalton, et al., model? How long do you think it would take to move on the Stage 2?

4. How might you use the Dalton model to establish goals for a merchandising internship?

Merchandising-Related Careers

Merchandising—especially retail merchandising—has long been the career focus of textiles and clothing academic programs. The first college-level merchandising program was offered by the Home Economics program at the University of Washington in 1917. The program included a combination of nutrition, home management, textile and non-textile merchandising, salesmanship, and an internship. Merchandising programs were designed to provide opportunities for women to move into business careers (Paoletti, 1985). "Collegiate education in retailing began in 1919 with the founding of The Training School for Teachers of Retail Selling (now the Institute of Retail Management) at New York University. Other Universities soon followed suit" (Hollander, 1978, p. 3).

In the retail sector, as with most businesses, women are still clustered in lower-level sales and clerical positions, while upper management remains well over 70 percent male. Annual managerial turnover in retailing has been estimated at between 24 percent and 54 percent. This means that up to half of total management level employees leave every year, denoting a rapidly changing work environment that provides much opportunity for young people. Retailers regularly recruit on college campuses and often have well established executive training programs for merchandising positions.

The recruiting process for merchandising positions in the manufacturing sector is much less structured. Manufacturers hire fewer new college graduates and thus are less likely to recruit on college campuses. They are more likely to advertise positions in the trade press or network to hire people with merchandising experience from retail executive training programs. New merchandising graduates *can* get positions with manufacturers, but the path requires more initiative on the part of the student.

In many people's minds, merchandising as a process and as a career is still associated only with retailing. Consequently, merchandising career-related research has focused primarily on the retail sector, in particular on the job of buyer. Only in the last 20 years have many textiles and clothing programs expanded their scope to include manufacturing and distribution in the discussion of merchandising-related career opportunities. This opens up career development opportunities throughout the business sector and throughout the world.

Nevertheless, the retail sector remains a primary on-the-job training ground for merchandising-related positions. Retail based part-time jobs, summer work, field experiences, and internships are valued by both manufacturers and retailer recruiters because potential executive/managerial trainees have been exposed to the nature of the merchandising process, the intensity of product change, the challenges associated with working with a variety of opinionated people, and the difficulty of satisfying customers. Research has shown that retail executive and managerial recruits who have merchandising coursework and work experience are more likely to be retained and promoted buy their initial employer. Primary factors contributing to retention are 1) realistic expectations of the graduate related to the job; and 2) improved ability of the graduate to select an employer that can offer the opportunities desired.

Taxonomy of Merchandising Careers

The Taxonomy of Merchandising Careers represents the system of career development in merchandising related to the retail sector. It was developed as part of a larger project entitled Career Development of College Graduates Employed in Retailing (Kunz, 1986), as well as a follow-up study conducted by Kunz in 1990 (See Table 12.2). The Taxonomy identifies (1) areas of specialization of apparel-related retail firms as associated with career development; (2) levels of career development within these areas of specialization; (3) job titles within levels; and (4) the relationships in career opportunities among areas of specialization. Job titles in the merchandising area of specialization have been updated to include retail product development and Quick Response based on Gaskill (1992), Hare (1993), Parr (1993) and Wickett (1995). Interestingly, many of the job titles related to merchandising are the same in both the manufacturing and retail sectors. The actual job description associated with the title varies firm by firm in both sectors.

The Taxonomy emerged as a result of the process of constantly comparing data reflecting the diverse experiences of the informants. Since about two-thirds of the informants for this research spent most of their careers in stores or merchandising divisions, the depth of comparison in these parts of the Taxonomy is greater than that of the other areas of specialization. In the Kunz study, in-depth interviews with 42 retail executives allowed them to describe their career development experiences in their own language, thus revealing the "insider" perspective of career development. Table 12.3 provides profiles of the retail executive participants. Notice the range of education levels, diversity of majors, and salary ranges in relation to years in retailing. Retailers have traditionally recruited candidates with a variety of backgrounds into their executive training programs.

Relationship of the Taxonomy to BTAF

The Taxonomy can be regarded as a description of retail merchandising career development within the context of Behavioral Theory of the Apparel Firm (Kunz, 1995). The Taxonomy of Merchandising Careers was derived using qualitative, inductive research methods and insider perspectives similar to those used for development of BTAF. The areas of specialization in

TABLE 12.2

Taxonomy of Merchandising Careers.

Career Code	MERCHANDISING SPECIALIZATION	Career Code	STORES SPECIALIZATION
10	merchandise clerical; merchandise detail; merchandise technician; advertising coordinator	20	sales associates; display, stock person; commission sales
11	intern; buying trainee, merchandising trainee; allocator	21	intern; manager in training; assistant sales, department, counter manager; head of stock
12	assistant buyer; supervisor of stores, assistant designer	22	department, receiving, customer service, sales manager; personnel coordinator; small store assistant manager
13	associate buyer; planner-distributor; branch store coordinator; product development coordinator, technical designer	23	branch personnel, group sales, area manager or leader; customer service supervisor
14	buyer, product manager, product development manager; designer; brand development manager; purchasing manager, quick response liaison	24	merchandise, display, office, assistant, visual merchandising coordinator; small store manager
15	senior buyer; planning-distribution manager; merchandise counselor	25	personnel, group, operation, assistant, branch manager
16	divisional merchandise manager; merchandise administrator	26	store manager, store general manager, senior store manager
17	senior merchandise manager; product development manager	27	district, cluster store, creative display manager; senior district manager
18	vice-president of merchandising; general merchandise manager; vice president of product development; vice president of design	28	vice-president; regional administrator or manager; visual merchandising manager, branch store director
19	senior vice-president; design director; fashion director; quick response director, executive vice-president	29	senior vice-president, director of stores

Career Code	PERSONNEL SPECIALIZATION	Career Code	ADVERTISING AND SALES PROMOTION SPECIALIZATION
30	training instructor; employment clerical; employment coordinator; college relations representative	40	advertising copy writer; color coordinator
31	regional representative	41	account executive
32	college relations, assistant, training director or manager; personnel administrator	42	advertising assistant
33	employment representative; training coordinator; associate manager staff training	43	special events coordinator
34	executive training manager; senior recruiter	44	fashion, advertising, sales, promotions, special events director

TABLE 12.2 (continued)

Taxonomy of Merchandising Careers.

35	corporate training director or counselor; personnel, training, employee standards manager	45	
36	divisional manager executive placement; executive development administrator	46	
37	general manager of personnel	47	
38	vice-president of personnel	48	vice-president of sales promotion; vice-president of trend merchandising; special events director
39	senior vice-president; director of personnel or human resources	49	senior vice-president; director of sales promotion

Career Code	MANAGEMENT INFORMATION SYSTEMS SPECIALIZATION	Career Code	OPERATIONS and FINANCE SPECIALIZATION
50	clerical	60	clerk; credit counselor
51	sales leader	61	control trainee
52	supervisor; assistant manager	62	auditor; credit, department manager or supervisor
53		63	accounts payable manager; systems, shortage, financial analyst
54	consumer affairs; telemail manager	64	inventory control manager; shortage auditor
55	MIS system manager	65	shortage, charge, controller or coordinator
56	administrator	66	divisional cash, shortage control manager or administrator or controller
57		67	assistant corporate controller, quick response administrator
58	vice-president	68	vice-president of control administration
59	senior vice-president	69	senior vice president of operations

Career Code	SENIOR EXECUTIVES	Career Code	JOBS OUTSIDE RETAILING
100	president	200	not in work force
101	chief operating officer	201	student
102	chief executive officer; chairman	202	homemaker
103	co-owner	203	secretary, receptionist, clerical
104	owner	204	sales, showroom representative; social worker
105	owner-manager	205	merchandiser
106	owner, vice-president	206	marketing manager
107	owner, president	207	self employed
108	owner, chairman	208	other
109		209	other

TABLE 12.3

Profiles of Informants for Taxonomy of Merchandising Careers.*

Informant Number	Job Title	Store Type
4	Owner & Vice-President	Specialty
5	Owner & President	Specialty
7	Store Manager	Specialty
11	Senior District Manager	Specialty
12	Co-owner, President & Manager	Specialty
14	Buyer	Department
15	Assistant Store Manager	Specialty
17	President, Chief Operating Officer	Department
18	Divisional Merchandise Manager	Department
19	Buyer	Department
22	Customer Service Manager	Discount
24	Operations Manager	Discount
25	Store Manager	Discount
37	Owner, Manager	Specialty
40	Planning, Distribution Manager	Department
41	Buyer	Specialty
42	Vice-President & Retail Consultant	Department
44	Training & Employment Standards Manager	Department
45	Vice-President, Merchandise Information	Department
46	Vice-President & Store Manager	Department
47	Senior Buyer	Department
48	Divisional Merchandise Manager	Department
58	General Store Manager	Department
74	Owner & President	Specialty
90	President & Chief Executive Officer	Department
103	Assistant Buyer	Discount
104	Group Manager	Department
105	Divisional Merchandise Manager	Department
109	Vice-President & Control Administration	Department
130	Divisional Merchandise Manager	Department
132	Senior Buyer	Department
133	Merchandise Administrator	Department
134	Telemail & Consumer Affairs Manager	Department
135	Buyer	Discount
136	Group Department Manager	Specialty
144	Employment Representative	Discount
150	Corporate Training Director	Department
157	Divisional Merchandise Manager	Department
158	Assistant Buyer	Discount
159	College Relations Manager	Department
160	College Relations Representative	Department
161	Acting Store Manager	Department

*Kunz (1986 and 1990).

Years in Retailing	Age	Sex	Income Range (000)	College Degree	Major
21	44	m	75–100	BS	Agriculture
24	43	m	45–50	AA	Business
16	44	f	15–20	—	—
16	34	f	40–50	AA	Liberal Arts
13	32	f	15–20	—	Merchandising
12	30	f	25–30	BS	Design
11	31	f	10–15	—	—
30	52	m	75–100	BA	Business
24	50	f	50–75	—	—
5	24	f	20–25	BS	Merchandising
11	46	f	20–25	—	—
13	35	m	30–40	BA	Biology
13	30	m	30–40	AA	Retailing
8	31	m	20–25	BS	Business
14	36	f	NA	BS, MA	German
15	38	f	25–30	BA	Merchandising
12	34	m	75–100	BA	Psychology
8	32	m	30–40	BA, MBA	Psychology
9	34	f	75–100	MS+	Political Science
14	36	f	50–75	BS	Merchandising
11	33	m	30–40	BA	Sociology
11	33	m	40–50	BS	Business
25	NA	m	NA	—	—
9	42	f	30–40	BES+	Business
12	36	m	100+	BS, MBA	Marketing
8	28	f	40–50	BS	Merchandising
19	37	f	40–50	—	—
10	33	f	50–75	BBA	Business
18	40	m	50–75	BS, MBA	Business/Accounting
17	39	m	75–100	BS, MBA	Economics
16	39	f	25–30	BS	Merchandising
9	31	f	40–50	BS	Merchandising
11	33	f	20–25	BS	Merchandising
11	33	f	50–75	BS	Merchandising
5	28	f	20–25	BS	Merchandising
4	25	f	30–40	BBA	Business
6	35	f	25–30	BA+	Sociology
21	43	f	40–50	BS	Home Economics
6	28	f	40–50	BS	Merchandising
3	24	m	20–25	BS	Accounting
2	27	f	15–20	BBA	Business
12	36	f	15–20	—	

the model of the behavioral theory are intended to represent a generic apparel firm, whereas the Taxonomy of Merchandising Careers as it now stands is based only on the retail sector. Unfortunately, comparable career development research has not been conducted within the manufacturing sector.

Using the Taxonomy

Kunz developed a coding system to simplify the use of the Taxonomy to describe career development. A two-digit **career code** represents both the area of specialization and the career level within that specialization. The first digit in the career code represents the **area of specialization:** merchandising = 1; stores = 2; personnel = 3; advertising and sales promotion = 4; management information systems = 5; and operations/finance = 6.

The areas of specialization used in the Taxonomy are not necessarily consistent with the organization of any particular retail firm, but rather represent generic classifications according to specialization that relate to career development in retail organizations.

The second digit in the career code, a number from 0 to 9, represents a **career level** with the possible job titles at that level. For example, career code "25" means the responsibility falls within the stores specialization—2—and includes the jobs of personnel, group, operation or assistant manager, and small store manager—5. According to the Taxonomy, all of these jobs may be held by people that are on relatively the same career level in the specialization. Note that a "25" is similar to someone with a career code "15" in the merchandising division or "35" in the personnel division. Therefore, it is possible to describe moves from one job to another or one specialization to another in terms of major lateral or vertical changes in career status. In order to complete the career-development picture, job titles of top executive management, such as president or chief executive officer, are identified by a 100 number, while jobs outside of retailing have a 200 number.

As with BTAF, the areas of specialization identified in the Taxonomy are generic—they are not necessarily the functions identified in organizational charts of a particular retail firm. Whether a retail organization actually had organizational divisions similar to the areas of specialization identified in this Taxonomy was dependent on the size and type of retailer and the type of terminology the retailer used. Smaller stores did not necessarily have the formal areas of specializations, but still performed the functions identified by these areas in the Taxonomy. For example, in a small organization, a retail buyer (15) may perform the functions of department manager (23) and fashion director (19). Responsibilities that were a part of a particular job assignment were not necessarily all at the same career level but, according to informants, the primary responsibilities were what determined the career status in the organization.

None of the retail organizations included in the sample had all the career levels indicated by the Taxonomy. For example, the career ladder in the merchandising specialization in one department store included trainee (11), associate buyer (13), senior buyer (15), merchandise counselor (16), and general merchandise manager (17). The Taxonomy represents the diversity of career levels and job titles in retail organizations and is intended to include the areas of specialization within which any particular retailer's career path could be represented.

The Taxonomy is a useful tool for tracing career paths of merchandising managers and executives either for research purposes or for analyzing career development opportunities within or among retail organizations. A **career path** is the sequence of jobs held by an individual. It is possible to see the major area of responsibility and the steps for advancement by simply recording a series of two digit numbers. The career path of each informant was traced using the Taxonomy codes. This resulting information is included in Table 12.4.

TABLE 12.4

Number of retail employers and career paths of informants.

Participant Number	Sex	Years in Retailing	Number of Employers	Career path using career codes from the Taxonomy of Merchandising Careers
7	f	16	4	204,25,204,25
11	f	16	3	20,60,12,12,24,25,21,25,27,27,27
12	f	13	3	24,25,103
14	f	12	2	30,12,14,14,14
15	f	11	6	20,20,24,26,21,24
18	f	24	2	20,22,13,14,16
19	f	5	3	60,20,11,13,14
22	f	11	1	20,20,20,20,21,22,22,22,22,23
40	f	14	1	11,22,12,14,15,15
41	f	15	2	11,22,12,14,15,14
45	f	9	3	22,12,54,58
46	f	14	3	12,22,12,14,25,25,16,26,17,26,28
74	f	9	2	30,104
103	f	8	2	12,22,14,12,12
104	f	19	1	20,21,12,22,22,12,14,25,25

continued

TABLE 12.4 (continued)

Number of retail employers and career paths of informants.

Participant Number	Sex	Years in Retailing	Number of Employers	Career path using career codes from the Taxonomy of Merchandising Careers
105	f	10	3	12,12,14,25,15,16
132	f	16	2	11,20,22,12,12,14,14,15
133	f	9	1	12,22,14,26,16
134	f	11	3	21,11,12,62,12,22,52,54
135	f	11	4	11,12,12,14,14,14
136	f	5	1	22,22,22,23,23
144	f	4	2	31,30,31,32,33
150	f	6	5	204,204,204,204,204,12,35
157	f	21	1	20,12,13,14,14,16,16
158	f	6	2	11,22,12,14,15,12
160	f	2	1	30
161	f	12	1	20,21,23,24,25
4	m	21	4	11,12,204,26,106
5	m	24	5	22,14,26,15,25,25,26,26,14,107
17	m	30	7	14,16,16,19,100,100,100
24	m	13	2	20,22,21,24,25,24,25
25	m	13	2	20,22,22,22,25,24,24,25,26
37	m	8	3	204,25,14,105
42	m	12	2	12,14,26,28,29,19,209
44	m	8	2	12,23,14,54,35
47	m	11	1	11,12,14,14,14,15
48	m	11	1	12,14,14,14,16
58	m	25	5	20,14,16,17,26
90	m	12	3	204,16,18,19,100
109	m	18	4	63,64,66,64,67,68
130	m	17	4	11,22,12,14,26,26,16
159	m	3	1	60,20,12,22,32

For example, the career path of informant #133 was 12, 22, 14, 26, 16. This reflects that the individual started in the merchandising specialization as an assistant buyer, went to stores as a sales manager, returned to merchandising as a buyer, went to stores as a store manager, and returned to merchandising as a merchandise administrator. She made two changes between specializations at approximately the same career level as indicated by 12 to 22, and 26 to 16. The career path of another informant was 11, 12, 12, 14, 14, 14. This individual started as a trainee, became an assistant buyer and held two different assistant buyer positions, and then was promoted and held three different buying positions. It is immediately evident by the numbers that the experiences of the first informant interchange between the stores and merchandising specializations. All of the experiences of the second informant were within the merchandising specialization and career advancement had stopped at the buyer level.

Analysis reveals that women in this sample moved back and forth slightly more frequently between merchandising and stores than men. Women averaged 2.5 **lateral and backward moves** in their retail careers; men averaged 2.2. The backward moves often occurred with a change in specialization, and the next step was frequently an advancement for both men and women. These career paths suggest that the stereotypical perspective of successful career development as upward **vertical movement** in the organizational structure is inappropriate. Perhaps teachers as well as retail recruiters should discuss the importance of lateral as well as possible backward movement in the career path to gain diversity of experience upon which career advancement might be based.

Career path analysis of this sample supports Minor's (1992) suggestion that career development patterns differ between men and women and helps explain why it is not appropriate to use the same career development model for both genders. The increased career movement that women exhibited in this sample may be explained by Karelius' (1982) "rebirth of potential" concept where women make more frequent job changes due to a relocated spouse. This may necessitate women to start new jobs at lower levels than previously held, slowing career development, and taking longer to reach senior executive positions and salary equity.

Because this was a selected sample, one must use care in generalizing the findings. However, numerous issues for additional research were raised by the study:

1. How do lateral and backward movements in retail career paths vary by gender? Do women tend to accept these types of moves more frequently than men? If so, why? How do these differences affect promotability, earning power, and final career level attained?
2. How does the length of time in each *area of specialization* affect career path and final career level attained? How does length of time in each *position* affect career path and final career level attained? Does this vary with gender? Is it perceived to be more desirable to move frequently to gain a wide variety of experiences, or is an employee more valuable if they have significant depth in one specialization?
3. How do merchandising professionals progress to senior executive positions? What areas of specialization are most important in their career paths? Does the path to a senior executive position vary with gender?

The Taxonomy of Merchandising Careers needs further development through additional research related to merchandising responsibilities in the manufacturing sector. Of the areas of specialization now included in the Taxonomy, the management information systems (MIS) function may be changing most rapidly because of its relationship to information technology. The development of Quick Response business systems is closely tied to MIS because of requirements for electronic data interchange.

Learning Activity 12.3

Taxonomy of Merchandising Careers

1. Examine the sequence of job titles included in the merchandising area of specialization.

2. What is the meaning of a lateral career move? Give an example based on the Taxonomy. What are the advantages and disadvantages of a lateral career move?

3. What is the meaning of a vertical career move? Give an example based on the Taxonomy. What are the advantages and disadvantages of a vertical career move?

4. How do you see yourself in terms of career goals? Can you see yourself with senior management responsibilities or as CEO (chief executive officer)?

5. In the merchandising area of specialization, a buyer is usually viewed as middle management while a divisional merchandise manager, the buyer's boss, is often seen as the bridge position between middle and senior management. According to the Dalton, et al., model, what types of experiences does the divisional merchandise manager need to have to prepare to move into senior management?

Career Advancement

Kunz (1986) found the orientation of individuals within the retail organizations to be extremely vertical. For example, when an informant was asked who he or she worked for, the answer was often the immediate superior's name rather than the retail organization's name. When asked who he or she worked with, the interviewee reported a combination of the superior and his or her assistants. Seldom was there very much formal interaction with others at his or her own career level either within or outside their division or pyramid. This vertical orientation may be responsible in part for the informants' impatience toward advancement.

Many interviewees reported they had received increases in salary and/or job title every 9 to 18 months during their retail careers. Some retail organizations created job titles to give the illusion of **advancement** in situations where it was not possible to advance people to the next career level. For example, if the ranks of buyer and divisional merchandise manager were relatively stable with low turnover, it became a problem to sufficiently reward buyers who were doing a good job. In that situation, some stores created a position of "senior buyer," acknowledging the individual had given long and/or superior service to the organization. This title change may also have involved additional responsibility, more dollar volume, and/or more people to supervise. One of the department store organizations had "associate buyers" and "senior buyers" instead of "assistant buyers" and "buyers". When there was a question of titles, "associate buyer" and "senior buyer" had a higher-status sound to them than "assistant buyer" and "buyer." It was not clear whether the distinction was real, in terms of responsibility, or artificial, simply endowing status only. One informant said that the title "senior buyer" gave the buyer more impact in the market when working with vendors (Informant #26).

It is important to note that an individual may not have to move to the next career level in order to gain what is commonly called a promotion. A **promotion** was often identified by an upgraded job title, increased responsibility, or increased pay in the same job. For example, a buyer may be promoted by being assigned an additional department or by being transferred to a different area with larger dollar volume or more difficult merchandise. The individual remained a buyer but had a higher status because of increased buying responsibility. Promotions of this sort were common within career levels. However, the move to the next career level, as indicated by the Taxonomy of Merchandising Careers, was regarded by informants as a major change in career status.

Some organizations used the title "vice president" as a status reward for people in upper management. One informant, when asked what the title "vice president" meant in her retail organization said, "It means that you get better football tickets" (Informant #133). In another organization, when describing the conditions under which a woman was made vice president, one respondent said ". . . now vice-president of trend merchandising and fashion coordination . . . her title increased, job description remained about the same" (Informant #105). Other organizations use the vice president title much more stringently. The numbers of vice presidents in the retail firms studied ranged from 0 to 33.

The merchandising division is regarded as the place to be, the place where the decisions are made, where the action is. The merchandiser's job is often regarded as the "best job," the job that is closest to the pulse of the business. One company was described as a "buyer-run" organization (Informant #132). The concept, though, seems a little dated because in recent years several layers of management have been added between buyer and president and buyers have decreasing responsibilities in stores. As firms became larger, buyers had increasingly become selectors of merchandise, while others took on the responsibilities of how much to buy, how it was to be distributed to stores, how it was to be merchandised on the floor, and even when it was to be marked down for clearance. The process of buying merchandise had become a team effort.

Management Development

Retailers exhibited at least two **theories of management development:** 1) development of expertise through specialization; and 2) development of expertise through broad job experience, or "rounding out" the executive (Kunz, 1986 and 1990).

> If an individual indicates potential beyond that job (now held), management is forced to make a decision. Do we want to let this person mature for another year and dot the i's and cross the t's or would we benefit better from his taking the 85 percent and then growing into a larger job that would not only benefit him in terms of his growth and development, but also have his knowledge impact a greater area of our business ... The question is what are you trying to produce? Are you trying to produce managers for larger portions of your business or are you interested in developing a cadre or team or real expert, long-term buyers ... They are hungry for those people (managers). Retailing is a business that can respond very specifically and very dramatically to an individual's efforts ... (Informant #42)

The trend seems to be toward the **theory of specialization,** particularly as firms become larger. Each merchandising employee becomes responsible for more dollars, thus creating a need to be very good at what he or she does. For example, in some department stores, the buyer's job has been split to create a parallel position of planner/distributor. The role of the planner/distributor is to analyze the business, plan assortments, and distribute merchandise to stores. The planner/distributor also handles all communication with the stores about the merchandise (Informant #40). One buyer, when told about this organizational plan, agreed with this setup. "That frees you to do your job, buying" (Informant #19). It also means the only time the buyer sees or is involved with the merchandise is at the market or when he or she works with the sales representative. It seems the buyer would have an extremely limited view of the organization with such a narrow definition of responsibility.

Some of the retailers interviewed made it a point to move people from one division or area of specialization to another so that young managers/executives could gain broader experience. Other organizations, such as specialty chain stores, had most of their jobs within the stores themselves, with comparatively few in other divisions, thus making exposure to other divisions of the business nearly impossible. For example, one specialty chain had 150 stores and less than half a dozen buyers that supplied the merchandise for all of those stores (Informant #4). Obviously, there were few jobs available in the merchandising division as compared with the stores division. The advancement path was frequently trainee or manager in training, assistant manager, manager, district manager, regional manager, and vice-president of stores. Comparatively few people are able to make the jump from manager to district manager in the stores organization, with only about 10 percent of the number of store-manager jobs at the district-manager level. Promotion at the store-manager level normally involved moving to a store with larger volume. District and regional managers traveled daily, while a promotion to regional manager usually involved a move to the corporate headquarters.

The strategy of specialization may be effective in the short run, but may create problems in the long run. Who will occupy those top management positions that require a broad view of the total operation? Another view of the breadth of career path was provided by a vice president of control administration:

> . . . having worked in the financial side for a number of years . . . I took the opportunity to go out to the store line. I worked both merchandising and operations. Quite frankly, I probably would be in that line today had it not been for circumstances in '73 when the recession hit . . . They cut back greatly on their staffing. I was in the store line at the time and found myself working a minimum of 65 to 80 hours and six days a week. It was really taking a toll on me and my family . . . However, that experience has probably lasted through my career even though I am in the financial world now I am very sympathetic to the needs of the merchants and store line people . . . having been someone who has been on both sides of it has allowed me not to have tunnel vision and to keep in mind what merchants need. I know what the guts of the business is about. It is a merchandising business. We have to respond to their (stores and merchandising) needs. My areas here are purely support function and it's hard sometimes to keep that perspective in our area of the business (Informant #109).

Regardless of store type, a merchandising career required a high level of commitment to the business. Few informants were involved in any kind of community activities, only those at the very top of the executive ladder where such involvement was expected as a part of their job. When executives were asked how many hours they worked in a week, most had to figure it out and many did not include the hours that they worked at home. The job was not viewed from the standpoint of how many hours were worked weekly but rather "whatever it takes to get the job done." "Not enough time" was no excuse. A divisional merchandise manager said she usually stopped at a "branch" on the way home (Informant #18). The president of one department store reported that he often spent Sunday afternoons walking the floors of the competition—with his family. He said he did not regard that as work (Informant #90). One informant reported that the most important thing an executive had to learn to be successful was how to relax, how to leave the job, and not allow the job to dominate her life 24 hours a day (Informant #41). Interestingly, the firm where the executives worked the fewest hours per week expressed the greatest dissatisfaction with their employer, their jobs, and their careers (Kunz, 1986).

Computers and the Merchandising Environment

Many informants in the Kunz study regarded computer systems as a burden that slowed down information processing, limited their options, and provided information they didn't need and didn't want. One informant had recently changed jobs, having moved from a firm with one of the most advanced computer systems to a firm with very little computer support. The computer system of the former employer was regarded as "nice," but not essential to the informant's job success (Informant #41).

Perhaps the resistance to computerization is based on the fact that this transition was just beginning within retail organizations during the 1980s. A few firms had fairly well-developed systems. But all were in some state of development or improvement and recent observations suggest they still are. Some had just purchased new hardware and were phasing in the use of it over a one- or two-year period. Others were making major changes because of mergers and the computer systems were not compatible. Others were making existing systems more sophisticated to better meet their needs for decision making. Only one office, among the many that were visited while conducting interviews, had a computer terminal in it. This suggested that, while executives and managers were receiving computer output on a daily or even hourly basis, few were actively using the computer. All firms were in some state of transition regarding computers.

> POM (purchase order management) and MPS (merchandise processing systems) have been around for the better part of 10 to 12 years. All of our divisions have had MPS for probably 10 years, but they are very fragmented systems. Most of them are batch driven. The last few years IBM developed their PARIS (Planning Advanced Retail Information Systems) . . . That is the software we have acquired and are working with to jointly develop a system that is tailor made for us . . . We have very large computer applications right now. Our payable systems are all automated, our information systems are all automated

but how these systems feed each other and the interfaces is what we are stream-lining and getting into a data base environment . . . Of what they (IBM) have provided in software, maybe 80 percent can be applied generally to all retailers across the country. The other 20 percent we have to develop and tailor in-house with our processing staff to meet our needs. That takes a lot of time and with 200 plus departments we will phase in each of our group's departments over a period of time as we bring them onto the system. So we will not turn-key all of the departments at the same time. It would be virtually impossible to do (Informant # 109).

The necessity of phasing in and phasing out various computer systems is one of the sources of frustration for the executives. It means that some maintain their old manual, "black-book" systems on the side because the computer-generated data was regarded as unreliable. Thus, technology contributed to the other sources of turmoil in the environment.

Some vendors believe that retail merchandisers are more sophisticated today because of the quantity of information that is available (Chanil, 1992). Certainly higher-level analytical skills are required to manage the technology (Kean, 1987). Large-store buyers have been found to be more quantitatively oriented and small-store buyers more customer oriented (Fiorito & Fairhurst, 1993). At the same time retail buyers report that negotiating with sales representatives is still one of their most important competencies (Kotsiopulos, Oliver, & Shim, 1993). Some buyers, however, lament being more of an analyst than a buyer due to the huge amount of paperwork (Chanil, 1992).

Other buyers and account managers have indicated that technology has freed up time so they can concentrate on their important jobs of selecting, placing, and evaluating new merchandise. Buyers at Boscov's bring their portable PCs to do purchase order allocation while on major market trips (Robins, 1992). This makes it possible to tailor assortments to individual mar-kets—"things that really matter," according to Herb Kleinberger, a Manage-ment Horizons partner (Hartnett, 1993, p. 53). Computer-based inventory management systems encourage merchandisers to make decisions based on information, not instinct (Hartnett, 1993). Retail merchandisers and their vendors have concerns, however, regarding the increased reams of informa-tion they are expected to review and analyze. Some say the advances in technology have caused the buyer to be "less of a merchandiser and more of a financial problem-fixer" (Chanil, 1993). Some designers feel merchandisers are overworked and are concerned they are losing touch with the market be-cause of this (Parola, 1988). Other buyers, such as Jennifer Williams of Macy's, states that she is able to spend more time in the market and stores due to their new Buyer-Planner-Store, (BPS) system (Hartnett, 1993).

In some firms, traditional retail buying responsibilities have been segmented and are now handled by two or three people. For example, the Macy's merchandising system noted above enables the team of three BPS employees to identify short-term sales opportunities and exploit them (Hartnett, 1993). The retail buyer is responsible for doing market research, buying, and developing price; the planner does the assortment planning and the allocation process (Solomon, 1993). Assistant buyers may be involved with expediting—tracking goods, handling questions from the field, executing promotions, and following up on price changes (Hartnett, 1993) —and they are using technology to accomplish these tasks.

Keys to Career Advancement

For those who see themselves in top management, timely career advancement is extremely important. When informants were asked for criteria that provided the basis for promotion, all responded the same way: job performance. Job performance was measured by individual contribution to gross margin and company profits (Kunz, 1986). However, from the complete interviews emerged several other factors that contributed to the speed of career advancement. These included:

- *Educational background*—Little credit was given to education for career success by the Kunz informants, but most informants with advanced degrees were on the fast track, the firms were moving those people very quickly up the career ladder—and most informants with no degrees or two-year degrees were clustered in low paying stores positions.
- *Mentoring*—People in power who know young people and value their potential can recommend them for special opportunities and provide strategic guidance for their careers.
- *Choosing an employer that offers advancement potential*—Some firms have more room for young people than others and are structured so they can provide a diverse group of professional experiences in a single setting. This can provide better preparation for advancement either within or outside the firm.
- *Networking*—Taking advantage of opportunities, projects, and jobs that provide growth experiences, visibility, and chances to meet professionals in and related to your field is essential. "Its who you know. . ." Some say 80 percent of job opportunities are never advertised. People are promoted or invited to apply via internal and external recommendations.

- *Recognizing the necessity for self-marketing*—Presenting oneself in the best possible light is an on-going challenge. Talking about one's ability and successes in an interesting and convincing manner is difficult, but necessary. It takes practice. If you want a new opportunity, you have to convince others you can do it. If you want more money, you have to ask for it.
- *Intent of the organization toward the individual*—Department-store retailers have an intense need for career department managers. Specialty chain retailers have an intense need for career store managers. Firms must have employees that fulfill their needs. Employees need to understand their employers' needs and how they can maximize their opportunities within those constraints.
- *Intent of the individual toward the organization*—Not everyone wants to be in or is suited to top management. Finding an employer who has opportunities to match an individual's career aspirations and can draw out his or her best performance is a real challenge.

Learning Activity 12.4

Career advancement

1. Who holds the primary responsibility for an individual's career opportunities and advancement?

2. What career advancement strategies should college students be working on during their academic careers?

Selecting an Employer

Firms that are growing and making money are the best employers for young people. Conversely, stagnant and struggling firms tend to have too many middle management employees and little room for career advancement of new recruits. Having the power to be able to decide where to begin the post-college degree segment of one's career is a challenge. The power is dependent on the efforts of an individual to create a **marketable combination** of educational background, professional experiences, and personal attributes that is attractive to multiple employers. A four-year college degree is often now a minimum requirement for a merchandising-related executive training or management training position. But it is still not a guarantee of a position. Getting a good job, merchandising related or otherwise, is just plain hard work. It requires planning, organizing, practicing, presenting, persisting, accepting criticism, and dealing with rejection. Taking six months to a year to select the first full-time employer is common; and it can take six months to two years thereafter to make job changes. Many people change employers several times before they find the best match between their abilities and available career opportunities in environments offered by different firms.

Environments for Merchandising-Related Careers

Business in general, and apparel firms in particular, have experienced a great deal of turmoil in recent years. Mergers, downsizing, information technology, management philosophy, verticalization, and global competition have all been sources of change.

Retail Environments

The six Midwest-based **department stores** included in the Kunz (1986) study provide examples cited here. One had been on the brink of financial disaster, brought in new management, closed several stores, and restored order. Another had merged with another large department store division, resulting in the consolidation of the merchandising divisions in one city and the development of all new operating systems. Another had been taken over by a large non-retail corporation. The department store that gave the impression of being extremely dynamic and had the highest level of satisfaction and security among its employees merged with another department store division and moved the headquarters to another city. Finally, the long-time president of another department store was asked to step down, a move that was followed by a dramatic shake-up of middle and upper management.

Many Kunz informants pointed out the pressures present in the retail environment, including the expectations of superiors:

> We do an annual meeting in November that is really a "state of the union" when various assorted directors of the company talk about their various accomplishments and look to the future. In that meeting every year the chairman gives the ending address. Each year he speaks about the track getting faster. The reaction in the organization is always very stimulating. Good people are very challenged by that. Mediocre and bad people are threatened (Informant #45).

Another source of pressure is created by major changes such as mergers and reorganization. These changes force executives to deal with larger volume, more stores, and more departments. At the same time, cost cutting moves like the reduction of clericals and assistant buyers and withdrawing salespeople from the selling floors were implemented. This resulted in less assistance for executives during stressful times and less customer service to support badly needed sales. Buyers indicated that it was very frustrating to "... put all that energy into selecting, assorting, and distributing the merchandise only to have no one available to sell it." One major retailer reversed the trend of fewer people on the sales floor and ordered dramatic increases in sales staff, heralding the beginning of a trend that continues for some department stores today with a strong focus on customer service.

Specialty stores, particularly specialty chain stores, offer different types of career experiences than department stores. The ten different specialty stores included in the Kunz study were located in several different urban areas. The type of ownership and organization of the specialty stores varied. Some were independent, single-unit, privately owned stores; others were multi-unit privately owned stores; still others were corporately owned chain organizations. Some of the single-unit stores were very small, others comparatively large. The number of stores in each firm ranged from 1 to 150. Two female informants and three male informants owned or co-owned their stores.

Turnover of store management personnel seemed to be the most disruptive influence in the **specialty chain stores.** Recruiting, training, and motivating store personnel to perform at a necessary level was an on-going problem. Young people with or without college degrees sometimes became store managers after less than six months on the job. That may seem desirable from a career standpoint, but only if the employee could actually handle the job. Insufficient training and too much responsibility too soon appeared to be major contributors to the turnover problems in some organizations. In specialty chain organizations, district managers who supervised a group of store managers played key roles in the longevity and effectiveness of store managers.

Some specialty chains tried to deal with inexperienced managers by centralizing decision making. This left some store managers feeling underutilized and ineffective because their responsibilities were to implement instructions that had "come down" from corporate. They felt their lack of opportunity for innovation and lack of flexibility to adapt to the local market inhibited the success of the store. At the same time, some specialty stores had the ability to generate a fierce loyalty among their employees. The managers told "war stories" about long hours and unreasonable demands and then, in the next breath, would swear they did not want to work for anyone else.

In specialty chain organizations it was common for a person who started in sales to take a cut in pay when they moved into management. In sales, they received hourly pay, frequently with overtime, and sometimes sales commissions; as a manager they were salaried, so there was no additional compensation for overtime. Managers were also responsible for controlling selling costs, so they frequently took additional shifts on the sales floor, increasing their time on the job to 60 to 80 hours a week with no increase in pay.

Discount stores tend to offer yet another set of priorities. The Kunz discount store respondents worked for one discounter retailer, three in the headquarters and four in stores. They talked of long hours and hard work, as did most respondents, but they were also very enthusiastic about their employer, their work environment, and their career opportunities. As with the specialty chain stores and some of the department stores, there was a clear separation between career paths in stores and merchandising; in fact it was very unusual for someone to make a transfer from stores to the corporate division merchandising organization. This limitation in career opportunities was not seen as a problem by the discount store employees. They not only liked their jobs, but thought they worked for the best retail organization in the country. On a job-for-job basis, they had the highest salaries among the respondents. This is not to imply that all employees of discount retailers are satisfied with their jobs and receive high salaries. However, discounters are an important source of employment in today's retail sector and should not be overlooked.

It was unusual for employees to move between the major types of store organizations (department, specialty, and discount) when they changed jobs, yet job changing was very common. Of the 42 respondents, 16 had had three or more retail employers; only 14 had been employed by the same organization throughout their retail careers. For the most part, respondents tended to seek or be sought by stores of similar organization and merchandise type when they were changing jobs.

The major exception to "staying within the store type" was the discount store that hired regularly from the department store ranks for their corporate organization. The people who were able to accept the challenging opportunity in the discount organization needed to disassociate themselves from the strong merchandise orientation they had known in the department and specialty stores. The discount stores' orientation, instead, was "on the numbers" rather than on beauty, fashionability or quality of the merchandise. They recognized that the purpose of being in business was to make money—and money was made by serving the customer and by having the most effective merchandising and stores organizations. The "best merchandise" was the merchandise that provided the necessary gross margin to cover costs and sufficient turnover to make a profit.

Product Development and Manufacturing Environments

Information technology, verticalization, and global competition have been major sources of change for textile and apparel manufacturers. The following two cases exemplify some of the impacts of these factors on career opportunities.

Mervyn's Takes on Product Development

from The Quick Response Handbook (1994, March).
Apparel Industry Magazine, p. 18.

Remember when apparel manufacturers would call on retailers with sample garments? At Mervyn's, those days are in the history books. The Hayward, CA, division of Dayton Hudson today designs clothing, makes patterns, and fits, approves, and engineers garments before even starting to source them. Manufacturers who are put off by that independence or who can't keep up with Mervyn's technology simply don't do business with the chain.

That new approach had its genesis in 1991 when Mervyn's began to plot ways to cut into the year it took from creation of a garment to actually stocking it. Three months seemed more reasonable to Mervyn's management. So did the computer capability to conduct thorough cost analyses on a single garment, replacing a sleeve or bodice that couldn't meet standards.

It struck Mervyn's managers that the sensible thing to do was engineer clothing in-house before sourcing, to achieve the lowest price before the manufacturer even saw the pattern. That sparked a multi-million-dollar reengineering to eliminate paper and time.

The end result: Mervyn's employees now work with what is essentially a computer pyramid, with a ACS system at the base. A Microdynamics PDM graphics system is the apex. In between are a Gerber AccuMark system, Methods Workshop GSD software, Animated Images CAD system and Hunter Labs color palettes. Integrating it all is an IBM AS/400 system driven by software called ORO from John Nichols and Associates in Los Angeles.

More importantly, here's how all that expensive hardware and software is put to work. ORO, an auto-mated production planning and tracking package, tells patternmakers their production goals and deadlines and whether the previous week's goals were attained. It also reminds vendors of their daily commitments, the production department of tasks prior to delivery, and every department and employee of their individual daily and weekly assignments.

Also integral is the GSD system, which store's information on all operations, fabric costs, suggested vendors, plants, duties and freight, so Mervyn's can turn around and calculate labor per minute for each operation.

The Animated Images software lets Mervyn's operators design fabrics and silhouettes. They compare fabric samples and their shades and brightness with Hunter Labs software. The Gerber's Silhouette system lets patternmakers sketch patterns on a table and call up the results on a computer screen.

This puts the onus on manufacturers to keep up technologically. For several thousand dollars, they can access Mervyn's system with Excel software, a modem, and a PC. At the very least, they must be ready to communicate with Mervyn's via E-mail within three months of starting the relationship. A CLI videoconferencing system establishes a link with manufacturers in particularly remote corners of the world.

So far, Mervyn's says, the effort is producing impressive results. The company has achieved more than half of its turnaround time-cutting goal. Companies like Microdynamics [now merged with Gerber], Gerber Garment Technology, and Methods Workshop have integrated their systems with Mervyn's AS/400. Productivity in Mervyn's departments such as fit assurance has doubled. E-Mail has boosted productivity another 20%–30%.

Learning Activity 12.5

Environments for merchandising careers

1. Based on the previous discussion, make a list of words that describe environments surrounding merchandising positions. Make a corresponding list of personality characteristics that would seem to be compatible with these environments.

CASE 12.2

M & F Girbaud's Real-Time Integration

from The Quick Response Handbook (1994, March).
Apparel Industry Magazine, p. 3.

With the figurative flip of a switch on July 6, 1992, Girbaud turned on the most seamless, completely integrated computer system in the apparel industry. The result: Workers in every Girbaud department—design, finance, sales and production—have access to the same business data, on-line and in real time, regardless of whether they work in New York or Greensboro, NC.

Salespeople enter orders directly into the computer system so anyone in the company can tap into the data. Computers handle previous paperwork such as credit checks, so that evening garment orders can be shipped the next morning, and morning orders go out by noon.

And Girbaud's retail customers can watch audio/visual sales presentations, complete with garment drawings in full color, projected by computer onto large screens in company showroom theaters. It is almost a paperless environment.

The sophisticated system is built around an IBM mainframe and AS/400 midrange computers in several locations. Linked in real time to that central equipment are OS/2 graphic workstations, IBM token-ring local area networks, personal computers running on Microsoft Windows and PC-DOS and dumb-text terminals.

Girbaud is trying to share its advances with retail customers, which include Dillard's, Dayton Hudson, May Co., and other department stores. Three times a day, retailers dump point-of-sale data into an MRIS/View system maintained by Girbaud's parent, VF Corp. That POS information has helped Girbaud join the growing ranks of VF subsidiaries that provide automatic stock replenishment. Another feature lets Girbaud trap retail prices from a purchase order and print them on a hang tag, so each pair of jeans is ready for a retailer's floor. Still other aspects of Girbaud's EDI program benefit suppliers by allowing paperless invoicing, advance shipping notices, and electronic funds transfer payments to Girbaud suppliers.

Girbaud is unusual among apparel companies plunging farther into EDI in that it has no production; it is totally outsourced, with about 80 percent of shipments coming from the United States and 15 percent from the Far East. Microdynamics CAD systems form the backbone of product development, along with GMS software to help grade patterns and make markers.

Also crucial to the grand design is a 195,000 sq. ft. distribution center in Greensboro, where radio transmitters and an automated conveyor system support same-day shipments and preparation of floor-ready merchandise.

Girbaud is still not close to its ultimate goal—75 percent of production triggered by consumers buying garments off the shelf or rack—but that target lingers in the back of managers' minds.

In the future, Girbaud wants to further enhance connectivity with retailers, letting customers have simultaneous access to its data. And the company has started to focus more on suppliers, with a futuristic vision of fabric companies changing production based on the rate that garments leave the shelf. Girbaud is just scratching the surface of that relationship, aiming for electronic mail, work-in-process updates and advance shipment notices by mid-1994.

Recruiting for Merchandising Positions

Three major components are usually part of the screening criteria for recruiting merchandising personnel: formal education, work experience, and personal attributes. Table 12.5 provides lists of possible standards related to the first two of these criteria. The standards a particular firm/recruiter uses depend on their perception of the value of formal education and previous work experience relative to job requirements.

TABLE 12.5

Possible standards related to formal education and work experience that might be criteria for recruiting merchandising personnel.*

Formal Education	Work Experience
• no degree	• none
• AA degree, one or two year degree	• any paid activity that develops transferable skills
• any BA, BS, or BBA four-year degree	• customer service related work experience
• any BA, BS, or BBA from selected schools	• retail or manufacture merchandising related work experience
• any BA, BS, or BBA in business or textiles and clothing	• informal internship/field experience
• BA, BS, or BBA in business or textiles and clothing from selected schools	• formal internship/field experience
• any MA, MS, or MBA in business or textiles and clothing	• retailer or manufacturer related management level experience
• MA, MS, or MBA in business or textiles and clothing from selected schools	• retailer or manufacturer management level merchandising related experience from firms with nationally respected training programs

*Developed by Grace I. Kunz.

Recruiting standards related to educational background range from no requirement for a degree to preference for advanced degrees from selected schools. Some firms also have preferences for a particular major as well as grade-point requirements. Grade point average (GPA) is sometimes used as a measure of work ethic, rather than valued as a measure of academic achievement. Interviewees should be prepared to talk about their GPA in a positive manner regardless of whether the firm has this requirement. A recruiter may use the grade point discussion as a measure of how able an individual is to take responsibility for his or her own actions.

As indicated by Table 12.5, standards for work experience may range from no requirements to managerial level on-the-job training. Some firms may have their own training programs where a new employee is regarded as a trainee for six months to a year. New recruits are moved systematically around the company to observe and experience all facets of the operation before they are assigned to their first job in the career-development system. Other firms have only a few hours or a few days of orientation before the first job assignment begins. These firms may be more dependent on training and transferable skills gained in previous work experience.

Personal attributes are the primary selection criteria in some interview situations. Recruiters look for enthusiasm, intensity, articulateness, purposefulness, listening skills, and a sense of humor. Some use "pressure tactics" during interviews to test poise. They view interviewees' non-verbal communication as evidence of self-worth and confidence. For the most part, recruiting is treated as more of an art instead of a science, although increasing numbers of companies are using tests of various kinds to provide some substantive evaluation of potential employees' worth to the company. Interviews require practice in talking about oneself and what you have to offer.

Recognition of Transferable Skills

Obvious key components when preparing to select an employer include academic background and career related work experience. Creating the ability to choose an employer requires effort beyond the obvious. Individuals must recognize transferable skills and be able to articulate those skills in resumes, cover letters, portfolios, and interviews. **Transferable skills** are abilities gleaned from life's experiences that can be applied in multiple settings. For example, recognizing and articulating that waiter/waitress jobs provide experience in time management, judging priorities, accepting praise and criticism, managing stress, and problem solving helps recruiters see value in this previous work experience. Because of the variety of transferable skills acquired, diversity of work experience can often be presented as an advantage.

Resumés, cover letters, portfolios, and interviews are tools for communicating with potential employers. All require thorough preparation. Effective **cover letters** reflect knowledge of the company and communicate what the applicant can bring to the business. Recruiters may receive hundreds of resumés for one open position. One criteria for evaluating a **resumé** is to make note of what you see if you look at it for 10 seconds. Make sure a recruiter or employer sees active verbs describing experiences resulting in transferable skills. Describe your leadership and management skills, training, creativity, and initiative. Present information in such a way that exemplifies how education and work experience can be applied to new settings.

Portfolios have long been part of the job hunt for designers, architects, and graphic artists. Today, merchandisers can also use a portfolio effectively. The portfolio might include projects from coursework, including merchandise plans, product development projects, concept boards, etc. Or use photographs or videotapes of work-related or internship activities and projects, such as visual merchandising, fashion shows, departmental layout, etc.

Summary

Merchandising-related career development is a process that evolves through a series of vertical and lateral moves throughout the organization and industry. Kunz developed the Taxonomy of Merchandising Careers to provide a framework for tracing this movement by examining the levels and areas of specialization chosen by retailing executives. The Taxonomy evolved by using the constant comparative method of data analysis to create areas of specialization, job titles, career levels, and the relationships among areas of specialization. It is now possible to trace the career paths of merchandising executives, which will be helpful to the career development of industry employees. The Taxonomy is also a useful tool in organizational analysis, can serve as a framework for career development research, or assist students in better understanding merchandising-related career opportunities.

Merchandising careers are characterized by high pressure, fast pace, long hours, frequent travel in some jobs, and total involvement with the business. Present market conditions, management and organizational changes, and developing technology have created additional dimensions of stress as well as opportunities for people in merchandising careers. The vertical orientation within the career path has been moderated in those organizations creating product teams that include a merchandiser, a marketer, a production liaison, and a product manager. The product teams are responsible for the product from conception to delivery to the stores. The use of teams improves the breadth in career experience necessary for advancement into top management. In spite of the pressures and degree of commitment that is required in merchandising, many people are thriving in the environment and would seek merchandising careers if they were to begin all over again.

Key Concepts

adult life roles

backward career movement

career

career advancement

career choice

career code

career development

career level

career path

career-related work experience

cover letter

educational background

lateral career move

life structure modifiers

marketable combination

organizational theory

personal attributes

portfolio

promotion

rebirth of potential

resumé

stages of career development

theories of management development

theory of specialization

transferable skills

vertical career move

Integrated Learning Activity 12.6

Develop a resumé suitable for applying for a merchandising-related internship. Be sure to include educational background, career-related work experience, and personal attributes, with an emphasis on transferable skills related to merchandising responsibilities. Make the presentation as concise as possible while using active verbs to present your transferable skills.

Recommended Resources

Avery, C. E. (1989). Profiling the career development of women fashion merchandising graduates: A beginning. *Clothing and Textiles Research Journal, 7*(3), 33–39.

Bluestone, B., Hanna, P., Kuhn, S., & Moore, L. (1981), *The Retail revolution: Market transformation, investment, and labor in the modern department store.* Boston: Auburn House.

Fiorito, S. S., & Fairhurst, A. E. (1993). Comparison of buyers' job content in large and small retail firms. *Clothing and Textiles Research Journal, (11)*3, 8–15.

Gaskill, L. R., & Sibley, L. R. (1990). Mentoring relationships for women in retailing: Prevalence, perceived importance, and characteristics. *Clothing and Textiles Research Journal, 9*(1), 1–10.

Go For Apparel, American Apparel Manufacturers Association.

Hare, D. (1993). The role of the quick response director. *Proceedings of the Quick Response 92 Conference,* 243–248.

Hartnett, M. (1993, September). Buyers: Endangered species? *Stores, 75,* 53–55.

Parr, M. (1993). The role of a quick response director. *Proceedings of the Quick Response 93 Conference,* 15–32.

References

"Born Free": A World of Options (1978), Department of Psychoeducational Studies, College of Education, University of Minnesota.

Chanil, D. (1992, July). Partnerships: Illusion or reality? *Discount Merchandiser, 32,* 20–26, 58.

Chanil, D. (1993, July). Grappling with changes in retail. *Discount Merchandiser, 33,* 28–32, 37, 71.

Courtless, J. C. (1990, November 28). Developments in apparel, textiles, and fibers affecting the consumer. *Annual Agricultural Outlook Conference.* Washington, DC: U. S. Department of Agriculture.

Dalton, G. W., Thompson, P. H., & Price, R. L. (1977). Research: The four stages of professional careers—A new look at performance by professionals. *Organizational Dynamics, 6*(3), 19–42.

Erikson, E. H. (1959). Growth and crisis of the healthy personality. *Psychological Issues, 1*(1), 50–100.

Fiorito, S. S., & Fairhurst, A. E. (1993). Comparison of buyers' job content in large and small retail firms. *Clothing and Textiles Research Journal, (11)*3, 8–15.

Gaskill, L. R. (1992). Toward a model of retail product development: A case study analysis. *Clothing and Textiles Research Journal, 10*(4), 17–24.

Glaser, B. (1968). *Organizational careers.* Chicago: Aldine.

Hall, D. T. (1976). *Careers in organizations.* Glenview, IL: Scott Foresman.

Hare, D. (1993). The role of the quick response director. *Proceedings of the Quick Response 92 Conference,* 243–248.

Hartnett, M. (1993, September). Buyers: Endangered species? *Stores, 75,* 53–55.

Holland, J. L. (1973), *Making vocational choices: A theory of careers.* Englewood Cliffs, NJ: Prentice Hall.

Hollander, S. C. (ed.). (1978). Retail education {special issue}. *Journal of Retailing, 54*(3), entire issue.

Karelius, K. L. (1982). *A study of early adult development and motivation for enrollment of women and men who enrolled in graduate school during the age thirty transition (Ages 28–32).* Unpublished doctoral dissertation, Michigan State University.

Kean, R. C. (1987). Definition of merchandising: Is it time for a change? In R. C. Kean (Ed.), *Theory building in apparel merchandising* (pp. 8–11). Lincoln: University of Nebraska-Lincoln.

Kotsiopulos, A., Oliver, B., & Shim, S. (1993). Buying competencies: A comparison of perceptions among retail buyers, managers, and students. *Clothing and Textile Research Journal, 11*(2), 38–44.

Kunz, G. I. (1987). Apparel merchandising: A model for product change. In R. C. Kean (Ed.), *Theory building in apparel merchandising* (pp. 15–21). Lincoln: University of Nebraska-Lincoln.

Kunz, G. I. (1986). Career development of college graduates employed in retailing. *Dissertation Abstracts International, 46,* 3619-A. (University Microfilm No. DA604886)

Minor, C. W. (1992). Career development: Theories and models. In Montross, D. H,. & Shinkman, C. J. (Ed.), *Career development: Theory and practice* (pp. 7–34). Springfield, IL: Charles C. Thomas.

Paoletti, J. B. (1985, May). The origins of fashion merchandising programs in home economics. *ACPTC Newsletter,* No. 8.

Parola, R. (1988, October 17). The anatomy of design. *Daily News Record,* pp. 41–45.

Parr, M. (1993). The role of a quick response director. *Proceedings of the Quick Response 93 Conference,* 15–32.

Proceedings of the Quick Response 93 Conference. (1993). Pittsburgh, PA: Automatic Identification Manufacturers, Inc.

Robins, G. (1992, December). KIN II: A new generation. *Stores, 74,* 34–35.

Solomon, B. (1993, July). Will there be a miracle on 34th Street? *Management Review, 82,* 33–36.

Spradley, J. P. (1979). *The Ethnographic interview.* Chicago: Holt, Rinehart and Winston.

Stevens-Long, J. (1979). *Adult life developmental processes.* Palo Alto, CA: Mayfield.

Super, D. E. (1957). *The psychology of careers: An introduction to vocational development.* New York: Harper.

Van Maanen, J. (Ed.). (1977) *Organizational careers: Some new perspectives.* New York: Wiley.

Wickett, J. L. (1995). *Apparel retail product development: Model testing and expansion.* Masters thesis, Iowa State University.

MERCHANDISING GLOSSARY

above-market price Price set in the upper range of prices for a particular product type; includes additional markup on first price or higher than average initial markup.

accurate response Determining what forecasters can and cannot predict well and redesigning merchandise planning processes to minimize the impact of inaccurate forecasts (Fisher, Hammond, Obermeyer, & Raman, p. 84).

adaptive corporate culture Organization capable of operating profitably in a competitive environment of continually changing customer opportunities (Goldman, Nagel, & Preiss, 1995).

additional markup Difference between first price and above-market/premium price.

additional markup cancellation Reduction in above-market/premium price to first price.

aesthetic benefits Includes sensual pleasure, beauty, aroused emotion, creative expression and identity; result in pleasure or satisfaction (Fiore & Kimle, 1997).

agility Dynamic, context-specific, change-embracing and growth-oriented (Goldman, Nagel, & Preiss, 1995); requires information based decision-making along with flexible supply and distribution systems.

airway bill of lading (AWB) A written receipt given by an air carrier for goods accepted for transportation.

alternate selling Showing concern about not meeting customer's needs and suggesting different kinds of merchandise the customer might like.

Americas trading bloc The combination of North America (Canada and the U.S.) and Latin America (Mexico, Central and South America, and West Indies).

Asian/Pacific Rim trading bloc Countries in the East, Southeast, and South Asia.

assist An item or service supplied free of charge (or at reduced cost) to a contractor (e.g. rivets, buttons).

assortment Range of choices offered at a particular time; usually determined by style, size, and color (Glock & Kunz, 1995).

assortment dimensions Traditional terms are assortment depth and breadth; measurable assortment dimensions include assortment factors, stock-keeping units, volume, and assortment variety.

assortment distribution The allocation of volume across assortment factors at the classification level.

assortment diversity The range of relationships that can exist between assortment volume and assortment variety; a combination of the total number of units in the assortment (assortment volume) and the number of SKUs in the same assortment (assortment variety).

assortment diversity index (ADI) A predictor of the impact of volume per SKU for the assortment on financial productivity.

assortment error Difference in distribution of assortment factors (usually style, size, and color for apparel) between planned and actual demand.

assortment factors Dimensions defining the characteristics of a product for purposes of identifying and describing it; usually style, size, and color.

assortment planning The process of determining the range of merchandise choices to be made available at a given time.

assortment plans Documents that may include model stocks, basic stocks, and automated replenishment.

assortment variety The total number of SKUs in an assortment.

assortment volume The total number of units in an assortment.

assumption Something believed to be true but not necessarily proven to be true; the foundation from which theory departs.

at-market price   Similar to competitors offering the same products.

audit   Methodical quality and/or quantity examination applying pre-established company guidelines.

average inventory   The average number of units in stock during a selling period (Poindexter, 1991).

back-end merchandising activities   Related to the inventory management phase; takes place after resources are committed.

backward career movement   A move to a lower career level than the previous one.

balanced assortments   A well-planned variety of styles, sizes, and colors for special appeal to a specific market; must result in satisfied customers and meet merchandising goals.

basic goods   Classifications that experience little demand for change in styling from one merchandising cycle to the next.

behavioral theories of the firm   Emphasizes the role of human behavior in explaining the activities of the firm; addresses issues like how organizational objectives are formed, how strategies evolve, and how decisions are reached within those strategies.

behavioral theory of the apparel firm (BTAF)   Views the apparel firm as a coalition of employees that share some common goals; the apparel firm is divided into five areas of specialization known as internal constituencies.

below-market price   Less than competitors offering the same products; may be based on lower than normal markup.

benchmarks   Points of comparison; indicators of levels of success.

bill of lading (B/L)   A written receipt given by a carrier for goods accepted for transportation.

billed cost   List price less quantity, trade, and other discounts as stated on an invoice.

bottom-up planning   Merchandise planning beginning with people at the lowest levels of the organization in closest contact with customers.

breadth of assortment   Commonly used term with a variety of meanings; may refer to the number of categories, brands, product lines, or styles in an assortment.

broker's delivery order   Instructions issued by a Customs House Broker to an inland carrier to move cargo that has been cleared through U.S. Customs from the dock, to the port of entry, to a specified location.

browsing customer   The customer who has no item in mind; he or she entered the store for pleasure or to collect information for future shopping trips.

buyer   Employee of a manufacturing or retailing firm who commonly purchases designer name, brand name, and/or private-label goods to fill out their line plans.

care label   A label sewn into a garment showing the care instructions and plant identification code; may also contain product code, fiber content, size, country of origin, etc.

career   The individually perceived sequence of attitudes and behaviors associated with work-related experiences and activities over the span of the person's life (Hall, 1976).

career advancement   A move to a career level higher than the previous one.

career choice   The process of selecting an area of specialization as a focus of one's work.

career code   A two-digit number representing both the area of specialization within which a job responsibility is held and the career level within that specialization according to the Taxonomy of Merchandising.

career development   The lifelong process of examining the possibilities for work-related experiences and activities and deciding with awareness what one wishes to do with one's life (*"Born Free." A world of options, 1978*).

career level   A stage in career advancement.

career path   The sequence of jobs held by an individual.

career-related work experience   Past jobs relevant to one's career that enrich one's experience, expertise, and transferable skills.

carton tag   Coded tag attached to cartons of finished garments identifying contents.

cash discount   Reduction in billed cost as incentive to pay the invoice on time.

cash on delivery (COD)   Payment term; no discounts are allowed and merchandise must be paid for in cash or by certified check when delivered.

certificate of origin   A document that certifies the goods referred to were manufactured in a specific country.

change-intensive products   Products that change very frequently due to fashion and seasonal influences.

chargebacks   Credits against an invoice because of late shipment and/or incorrect, poor quality or otherwise unsalable merchandise.

classification analysis   Establishing priorities for weeks of sale, price points, size ranges, and size standards for groups of merchandise as a basis for merchandise planning.

clearing a shipment   Process to validate duty rates and ensure quota is available for goods subject to quota restriction.

close-ended questions   Questions that can be answered by "yes" or "no" and do not encourage the customer to elaborate when responding.

closing the sale   Getting the customer to agree to buy the product.

commercial software systems   Computer programs available for sale from computer software and consulting firms.

comparison price   Price offered in advertising or on price tickets as representative of "regular price" or the value of the product.

conference carriers   An organization of ocean carriers that fixes rates and sailing times.

constructs   The fundamental variables of a theory.

contract dating   Determines when a cash discount can be taken and when an invoice is due to be paid.

contractor evaluation   A procedure to evaluate a potential contractor's ability to meet standards of product quality and cost, delivery reliability, and financial stability.

cost   The value given up in order to receive goods or services; the amount invested in order to have a product.

cost and freight (C & F)   Seller includes price of the merchandise and freight charge in the price to the sourcing company.

cost, insurance, freight (CIF)   Shipping term; ownership is transferred as soon as merchandise is shipped; billed costs includes merchandise cost, insurance, and freight.

cost of goods sold   the amount the firm has paid to acquire or produce the merchandise sold (cost of merchandise available for sale minus cost value of remaining inventory).

cost-plus pricing   Pricing process that realizes a specified level of markup from each product offered for sale.

counter sample   A copy of the prototype garment made by the contractor.

cover letter   A tool for communicating with potential employers; reflects knowledge of the company and communicates what the applicant can bring to the business.

customer-driven business systems   Firms that focus on their customers and satisfying their customer's needs within the business definition of the firm.

customer needs   Something necessary to the customer, including merchandise type, style, and price; customer service, including responsiveness, promptness, knowledgeable people, accuracy, and accessibility.

customer response system (CRS)   Merchandise assortments that are truly customer driven by determining what customers want in advance and planning assortments so the merchandise the customer wants is available when he or she wants it.

customer returns and allowances   Cancellation of sales because of merchandise returns and refunds or price adjustments because of customer dissatisfaction.

customer service   Any interaction between a customer and a firm's personnel.

customer wants   Something the customer desires.

customer's objections   Negative comments coming from the customer about the merchandise, the store, the service and/or willingness to buy.

Customs House broker   An agent in a port who facilitates Customs clearing on behalf of a company; a person or a firm licensed by the Treasury Department to prepare and file

Customs entries, arrange payment of duties due, take steps to release goods from Customs, and represent clients in Customs matters.

cut, make, pack, and quota (CMPQ) sourcing Defines basis of contract costs when sourcing production; the sourcing company is responsible for product development including development of designs, patterns and product specifications, and sourcing materials; the contractor provides labor and equipment to cut, sew, and pack products and includes quota rent in total costs.

cut, make, and quota (CMQ) sourcing Defines basis of contract costs when sourcing production; the sourcing company is responsible for product development including development of designs, patterns and product specifications, and sourcing materials; the contractor provides labor and equipment to cut and sew products, and includes quota rent in total costs.

cut, make, trim (CMT) sourcing Defines basis of contract costs when sourcing production; the sourcing company is responsible for product development including development of designs, patterns and product specifications and sourcing materials; the contractor provides labor and equipment to cut, sew, and finish garments.

data integrity Information that accurately represents reality.

demand re-estimation Recalculation of sales forecasts based on point-of sale (POS) data.

depth of assortment Commonly used term with a variety of meanings; may refer to quantity of each item, number of stock-keeping-units in each brand, or number of pieces in each style in an assortment.

dimensions of product lines prices, assortments, styling, and timing.

display Physical arrangement of goods that are available for sale.

displaying The process of making merchandise accessible for a customer to buy.

distressed goods Merchandise not salable at the intended first price; seconds, overruns, samples, last season's goods, and retailer returns.

distributing The process of receiving, sorting, storing, allocating, picking, and shipping merchandise.

dollar open-to-buy The difference between planned merchandise to receive and merchandise on order at retail.

dollar open-to-buy at cost The amount of dollars planned for spending at wholesale in the market.

dollar plans Traditional form of merchandise budget; the dollar allocation to departments or merchandise categories; determines the amount of merchandise that can be made available for sale, but does not outline strategies to support other improvements in performance.

duty Tariff; tax levied on articles of foreign manufacture imported into a country.

duty classification One element of a system for applying taxes related to importing goods.

dynamic merchandising process Planning, development, and presentation of product lines that is continuously integrating new information.

economic theories of the firm Theories of the firm based on micro-economic assumptions; emphasizes profit maximization.

educational background Degrees or other formal educational experiences in an educational institution.

electronic data interchange (EDI) The computer-to-computer exchange of business documents, such as sales information, purchase orders, or invoices in a standard format.

end of month (EOM) dating Merchandise purchase contract term; discounts and due dates are calculated from the end of the month when the invoice is dated rather than the invoice date itself.

European Economic Community (EEC) Formed in 1952 includes twelve nations—Belgium, Denmark, England, France, Germany, Ireland, Italy, Luxembourg, Netherlands, Portugal, Scotland, and Spain.

everyday low pricing (EDLP) Pricing strategy that focuses the attention of customers on fair value at their convenience.

executive constituency Management of an apparel firm, generally consists of heads of functional areas of specialization/constituencies and the owner/manager or chief executive officer/president.

external coalitions According to Behavioral Theory of the Apparel Firm (Kunz, 1995), outside groups with which the firm interacts; competitors, customers, families of employees, shareholders, and suppliers.

fabric booking confirmation Letter of intent used to block or book fabric for use by specified contractors.

fabric testing Series of lab tests to identify a fabric's characteristics (shrinkage, tear strength, fading, water absorption, etc.) so that appropriate care instructions can be determined and to ensure standards are met.

fashion goods Merchandise classifications that experience demand for change in styling from one merchandising cycle to the next.

fashion theory Explanation for on-going demand for the change in appearance of apparel.

finance constituency One of the five internal constituencies of the firm, according to the Behavioral Theory of the Apparel Firm; evaluates the profitability of past business and helps set goals for future business.

finished goods buying/sourcing Determining the most cost-efficient vendor of finished goods at the specified quality and service level.

firm A coalition of individuals who have some common goals in relation to production, inventory, sales, market share, or profit.

first price Original retail price; may or may not be the same as list price or the price the customer first sees on a price ticket; first price is the base price for retail price structures.

forecasting Predicting the future based on several factors from the past integrated with current trends and environmental factors.

free alongside the ship (FAS) Merchandise purchase contract term; the vendor will pay for transportation of goods to the dock where the ownership is transferred to sourcing firm; all shipping costs are borne by the sourcing firm.

free on board (FOB) Shipping term used in merchandise purchase contracts; FOB origin or FOB factory means ownership is transferred when goods are loaded on a transporting vehicle and the buyer bears the shipping costs; FOB distribution center or FOB store means ownership is transferred when the goods are delivered at their destination and the vendor bears the freight costs.

freight forwarder An agent who facilitates the movement of goods from Customs to inland transportation

frequency of additional deliveries (FAD) The number of additional deliveries after the original delivery in a selling period.

front-end merchandising activities Related to the planning phase of merchandising and takes place before resources are committed.

full package sourcing (FPS) Merchandise purchase contract term; the contractor provides everything required to make the garment (purchases materials, develops samples, makes garments, and ships first quality goods to the sourcing company); no fabric or findings are owned by the sourcing company.

garment purchase agreement (GPA) Legal contract to purchase a stated quantity of goods at a certain price, within specified dates, and on stated terms and conditions.

General Agreement on Tariffs and Trade (GATT) A worldwide trade agreement whose fundamental purpose is to promote free trade by reducing trade barriers.

globalization From a business standpoint, the term globalization is associated with viewing multiple sites in the world as markets and/or sources for producing or acquiring merchandise.

globalized industry A business sector that operates and competes worldwide.

greeting a customer Welcoming a potential purchaser of goods and/or services.

gross margin (GM) The revenue available for covering operating expenses and generating profit; sometimes called gross profit (net sales minus cost of goods sold).

gross margin return on inventory (GMROI) The financial ratio that shows the relationship between the gross margin in dollars and the average inventory investment.

gross sales   The total revenue received by a firm from sale of goods and services in a period of time including both cash and credit sales.

group concepts   Factors that give unanimity to merchandise groups and make them salable together.

Harmonized System of Tariffs   A globalized international trade taxation system; recently replaced the Tariff Schedules of the United States.

high-low pricing   Pricing strategy that involves periodic and sometimes very frequent temporary markdowns to stimulate customer traffic; also known as promotional pricing.

implementation of technology   One of the two phases of the diffusion of innovations, according to Rogers (1983); occurs as the technology is put to use.

in-stock   The particular stock-keeping unit (defined by style, size, and color) is immediately available to buy.

in-store shopping behavior   A behavioral model looking at how situational factors, shopping intentions, and stock situations affect in-store purchase decisions (Kunz & Song, 1996).

income measurements   Different expressions of revenue gained while running a business for a defined period; gross sales, net sales, gross margin, operating profit, and net profit.

income modifications   The reasons for the differences in income measurements; customer returns and allowances, cost of goods sold, operating expense, and other income and/or expenses.

income statement   A summary of a firm's revenue and expenses for a defined period of time; usually prepared on a monthly, quarterly, and/or annual basis.

initial delivery   Part or all of the initial order that is shipped at the beginning of the selling period.

initial markup   Difference between wholesale price and first price.

initial order   A request to receive merchandise not previously stocked.

initiation of technology   One of the two phases of the diffusion of innovations, according to Rogers (1983); represents the decision to adopt the technology.

interactive planning   A teamwork activity with input from all of the firm's constituencies; a combination of top-down and bottom-up planning.

internal constituencies of the firm   Areas of specialization within a firm according to Behavioral Theory of the Apparel Firm (Kunz, 1995).

internal line presentation   Presenting the line inside the firm in order to develop consensus and support for the proposed applications of specific products to the line plan.

inventory   The stock of merchandise available at any given time.

inventory and profitability (IP)   Performance measure of multiple delivery strategies; composed of five measures including percent jobbed off, percent gross margin, percent adjusted gross margin, gross margin return on inventory, and average inventory (Lin, 1996).

Item 807/Chapter 9802   A special provision in the U.S. tariff schedules that allows products to be designed and cut in the U.S., exported, sewn in a foreign country, and then imported with tariffs assessed only on value added.

job-off price   Price for selling distressed goods to a jobber or diverter; may be sold by the piece or by weight.

joint product development   Key component of merchandising in a Quick Response environment; retailer merchandisers work with manufacturer merchandisers and designers to develop the line concept, establish line direction, and to plan and develop products.

just-in-time (JIT)   A business philosophy that focuses on removing waste from all the organizations' internal activities and from external exchange activities (O'Neal & Bertrand, 1991).

keystone markup   Traditional markup on apparel; 50% markup on retail; 100% markup on cost.

knockoff   Adaptation or modification of a style from another firm's line; usually offered for sale at a lower price than the original (Glock & Kunz, 1995).

labor exploitation Making profit from the labor of others without giving just return.

landed cost The cost of goods up to the time they are delivered to the distribution center of the buyer.

lateral career move A move between specializations or job titles maintaining the same career level.

lead time The time between placing the initial order or reorder(s) and receiving the merchandise.

leadership Embodies empowerment, including directing, motivating, and inspiring (Kotter & Heskett, 1992).

learning The result of educating for longer-term outcomes (Barr & Tagg, 1995).

learning organization An organization that continuously improves; employees determine the next logical step and initiate on-going improvements.

letter of credit Written document issued by a bank at the request of a buyer authorizing a seller to claim payment in accordance with certain terms and conditions; may or may not be irrevocable or transferable.

life structure modifiers Event(s) that change the way someone lives but, at the some time, allow continuity.

limited service Combines some aspects of self service and full service environments; requires customers to self select merchandise.

line adoption Determines what merchandise groups will be applied to the line plan; what designs will become styles in the line, model stocks, gross margins, prices, and expected volume for each merchandise group.

line concept Includes the look and appeal that contributes to the identity and salability of the line.

line development The process of determining the styles, fabrications, colors, and sizes to be offered for sale; applying real merchandise to the line plan.

line direction An element of line concept; relates to trends in color, styling, and fabrications as interpreted for a firm's target customers.

line evaluation Offering merchandise for consideration both internally and externally.

line preview Time when a season's line is presented to the sales staff by the merchandising and marketing constituencies (Glock & Kunz, 1995).

line release Time when a new line is first shown to buyers.

list price Suggested retail price used in manufacturer's/wholesaler's catalogs and price sheets; an estimate of the value of the product to the ultimate consumer; the base for wholesale price structures.

lost sales Result when a customer goes to a different source or quits shopping.

management Embodies budgeting, organizing, and controlling.

manufacturer A person or company in the business of producing something by hand or by machines usually in large quantities and with division of labor.

manufacturer's wholesale price List price less quantity, seasonal, and trade discounts.

markdown Difference between first price and promotional or clearance price.

markdown cancellation Elimination of a markdown to restore first price; may be accompanied by another markdown or an additional markup to establish the next price a customer will see.

market driven A company that identifies and evaluates unmet needs of the customers in relation to the firm's capabilities, and then merchandises, produces, and markets accordingly.

marketable combination A mixture of educational background, professional experiences, and personal attributes of a certain individual that is attractive to multiple employers.

marketing concept A philosophy of the firm as that directs the agendas and activities to satisfy the needs and wants of external coalitions that are exchange partners, particularly their customers (Houston, 1986).

marketing constituency One of the five internal constituencies of the firm according to the Behavioral Theory of the Apparel Firm; responsible for broadly defining a company's market, shaping and strengthening the image of the company and its products through promotion, optimizing sales opportunities, and developing alternate strategies for corporate growth.

materials sourcing Determining the most cost-efficient vendor of materials at the specified quality and service.

matrix buying Tool used by large retailers for improving the effectiveness of their line development processes; the merchandising group identifies its best and/or most dominant suppliers and creates a list of preferred vendors for each merchandise classification.

maximum inventory The amount of merchandise needed on hand during a selling period.

mean Statistical average; sum of entries divided by number of entries.

measurable assortment dimensions Quantitative descriptors that can provide a basis of assortment planning including assortment factors, stock-keeping units, volume, and assortment variety.

merchandise approach One of the three techniques of retail customer approach used when the shopper seems to be viewing specific merchandise; the greeting usually includes a casual "Hello" and a comment about the merchandise.

merchandise assortment The relative number of styles, colors, and sizes.

merchandise budget Planned sales, dollar investment, and open-to-buy by merchandise category or classification.

merchandise categories Major components of the total merchandise mix.

merchandise classification Group of products within a merchandise category.

merchandise group Products that are reasonable substitutes for each other from the perspective of customers; products that are similar in function, selling period, and price.

merchandise/line development The process of determining the styles, fabrications, colors, and sizes to be offered for sale; applying real merchandise to the line plan.

merchandise/line plan Combination of budgets and assortment plans; based on sales history, goals, and forecasts; framework for line development.

merchandise/line planning Combination of budget and assortment plans based on sales history, goals, and forecasts; framework for line development.

merchandise/line presentation Process required to evaluate the line and make it visible and salable.

merchandise mix The complete offering of products by a particular manufacturer or retailer.

merchandise plan See line plan.

merchandise/product line Consists of a combination of styles that satisfy similar or related customer needs, can be sold within the targeted price range and marketed with similar strategies.

merchandise replenishment The process of planning and placing reorders, as well as handling, shipping, receiving, distributing, if necessary, and displaying merchandise (Lin, 1996).

merchandise selection assistance Showing the merchandise and discussing its benefits and features.

merchandise subclasses Groups of merchandise within classes.

merchandise to receive Products expected to be received at the retail level in order to achieve planned sales; could be measured in dollars, units or SKUs.

merchandising Planning, developing, and presenting product lines for identified target markets with regard to pricing, assorting, styling, and timing (Glock & Kunz, 1995).

merchandising constituency One of the five internal constituencies of the firm according to the Behavioral Theory of the Apparel Firm; responsible for interpreting customers' apparel preferences for the rest of the firm; planning, developing, and presenting product lines.

merchandising cycle One-year period from the first week of February to the last week of January.

merchandising technology The systematic application of information technology and telecommunications to planning, developing, and presenting product lines in ways that reflect social and cultural value.

model stock A plan for a merchandise assortment according to assortment factors; identifies how many of each assortment factor should be included in the assortment.

Multi-Fiber Arrangement (M-FA) Trade regulation operating as a system of quotas for textiles and apparel based on bilateral agreements among about 50 member countries; designed to protect the textile and apparel industries in developed countries from excessive imports from low-wage developing countries.

multiple delivery strategy Using more than one shipment of a given merchandise assortment based on an initial order and reorder(s).

net profit before taxes The figure on which a firm pays income tax.

net sales Actual revenue from sale of goods and services (gross sales—customer returns and allowances).

North American Free Trade Agreement (NAFTA) Trade agreement enacted in 1994 between U.S., Canada and Mexico; purpose is to promote economic growth through expanded trade and investment.

number of stock-keeping units (SKUs) For most apparel assortments, number of styles times number of sizes times number of colors.

on the water or shipping report A report notifying merchandisers that products are being shipped.

open-ended questions Questions that begin with what, why, how, or tell me and encourage elaboration when responding.

open-to-buy A means of controlling merchandise investment before and during a selling period; planned merchandise to receive minus merchandise on order

operating expense All costs associated with running a business other than the cost of merchandise sold.

operating profit What remains after all financial obligations related to running the business are met (gross margin minus operating expense).

operations constituency One of the five internal constituencies of the firm, according to the Behavioral Theory of the Apparel Firm; manages the organization's resources of people and physical property.

other income and expenses Additional revenue or costs related to operating the firm other than from selling goods and services.

pattern check run (PCR) Production of samples to ensure all aspects of construction and sizing have been clearly communicated and can be properly executed by the contractor.

penetration pricing Pricing strategy designed to establish a value image in the mind of the customer while increasing market share.

percentage variation method of planning inventory Adjusting stock levels in relation to actual variations in sales; appropriate for basic/seasonal and fashion/staple goods.

perceptual map Two-dimensional diagram of relationships among concepts.

performance measures The indicators that help a firm judge the efficiency and effectiveness of their strategies.

periodic replenishment method of planning inventory Automated replenishment with computer—generated orders managed either by the vendor or the retailer; appropriate for basic/staple goods.

permanent markdown Reduction in price reflecting decline in merchandise value based on salability.

personal/informal/social approach Used if the retail customer approaches the seller or if the customer appears to be browsing; the greeting might be a positive statement such as simply "Hi," or include a comment on the weather, business, merchandise, customer's clothing, or customer's children.

personal selling service Close interaction of the seller and customer to assist with the selection and purchase of merchandise.

planograms The output of retail space management technology originally developed for grocery stores.

port of entry A place with Customs authorities designated for the entry and clearance of vessels and goods; major ports include Oakland, Los Angeles, New York City, and Miami.

portfolio A tool used in presenting oneself to a potential employer; might include photographs, drawings, videotapes, projects from coursework, etc.

postadoption product development Includes a group of processes required to perfect a design into a style and make the style producible; part of the line development process.

potential sales Exist if the customer postpones purchases or browses.

preadoption product development Focuses on analysis, creativity, and the formation of product groups that are unique but reflect the line concept; part of the line development process.

preliminary inspection certificate (PIC) Authorizes shipment of goods when they have passed a final audit at the offshore contractor; required by the bank to release funds to pay the contractor.

premier service Provides intensive interaction with customers where few limits are placed on what sellers can do to satisfy customers; first priority of the company is to satisfy customers.

premium price See above-market price.

prestige pricing Pricing strategy intended to reflect a quality/value/service image for people willing to pay "regular price"; also known as status, psychological or above-market pricing.

price The amount asked for or received in exchange for a product.

price elasticity The relationship between price and quantity purchased.

price lining Offering merchandise at a limited number of price points that reflect differences in merchandise quality (Mason, Mayer, & Ezell, 1984); selling items of varying costs for the same price.

price points Specific prices representing a price line.

pricing strategy A particular combination of pricing components designed to appeal to a firm's target customers and contribute to achieving a firm's goals.

private label Private label is "merchandise that bears a retailer's own name brand rather than that of a designer or manufacturer " (Jernigan & Easterling, 1990, p. 565).

product benefits What the product will do for a customer.

product development The design and engineering of products to be serviceable, producible, salable, and profitable (Glock & Kunz, 1995).

product development package Basis of counter sample and costing; sketch and fabric descriptions or prototype and swatches along with sample size specifications and size range.

product features Characteristics of the product such as color, style, fabric, etc.

product velocity The speed with which a product passes through the industry matrix; average inventory during a selling period.

production activity report (PAR) A status report summarizing contractor production activity for use of merchandisers.

production driven Making goods that can be produced conveniently and efficiently with little consideration of market demand.

production sourcing Determining the most cost-efficient vendor or sewing contractor at the specified quality and service.

promotion An upgraded job title, increased responsibility or increased pay in the same job.

promotional price Price intended to increase total revenue by generating additional customer traffic.

proprietary software systems Computer programs and technology developed by individual firms for their own use.

prospecting The first stage of the selling process; includes two phases, personal preparation and evaluation of potential customers.

purchase of finished goods Acquiring goods ready for use by the ultimate consumer.

purposive customer A customer that has a specific or general item in mind and intends to make a purchase.

quantity discount Reduction from list price related to efficiencies of volume of purchase; incentive to make larger or multiple purchases.

quick markdown pricing Pricing strategy designed to provide high value for the bargain shopper; used for fashion and seasonal goods that have several selling periods per year.

quick response (QR) A comprehensive business strategy incorporating time-based competition, agility, and partnering to optimize the supply system, the distribution system, and service to customers.

quick response merchandise replenishment A customer-driven process of planning and placing reorders, as well as handling, shipping, receiving, distributing, if necessary, and displaying merchandise with the shortest possible lead time.

quota rent Purchase of quota from a firm that has excess quota for import of a specific classification of goods from a specific country; cost depends on market demand at a particular time and place.

rebirth of potential An event that causes a radical change in one's life; starting all over again.

receipt of goods (ROG) dating Invoice payment term meaning that the cash discounts and due dates relate to the date the goods are received by the store or distribution center rather than the invoice date.

reductions Anything other than sales that reduces the value of inventory; markdowns, theft, inventory damage, etc.

regular price Price perceived to be the "usual" or "normal" price for a product.

reorder A request to replenish merchandise previously stocked.

resale price maintenance Also known as vertical price fixing, occurs when manufacturers control the retail prices of their product; it is an illegal practice.

resources People, money, and physical property required for operation of the firm's business.

retail merchandise cost Wholesale price less discounts and allowances; may include transportation costs.

retail method of inventory The value of inventory as determined by retail prices.

retailer A firm that sells goods and services to the ultimate consumer.

retailer product development "The process of creating research-based private label merchandise manufactured or sourced by a retailer for its exclusive sale to an identified target market" (Wickett, 1995, p. 59).

sales Dollars generated by transfer of ownership of goods.

sales goals Expected sales of goods or services to a target market for an identified period of time.

sales per square foot Dollars generated for each square foot of a particular store, showroom, or other space.

sales promotion A marketing strategy intended to increase total revenue.

scanning Electronic interpretation of information via bar-codes, pictures, or other documents.

seasonal discount Reduction from list price relating to time of purchase in a selling period; a manufacturer may offer pre-selling period, late-selling period, and end-of-the-selling period discounts.

seasonal goods Classifications that experience changes in market demand during a merchandising cycle related to ethnic and cultural events, holidays, and weather changes.

self service Customers provide their own selling service.

selling The process of changing ownership of goods or services.

selling period Time period during which a particular product line or merchandise assortment is salable.

selling price Price a customer pays for a product; wholesale price in the manufacturing sector; may be higher or lower than first price in the retail sector.

service approach The standard "Can I help you?" greeting.

ship date The date a bill of lading is signed and the goods are physically in transit.

shipping terms Determines who bears the transportation costs and when the buyer takes title/ownership of the merchandise; free on board (FOB); cost, insurance, freight (CIF); free along side the ship (FAS).

shopper's intentions Relate to the purpose of the shopping trip; relate to product type and have three forms: specific item in mind, general item in mind, and no item in mind (Song & Kunz, 1996).

single delivery Shipment of 100% of a given merchandise assortment based on an initial order.

situational factors All those factors particular to a time and place, excluding personal preferences and choice alternatives (Belk, 1975).

six-month plan Traditional merchandise dollar plan; establishes the levels of investment to be available for merchandise lines and product classifications for each selling period and each month of the year.

sourcing Determining the most cost efficient vendor of materials, production and/or finished goods at the specified quality and service level with delivery within an identified time frame.

sourcing company A firm that is seeking a vendor of materials, production, and/or finished goods.

square meter equivalents (SME) The amount of fabric required to make a garment or a group of garments.

standard deviation Twice the square root of the variance; useful statistic for forecasting.

staple goods Classifications that are in continuous demand throughout a merchandising cycle; demand is not greatly affected by the time of the year.

stock on hand Current inventory.

stock turnover The number of times the average stock is sold within a given period of time.

stock-keeping unit (SKU) Designation of a product at the unit level for merchandise planning or inventory purposes; usually represents a combination of style, size, and color (Glock & Kunz, 1995).

stock-to-sales ratio method of planning inventory Is done by dividing the total inventory for the period by the sales for the same period; appropriate for fashion/seasonal goods.

stockout The particular stock-keeping unit desired by the customer is not immediately available.

strategic partnering Establishment of collaborative and cooperative relationships among business partners; an informal form of vertical integration.

style sheet Describes products to Customs for establishment of duty rates and quota classifications; requires merchandiser input to describe garment's construction and fabric.

styling Characteristic or distinctive appearance of a product; the combination of features that make it different from other products of the same type.

suggestion selling Expanding a sale with companion products or other merchandise.

taxonomy A classification system describing some phenomena.

technical package Product specifications supplementing the Garment Purchase Agreement detailing construction, measurement, patterns, and markers.

technology The application of scientific and other knowledge to practical tasks by ordered systems that involve people and organizations, living things and machines (Pacey, 1983, p. 6).

temporary markdown Reduction in price for sales promotion; markdown will be canceled at end of special price period.

theories of management development Ways in which managers develop inside the organization; development of expertise through specialization and/or development of expertise through broad job experience.

theory of diffusion of innovation A process model for adoption of innovations within the organization that divides the innovation process into two sequential stages called initiation and implementation (Rogers, 1983).

theory of specialization The employee's responsibilities are increased and his/her area of specialization gets more focused allowing the employee to become very knowledgeable in that specific area.

theory-x management style Managing a firm based on top-down communication; based on the assumptions that employees really don't want to work and that the primary motivation for work is money.

theory-y management style Incorporates multidimensional communication, problem solving, and empowerment in all parts of the organization.

tiers in organizational pyramid Hierarchical levels in the organizational structure influencing the manner in which merchandise might be planned.

time-based competition Time is recognized as the firm's most fundamental resource

top-down planning The executive constituency develops the business plan; usually based on growth plans and prescribes sales goals and dollar investment in merchandise usually for a six month period or a year; focus is on sales goals.

total quality management (TQM) Organizing an operation to give timely response, deliver first quality and get the order right the first time and on time.

trade discount Reduction from list price granted to a firm that performs some marketing or distribution function.

trade universe All firms, collectively, that are subjects of consideration at once.

training A relatively short-term activity involving teaching how to produce specific, predetermined results as quickly as possible.

transferable skills Abilities gleaned from life's experiences that can be applied in multiple settings.

transfers Physical movement of goods from one retail unit to another.

U.S. Customs Service Agency responsible for establishment of duty rates and quota classification.

U.S./Canadian Free Trade Agreement Free trade agreement between U.S. and Canada enacted in 1988 with the purpose of promoting free trade between the two member countries.

unit A single piece of merchandise.

unit plans Traditional assortment plan; the quantity (units) of goods that could be made available during the selling period; dollar allocated divided by average merchandise price.

universal product code (UPC) A 12-digit code representing a unique product item.

utilitarian benefits Relates to aesthetic theory; comfort, protection, quality, social acceptance, status, efficiency, and value and provide social or economic gain (Fiore & Kimle, 1997).

vertical career move A vertical career move can be either in the same specialization or in another one; a switch to a higher level, better paid job, with more responsibility, authority, and benefits.

visual merchandising Creating an environment for and displaying goods so they can be viewed and purchased by customers.

volume error Difference between the quantity planned and actual sales.

volume per assortment factor The allocation of units per style, units per size, and units per color for an assortment distribution.

volume per SKU Number of units for each unique SKU.

volume per SKU for the assortment (VSA) Average number of units per SKU for the assortment.

volume per SKU for the initial delivery (VSID) The number of units allocated on the average for each SKU in the initial delivery.

wants Emotional desires.

weeks of sale Time period during the merchandising cycle when a particular classification of merchandise is salable.

wholesale line presentation Offering a line at wholesale markets or during calls by sales representatives; may occur in two phases—line preview and line release.

wholesale line preview The training of sales representatives by the manufacturer merchandisers on how to present assortments and sell a line.

wholesale market A site where manufacturers show lines to retail buyers.

wholesale price List price less quantity, seasonal, and trade discounts.

wholesale price structures Based on list prices and determines the price of the line at wholesale.

World Trade Organization (WTO) Worldwide trade regulation organization replacing GATT, whose fundamental purpose is to increase international trade by reducing trade barriers.

zero-based budgeting No previous levels of sales or productivity are assumed.

INDEX